Ethical Decision Making in Social Work

Wade Robison

Rochester Institute of Technology

Linda Cherrey Reeser

Western Michigan University

Allyn and Bacon

Boston ■ London ■ Toronto ■ Sydney ■ Tokyo ■ Singapore

Senior Series Editor: Judy Fifer
Editor-in-Chief, Social Sciences: Karen Hansen
Editorial Assistant: Julianna Cancio
Marketing Manager: Jackie Aaron
Editorial–Production Service: Shepherd, Inc.
Composition and Prepress Buyer: Linda Cox
Manufacturing Buyer: Julie McNeil
Cover Administrator: Jenny Hart
Electronic Composition: Shepherd, Inc.

Copyright © 2000 by Allyn & Bacon
A Pearson Education Company
160 Gould Street
Needham Heights, MA 02494

Internet: www.abacon.com

Between the time Website information is gathered and then published, it is not unusual for some sites to have closed. Also, the transcription of URLs can result in unintended typographical errors. The publisher would appreciate notification where these occur so that they may be corrected in subsequent editions.

Library of Congress Cataloging-in-Publication Data

Robison, Wade L.
    Ethical decision making in social work / Wade Robison, Linda
Cherrey Reeser.
        p.   cm.
    Includes bibliographical references and index.
    ISBN 0-205-30779-5 (alk. paper)
    1. Social service—Moral and ethical aspects—United States.
2. Social workers—Professional ethics—United States.   I. Reeser,
Linda Cherrey.   II. Title.
HV10.5.R64   2000
174'.9362—dc21   99-36052
                                                                          CIP

Printed in the United States of America

10 9 8 7 6 5 4 3 2 1   04 03 02 01 00 99

Linda Reeser dedicates this work to Lillian, Morris, and Barry.
Wade Robison dedicates it to April and Kelly.
And we both dedicate it to the many colleagues and students
who shared their wisdom about ethical thinking and practice with us.

CONTENTS

v

C A S E S

5 Agencies 156

6 Justice 194

PREFACE

Many cases that social workers face present an ethical issue. How such a case is handled will either benefit or harm the persons involved, and so, for that reason alone, what a social worker decides to do in response to a case is an ethical decision.

The question is how best to help social workers and students wrestle with the ethical aspects of social work practice. They need to make the best ethical decisions they can. There are two ways to proceed. We can study ethical theory and apply it to practice, or we can examine the practice to tease out the ethical issues involved. Each method has its advantages and its disadvantages.

In either case, we ought to resist the temptation to light upon one ethical theory as "the best" and use it to answer all ethical problems that arise in practice. Such a method prescribes a clarity where often clarity cannot be achieved. The Code of Ethics of the National Association of Social Workers says that it:

> does not specify which values, principles, and standards are most important and ought to outweigh others in instances when they conflict. Reasonable differences of opinion can and do exist among social workers with respect to the ways in which values, ethical principles, and ethical standards should be rank ordered when they conflict (Code of Ethics, Purpose).

Appealing to one ethical theory as "the best" will guarantee a rank ordering of ethical values and principles, but in doing so, we will lose the ethical ambiguities inherent in social work practice and obtain clear answers at the cost of misunderstanding the complexities that some ethical problems present to us. The Code of Ethics is clear again when it says that:

> There are many instances in social work where simple answers are not available to resolve complex ethical issues (Code of Ethics, Purpose).

We have chosen to examine social work practice and tease out the ethical issues involved by using a method we call "tracking harms." Among its other virtues, this option confronts the reader with real cases, gleaned from hours of interviews with social work practitioners. In each case, we put in the information the practitioner had. So one virtue, we found, is that the cases resonate with the experiences of practitioners.

Another virtue is that when used in a group or a class, the cases engender lively discussions about what ought to be done. Participants discover that what they think is obvious others think is wrong. They discover that they will need to provide reasons for their views if they are to have a hearing.

It is helpful to have someone leading such a discussion, but the role should be primarily as an organizer of others' thoughts, writing on the board or on an overhead projector what is being discussed—for instance, who is affected by the case. The leader can always intervene in the discussion when it seems to be going astray and say something like, "O.K. I've lost track of where we are here. I'm trying to write all of this up on the board, but we were talking about such-and-such and now I'm not sure what we are talking about."

Patience and a persistence in ensuring that the method is followed will almost always produce an answer from the participants—whether they are experienced practitioners or students in social work. The most difficult part for the discussion leader is to learn the right touch of deftness in figuring out when to say anything, and then in knowing what to say.

One permanent feature of discussions about ethical issues is the underlying assumption, perhaps too often voiced, that ethics is just a matter of personal belief. "No one has the right to tell me what to do, and I have no right to tell anyone else what to do." That assumption is especially likely to be voiced when disagreement arises about what ought to be done.

Living by the creed of that assumption, however, would undermine professional ethics. In becoming professionals, we agree to abide by the code of ethics of our profession. The codes do not assume that ethics is a matter of choice. They assume that sometimes there is a right and sometimes a wrong. For instance, we start Chapter 1 with the following scenario: Someone tells you about a confidential case while both of you are standing in a line at a restaurant where others can overhear. The NASW Code of Ethics prohibits such discussions. These kinds of discussions are wrong—no ifs, ands, or buts.

Discussion of a case leads either to an answer or to the discovery of a conflict of values within the profession, a deep tension between, for example, limiting a client's confidentiality and demonstrating a commitment to the client's well-being. We then have a case in which either of several responses is acceptable, with a recognition that we are in deep water. Even in such a case, participants come to see that ethics is not just a matter of personal belief. In such a situation, we are not free to believe what we wish. We must have reasons for our choice, reasons founded in the nature of the profession and in our commitment to its mission and goals. If we must break confidentiality to protect a client, and we fear the loss of trust in the relationship in which we had confidentiality, we need to think through the full implications of the alternatives and make a decision based on our best judgment about what a social work practitioner ought to do in such a situation. That is what ethics requires—that those whom we affect by our judgment can trust that we did what we thought was best in accordance with the goals and values of the social work profession.

So the discussion of a case that is interesting enough to generate lots of discussion may not lead to any clear resolution. Just as life sometimes does not provide us with all the facts we need to make a thoroughly informed decision, social work life sometimes provides us with competing values. The model we propose, however, does help us come to grips with cases that can seem incredibly messy and overwhelming upon our first encountering them.

We should mention another feature of our exposition that also mirrors life. We have made use of first person, second person, and third person pronouns, carefully switching between the three as the occasion requires. We may use "we" when we think a value is fully shared or are speaking for an identifiable group. We use the third person when, for instance, we are trying to remind the reader of the kind of objectivity ethical decision making requires. We may use the second person when we are trying to cajole the reader into adopting the point of view of a participant in order to understand more fully why the participant might have done what he or she did. Ethical decision making is a peculiarly personal process. You must decide what to do, and if you decide not to do anything, you will have to live with what happens from your not deciding. In our use of pronouns, we are trying to engage each and every reader in that peculiarly personal way that ethics requires.

We lay out the method of tracking harms in Chapter 1; Chapter 2 is devoted to detailing the crucial assumptions of our method—the need for providing reasons in making a decision about what to do, the requirement that the reasons be of a specific kind, and so on.

Chapters 3 through 5 cover the various kinds of relations social workers can be in—with clients (Chapter 3), with their peers (Chapter 4), and with their employers (Chapter 5). Chapter 6 is on justice and concerns both particular issues about justice within our system and the general issue of what kind of social system we ought to have and what kinds of ethical relations to our current system social work practitioners ought to have. Chapters 3 through 5 are thus about issues internal to our ongoing social system; Chapter 6 raises an ethical issue about the social system itself. Each chapter is case-driven; the cases are used to present the kinds of ethical issues that social workers have faced and will face.

We have not aimed at completeness of coverage. We have aimed to cover the most general sorts of ethical issues that social workers face. These are the sorts of issues identified through our discussions with social workers as central to their practices. We have included extra cases in Appendix II. These are sample cases to practice on, and, in some instances, they raise issues other than the ones we examine. We have found that practitioners are a sure source of cases, and we encourage readers to develop their own cases.

We have also not aimed at thorough coverage of the issues raised in any one case. We have instead used the cases to provide material to begin the dialogue and work that needs to take place to appreciate fully the complexities of these issues. As we have discovered, the cases are fecund in their capacity to generate discussion on any one issue. In addition, issues cannot be readily isolated from one another, and so, though we use particular cases to raise a particular issue, discussion quickly leads into the implications for other issues in social work practice. For instance, we provide a case of a social work practitioner having sexual relations with a former client. Pursuing that issue to its fullest extent would require, among other matters, examining what agencies ought to do about setting standards for social work practitioners. It would also require determining what kinds of enforcement mechanisms would be appropriate and could be effective to ensure compliance regarding what is a private relationship, one not likely to come to the attention of other social work practitioners. All cases we examine, that is, are pregnant with implications. That is one of their virtues. Their discussion produces lines of investigation for further work.

We have tried to stick as closely as we can to what we take to be the main issue that each case raises, without pursuing its implications and without necessarily drawing a conclusion about what ought or ought not to be done. We take seriously the admonition that, regarding such issues, "reasonable differences of opinion can and do exist among social workers" (Code of Ethics, Preface). We think one reason for this is that, as with other professions, the values of social work ethics can be in tension in particular cases. For us to impose a solution would be for us to impose our particular choice about how to resolve the tension among differing values.

Although we have not attempted to provide a thorough bibliography on all of the issues in social work ethics, we do direct the reader's attention to material that itself contains further references. By pursuing these leads, readers will quickly be able to home in on whatever specifically interests or concerns them. We also refer to the NASW Code of Ethics often; a copy is available at www.naswdc.org/CODE.HTM.

We thank the social workers who gave their time to be interviewed and were open about the ethical problems they experienced in their practice so that others could learn from them. They were open even when they were unsuccessful in resolving the ethical problems or had made mistakes. We cannot provide names for reasons of confidentiality; therefore, we have carefully removed all identifying references in the cases.

We also thank the students and practitioners who helped with comments in the classes and workshops in which we tried out various versions of the text. We can only issue a blanket "Thanks!" for the help provided by so many. We thank as well the following reviewers, who provided critical comments about how to improve the text: Sally G. Goren, University of Illinois at Chicago; Glenda Dewberry Rooney, Augsburg College; and David A. Spruill, Louisiana State University.

We would appreciate any constructive comments readers may have as well as any cases they may wish to send (with all identifying references removed). You may send those by e-mail to Linda Reeser at Linda.Reeser@wmich.edu or by mail to Professor Linda Reeser, School of Social Work, Western Michigan University, Kalamazoo, MI 49008, or to Wade Robison by e-mail at wlrgsh@rit.edu or by mail to Professor Wade Robison, Department of Philosophy, Rochester Institute of Technology, Rochester, NY 14623.

1 Ethics in Social Work: Tracking Harms

Y ou are standing in line one day at a local restaurant and a colleague from work joins you and starts chatting away about a case she had that morning—how the woman in the case has AIDS, how she does not want anyone to know, how hard it will be to keep that quiet because she has children who are going to be affected by her condition, and so on. You ought to be upset at your colleague telling you these things. After all, by telling you, your colleague has just broken the confidence her client placed in her not to tell anyone. For all your colleague may know, you may have seen this woman going into her office, and you may know her. In addition, your colleague's relating all of this in a public place means that others may now know about this case.

The Code of Ethics of the National Association of Social Workers specifies as a standard of professional conduct that "social workers should protect the confidentiality of all information obtained in the course of professional services, except for compelling professional reasons" (1.07[a]), and it goes on to say that "social workers should not disclose confidential information in any setting unless privacy can be assured" (1.07[i]).[1] It specifically lists restaurants as public places in which disclosures should not occur.

So your colleague ought not to be talking to you about this case—certainly not in that place. No law prohibits her telling you this or her telling you this in a restaurant. Although your colleague might be sued by her client because she broke confidentiality, the issue here is not one of the legality or illegality of what she is doing. It is just ethically wrong for her to do what she is doing.

We can all make the distinction between what is ethically wrong and what is illegal. If a friend tells you something, asks you to keep it in confidence, and you agree, then if you tell someone else, you break that confidence. You have broken a promise and so have done what is ethically wrong. But no law prohibits our telling others what friends have told us in confidence, and it is not likely a friend could win any legal suit for your actions. We can distinguish, however, ethical norms from legal norms. How we do that, and what the basis of ethical norms may be, are not issues we need consider. It is enough for us to know that it is ethically wrong for the colleague to say anything about her client.

It is equally wrong, ethically, for you to chat about your cases at parties. It is wrong for you to write up a case for the local newspaper, using the case to make a point about the need for more funding, for instance, unless you have the informed consent of the client. It is wrong for you to talk over the case with your spouse, even when seeking advice. You can only talk about the case if you have compelling professional reasons—as when there is child abuse, for instance, or when the client gives you permission.

We can understand why. First, the social worker may cause the client harm. Others may come to know what the client told her in confidence, and that may cause the client to be fired, to lose trust in the social worker or social workers in general, and so on—all harms to the client that come about through no fault of hers. These are *extrinsic harms*, the harmful *effects* of the act in question.

Second, the client told your colleague with the understanding that what was being told was to be held in confidence. So your colleague causes a special kind of harm in revealing what was told. She wrongs her client. This is an *intrinsic harm*, a harm produced by the act itself, independently of whatever effects the act may have. In taking on a client, you effectively promise not to say anything about what you are told, and in saying something, you break your promise. The client has an ethical right that you not reveal what the client has told you in confidence.

The client is harmed intrinsically even if she is not harmed extrinsically. Even if no bad effects result, even if only good comes from your colleague's telling, she has still wronged her client. It is ethically wrong to reveal a confidence you are supposed to keep.

Your colleague is making at least two ethical mistakes—telling you without a compelling professional reason, and telling you where others can overhear—and the judgment that she is wrong is an easy one. Unfortunately, many of the ethical issues that social workers face are hard,[2] and not all can be settled by appealing to the Code of Ethics.[3] There are cases that raise difficult ethical issues, and our concern is how we ought to handle these sorts of cases.

Difficult Ethical Cases

Consider the following case, drawn, as are all cases in this book, from real-life problems that social workers have faced:

CASE 1.1

The Death of a Baby

Sue had just bathed her five-week-old son, Jack, and put him in the middle of the double bed when one of her other three children called. She left Jack with her husband, Hal, who was playing with him when she left.

When she returned, she found Jack lying beneath Hal, who was sound asleep, and all she can remember is that Jack was blue and she had to pry him out from under her husband, who did not awaken.

She called 911, and what followed were three days of intensive care at the local hospital and then at the intensive care unit of the nearest major hospital. It took the medics ten minutes to get a heartbeat back when they first arrived after Sue called, and Jack had sporadic brain waves for a while, but he was declared brain dead on the third day.

The physician ordered a drug test on the baby and a body scan to see if there were bruises or broken bones. Nothing unusual showed. So the physician wanted to call the death a "SIDS," a sudden-infant death syndrome of the sort that can occur to a child while sleeping in a crib.

The social worker involved, Deborah, thought that wrong. "There *is* an explanation. We just don't know what it is. There are some missing pieces here." Sue said that Hal had had two beers, and Hal admitted he had been drinking. But Jack was a big baby—eleven pounds at birth and thirteen pounds at five weeks. It seemed odd that Hal would not have sensed Jack's struggles as he tried to get air. But Deborah did not think that Hal had intentionally suffocated his son. He showed great remorse and guilt, he had stayed at the hospital the three days it took Jack to die, and the family seems to be a good family. They cared for their other children, and there were none of the usual causes of family disruption. He had a job, they had insurance, and so on.

Deborah felt she had a dilemma. If the death was reported as suspicious, Hal would be investigated, the parents might lose their other children, and they had clearly suffered a great deal already. But if the death was reported as a SIDS, a death that had an explanation would not be explained. "The doctor would be stretching the definition of SIDS." More importantly, Deborah felt she might be countenancing a situation in which the other children might be harmed. Unfortunately, a death certificate must be filed within forty-eight hours after death, and so Deborah had little time to make a decision about what to do.

If Hal had beaten his son to death, Deborah would have no trouble making a judgment about what to do. But Hal is remorseful, and he was at the hospital while Jack was under medical treatment. He did not act like a man who had intentionally killed his son, and the family has no history of anything that might make one suspect a problem, even though they have three other children. So Deborah is unsure about calling in the police, as though Hal were guilty.

Yet Hal did not awaken. We think a normal person under normal circumstances would have, and so Deborah wonders, "Maybe he was drunk." But not being sure what happened causes her, and us, to be unsure about what sort of ethical judgment to make about Hal's responsibility.

This is a difficult case. In fact, it raises all three of the problems that can, even individually, make a case difficult:

- It raises an ethical dilemma.
- It is factually problematic.
- It is conceptually problematic.

Let us consider these three sorts of problems in turn.

Because Deborah is not sure whether Hal is responsible for his son's death, she faces the ethical dilemma of whether to inform the authorities or let the matter go. These options can both cause harm. If she does not inform the authorities, she may be failing in her legal and ethical obligation to inform authorities about suspected abuse and her failure may lead to Hal's harming the other children. But if she does call the police, she will cause the family harm. One sort of problem we can face, in other words, is that, like Deborah,

    a. We may have an ethical dilemma.

Ethical dilemmas arise when the options concern what we ought to do. Deborah's dilemma is ethical because she has a legal and an ethical obligation to report the circumstances of the death, but risks harm to the family if she does.

Some ethical dilemmas are easy. This one may look easy because of Deborah's legal obligation, but she has no real evidence to justify her suspicion. She sees no signs of abuse, but wonders how the father could have caused his baby's death without knowing it. She lacks the information she needs to be sure of what she ought to do. We shall need to examine further the harms that come from taking either course of action to determine what kind of decision she has to make. It may turn out that her ethical dilemma is difficult. It would be that if she had two options so evenly balanced in terms of the harms either causes that neither is obviously worse than the other. We may then be at a loss to know what to do.

In any event, whatever we do, we will do something ethically dissatisfying. If I promise to do two different things at the same time that I cannot do at the same time, I must break one promise to keep the other. Because I ought to keep the promises I make, I will thus fail to do something that, but for the ethical conflict, I ought to do, and that is ethically dissatisfying. It is better, if we can, to arrange matters so that we do not face ethical dilemmas.

The problem of resolving ethical dilemmas requires making a judgment between alternatives, and that problem is compounded when we have no clear way to determine the correct choice. Such problems permeate social work, as they do any profession. Consider the following case:

CASE **1.2**

Dancing a Legal Dance

Martha and Kathy are twelve and fourteen years old and had been placed away from their home by the Juvenile Court because they claimed that their father sexually and physically abused them. Their father, Henry, then moved away from their original home. Hating where they were, the girls were placed back in their original home.[4]

All of the members of the family were individually seeing Mary Todd, a social worker in private counseling under contract with Children's Protective Services. After asking Mary not to tell anyone, Martha told her that her father was sexually abusing her again. Mary had to put the information in her report,[5] and the issue was taken to court where both Kathy and Martha were called to testify. The judge refused to see them in chambers, and faced with having to tell her story in front of her parents, and especially her father, whom she fears, Martha retracted it.

Kathy continued to insist that her sister was being abused, but the judge, given Martha's denial that her father was abusing her, declared that Martha was not sexually abused. When Mary Todd was called upon to testify about what Martha had told her and what she knew, the judge cut her off when she began reporting on the sexual abuse, saying that he had already declared that the child was not sexually abused and that only evidence of new sexual abuse would be admitted.

Henry is so obsessed with seeing the children that he has been coming over whenever he pleases. He has been there at least four times and was caught three times, and although the judge finally put him into jail for a month, he is still coming over whenever he wishes.

Martha has told Mary that she thinks Mary has betrayed her, and she has become extremely defiant. Whenever they meet for their counseling sessions, Martha stands with her hands on her hips, cusses Mary out, and flips out whenever sexual abuse is mentioned. She cannot trust her father; her mother cannot protect her; and now she cannot trust her social worker. Mary thinks that Martha has almost totally disintegrated. Martha cusses out everyone, hits and batters her mother, lies, and goes to the houses of friends and stays for days at a time. Her sister seems to be doing acceptably. Kathy is sticking to her story and is not being abused. "He won't mess with me 'cause he knows I'll tell."

No one is willing to consider criminal prosecution against the father because everyone except Kathy lies. The mother is a person with mental illness and will lie, for example, about the bruises on her arms caused by Martha. She will also lie about her husband. She was abused by her father and was picked up and cared for by Henry when she was 18. So she feels obligated to him.

Mary's coworkers keep asking her about the father, "Can you get him to confess?" But a caseworker at Children's Protective Services has suggested the case be dropped. "You're spending a great deal of time and getting nowhere. We've got other people to serve."

Mary does not know what to do. The judge is "dancing a legal dance," and she is forced to wait until the child is sexually abused again, but then has no guarantee the child will testify. "It is so unfair."

Mary has a dilemma about whether to report the abuse or not. If she reports it, she risks the loss of Martha's confidence, and if she does not, she breaks the law. Either way, Mary will have done what is right only by doing what normally would be considered wrong, for Mary will either break the confidence or the law.

This looks to be an easy dilemma to resolve. After all, there is always an ethical obligation to obey the law, and the law to report suspected child abuse is there to protect children and is not to be denied except for very compelling reasons. Unlike the case with Deborah, where it was unclear whether there was abuse or not, both of the children—Martha and Kathy—said that Martha was being abused. Martha took it back in open court, but Kathy insisted that Martha was still being abused. So we have in this case far more compelling evidence of abuse than Deborah had.

But the case is unclear in other ways. For example, Mary presumably knows what happened before Martha told her of the incest, but we do not. We do not know whether Martha blurted out the details before Mary had a chance to warn her that she would have to inform the authorities, or whether Mary intentionally misled Martha in order, perhaps, to encourage her to be open, or if Mary just did not think about telling Martha that she would have to write up a report, whether she did tell her, but Martha did not pay attention, or what. It can make an ethical difference. If Mary led Martha to believe that the information would be kept confidential, she would have acted irresponsibly. So the case is problematic for us because we lack some ethically relevant factual information.

Such information may be about what a person did, as in this case, or about what caused a person to do something, or about what the consequences of various courses of action may be. In any event, we may find ourselves having to make an ethical judgment without information that we know or think is ethically relevant, and there is thus another kind of problem that can arise:

> **b.** The situation may be *factually problematic.*

In *The Death of a Baby,* Deborah does not know why Hal did not awaken when he was laying on his son. With enough time and effort, she might be able to find out, but she must tell the physician quickly if she is to say anything because the physician will fill out a death certificate at any time within forty-eight hours of the baby's death. She has a suspicion that is relevant to what the physician puts down as the cause of death, and so she has an obligation to inform the physician so that the physician does not make a mistake. So she must resolve her ethical dilemma without the information she needs in order to know she is doing the right thing. She thus faces an ethical dilemma in a factually problematic case.

There is a third kind of ethical problem we can have. Look again at *Dancing a Legal Dance.* According to the Code, Mary ought to have explained to all of the members of the family the "limitations of [their] right to confidentiality" (1.07 [e]).[6] We do not know from the case whether she did this, and we do not know how she did it if she did. We do not know, for instance, whether she made a general statement to the entire family or to each member individually, or whether she explicitly told Martha and her sister that if they were to report abuse to her, she would be legally obligated to tell.

Mary would have been ethically irresponsible never to tell Martha that she would have to pass on any information Martha gave her about abuse. But would it be enough for Mary to tell Martha once, when they first began? Or from time to time? Or whenever she thinks something is to be given in confidence? Or whenever they meet? And is it enough just to tell her, or ought she ask her, at least once, to repeat what she was told to be sure she understood? Or put it in her own words? Does it matter that Martha is a young child? What does Mary need to do, in other words, to be ethically responsible in such a situation? We may be clear that she needs to tell Martha, but unclear about how and how often. One kind of general problem we may thus face is conceptual unclarity—what would *count* as being responsible:

c. The situation may be conceptually problematic.

We can see how these three different kinds of ethical problems arise in the two cases we have so far looked at. In *Dancing a Legal Dance*, Mary was told by a caseworker at Children's Protective Services that she should consider dropping the case.[7] She may not have any choice if the caseworker is speaking for the agency and insists, but if the choice is hers, she faces a more difficult ethical dilemma than the one she faces in deciding whether to tell the authorities about the suspected child abuse. She faces using resources in what appears to be a fruitless enterprise when she could be helping others. Mary is failing to help no matter what she does. She either fails to help her current clients or fails to help others.

If she knew she could solve the problem in another day or so, or if she knew she really could help another family and not cause further harm to Martha or her family, she would have no ethical dilemma. But she cannot know these things and so must decide in ignorance. The situation is factually problematic. Such a dilemma is typical.

Deborah also has a dilemma, one made more complicated because the situation is factually problematic (in that she does not know what Hal actually did in the bedroom). But it is also conceptually problematic.

We hold others responsible if they put themselves in a position where they can cause harm—like someone getting in a car to drive and drink. So we would feel ethically uncomfortable if we found that Hal, while fully awake, had told his wife that he would take care of their child and then drank himself into a stupor and fell asleep on the child. But we do not hold someone responsible for something he or she cannot control. So it is ethically wrong to hold Hal responsible if he had a seizure that caused him to fall asleep. These two sorts of cases are clear, but because Deborah is not sure what happened that evening, the case is factually problematic.

Even if Deborah knew what had happened, she must still consider what would make Hal responsible for his son's death. That is to consider something that is conceptually problematic. We should think that Hal should have taken due care to be sure that he did not put his child at risk. But is it taking due care never to put oneself in a position where one can cause an accident? Or is that too high a standard? Much depends upon the details—on how strong a drink one has if alcohol is at issue, on one's level of tolerance, and so on. Because Deborah does not know exactly what happened, she faces too many possibilities to come to any determinate conclusion. Though hesitant to inform the authorities, she is also hesitant to let the matter go.

Such hesitation is the usual reaction to such ignorance, and it is appropriate. Such circumstances ought to make us cautious about the ethical judgment we make.

Ignorance creates appropriate uncertainty. Once we get away from a clear case where harm is intentionally caused to one person by another person who knows exactly what he or she is doing, an ethical judgment can be a difficult matter, requiring a great deal of detail about the situation. The ways in which we can fail to be ethical are numerous, and, in addition, some ethical failings are a matter of degree.

It is also an ethical wrong to make the wrong ethical judgment—to judge that someone has caused ethical harm when he or she has not or to judge without good evidence that someone has done wrong—and so we have to take special care. If Deborah judges wrongly in this case, Hal and his family, who have already suffered an enormous loss, will suffer even more.

Whatever Deborah does, she needs to give *reasons*. Because whatever we do may cause harm to others, we must take special care to justify what we do. Justifying something ethically requires giving reasons for it, reasons that will provide an understanding why one choice was made rather than another.

So Deborah and Mary both need to appeal to reasons and to *reasons of a special kind,* for the reasons need to be ethical reasons that will justify one ethical choice over another. If Mary chooses to drop the case, that ought to be an ethical choice, for that decision may involve harm to Martha and her family. But what, we must ask, is an ethical reason?

To answer that question, we shall need to lay out our method for determining ethically what we ought to do if we have an ethical dilemma, or if the situation is factually or conceptually problematic and appealing to the Code of Ethics does not provide enough help. The method involves, as we shall see, tracking the harms likely to occur regarding our various options in a case.

The Method of Tracking Harms: Working through a Case

How the Method Works

Suppose one person intentionally does something to someone else that is itself harmful to that person's interests and will predictably cause much additional harm (is intrinsically and extrinsically harmful). Suppose in addition that the harm is of great magnitude, that the person causing the harm knows that what he or she is doing is harmful and does it because it is harmful, and that he or she sets a precedent so that others will cause similar harms in similar situations. This sort of situation has as many footholds for immorality as one can find.

We can imagine an ethically less harmful situation by supposing, for instance, that one causes just a little bit of harm or that one causes great harm intending to do a great deal of good. In short, an ethically wrong situation may be ethically wrong for a variety of different reasons, and changing the situation, even ever so slightly, may make it ethically better.

Similarly, a variety of different features is necessary for the very best of ethical cases, and changing any one of them, even ever so slightly, may make the case ethically worse. The very best of ethical cases, in which no ethical problems seem to have a footing, occurs when a person intends what is good for someone (knowing that it is good and doing it because it is good) and then works to ensure that what is intended comes to pass and has no harmful effects.

These descriptions of the worst sort of ethical case and the best sort provide us with clear examples that we can hold up as standards of comparison for judging what kinds of problems we can have in deciding what we ought to do when we are involved in a particular difficult case. As we shall see, the ways in which we can go ethically wrong are many.

The cases that cause difficulties always involve harms to various individuals, to organizations, or to society as a whole. It may help to think of a harm as a setback to an interest.[8] We all presumptively have an interest in living, and so, presumptively, the baby's interest was set back in *The Death of a Baby*. Similarly, Deborah faces a choice between risking the setback of the interests of the other children in not being killed or hurt—should Hal have killed the baby intentionally—and setting back the interests of the family in staying together in the face of a terrible accident. She faces a choice, that is, between two different ways of causing harm.

We can weigh harms, or setbacks, one against another.[9] In explaining why Deborah did not inform the authorities right away about how the baby died, we attributed reasoning to her that led to the conclusion, "I will cause harm if I inform and may cause harm if I do not." If we must weigh a real setback to someone's interests to a possible setback to their interests, then, at least if the interests are roughly of equal weight, we opt for not causing a real setback. Our justification for doing that is straightforward. We ought not knowingly cause harm when we can avoid it.

But the interests that Deborah is concerned about are not of equal weight. The children will be harmed if they are removed until Protective Services investigates the case, but they will be harmed significantly more if they stay and end up dead or severely beaten. It is the different weights of these interests that presumably cause Deborah to hesitate in choosing between a real harm and the risk of harm. She would choose not to cause real harm except that the risk to the children if she does not inform is of a very great harm.

In beginning to understand a case that appears difficult, we thus begin by focusing on the harms, or setbacks to interests, of those involved, and our aim is to try to understand what they are, how they affect everyone involved, and how they weigh one against another. We must thus answer a variety of questions just to begin to understand a case:

- Who are the participants in the case, and who else is affected?
- What is it the participants have or have not done or are or are not doing—particularly insofar as they cause harms?
- Why are they doing what they are doing?

In *The Death of a Baby*, the participants include at least the parents and Deborah, and among those affected are the baby and the other children though, obviously, in different ways. For instance, the baby is dead, and the children are at possible risk. The physician will certainly be affected by whatever it is that Deborah decides to do, and he or she may become a participant, willing or otherwise. If Deborah's decision, whatever it is, becomes a precedent for future cases, then others facing similar situations will be affected as well. That is, we must keep in mind that whatever Deborah ought to do is what anyone else, similarly situated, ought to do.

If we turn to what the participants are doing, we need to examine the case in detail, sorting out both what was done and what was not done. Your immediate response to a case may not be the right one, and you will need to sort out your reaction from what is true. You will need to distinguish what someone says is true from what is known independently to be true. For instance, in *The Death of a Baby*, Sue, the mother, says that Hal fell asleep on the child, and although Deborah has no reason not to believe her, still, she must remember that she has no independent way of knowing whether that is true. From what Deborah knows, it is possible that Hal purposefully smothered the child and Sue is trying to cover for him. Deborah would be inferring from what she knows that Hal did not fall asleep on the child on purpose, and her inference may be mistaken.

We must also remember that it is easy to overlook features of a case that we later realize are relevant. So understanding what the participants are doing in a case is, as with every step in the method, a continuing process, requiring that we revisit the case regularly.

When we work through a case to determine what was done and not done, we will have questions. For some questions, the case will provide answers. For others it will not. For instance, we do not know why the father did not awaken when he fell asleep on the baby. The case does not tell us. When we do not have adequate information, and cannot expect to obtain it before we must make a decision, we must realize that any decision we make is chancy—open to criticism when the missing facts come to light, if they ever do.

We may also wonder why Deborah did not tell the authorities right away what she knew about the cause of the baby's death. In considering possible answers, we cannot avoid making some presumptions about Deborah. She could be so concerned about her own interests that she thinks it better to pretend not to know anything. Or she could be evil, holding off so that she can figure out the best way to cause the greatest harm to the parents.

So what ought we to presume about Deborah—this in partial answer to the query of why the participants are doing what they are doing? We should begin by presuming that she wanted to do what was best. Our presumption may be wrong, but without any evidence to the contrary, it is best to begin by presuming the people involved are reasonable and well-intended. We then ask, "What would have to be the case for such a person to do *that*?"—where "that" is what needs to be justified.

We thus presume that Deborah did what appeared reasonable and right to her at the time. If it turns out that we cannot explain her actions, except by assuming that she was unreasonable, or unethical, or ignorant of some crucial feature of the situation, that will be the time to make those inferences. By presuming whatever we need to explain how someone who is well-intended and reasonable could have done what was done, we are more likely to uncover what it was about the situation that went wrong. We shall then be in a better position to know what someone who is well-intended and reasonable ought to do so that, if we were similarly situated, we would know how we ought to act.

What we are trying to do in making such presumptions about the participants is to build for the participants the arguments they would have to give to justify their actions or omissions. If they did something, they should be able to provide reasons for what they did, but because it is rare that such reasons are fully articulated, we have to articulate them.

Consider one of the unclarities in *The Death of a Baby*. The case does not tell us that Deborah did not inform the authorities right away. But her puzzle about what to do in the short time she has before the physician signs the death certificate would not make sense if she had informed the authorities. So we presume she did not, and we ask why not.

We gave, as a justification, her lack of knowledge about what Hal had done and her knowing that if she informed, Hal and the family would suffer even more. So we attributed to her roughly the following reasoning:

> I ought to minimize the amount of harm that I cause.
>
> If I inform the authorities about how the baby died, I will cause harm to the family.
>
> If I fail to inform the authorities, I risk allowing the children to be in a situation where they may be harmed.
>
> Thus, I will cause harm if I inform and may cause harm if I do not.
>
> So, therefore, I will not inform—at least for awhile.

Anytime we attribute reasons to a participant, we need to do our best to choose true premises—such that a reasonable and well-intended person in that situation would act on them. So not just any speculation will do. We need to look closely at the situation and determine, if we can, what is most likely, given what we know happened.[10]

But what seem the most likely reasons to attribute to someone may not be true. So even after we determine how we think someone in a particular situation must have reasoned—because otherwise we cannot explain why he or she did what was done—we may question whether the premises of the argument we have attributed to that person are true. Deborah seems to be in a quandary about what to do at least in part, it appears, because she has not weighed in the law requiring her to tell the authorities. She is so focused on not causing harm to the family that she has ignored both the legal obligation she has to report and the consequent harm to herself that may result from her not telling the authorities.

But, more importantly, she seems not to have asked herself *why* there is such a law. Oftentimes, when we are at a loss to know what to do in a specific case, we can find some rule that tells us how people who have similar problems have responded. The point of the rule is that it has been found that responding in the way the rule requires leads in general to less harm than responding in some other way. The admonition that we ought to tell the truth tells us that, as a rule, telling the truth is less harmful than not telling the truth. Codes of ethics generally contain such rules—the accumulated wisdom of a profession. In the same way, the law that social workers ought to inform the authorities when in the sort of situation Deborah finds herself in does not just make it legally obligatory for her to tell. It also tells her that, as a rule, telling the authorities leads to less harm than not telling.

It is often not easy to figure out what reasons people have for doing what they did. On the one hand, although we should strive to attribute to a person only what is true, we should always realize that we can make a mistake, that the person may have reasons that did not occur to us. On the other hand, it sometimes is difficult to see how participants could have done what they did without acting on what we can see are false assumptions. In struggling to construct a good argument for the participants, we may find that we force out assumptions people are making that we ought to question.

In *Dancing a Legal Dance,* for instance, why would Martha go to the houses of friends and stay "for days at a time"? No reason is given in the case, but put yourself in her shoes. You are being sexually abused in your own home, and neither your mother nor the outside authorities, represented by Mary, can protect you. It is reasonable to get away from the place where harm is occurring. So Martha's going to friends "for days at a time" may be the best evidence available that she is reasonable and knows what she is doing. She is doing what no one else is capable of doing, namely, getting herself out of harm's way. Mary is taking that behavior as evidence of Martha's defiance or disintegration, and she may be making a mistake.

What we are trying to do is to get inside a case by figuring out why the participants are acting the way they are acting. Consider, in this regard, the following case:

CASE 1.3

Adoptive Children

The state has a registry for natural parents and adoptive children. A natural mother, for instance, may consent to have information about her given to the child she gave up for adoption if the child seeks it, or she may file a denial at the registry, refusing the child any information. But most people do not know about the registry since it is poorly advertised and underutilized by social work agencies.

LaShonda supervises adoptions for the county, and she often has adoptees come to her asking for information about their natural parents. She has a great deal of that information, but adoptees are only entitled to nonidentifying information. The law of the state she is in requires that, and when the natural parents gave the child up for adoption, the state agency promised them secrecy.

One woman came to see LaShonda. She had been to the registry without success and had tracked down the name of her natural mother, but it was a common name and she could not find her. So LaShonda gave her the father's name—a piece of identifying information. LaShonda is concerned about the interests of the natural parents, and so she does not give information to everyone who seeks it. She gives it only to those she judges will be sensitive to the needs of their natural parents. She gives it to those who do not act only for selfish reasons, but work to change the law, and to those who work actively in support groups that exist for adoptive children, showing in that way that they care about others.

A young brother and sister showed up one day, without making an appointment, and asked her for help. She was concerned that they had not called her ahead of time. "That shows a lack of concern for me. I can't just see anyone who walks in the door!" And they said they would do whatever they had to do to find out who their natural parents were. LaShonda did not give them the information even though she knew.

LaShonda is concerned about what she does. She is breaking the law, and she knows it. "Do I really have the right," she asks, "to go above the law and say this person deserves it and this one does not?" Doing that puts her job at risk. At one time, the Court would contact the natural parents when they were sought by an adopted child and ask the parents if they wanted to use the registry. But a judge ruled that the State "has no right to interrupt their lives in that way." So LaShonda sometimes gives extra information.

She does it because she thinks the law as it now stands is unfair. Some are able to find out about their natural parents and others are not, based purely on accidents like whether the natural parents have heard of the registry.

This case raises the issue of whether we are obligated to obey the law and whether a social worker, in particular, can disobey the law for a supposedly higher good.[11] It also raises the question of how to break the law if we decide to break it. Who gets the illegal information, and who does not? It is unclear why LaShonda does not give information to the brother and sister who come to her, and as we try to determine what argument she could have for not doing that, we find ourselves forced to question what she says are her reasons for giving information. It seems too high a standard to require that the brother and sister be politically active or work for support groups. So, to justify her action, we are forced to wonder if she is not somehow prejudiced against them for not having called to set up an appointment or is inappropriately using that failure as evidence that they are not concerned with the interests of others.

In querying what LaShonda is doing, we are proceeding with the first step in working through a case:

1. *Try to understand why the participants are doing what they are doing by constructing arguments that would justify their acts or omissions.*

This is a complex step.[12] As we have pointed out, it requires asking the following:

- Who are the participants in the case, and who else is affected?
- What is it the participants have or have not done or are or are not doing that they ought to be doing—particularly insofar as they cause harms?
- Why are they doing what they are doing?

Step 1 summarizes these questions while adding another:

- Are the reasons that seem most plausible to attribute to the participants sufficient to justify what they are doing?

Step 1 tells us to begin by asking, "Who are the participants?" If we are to understand the case from the perspective of the participants, we must get so far inside a case that we can understand it from their points of view. We must determine as best we can what has been done—what the facts are—and put ourselves in Martha's shoes, or Mary's, or LaShonda's and try to see what they would say, as rational and well-intended people, to justify their actions. Of course, a case may be so problematic that we cannot be sure why a participant has done what he or she has done. In such a situation, we may have to propose several possibilities and work out the implications of all of them. We may also discover later that some feature of the case we thought unimportant or had not noticed turns out to be crucial. Discovering the facts is, as we have said, a continuing process.

In determining what reasons a participant had for doing what he or she did, we need to make explicit, and keep clearly in mind, what the participant ought to be trying to do and what means are the most appropriate for that. It helps in achieving that end to determine, if we can, what the participants thought their goals were and how they were going to achieve them. The second step in working through a case, in other words, is the following:

2. *Determine what goals the participants had and what means they thought would achieve those goals; then determine what goals ought to be achieved and determine what means are best for achieving those goals.*

Is the end in mind reasonable and ethical, and are the means to that end reasonable and ethical as well? Determining what ought to be our goals, and how to achieve them, is a complex undertaking that is fraught with the possibility of mistakes, ethical and otherwise. We need to do the following in determining what the goals in a case ought to be:

- Distinguish short-term goals from long-term goals.
- Assess whether the various goals are compatible with one another.
- Determine whether the goals in mind actually resolve the initial problem or introduce new ones.

We need to do all this keeping in mind how best to achieve the goals we ought to have.

What are Mary's goals, for instance?[13] One goal is to stop the abuse by Martha's father. It is to keep Martha from harm, that is, and that is one of Martha's goals as well. It is that common goal that ought to give us an understanding of what Martha is doing and what Mary ought to do. If you are Martha, you want to get out of harm's way, and you believe that the system that is supposed to protect you has let you down. After all, the judge has told you that you were not sexually abused even though you know you were. What can you do? You can stop the abuse by staying with friends. What better way for you to get out of harm's way—given that you no longer trust Mary or, presumably, any authority that purports to be of help? You are thus accomplishing what ought to be one of Mary's goals, and if Mary is clear that her goal is to protect you, and if she understands how you are protecting yourself, she has a better chance of understanding what you are doing and of determining whether your means are best or whether some alternative is better.

Confusion about one's goals and about how best to accomplish them is all too common. Consider, in this regard, the following case:

CASE **1.4**

Doing What the Judge Orders

Jane got AIDS through a transfusion and is suspected of incestuous involvement with her fifteen-year-old son, Al, who is in foster care. Jane informed a social worker that she has AIDS, and when the social worker said, "There are people who ought to know about that," Jane told her, "If you tell anyone, I'll sue. I would rather my children find me dead than find out that I have AIDS." But the social worker told the caseworker for Al because Al may be a carrier. He has a girlfriend and claims to be sexually active, and his foster family may be at risk.

The caseworker, John, went to his supervisor and presented her with a hypothetical case. "If I knew that the natural mother of a young boy in my care has AIDS and might be involved incestuously with the boy, but I am not supposed to know that she has AIDS, what should I do?" They both went to the judge who had put the child in foster care and posed the same hypothetical. Al was up for review at the time, and he had been acting out. So the judge ordered a complete physical, asking that every test possible be done to see why he is acting out, including a test for HIV. Such a test is not a normal part of a physical, and the child is not to know.

John argued that "that will cover us for having a complete physical because it's a court order," and he remarked, "I've gone through all my channels so that if it came back on me, I could say, 'Hey, the judge told me to do it!' "

John succeeded in having Al tested to determine if he was HIV-positive. The case suggests that he thought that if Al did not test positive for HIV, he would not have to do anything and could sidestep the ethical dilemma he faced of choosing between putting his client at risk and breaking the confidence he had. But things will not work out that way. As we shall see, he did not achieve the goal he seems to have had in mind, and, in addition, the means he used in trying to achieve that goal caused unnecessary harm.

For if the test is positive, Al may be putting his girlfriend and foster family at risk. John will have the same ethical problem he thought he had when he began. He must risk harm to innocents or break the confidence he was given.[14] And he will not know if Al was infected by his mother because he claims to be sexually active with a girlfriend and she may be a carrier. So John gains nothing ethically or practically if the test is positive.

And if Al tests negative? John will not know Al is HIV-negative. The test may produce a false negative. AIDS can be difficult to detect, and Al may have it without any virus being in any particular sample of blood. Or, because it takes up to six months after infection for any virus to appear in the blood, not finding it may mean only that Al may have become infected within the last six months. And having Al tested does nothing to keep Al from continuing to be at risk. If Al is in a relationship with his mother, he may become infected at any time. So, if the test is negative, John cannot be sure Al is not HIV-positive, and he still has a client who may become HIV-positive at any time.

John thus gained nothing ethically by trying to get Al tested. Whatever the result, he faces the same sort of ethical problem he had. What ought to be John's long-term goal of protecting Al and those who come into contact with him is not helped by John's having Al tested. Indeed, the means to that end introduces a new harm—testing Al without his consent .

The crucial problem is that Al may be at risk, and he may be at risk because he may be in an incestuous relationship with his mother. To solve that problem, John or the mother's social worker must come to grips with the suspected relationship. It seems they think enough of the evidence they have to pursue the matter to court, but if they do have evidence of such a relationship, why do they not report the mother as a suspected child abuser? That may bring out that she has AIDS, but even if it does not, the suspected abuse may be stopped. It will then be appropriate to get Al tested to determine if his girlfriend and foster family need protecting.

This analysis of John's goals in *Doing What the Judge Orders* illustrates what often happens when we begin to untangle a case. In trying to understand why someone has done what he or she has done, in laying out the harms to all affected, determining their kinds and assessing their magnitudes, and in determining what ought to be the goals in the case and how those ought best be achieved, we can come to clarity about what went wrong. John gained nothing practically or ethically by so arranging things as to have Al tested. Because he caused Al to be deceived for no good reason, he caused harm he need not have caused. So he was wrong to do what he did.[15]

John is right back where he started, ethically and practically, but we now know that the real concern is with Al's purported relationship with his mother.

We have clarity about what John ought not to have done. Now, were we in his shoes, we would need to determine how best to proceed given what he has done. Similarly, in *Dancing a Legal Dance,* if Mary wants to protect Martha from her father, we can see that she should try to obtain clinical evidence of any sexual abuse. That is what she should have done initially. Then the case would not turn on Martha's willingness to testify. But although we have clarity about what Mary ought to have done, the very way her problem is posed shows how complicated it is. She must await new abuse by the father if she is to make use of the law to prevent more abuse. If we ask what Mary ought to do now, given what has happened, we can see how constrained her choices are.

Having come to understand a case as it is understood by its participants and having clarified what our goals ought to be—having followed steps 1 and 2 of the method of tracking harms, that is—we have arrived at the stage where we need to explore what is now possible. How are we to get ourselves out of the ethical mess we find ourselves in?

The cases we are considering would not be difficult if this next step were easy and the solution presented itself as obvious once we went through the first two steps. If it does, then that is the end of the matter, and we have a case that appeared difficult but turned out to be easy. But in a difficult case—difficult because we have a dilemma and must choose between harms or because the case is factually or conceptually problematic—we shall need to brainstorm possible solutions, laying out as many as we can conceive and assessing each of them, in turn, for the harms they will cause. It is thus a crucial step in our method to:

3. *Determine what the harms are of various courses of action. To whom would they occur, what kinds are they, and what are their magnitudes?*

We should always presume that a difficult case has a solution. We will then presume that a failure to find a solution means that we have not thought enough about the case or thought about it in the right way. But finding a solution can be difficult. What, after all, is Mary to do in *Dancing a Legal Dance?* Finding a solution requires creative imagination—an ability to get outside the box presented by a dilemma, for instance, and see if there is some way to rework the problem so that the dilemma does not occur.

The latter is what John tried to do in *Doing What the Judge Orders.* He thought he faced the ethical dilemma of choosing between putting his client at risk or breaking the confidence he had, and so he attempted to sidestep the dilemma by convincing the court to order a complete physical for Al. That way John would find out whether Al was HIV-positive without appearing to break the confidence he had from the mother's social worker. But, as we saw, he failed to sidestep the problem.

What helps our creative imagination are the first two steps in the method. If we concentrate on what our goal ought to be and understand the case fully from the perspective of those in it, we are as well positioned as we can be to determine how best to achieve the goal given the situation. Having clarity about the goal gives us a target, something we are aiming for when we consider how to get from where we are in a case to where we ought to be. It is laying out as many possible ways as we can of getting from here to there that requires creative imagination, and there is no simple formula for imaginative solutions to problems.

There are some simple guidelines:

- Do not assume that the first possible solution you come up with is the right one.

Often it is. Your intuitive reaction to a case may be more on the mark than the solution you arrive at after getting into the case and then trying to figure out how to get out. The more experience we have in handling such cases, the more likely it is that our gut reaction is the correct reaction. But even so, we need to know that it is, and that requires thinking through the case and coming up with as many possibilities as you can.

- Put as much thought into it as you can and do not constrain your thought by any difficulties you may see. Let the criticisms come later.

Talking through a case with colleagues helps. That both increases the brain power brought to bear on a case and helps to ensure that any of one's own biases about how to proceed are brought to light.[16]

But the best advice about how to proceed is to follow the first two steps of the method:

- Get as clear as you can on the case itself because understanding it not only tells you what has been done, but suggests what can be done.
- Then make sure you understand what the goals ought to be so you can keep those in mind as you turn the case over and over, hunting for ways to get out of the ethical mess you have to the goals you need to achieve.[17]

Unfortunately, the solution you find may not be right. You may have overlooked something important in the case and solved a different problem from the one you fail to realize you have. Not finding a solution to a difficult case may mean that you need to work on it more, in different ways, perhaps, but it also may mean that the case reflects ethical tensions within the profession itself between competing values. In such a situation, no clear solution may exist.

For instance, the two values of obtaining trust in the relationship between a social worker and a client and of ensuring that harm does not befall one's client are both important, and when the two conflict, no easy solution may present itself. This is the standard problem when a social worker discovers that the client may cause harm and has to make a complicated set of judgments.[18] "Is the client just mouthing off, or is this serious?" "If it's serious, how serious is it: what's the risk?" "Can I best work this out by keeping within the relationship and not going to the authorities?" And so on, and so on. No obvious answer about what to do may emerge from this series, and that may reflect deep tensions within the profession itself about the status of these values and how they are to be ranked one against another.[19]

Once we have identified various courses of action, however—what we could do to get from where we are to where we ought to be—we will need to be sure that we lay out all the harms attached to each of the various courses of action:

- To whom would they occur?
- What kinds are they?
- How weighty are they?

Although we have not made the point explicit, we should also mark out what good comes from the various courses of action. Few things come without some silver lining, however small, and a proper assessment of the various courses of action—a ranking of them in terms of which is ethically preferable—requires that we take into account what good comes from doing each as well as what harms come.

Consider *Dancing a Legal Dance* again. Mary has to choose between sticking with the case or dropping it and going on to a new one. When we map out what is likely to happen if she chooses to stick with the case—if the agency lets her do that—we will have to take into consideration how that may affect other potential clients whom she will not be able to see. We shall have the good she might accomplish by sticking with the case, that is, and then, as best we can, we will have to weigh those goods against the harms of those not being helped. We shall then need to compare the result of that weighing against a weighing of the harms that would occur to those she is currently trying to help if she were to drop the case and the good that would occur to those she would then be able to help.

To call a harm "weighty" is to speak metaphorically. Harms are neither heavy nor light, but they can be compared with one another—the harm of Martha's being deceived compared with the loss of the relationship of trust between Mary and Martha, the harm to Martha of being sexually and physically abused compared with the harm of Martha's running away from home and staying with her friends, and so on. Sometimes we can readily judge which harm is heavier, as it were, and must be avoided. A choice between your money or your life is easy unless you had been planning on committing suicide and want to take advantage of this offer. But sometimes we cannot readily make a judgment. As we said, there is often no easy way to choose between two values when the values are in tension and both are of great importance to the profession.

Yet issues that appear so complex that we hardly know what to do can become so clear as we work through the three steps we suggest that we do not self-consciously need to do anything further. But even in these clear cases, we are making a judgment at the end, and that is the fourth step:

4. *Back off from the case and judge what is best to do. What will minimize harms?*[20]

When we try to understand why the participants are doing what they are doing—why Martha is staying away for days at a time, for instance—we are putting ourselves in her shoes. But step 4 requires us to step out of the shoes of the participants and, as an observer of the case—but now understanding the point of view of those who are participants—judge what is ethically right and what is not. We must be sure that we judge as observers. This is especially difficult when we are ourselves participants in the case, for we must back off and try to make an unbiased judgment, one that does not unduly reflect our own self-interest and our own point of view.

Such judgments often come without any difficulty when we explore a case in detail. An analysis of the various harms and their weights in a case may make it easy to determine what ought to be done. At the least, no one ought to cause harm to others for no benefit at all—as John does to Al. Once we back off from what John is doing, we are able to judge that he is making an ethical mistake, causing harm for no benefit because he apparently has not thought through what his goals are and how best to achieve them.

But suppose a test for HIV would give us useful information. Would it then be appropriate for John to be concerned about Al's giving informed consent for such a test? Ought he act for Al without Al's consent because Al is a minor, or ought he seek Al's consent since Al is fifteen years old?[21] What is at issue is the proper weighing of the values of self-determination and harm when the subject is fifteen years old, and reasonable people may disagree.[22] Some may argue that those who are fifteen years old must be presumed to be reasonable enough to make decisions about their own health unless there is good evidence that they are not. Some may argue that the potential harm to others is so significant that were Al to decide he did not want to be tested, the Court would be justified in ordering a test and so denying his self-determination. If so, the argument continues, why give him a choice to begin with? It is not *obvious* which view is correct, and so if testing were a real issue in *Doing What the Judge Orders*, working through the case would not give us a clear answer. It would only give us a clear problem. But that is a huge gain. We now know what to focus on, and we can begin to work through the reasons for and against obtaining informed consent from a fifteen-year-old so we will be able to make a judgment.

When we have a clear ethical judgment, and determine exactly what we ought to do, we still have to do it and do it properly. There is thus a final step in the method of tracking harms:

5. *Determine how to do what ought to be done in a way that will itself produce more good than harm.*

This is not by any means always easy to do. It may seem that deciding what to do is the hard part, and, once that is done, it is just a matter of doing it. But we can fail to do something well, causing more harm than good, even when we know what it is we are supposed to do and try to do it. For instance, if Deborah were to decide that the right thing to do was to inform the authorities about Hal and the death of his baby, she may have a difficult time doing this after spending so much time with him and his family as they worried over the baby and then grieved his death. It might be all too easy for her to become angry with Hal, and so make herself feel better about informing on him, even if she were not quite completely sure he was responsible. But informing the authorities while angry at Hal might give just the wrong sort of impression to them regarding her own doubts in the issue. It is, in short, not ethically neutral how we do what we ought to do. A child's yelling, "Thank you for the stupid gift!" will not do even though thanks is called for.

We are concerned in this book primarily with steps 1 through 4, with determining what it is we ought to do. Step 5, determining *how* we ought to do what we ought to do, is a topic in itself, and our putting it to one side is not meant to indicate that it is any less important. Indeed, we will address the issues raised by step 5 when it is necessary and opportune.

Learning a Skill

It is not easy being ethical, and even with the best of intentions, we can still do wrong. It is an underlying assumption we make that determining the right thing to do in any ethically difficult case is a matter of skill that needs to be honed by continuous work. We have laid out five steps that, if followed, will help in coming to a proper ethical decision and in doing what is right:

1. *Try to understand why the participants are doing what they are doing by constructing arguments that would justify their acts or omissions.*
2. *Determine what goals the participants had and what means they thought would achieve those goals; then determine what goals ought to be achieved and determine what means are best for achieving those goals.*
3. *Determine what the harms are of various courses of action. To whom would they occur, what kinds are they, and what are their magnitudes?*
4. *Back off from the case and judge what is best to do. What will minimize harms?*
5. *Determine how to do what ought to be done in a way that will itself produce more good than harm.*

Each step involves learning a skill, with steps 1 through 4 being crucial in determining what we ought to do, and step 5 being crucial in doing in the right way what we have decided we ought to do.

Each of these steps can be complicated because of features we bring, and features that those we are working with bring, to any ethical problem. It will make our problems that much more difficult, for instance, if those we are helping see us as representatives of an oppressive social system, or if they have been ill-treated in the past by other social work practitioners, or if we do not listen well to others or do not respond with empathy to a client's plight. To the extent that we do not come to understand ourselves, or how we may be perceived by those we are trying to help, we will have a harder time understanding how to act so as to help them.[23]

At the same time, certain character traits we should encourage may alert us to ethical problems or to difficulties our clients are having. When we bring empathy and self-understanding to our relations with others, we are far better positioned to understand what their problems are and far better positioned to help them.

We will also need to understand how working with a client can change our relationships. Deborah may become more empathic to Hal from being with him for those days he suffered as his son died, and so less likely to think him guilty of his son's death. Working with someone can change how you each see each other and can change as well the ethical problems that you face. What might have been a clear decision, when Deborah first saw the harm Hal might have done, becomes harder as she realizes how much he is suffering. Just so, Hal may become more dependent upon Deborah as she helps him through the problems he has, and so he will be the more surprised if she informs the authorities. So understanding our ethical situation is an evolving problem, one that may well change as we come to grips with it and one that requires us constantly to remind ourselves to back off from the problem to try to get a more objective view.

But besides cultivating those character traits of empathy and self-understanding, for example, that will help us understand our clients' problems, and realizing how our work with clients can change our relationships with them, it will also help for us to cultivate the habits of thought and ways of looking at problems that our method articulates. So we want to develop habits, ways of thinking about ethical problems and responding to them, that may assist us in recognizing the ethical issues involved and resolving them properly. The more habitual our behavior, the less time we have to spend thinking about what we ought to do. We thus need to get into the habit of trying to understand what the various parties to an ethical problem are doing. We can do this by constructing arguments that would justify their acts, determining what goals ought to be achieved, looking at the various harms that have occurred and may occur from the perspectives of the various participants, and then backing off and asking what we ought to do.

It would be nice if practice made perfect, but even long practice cannot guarantee that mistakes will not be made, either in analyzing a case to determine what ought to be done or in responding in the morally best way after deciding what ought to be done. Practice will produce habits of thought that can serve us well when we face problems. Oftentimes we do not have time to work through a problem in any great detail, but must make a quick decision, and if we have had experience in working through difficult cases, we will have learned what to hunt for and how to respond and so can trust our quick judgment. That we have an intuitive response to a moral difficulty does not make our response correct. The only test for its being the right response is that it causes the least harm. But if our intuitive judgment is backed by practice in difficult cases, it is certainly more likely to be right than a guess, and it is better to rely on our experience when a judgment must be made quickly, than simply to throw up our hands.[24] When we have time, it is helpful to test one's intuitive judgment with one's colleagues when doing so will not risk a client's confidentiality. The more minds that are brought to bear upon a case, the more likely it is that all its problems will be seen. But, again, even agreement by one's colleagues is no guarantee that our response is correct. Again, the only test is that it causes the least harm.

In short, there are no shortcuts in making ethical decisions. We provide a guide—the method of tracking harms—but the guide may make things look simpler than they are—as though we only had to follow it and a decision would emerge. But, as we have seen, matters are not so easy. We shall make use of the guide in what follows just as we have made use of it so far—not as a recipe to be followed step-by-step for ethical success, but as a reminder of the sorts of considerations we must come to grips with when facing ethical difficulties.

It is worth reminding ourselves that analyzing an ethical problem is a continuing process. We may not realize until we are deep within a case that something we thought irrelevant is really quite relevant. Or we may discover only after analyzing a case that no real ethical problem exists. Once we clarify what we thought was an ethical problem, the disagreement may not turn out to be ethical. So we are not providing a checklist of things to do. We are rather providing factors that are relevant to coming to grips with a case, and you must keep these in mind all the time.

A Synopsis of the Guide to Ethical Decision Making

It will be helpful to have a guide readily available for the method of tracking harms. This can hardly stand alone without the explanations we have provided in this part, but with that background in mind, a quick summary is useful.

1. *Try to understand why the participants are doing what they are doing by constructing arguments that would justify their acts or omissions.*
   a. Who are the participants in the case, and who else is affected?
   b. What is it the participants have or have not done or are or are not doing?
      i. Be objective and distinguish
         1. your immediate and perhaps biased response from what is true.
         2. what is said from what is known.
         3. what is known directly from what is inferred.
      ii. Discovering the facts is a continuing process. Facts thought to be irrelevant may be seen later to be relevant.
   c. Why are they doing what they are doing? What premises, that is, need we attribute to the participants of the case to make their acts (or omissions) reasonable and, if possible, ethical to them?
2. *Determine what goals the participants had and what means they thought would achieve those goals; then determine what goals ought to be achieved and determine what means are best for achieving those goals.*
   a. What are the goals of the person(s) facing the problem(s)?
   b. What are their means?
   c. What ought to be their goals?

        i. Distinguish the short-term goals from the long-term goals.

        ii. Assess whether the various goals are compatible with one another.

        iii. Determine if achieving these goals will actually help resolve the initial problems.

        iv. Determine whether achieving these goals will create new problems.

    d. What is the best way to achieve the goals that ought to be achieved?

3. *Determine what the harms are of various courses of action. To whom would they occur, what kinds are they, and what are their magnitudes?*

    a. A helpful way of entry into a complex ethical problem is to track the harms that have occurred and are likely to occur without intervention. It is useful to ask:

        i. Who is affected—not just who is involved?

        ii. What interests, of which people, have been harmed so far—both short-term and long-term?

    b. Not all harms are ethical harms, and so we must ask which harms are ethical. We may proceed by identifying particular important interests people have, including, but not limited to the following:

        i. A person has an interest in deciding for himself or herself what to do or omit from doing regarding those matters that affect him or her. Such decisions are (best) made voluntarily when fully informed and competent.

        ii. A person has an interest in not being harmed by others.

        iii. Each of us has an interest in others helping us, either by mitigating harmful conditions or by providing benefits.

        iv. Each of us has an interest in being treated in the same way others similarly situated to us are treated and being treated differently from those differently situated.

    c. The most difficult ethical problems are of the following sorts:

        i. It may be an ethical dilemma—in which we have incompatible choices so that no matter what we do, we will cause harm.

        ii. It may be factually problematic—in which we are ignorant of certain relevant facts.

        iii. It may be conceptually problematic—in which we are unsure what we ought to mean by something—such as "acting responsibly."

4. *Back off from the case and judge what is best to do. What will minimize harms?*

    a. Be sure a real ethical problem exists. Disagreements often occur that, for all their emotion, are not really ethical problems because no ethical conflict exists.

    b. If the problem is that an ethical harm has been done—*for no good ethical reason* (that is, nothing ethical justifies what is causing the problem), no ethical problem exists. Causing harm is just wrong.

    c. If an ethical dilemma exists or if the case is problematic, much depends upon the details of the case. In any event, we ought to lay out the alternatives by determining as best we can the long-term effects of possible solutions to the problem.

      d. In deciding what to do, always act to minimize harm—for everyone involved.[25]

      e. One short way to test a solution is to ask, "Would I agree to be treated in the way I am treating those involved?" The proper answer presupposes that one is objective and unbiased.

5. *Determine how to do what you have determined ought to be done and do it in a way that will itself produce more good than harm.*

QUESTIONS

1. Provide an example of something we ought to do ethically where the failure to do it would not be illegal.

2. Once we have a law about which side of the road to drive on, it is an ethical and legal issue to drive on the wrong side. But the decision of which side to drive on is not an ethical issue. The British are not any less or any more ethical than Americans because they drive on the left-hand side and we drive on the right. Provide a similar example where making a choice has legal and perhaps ethical consequences but is not itself an ethical matter.

3. Look at Case 1.3, *Adoptive Children* and distinguish one ethical issue from one legal issue.

4. Confronting a parent about suspected child abuse can be painful, but the results may be generally beneficial. The parent may cease to abuse the child. An act can thus be harmful in and of itself, but can have good consequences. Provide a similar example.

5. Now provide an example of something that can be good in and of itself but has harmful consequences.

6. In the restaurant example at the beginning of this chapter, does it matter whether your colleague uses the name of the person whose case she is talking about? Distinguish, in this regard, between names (e.g., Santa Claus) and identifying references (e.g., the man who comes down the chimney at Christmas). Consider, for discussion, whether any description of a case would be too likely to provide identifying references (e.g., "the woman with three children, one adopted and two from two different men") to make it safe to discuss a case in public.

7. What is an ethical dilemma? Explain clearly why it is a dilemma and why it is an ethical dilemma. Provide three examples and rank them in accordance to how difficult they are to resolve in an ethically acceptable way.

8. When you ranked the ethical dilemmas you provided in the previous question, what criterion or criteria did you use? Suppose someone were to say, "I always rank my dilemmas in terms of how much trouble their resolutions are going to cause me. The ones that cause me very little trouble are the easiest even if they cause others a lot of trouble, and the ones that cause me a lot of trouble are the hardest even if they cause others little trouble at all." How would you defend your criterion or criteria against this person's?

9. From your own experience, give an example where you had to make an ethical decision without sufficient information on the basis of which to make the decision. What criteria did you use to make the decision?

10. What does it mean for something to be conceptually problematic? Provide an example. (You might think about legal cases regarding whether someone is responsible or not.)

11. Pick a troublesome situation from your own experience, determine what the options are or were, and track the harms, that is, apply the method for determining what we ought to do.

12. Pick out an example of odd behavior—something that does not seem rational, but which the person involved is clearly doing on purpose—and construct an argument for that person that would justify what it is that he or she is doing.

13. Give an example of a goal you want to reach in your life and specify the means by which you hope to achieve it. Examine alternative ways of achieving that goal and explain why your way is the best way (if, after looking at alternatives, you still think it is).

14. Provide an example of how you have been harmed recently. Compare it with other sorts of harms—someone's hitting you, the IRS telling you that you owe lots of money—and assess its magnitude on a scale of one to ten, with ten being the worst thing that could happen to you.

15. Give an example of how someone does the right thing, but in the wrong way (such as a child yelling "I'm sorry!" to a sibling).

16. What are the advantages of cultivating the habits of thought that our method articulates?

17. What are the five steps in the method? Using one of the cases so far discussed, explain why each step is important.

18. Apply the method to one of your own cases, first describing the case and then laying out, step by step, how the method applies to it.

19. Why is it important to try to understand what the participants were doing from their points of view? Why is it not enough that what was done was wrong, for example?

2 Reasons for Acting

In the first step of the method of tracking harms, we are to:

1. *Try to understand why the participants are doing what they are doing by constructing arguments that would justify their acts or omissions.*

As we have seen, this step involves trying both to understand what a participant was thinking that could explain the action or omission and also to see how the participant could think that the action or omission was justified. We can understand why someone does something without thinking the action is justified. One child may hit another who took a toy, and we can try to understand why the one child took the toy and why the other child hit the first one. But understanding why they acted as they did does not mean we think either child was justified. If we are to determine whether a person is ethically justified in some action or omission, we need to assess the premises that we can plausibly attribute to the person to determine if they are good reasons—if, that is, they are ethically right.

So Step 1—the first step in our method of tracking harms—requires that we be clear about what kinds of reasons can be given for acts and omissions. Among all of the possible reasons that someone may have for doing or not doing something, we want to focus on the kind of reason that provides good ethical grounds. We shall find that we can have all sorts of good reasons for acting that are not in themselves ethical although they may be consistent with what is ethical. As we shall see, it is easy to confuse nonethical reasons with ethical ones.

It is also easy to think that ethical reasons are so distinct from nonethical ones that one can never have a nonethical reason for doing something ethical. That would be a mistake. We often have a number of different reasons for doing something. We may eat breakfast because it is good for us, because we like having breakfast, because we can see the family, and so on. We will then have more than one reason for eating breakfast, and if any one of two or more of these reasons suffices to explain what we are doing, what we are doing is *overdetermined*. When our doing something is overdetermined, at least two reasons are sufficient to explain our doing it and we would do it even if one of those reasons disappeared. If our eating breakfast is overdetermined, we would still eat breakfast even if everyone else in the family is sleeping late, for example.

Just so, doing what is ethically right may be overdetermined. You may do something ethically right that also serves your self-interest, provides you with pleasure, is prudent, satisfies the Code of Ethics, is standardly what anyone in your situation ought to do, and so on. Although it would be wrong to do what is not ethically right just because you want to, for instance, it is not wrong to do what is ethically right if you do it for the right reason and it also happens to satisfy your self-interest, gives you pleasure, and so on. Indeed, we should all hope for a world in which doing what is right is also prudent, satisfies our self-interest, and gives us pleasure. We do not have such a world, and so, oftentimes, doing what is ethically right conflicts with other interests we have. But when it does not conflict, that does not make it wrong. It makes it overdetermined, reasonable to do, that is, on at least two different grounds.

So when we distinguish between various kinds of reasons for acting and argue that certain kinds of reasons are not ethical reasons for acting, we leave open the possibility that when we act ethically, we may also act for other reasons. It may be thought, for instance, that one must always give up one's self-interest in acting ethically, but that is not true. What is ethical may be just what is in one's self-interest.

The goal of sorting out reasons for acting is to put us in a position to distinguish the sorts of reasons individuals have in particular cases. But applying the distinctions to particular cases is complicated by at least two factors.

First, it is difficult to be sure we know people's reasons for acting. We must make judgments of what they are thinking and believing based on how they act, and these judgments are prone to error. The possibility of an act being overdetermined means that people may do something ethically right only because it is in their self-interest, for instance. Since a single act may be explained by a variety of different reasons, that is, judging which reason or reasons count for the persons acting is a delicate matter in which it is easy to err.

Second, it is even harder to be sure we have gotten things right when we are ourselves parties to a case. It might seem easier. "After all," we may think, "who is better positioned to know our own reasons for acting than us?" But what is needed for us to be sure that what we are doing is ethical is objectivity. We need to back off from the case and, as an observer, come to understand the reasons each person involved in the case has for doing what he or she is doing. But if I am involved in a case, that means that I must (a) back off and try to see my behavior as others are seeing it and then (b) try to understand what my reasons are for doing what I am doing. Both of these enterprises are difficult.

    a. Consider, for instance, how difficult it can be to get someone to see that he or she is being abusive or passive-aggressive. Even well-intended men, who say they would not harm anyone for the world, have trouble seeing their anger or sharp words as abusive.[26] And we can all surely think of examples in which someone thought we were angry or sad, say, when we had not realized we were until asked about it. Seeing our behavior as others see it is little easier, if at all, than seeing how we look, front or back or side, to others. When we are a participant in a case, it does not give us a special inside track to understanding the case. It seems as likely to cause us more difficulty in understanding at least our own behavior.

In addition, since we are involved in the case, and so presumably have an interest in the outcome, we may find it difficult as well to be objective about what others are doing. After all, the more disreputable the behavior of others, the better one's own behavior may look, and when the outcome of the case can cause real harm to one's reputation, or when one has not acted well, it seems only human nature to try to put a better face on what one has done. We can do that by downplaying the harm one has done or by magnifying the harm others have caused.

b. Even if we come to see our behavior as others see it—and that assumes it is unambiguous enough that others see it in a single way—we have the additional problem of trying to understand our reasons for behaving as we do. Sometimes we do not do well in understanding the reasons for our own behavior. We might think that we are acting unselfishly when we are being selfish; we might think that we are acting selfishly when we are being unselfish. These are not universal truths, but we find them true often enough in the case of others, at least, that each of us must admit that they may well be true in many cases for us too. The consequence is that we can never be sure that we have come to understand correctly the reasons for our actions.

In addition, just as with understanding our behavior and that of others, we may find it difficult to be objective about the reasons others have for their behavior. After all, the more disreputable their reasons seem, the better one's own reasons may look. When one does not have good reasons or when the case may cause one real harm, it seems again only human nature to try to put a better face on the reasons for one's doing what one has done. There may thus be a natural tendency to see the reasons others have as less than pure as well as a tendency to see one's own reasons in a better light.

But as difficult as it can be in a particular case to sort out our own and others' reasons for acting, we can do no sorting until we have a checklist of the kinds of reasons we generally provide for our acts and omissions. We shall thus work our way through some of the kinds of reasons people have for acting, coming, at the end, to ethical theories and the reasons they provide. We are not concerned with providing an exhaustive list of all of the kinds of reasons people can have for acting, but only the subset of those reasons that we are likely to mistake for ethical reasons or that we will be tempted to use in difficult ethical cases. One aim is to make it clearer what counts as ethical reasons and what does not.

Self-Interest and Self-Sacrifice

Making an ethical judgment requires being like a judge. In deciding a case, a judge must come to see the situation from the point of view of the plaintiff, to see why the plaintiff has taken the case to court. Then the judge must do the same for the defendant, understanding why anyone should be willing to defend against such a charge. After seeing the case from the points of view of the defendant and the plaintiff, the judge must back off to make an objective judgment, determining not what is in the interests of either the plaintiff or the defendant, but what is right.

When we make an ethical judgment, we must extricate ourselves from the emotions of a particular situation to look at the matter objectively. But when we are involved in a situation, it is extraordinarily difficult to back off and, just as important, to *know* that we have backed off and are making objective judgments. It is like trying to be a judge between a defendant and a plaintiff when one is the defendant or the plaintiff. Among other problems, our self-interest can get in the way.

It is particularly likely to get in the way when we are unsure about what to do, as we ought to be when facing a hard case. If we are at a loss to know what to do ethically, but know we may cause great harm if we just act without clarity about our aims, we may think it best to further the interests we know. When we are confused, our immediate self-interest may seem the only clear guide for action.

Some take the opposite view. Confused about what morality requires, and knowing that morality and self-interest are not identical, they adopt the principle that in such a situation we ought to act so as *not* to further our self-interest. They think we can fish some morality out of the confusion by self-sacrifice.

We may luck into what morality requires when we sacrifice our immediate interests or act on them. Acting out of our immediate self-interest may be just what is required in a particular case to achieve morality, for instance, but this would be luck, and we would do what is ethical for the wrong reason. Doing what is ethical because it is to our immediate self-interest is not to make an ethical decision, but one based on our immediate self-interest.[27]

That is not to deny, as we have seen, that we can do what is ethical while acting in our immediate self-interest. In *Dancing a Legal Dance,* Mary had to consider that the law requires her to inform if Martha told her of child abuse, that we generally have an obligation to obey the law, and that a failure to inform might thus lead to Mary having legal problems. So besides having an obligation to obey the law, she had a concern about her own interests that might lead her to inform. Mary also had reason to believe that less harm would come to Martha if she informed, and appealing to causing less rather than more harm is an ethical reason for acting. So the judgment that Mary should inform could be backed by an ethical reason and yet also coincide with her self-interest.

Of course, it could also not coincide with her self-interest. Indeed, generally, acting in our immediate self-interest may not only be unethical, but it is likely to be unreasonable. At the least we need to distinguish between acting in our immediate versus our long-term self-interest. Being inoculated would harm my immediate self-interest because the needle's going in is painful. Being inoculated may even harm some less immediate interests because sometimes an inoculation produces a painful persistent swelling. But my long-term interests are generally well served by being inoculated. Being inoculated generally means I am protected against having a particular disease and will not have the pain and suffering and expense it causes. Those gains far outweigh the harms of the inoculation, and it would thus not be reasonable not to have an inoculation just because of the immediate and even less immediate harms it may cause.

Acting out of Prudence

To be prudent is to act cautiously and in a way that does not harm one's long-term interests. It is imprudent to drink alcohol and drive, for instance. In *The Death of a Baby,* Deborah's not telling the authorities right away what she knew about Hal's suffocating the baby creates a problem for her that she has to consider if she is to act prudently. For her later to tell what she knows is for her to admit that she kept the information to herself, thus misleading the authorities. A concern for her own well-being should not be a decisive factor in her determining what she ought to do, but the case illustrates how we can complicate our own position, and compromise our own long-term self-interest, by not acting when it may be thought most appropriate to act.

Of course, we may not know what we think we need to know to act in a timely way and may not even know what is in our interests. In *Dancing a Legal Dance,* Mary may not know whether it is more prudent to drop the case or not. If she drops it, she may get the reputation of not being able to complete difficult cases and so may not be hired again for such cases. Or she may get the reputation of being someone who knows when to cut her losses and move on. The situation is complex enough that she may not know whether going on or staying is in her long-term interests and cannot know how others will see what she does.

Mary can gain some objectivity about her position by asking what professional interests of hers may be affected. Consider her interests in being Martha's social worker and about whether she ought to tell about the abuse. We tend ultimately to trust those who are honest and open with us. The core of the relationship of being a social worker to someone is trust. The social worker must be trusted by the client, and the client must be trusted to be telling the truth to the worker. Losing that trust damages the relationship. Mary's long-term interests in remaining Martha's social worker, and so helping her eventually, argue for her being honest and clear. "If you tell me about abuse, I will have to report it."[28] So focusing on her long-term professional interest of maintaining trust so that she can maintain the relationship allows her to back off and ask herself with more objectivity what she ought to do.

To act prudently, we must examine what interests we have in a situation and distinguish carefully between our immediate interests and our long-term interests. To act prudently is to give full weight and value to long-term interests, however powerful and compelling our immediate interests may be. We may be tempted to lie for immediate advantage, but, among other things, our concern about our reputation for honesty ought to weigh heavily against any such temptation.

Acting with prudence has value. For instance, we judge people in part by whether their conduct harms their self-interest. If it does, then we cannot be sure that they will not harm our interests. If they are not careful about their own interests, why would they be careful about ours? Acting in a prudent way also gives us a broader perspective on what ought to be done. Determining our long-term interests requires us to back off from the immediate situation and so creates some distance for us from the immediate situation. That distance provides some objectivity.

Yet what is prudent is not necessarily ethical, and vice versa. Acting in our long-term self-interest may be ethical, but not because it is in our long-term self-interest. Deciding not to help others because it is in our long-term self-interest is not to make an ethical decision, but a decision based on our self-interest.[29] And acting ethically may harm our own long-term self-interest. There is no guaranteed match between what is ethical and what is prudent.

Doing What Is Legally Permitted or Required

In *Dancing a Legal Dance,* Mary was legally required to report the information about child abuse given to her by Martha. So if, to keep Martha's trust, she had kept the information confidential, she would have broken the law. Mary had a conflict between keeping silent and doing what the law requires. Appealing to the law seems to lift the burden of decision-making from a social worker's shoulders and provide a way out of a complex problem.

In *Doing What the Judge Orders,* John thinks his interests are doubly protected by his going through channels. He thinks he is protected because no one can fault him for having made a professionally questionable decision on his own. In addition, the "right choice" becomes what the law requires, whatever John's self-interest may be and whatever others may think.

Appealing to the law can resolve an ethical problem; but although we may end up doing what is ethically right and protecting the self-interest of those involved, in this case appealing to the law does neither. John's supervisor and the judge knew exactly whom he was talking about, and so, though he never mentioned Jane's name, he identified her as having AIDS. He thus can be faulted for breaching confidentiality. The judge can be faulted for having Al tested without his permission, and John and his supervisor can be faulted both for following the judge's unethical decision and for so manipulating things as to make it appear to observers that the judge is at fault, not they. The case nicely illustrates how appealing to the law can provide a way of resolving our doubts about what to do, but does not guarantee an ethical resolution—even though self-interest, and even prudence, may encourage that resolution.

What is ethical and what is legal may diverge. We may be ethically obligated to do something that the law does not require. Someone who owes a debt, and is not able to pay it for awhile, and is also able to convince the person to whom the debt is owed not to sue will not be legally obligated after a certain period of time. The legal obligation will lapse, but the ethical obligation to pay the debt remains. We may also be legally obligated to do something that ethically makes no difference.

But although what is ethical and what is legal may diverge, we are not suggesting that social workers, or any professionals, not do what the law requires. We are suggesting that the law is not the final word on what a social worker ought to do to be ethical. Legislators do not determine what is ethical, and we cannot justify doing what is ethical by saying, "The law says I have to do that." We need to add, "And the law is ethically right in this case." Some laws may not be ethically right. Martin Luther King certainly thought so when he protested state and federal laws supporting segregation. Thus, although we must take what the law says about a situation into account in deciding what to do, what the laws says is not determinative of what we ought to do.

Doing What Is Standardly Done

A person trained as a professional is trained into a set of practices that constitute the standards of the profession and are normative for someone in the profession. A social worker's failure to honor confidentiality, for instance, subjects the social worker, at a minimum, to criticism—both from the client and from the social worker's colleagues and others.

We get a sense of the normative power of these standard practices by noting what should be a lawyer's first question to a physician accused of malpractice. "Did you do what any physician would do under the circumstances?" If the answer is affirmative, the lawyer has the first line of defense in hand. "You are indicting the entire medical profession, not just my client, for any physician would have done what my client did. It's standard medical practice!"

To become a professional we must learn the standard practices, and because standard practices serve as norms for professionals, a professional must follow the standard practices to practice well, it may be thought. They are sanctioned, and so legitimized, by countless professionals having done them. Yet, for all that, they may be mistaken. It may be standard practice for someone to counsel all of the members of a family, as Mary does in *Dancing a Legal Dance,* but it puts Mary in a position where she is tempted, and even told by a colleague, to encourage the father to confess. Although confession may be good for the soul, it is not obviously her job as social worker to urge a client to confess. Standard practice does not guarantee an ethical practice.

A professional is always faced with a dilemma, obligated to follow standard practice because those are the norms of the profession, and yet obligated to question those norms and to act otherwise if they are wrong. It takes courage to step outside the normal practice of the profession to do something contrary to that practice. We open ourselves to the charge that, as an opposing lawyer might put it, "It is not the profession itself we indict today, but only this person, who, instead of following standard practice for such a case, insisted on following whims, untried and untested by the countless, good professionals who would have saved my client harm by doing what the profession requires."

An appeal to the standard practice of a profession has weight in deciding what we ought to do because that practice supposedly represents accumulated professional wisdom—the way in which many different persons responded to the same sort of problem, presumably with some success.[30] If they all responded in the same way, despite their personal differences and the presumed differences in the situations they faced, that is some guidance to how anyone ought to respond. But appealing to the standard practice of social workers has its problems.

First, the situation we find ourselves in may be so unique that there is no accumulated wisdom and so no standard practice. How many times have social workers found themselves in a situation like that confronting John in *Doing What the Judge Orders*?

Second, even if there is a standard practice, we may not be able to find out what it is. Social work often takes place in private. The social worker's interactions with a client are generally unobservable by others, taking place in an office or during a home visit. The requirements of confidentiality may mean that cases never get discussed. We may not be able to discover any similar case.

Third, even if we do, we cannot be sure we have discovered the standard practice. Professionals are in a variety of communities. The professional community of a social worker stretches beyond the confines of the agency employing the social worker, the community within which the social worker actually lives, and the local or state professional organizations to which the social worker belongs. We cannot be sure these communities have the same standard practice for particular problems. What is acceptable in one community may be unacceptable in another. So even if we discover what others have done, we may not know whether it represents the standard way of handling such a situation, or whether it is the way those in a particular community handle such problems. Those who acted that way may have been as lost as we may find ourselves.

Fourth, even if there is a standard practice, and we can find out what it is, we may not know what it means in a particular case. The standard practice may be open to a variety of interpretations, or it may be clear, but we may be unclear how it applies in the case in question. In *Doing What the Judge Orders*, standard practice may require us to tell Al that he is to be tested for HIV, but we may be unclear whether that means we must ask him directly, "Is it permissible to test you for HIV?" or whether it is acceptable to ask, "Is it OK if we test you for everything you might have?" The standard practice may be consistent with both alternatives, but the latter would deny Al information he would need to give informed consent. In short, the standard practice may be itself conceptually problematic, consistent with different ways of understanding what is required or permitted, with different implications for what a practitioner ought to do.

So it is oftentimes not possible to appeal to a single accepted understanding of what is the standard practice for a particular kind of problem. But even in the best of cases, where there is an accepted understanding, doing what is standardly done is no guarantee that we are acting ethically. That a group of practitioners in a profession have come to act in a certain way in certain situations may provide the individuals in the group with legal protection, since they can cite the "standards of the profession" as a justification for their actions, but it surely does not ensure that their actions are ethical. Otherwise, we should have to admit that because slave owners were a group, what they commonly did regarding their slaves was ethical. Or, more pointedly, even if social work practitioners commonly talked about their cases in public, that would not make it ethical.

This point about common practice not being ethical merely because it is the common practice can be difficult to accept for someone trained into a set of professional standards, particularly when those are embodied in a code of ethics that clearly contains ethical pronouncements. But codes of ethics have histories—have changed, that is, as professions have changed—and the changes are evidence that at least some of a code's pronouncements are not the truths of ethics that some may imagine. It used to be common practice in medicine, for example, for medical practitioners to talk about their cases in public places. It is still common practice for those at admitting desks in hospitals and doctors' offices to ask, loudly enough for others to hear, whether one has insurance, and if so, with what insurer. That such practices were or are common does not make them right. It is a sign of the ethical maturity of a profession to critique its own code of ethics, as the social work profession has recently done, and make the changes it sees are needed to ensure that the code better accords with what is ethically right. That a code of ethics is ethically better obviously does not mean that it is ethically the best it can ever be. History teaches us otherwise.

But where a code of ethics does embody the standard practice of a profession, one may think that at least it provides clear guidance as to what the profession thinks we ought to do in particular cases. Unfortunately, although appealing to a code of ethics for a profession provides some guidance about the sorts of ethical considerations we should keep in mind in trying to resolve an ethical problem, it is no better than appealing to the standard practice in guaranteeing true ethical premises and not much help in resolving the difficult ethical cases we are considering.

Appealing to the Code of Ethics

In the best of cases, codes of ethics contain the essential values of a profession, making explicit the ethical commitments of those in the profession to those whom the profession is to serve. Those learning about a profession may look to its code to understand the profession's mission and how its practitioners see themselves as working to fulfill it in an ethical way. They will also find prohibitions against certain sorts of behavior (like speaking about cases in a public place) and admonishments to further certain goals (like furthering the self-determination of clients).

But what neither those learning about a profession nor those in the profession will find is much guidance for the sorts of ethical problems we laid out in Chapter 1. These problems arise in specific cases where the details make a difference, and no code of ethics can be expected to guide us in everything we must do. And these are hard cases, about which seasoned professionals may disagree, and the Code recognizes that such cases exist and does not attempt to resolve them by fiat.

Consider what John in *Doing What the Judge Orders* would find were he to look at the *Code of Ethics of the National Association of Social Workers* to help him determine what he ought to do when told by another social work practitioner that his client's mother, Jane, has AIDS. In the section of the social work Code concerned with confidentiality and privacy, we find the following rule:

> The social worker should protect the confidentiality of all information obtained in the course of professional service, except for compelling professional reasons (1.07[c]).

This provision tells a social worker that a client's confidence has great ethical weight, enough to make it wrong for Jane's social work practitioner to tell anyone that Jane has AIDS except for "compelling professional reasons."[31] So she is not to chat about it casually, and she is not even to pass it on in a professional setting unless she has a compelling professional reason. So the Code is helpful in giving us some guidance about what not to do. It does that in telling us what kind of reason we ought to have to deny someone's confidentiality.

It then provides an explanation of what counts as compelling professional reasons when it says that:

> . . . the general expectation that social workers will keep information confidential does not apply when disclosure is necessary to prevent serious, foreseeable, and imminent harm to a client or other identifiable person . . . (1.07[c]).

This is the right sort of reason to justify denying confidentiality. Causing harm to others if we retain confidentiality is arguably unethical if the harm is foreseeable and imminent and of sufficient magnitude.

But requiring that we know that harm will occur sets a high standard to meet, and so the Code will be unhelpful in the most difficult cases—the ones in which we know of a risk of harm, even a great risk, but do not know for sure that harm will occur.[32] Deborah's problem in Case 1.1, *The Death of a Baby* is of just that sort.

Second, if John is to act to prevent harm, what ought he to do?

- Tell Al that he may be HIV-positive?
- Tell Al that his mother has AIDS and that he may be HIV-positive?
- Tell Al that he may have something, but John is not sure what?
- Not tell Al anything, but tell others who may act for Al?

These are ethically different ways of responding to the problem. The first two respect Al's self-determination, giving him information he would need to make an informed decision. But they differ in that only the latter explains why John thinks Al may be HIV-positive—although only by implication, leaving it to Al to figure out that John thinks he and his mother are sexually intimate.

The third provides Al with no information about the source of a possible infection or about what the infection is. So it protects the confidentiality of Al's mother, but leaves Al without the information John has that makes informed consent possible for Al. If I am told I have something, but have no suspicion it will lead to AIDS, I cannot willingly consent to a procedure that will test for my being HIV-positive. So when I make a decision, I will have at best the illusion of self-determination.

The fourth alternative denies Al even the illusion. It is the one John chose, and it denies Al's self-determination. Others are deciding for him what ought to be done about him.

These four options differ ethically, and John made an ethical choice when he chose the fourth. Is there anything in the Code that might necessitate or justify that choice? Only one section is relevant:

> Social workers may limit clients' right to self-determination when, in the social workers' professional judgment, clients' actions or potential actions pose a serious, foreseeable, and imminent risk to themselves or others (1.02).

This Code gives John permission to limit Al's self-determination, and for almost, but not quite, the same reasons that must hold for the general expectation of maintaining confidentiality to be lifted.

We are justified ethically in breaching a client's right to confidentiality when there is "serious, foreseeable, and imminent harm to a client or other identifiable person." We are justified in denying a client's right to self-determination when there is "a serious, foreseeable, and imminent risk to themselves or others." Denying confidentiality requires knowing that harm will occur; denying self-determination requires knowing that a risk of harm will occur.

The Code thus sets different standards for denying self-determination and confidentiality. We are permitted to limit a client's right to self-determination when we believe there is a risk that harm will occur, and we are "generally expected" to deny confidentiality when harm will occur. It is thus easier to deny someone's right to self-determination than it is to breach someone's confidentiality. For the former, we need only know that a risk of harm will occur, whereas for the latter, we must know that harm will occur. The Code thus makes breaching confidentiality ethically worse than denying self-determination because we need more to justify breaching confidentiality than we do to deny self-determination. So when John chose to deny Al's self-determination rather than breach the confidence, he was acting consistently with the Code.

But it is not at all obvious that confidentiality ought to have more ethical weight than self-determination. The Code implies that it does, but that does not make it true.

And that is one problem. Even if it were true, its being in the Code would not be sufficient to justify John's behavior. Citing a provision of a code does not give the ethical *reasons* for doing what it says to do. It is not enough to say, "The Code told me so."

Second, John cannot properly cite the Code. The Code tells him to break a confidence only for a compelling professional reason, but he only has a compelling professional reason if harm is to occur. But he cannot know that harm is to occur without knowing the results of Al's test. He thus cannot use the harm's occurring as the reason for having Al tested. Indeed, even if we were to lower the threshold and require only an increased risk of harm, John would not be able to act because he cannot know before Al is tested that Al is putting anyone at risk. So John must find some independent basis, something other than the Code, to justify having Al tested.

In general, if a client has an ethical right not to have confidentiality breached except for compelling professional reasons, only an ethical reason can be the right kind of reason. In addition, the reason must be compelling *enough*, must outweigh—to use a metaphor—the ethical heft of a client's right to confidentiality. So we always need to ask the following two questions when we are considering denying a client's ethical right:

a. Do we have the right kind of reason for doing that?

Wanting your friends to know how difficult the case is that you are working on is not the right kind of reason for denying confidentiality, but even if we have an ethical reason, we must ask:

b. Is the reason compelling enough to deny the right?

We have the same reasons for ensuring that what a client says to a social work practitioner remains confidential as we do for ensuring that a patient's concerns are kept confidential by the physician and other medical practitioners who have access to them. Patients and clients need to be assured that they can speak freely, without having their remarks read or passed on to anyone, so that, among other things, physicians and practitioners can be sure that they have all the information they need to give informed assistance. That others may come to know of something the client finds embarrassing or wants to maintain private is an impediment to the client's engaging in the free and open exchange necessary for informed professional practice.

But besides this practical reason for maintaining confidentiality, clients have an ethical right, independent of the practical consequences, that what they tell to a social work practitioner will be kept private. The information they provide is about aspects of their lives that are not, presumably, general knowledge to the world at large, and just as we all have a right that others not disseminate private information about us, clients have a right that those whom they see professionally keep private what was private.[33]

But whatever we do, we must also—always—ask a third question:

c. Is our act or omission firmly enough grounded with ethical reasoning that it can properly serve as a precedent for others?

Every decision—to act or not to act—creates a precedent others may appeal to in determining and justifying what they do. Therefore, we need to be careful when we make decisions not to provide a precedent that can readily be misused. Otherwise, we may find our decision being cited as a precedent for someone's denying confidentiality, for example, for reasons we do not think relevant or for relevant reasons we do not think weighty enough. The latter difficulty is common to every distinction in which lines cannot be clearly drawn. If a particular reason is judged weighty enough to justify breaching someone's confidentiality, a similar reason almost as weighty may be thought weighty enough even if it is a closer call. This continues on down the slippery slope.

The problem of our judgments about what we ought to do creating precedents is compounded because judgments about what ethical weight various considerations have are subject to no clear calculus. Well-intended, well-informed, and bright individuals may disagree. Others may think your decision is an obvious precedent for what they ought to do even if you do not see it as such. What counts is not what you think or would say if asked, but how what you did is understood by others—even if you understand it differently.

In general, to summarize, codes of ethics fail to provide solutions to hard cases. They fail because of what a code is designed to do and because of the nature of ethical dilemmas and problematic cases. A code of ethics is meant to define a profession. For instance, nurses ought to act for the well-being of their patients. That concern is of such importance that it outweighs the self-interest of a nurse. But those in business would not long survive if they took as a primary obligation caring for their customers' well-being rather than their own. A complete and well-articulated code of ethics for a profession would distinguish one profession from another ethically.

Yet professionals can reach agreement about what defines their profession only if the provisions are of a high enough generality that their articulation does not cause disagreement. As soon as we begin to specify the *reasons* why a nurse is obligated to put the well-being of a patient above his or her own, or begin to specify exactly what it is that a nurse ought to do in such a situation, we discover disagreement. Is a nurse to care for a patient if the nurse is likely to get very ill—with AIDS, for instance? Such a question raises disputes about what counts as relevant reasons and about how weighty various relevant reasons are. Social workers must encourage as much self-determination as possible and yet intervene to help others, sometimes making decisions for them about what is in their best interest. Determining how much to intervene to encourage self-determination or prevent harm requires giving reasons and assessing them. No code of ethics can state how we are to resolve this sort of problem in the multitude of cases in which it occurs. We can see how this occurs in each of the three kinds of ethical problems we can face—ethical dilemmas, factually problematic cases, and conceptually problematic cases.

In *The Death of a Baby*, Deborah's problem was that she did not know what happened and yet had to decide how much she should hold Hal responsible. But merely knowing of a possible harm to others is generally not enough to justify denying a right.[34] When a case is factually problematic, its very nature—the state of our ignorance—makes appeal to the Code problematic.

The same is true for conceptually problematic cases. If John decided to break confidentiality, he would need to decide whether a fifteen-year-old is old enough to give informed consent and then whether *this* fifteen-year-old is an exception to whatever generally holds. He did not do either, but, in any event, the Code of Ethics would be no help. What it is to be "old enough to provide informed consent" is conceptually problematic, with people disagreeing whether the concept is applicable even when they agree on the facts. In addition, codes of ethics fail to be specific enough to be helpful, and, obviously, no code could help decide whether Al is an exception to whatever the general rule is.

Codes also fail to be specific enough to help with ethical dilemmas. Dilemmas are especially sensitive to details. If the harm to one side were just a little more, or were this kind of harm rather than that, we might be justified in deciding one way rather than another. We cannot know until we look at the details, but no code of ethics can provide detailed prescriptions for every case that may arise, let alone do that and be general enough to obtain the general assent of a profession.[35]

As we have mentioned, codes of ethics state, in one readily discoverable place, what a profession has presumably agreed upon as its essential values and norms. So codes can be used, among other things, to socialize members into a profession and to provide a basis for corrective measures and sanctioning members for violations in order to protect both individuals and the social good. And, as we saw regarding the situation in which a co-worker tells you in a lunch line about a case, the Code of Ethics provides clear and helpful guidance about what social workers are and are not to do in some kinds of cases. It provides a map to guide social workers about what is relevant and what is not in more difficult cases.

Doing What Is Ethical

When faced with an ethical problem, we ought to proceed in a systematic way to get a grip on what the problem is. No procedure will always lead to a single clear and obviously correct answer, but we ought to get into a position to see what the possible answers are.

Getting the Facts

As our method of tracking harm requires, we begin by determining what the facts are. This is often not easy. In *The Death of a Baby* we may never know why Hal did not awaken while he lay on his son. Perhaps he had an epileptic fit. If he did, it would make a difference in any judgment we would make about him, but if he is unaware of what happened, access to it may be lost forever.

We may also think we know something we do not know. Although Mary Todd has no reason not to believe Martha's story about her father's sexual abuse, and has good reason to believe it because it was substantiated by Martha's sister, still, there is no clinical evidence of such abuse. So we can at best say that Mary has good reason for *believing* that Martha has been sexually abused, not that Mary *knows* that.

Getting the facts right thus requires sorting things in different piles—what we know, what we think we know but may be wrong about, what we have good reason to believe, what we suspect but have no good evidence for, and so on. The borderlines between these categories are not clear, but even if they were, we can be unclear where to put what often does not fit neatly into a category. But we must make the attempt, for that tells us what we need to double-check and what more we need to know. We often find that we were assuming something we thought we knew or that the evidence we have for something is inadequate. For instance, Mary has good evidence that Martha is beating her mother. Her mother has bruises, and Martha says she is beating her. But her mother will not talk, and the evidence is consistent with the father's beating the mother and Martha lying to protect him—perhaps because he is forcing her to.

Even what seems obvious may not be. A woman was charged with first-degree murder because she stabbed her live-in lover with a butcher knife as he was being held by two policemen. He had been beating her again, and neighbors called. When the police came, they grabbed him, and she went to the kitchen and came back with the knife behind her. As he stood with the policemen holding his arms, she killed him before they had a chance to intervene. It looks like an open-and-shut case of cold-blooded murder, stupidly executed. If she wanted to kill him, why kill him in front of witnesses, and the very best sort of witnesses one can get?

Yet appearances can be deceiving. Suppose that he had been beating her for a long time, that this time he said he was going to kill her, and that she felt powerless to prevent him. She knew the police would not keep him long and believed he would return and beat her unmercifully, perhaps to death. She did not have the capacity to keep him away from herself and her children, whom he was abusing. So she killed him while he was helpless—the only way she thought she could. What at first appears to be stupid cold-blooded murder may be a desperate act of self-defense. This scenario does not justify her act, but does put it in a different light.

The context makes a difference. Often without really thinking about it, we assume a context for a particular set of facts, but with a different context, the *facts* look different. One can tell a variety of different stories that are consistent with a single set of facts, and yet those different stories make the facts different. What looks irrational may turn out to be the smartest thing to do in such a situation.

This sort of problem can be particularly acute in social work where a social worker from one culture may have a client from another. What is commonplace and obvious for one person, in one culture, may be odd and obscure to another, in another culture. The Code of Ethics thus mandates that social workers "should have a knowledge base of their clients' cultures" and "seek to understand the nature of cultural diversity" (1.05[b] & [c]).

The same sort of problem can arise when a practitioner is from one social or economic class and the client is from another or when the client is a person with developmental disabilities, for instance, and what seems obvious to the practitioner is not at all obvious to the client. Getting the facts does not mean listing bits and pieces of information, but understanding the full picture, understanding as fully as we can the context within which those bits and pieces fit.

Discounting Our Biases

In *Adoptive Children,* LaShonda had to make judgments about who should get her help and who should not. She decided to give help "only to those who would be sensitive to the needs of their natural parents" and then had to determine who was likely to be sensitive and who was not. She decided that those who work to change the law show they are not selfish and that those who work in support groups for adoptive children show they care about others. So she used those two factors to determine who should get information, but the way she used these factors in regard to the brother and sister creates a concern about bias.

She decided they should not get information, and one of her stated reasons was that they came to her without an appointment. But that seems a trivial and mistaken reason for treating them differently than others. It is a presumption of justice that like cases be treated alike, and so it would be unjust to treat anyone needing help differently from others for reasons that make no ethical difference. LaShonda did treat the two differently, and so she needs a good ethical reason for doing that.

But coming to see a public official without making an appointment is not evidence of a lack of concern for the official and thus of a lack of concern for others. The brother and sister may not have thought about needing an appointment to see a public official. Or, having thought about it, they may have been hesitant to call because they were afraid LaShonda might not see them, given what they wanted.

If we are to come to a proper ethical judgment, we must discount any feature of the situation or of ourselves that may cause us to bias our judgment. But LaShonda seems unduly sensitive to slights. So some feature of her may be biasing her judgment. And without checking, LaShonda does not know why the two did not make an appointment. Their failing to do so may be due to an insensitivity to the interests of others, but it also may be due to their youth, or to their concern about being rejected should they call first, or to their failure to realize one calls a public official to make an appointment—a failure common, we should think, to many of us. So a feature of the situation may be misleading LaShonda. The brother and sister may seem impetuous and selfish when they may be cautious and concerned.

LaShonda's other criteria for helping is that those who ask her are working to change the law and are in support groups. But that may be to hold the brother and sister to too high a standard. They are young and perhaps politically inexperienced. Working to change the law may not have occurred to them, or they may already be jaded enough by the political system to be skeptical about the possi-

bility of changing the law. Why should their immaturity, or their competing political judgment, be held against them, and similarly for not working with a support
group? They might think it important, but going to school and working to support
themselves, they may judge they should do it later. Why should a judgment about
timing or priorities be held against them?

What LaShonda needs to know are the reasons the two have failed to do
what she thinks they ought to do. Otherwise she is not entitled to make a judgment that excludes them from access to information she is giving others.

We may explain LaShonda's hesitations by her prudential concerns. Setting
high standards for those to whom she gives illegal information is a way of protecting herself. She may think that those who care about the well-being of their
natural parents, and are concerned to change the law, are less likely than others to
tell on her.

Yet the remark about the brother and sister not calling to make an appointment arouses a suspicion that she is not properly applying her own stated criteria
for determining who is to get help and who is not. The judgment she is making
not to give them help may be determined by her irritation at being treated in a
way she considers impolite. But if she has decided to give information to those
who deserve it, she should take into account only what is relevant. What is
required in making ethical judgments is that the judgment be *objective*, not in any
way biased by subjective factors.

It is not just ethical judgments that require objectivity. We ought to examine
how much money we have in our checking accounts by checking on what we have
put in and taken out, not by fantasizing about what we want there. Objectivity is
not usually problematic when checking how much money we have in our
account, but checking our ethical judgments is more difficult. They tell us how
things ought to be, not how they are, and so we cannot check them against the
world to see if they are true. They are also peculiarly prone to be biased by individual, social, and cultural biases.

A major difficulty in making ethical judgments is that some feature of ourselves may get in the way of being objective, and we are the worst positioned to
realize it. In making ethical judgments about others, it may matter that one is
white, or that one is female, or that one was born of relatively well-to-do parents.
We may so look at the world, and thus so look at the problems we face, that even
what we *see* is biased by those features of ourselves. What we must do to make a
proper ethical judgment is to discount anything about ourselves that might bias
our judgment. We must ignore our own economic position in making a judgment
about someone with more money or someone with less. Neither envy nor sympathy ought to bias us. If we are having a bad day, that ought not to make a difference in how we treat our clients. Someone who comes on a bad day ought not be
penalized for such bad luck.

The question to ask oneself in coming to an ethical judgment is always
whether others, differently situated regarding the relevant feature, would make
the same judgment. LaShonda should thus ask herself whether someone else who
is not offended by someone's not calling to make an appointment would judge as

she did. Asking whether someone else without that feature would agree is a way of assuring a judgment's objectivity. Just as we want, as it were, to look past our own personal characteristics to see a situation as others would see it, so we want to examine and discard whatever external features may prevent us from seeing the client in an unbiased way. We are trying to get rid of the contingent features of the situation that ought not to make a difference to the ethical judgment we make—that we got up on the wrong side of the bed in the morning, that the person is from another culture, and so on.

The problem of discounting our biases to try to obtain objectivity permeates every aspect of understanding an ethical problem. Even getting the facts right depends upon understanding the context within which they occur, and that context can be determined by cultural features, for instance, not easily accessible to someone from another culture. We must try to understand the situation from within that context and then back off from it, and from our own, to determine what we ought to do.

Giving Reasons

When we give reasons for doing or not doing something, we provide arguments. That word may make us think of people with loud voices disagreeing to no good effect. But an argument is a set of premises that provide support for a conclusion, and although people do use arguments in disagreeing with each other, they also must use arguments to provide reasons for doing what they think they ought to do. If Mary, in *Dancing a Legal Dance,* is not to engage in therapy with both the father and Martha, she needs reasons for choosing one or the other.

But the reasons given in the premises of an argument can fail to support a conclusion in two different ways. They may fail to support the conclusion because even if true, they are not relevant to the conclusion. Or a premise may be relevant, and so could support the conclusion, but does not because it is false.

The first kind of failure is one that depends upon the relationship between the premises and the conclusion. Could those sorts of premises support that conclusion? This is a question of the form of the argument and has nothing to do with whether the premises are true or false. For example, in the following example of what is called a deductive argument, the premises could support the conclusion:

> All social workers are overpaid.
> All overpaid workers are lazy.
> Therefore all social workers are lazy.

This argument is valid. The premises are such that if they were true, it is necessary that the conclusion be true as well. A mark of a valid argument is that we can put different premises of the same form in place of those in the argument and, no matter what premises we put in, we can never have true premises and a false conclusion. A valid argument preserves the truth of the premises so that we never go from truth to falsehood.

But we must start with true premises if truth is to be preserved, and the premises in this argument are false. Social workers are not all overpaid, and not all overpaid workers are lazy. So these premises do not succeed in proving the conclusion true. A good argument, one that gives good reasons for a conclusion, has true premises that provide support for a conclusion.

Consider John's conclusion in *Doing What the Judge Orders*. He concluded that he would not be responsible for Al's being tested for HIV because the judge told him to do it. So his argument goes roughly like this:

> The judge told me to have Al tested.
> We are not responsible for what we are told to do.
> Therefore, I am not responsible for having Al tested.

These premises, if true, would support the conclusion. If we are not responsible for what we are told to do, we are not responsible for doing something we are told to do. So the argument is valid. But is it true that we are not responsible for what we are told to do? Surely John does not think we should never question orders. Suppose someone ordered him to murder Al. If we are to understand why John thinks he is not responsible, we must understand him as implying something like this. When we are told to do something by someone who has the authority to tell us what to do, *and* what we are told to do is ethically right, then we are not responsible. But although this new premise is more likely to be true, the conclusion is not supported by it unless it is right to have Al tested without his knowledge and permission. John must be assuming that it is. But a judge's ordering it does not make it ethically right.

Trying to understand how John could argue for his conclusion allows us to see more clearly what is at issue in the case. As we try to see how John could have true premises for the conclusion he draws, we uncover the assumptions John is making that we must assess—including the premises John must take to be true. Such premises purport to be true of the world, and so we can look to the world to see if they are true. Premises that tell us what we ought to do do not tell us how the world is, but how it ought to be. The question arises, then, how we determine the truth and falsity of such premises.

Finding True Ethical Premises

As we have seen, we cannot be sure that what prudence, or the law, or standard practice tells us is ethical.[36] Even if what is ethical is prudent, legal, and standard practice, it is not ethical for those reasons. And appealing to the Code of Ethics does not give us sufficient guidance in difficult cases. So we need to determine on what basis we are to judge what is ethical.

Tracking Harms.   In each case we have had so far, the practitioner was trying to prevent something harmful from occurring. In *Dancing a Legal Dance*, Mary was concerned, among other things, with preventing the father from further harming

Martha. In *The Death of a Baby*, Deborah was concerned that no matter what she did, she would cause harm to the family, either by saying nothing when something should be said or by saying something when nothing should be said. In *Doing What the Judge Orders*, John tried to work through a mine field of different harms to his client, to his fellow social worker, and to the innocent persons who might become infected with AIDS. And in *Adoptive Children*, LaShonda thought the law harmed those children and their natural parents who would want to be reunited, and she tried to give information only to those she thought would not cause harm.

It is no accident that each case involves minimizing harms. Social workers and their clients are not often graced with the problem of choosing between different goods, and when they are, though the choice may be difficult, it is hard to complain about a mistake. The problem that most often confronts them is that of preventing harm and, unfortunately, of trying to determine which is the lesser of two or more harms.

One helpful way of entry into difficult ethical problems is thus to track the harms that have occurred and are likely to occur. This is why our method is designed to ferret out harms. In *Dancing a Legal Dance*, the number and varieties of harms are enormous—the physical and psychological harm by the father to his daughters, the deterioration of what is left of the family, the physical and psychological harm to the mother as Martha batters her, the harm to Martha and others caused by Martha's deterioration, what Martha took to be the deception by Mary in reporting what Martha thought she was telling her in confidence, the consequent loss of the relationship of trust between Mary and Martha, Martha's possible lack of trust in anyone who may now try to help her, the harm to others who are not being served because of the time spent on this family, and so on. Many different persons—Martha, Kathy, the mother, perhaps even Mary, who may get a reputation for not being able to do such therapy well—were harmed or are at risk of being harmed, in a variety of different ways—physically, psychologically, socially, and so on.

Suppose Mary were considering whether to deceive Martha about having to tell. What ought she to take into consideration? First, there is the deception itself. We are harmed by deceit whatever the consequences. Second, the relationship a social worker has with a client requires trust. Mary must weigh whatever good reason she thinks she has for deception against the likelihood that Martha will no longer know when she should believe Mary and when not. Third, Martha has already been deceived by her father, someone she should be able to trust. So in deceiving her, Mary is making it that much harder for Martha to trust anyone. Martha will learn that even someone professionally obligated to be trustworthy is not. Fourth, Martha will have been denied the opportunity to decide for herself whether to tell Mary what her father is doing.

As the list of harms grows, some immediate and some long-term, it becomes harder to justify Mary's not telling Martha what she is legally obligated to do. As we saw, the harm she is trying to prevent—Martha's being abused by her father—may not be prevented even if Mary gets the information she needs to go to court.

The harm that may result from the deception may be much worse—the continuation of the abuse and the loss of anyone Martha feels she can trust to help her. The dilemma Mary may have had, to tell or not to tell, is easier to resolve if we list the harms and consider whom they will affect, for we can more readily determine what course of action is likely to minimize the harms that may occur. Tracking the harms allows us to see that Mary ought to be honest with Martha because the gain in not being honest does not outweigh the harms caused by the deception.

In making this judgment, we are implicitly appealing to an ethical theory, and it is time to turn to an examination of the most plausible candidates. It is these theories that provide backing for the ethical premises we must use in making ethical judgments.

Ethical Theories. Suppose again a situation that has as many footholds for immorality as we can find—a person intentionally doing something to someone else that is itself harmful to that person's interests and will predictably cause other harms, the harms are of great magnitude, the person causing the harms knows that what he or she is doing is harmful and does it because it is harmful, and what is done sets a precedent for others to cause similar harms in similar situations.[37] We need to consider the harms of both the act itself and its effects, including the systemic harm that may result from an act's being a precedent. Within the act itself, we need to separate out the intention of the person who acted (or omitted acting when acting was called for), the knowledge or ignorance of that person regarding what was done (because we might do something intentionally, but without realizing that what we did was harmful), including the capacity to predict the normally expected consequences of the act, the kind of act that was done, and the magnitude of the harms committed.

With so many ways in which harms can occur, and so many different kinds of harm to compare with and weigh against one another, we can understand how saying we ought to minimize harms would be unhelpful in some cases. Not every issue will work itself out in the way we worked out what John ought to do regarding Al in *Doing What the Judge Orders.*

A major source of difficulty is that different ethical theories hold up different visions of what we ought to do. An act may further a particular vision, may fail to further it, or may positively harm its realization. But what sets back the realization of one vision, and so is a harm to it, will not necessarily set back another vision, and so will not be a harm according to it. Indeed, what is a harm by one theory may not even look like a harm by another or may look like a different sort of harm, of a different kind and different weight. So a participant who sees a situation according to one moral theory may not even *see* a problem—see something *as* a harm—that someone else, with a different vision, takes to be central. The situation is like that in the example we considered in which a woman stabbed her lover while he was being held by two police officers. What appeared irrational in one interpretation appears more reasonable, though desperate, under another. So one source of disagreement people may have in grappling with cases is that they presume different ethical visions, perhaps without realizing it.

We will find that many of the cases we consider lend themselves to resolution even when they are viewed in different ways by different theories, for often the theories produce the same result, though for different reasons. Each of the theories we consider provides reasons for minimizing harms, for instance. But sometimes the best we can do is to lay out how the competing ethical visions produce different ethical results. The difficulty we will have in resolving some hard ethical problems is that we have no way to choose between these competing visions.

One main divide between ethical theories regards the ethical import given to what happens in the world versus what is internal to the person acting in the world.

On the one hand, ethical acts are acts. When I turn the knob of a door, I act for some end—to open the door to go out, to see if the door is still stuck. By turning the knob, I may cause it to break, or to become stuck, or to open the door so a person lurking outside can enter. Ethical acts and omissions are like any other acts and omissions. They have consequences in the world, intended or not.

An ethical theory may take as ethically crucial what happens in the world and thus what is done to other people. After all, the argument would go, if by our acts we harm others, we have acted unethically. Any truly ethical theory, it is claimed, must take as of first importance how it is that we treat others when we act.

Yet, on the other hand, it is arguable that we can only be held ethically accountable for what we are responsible for. If I become so ill that I faint, and in fainting fall against you, I cannot be held responsible for falling against you or, if I am, only to the extent that I am responsible for making myself so ill that I faint. But if we are only ethically accountable for what we are responsible for, then, the argument goes, we can only be held accountable for what we decide to do. We surely cannot be held accountable for the consequences of our actions that no one could reasonably have predicted, and it is not even obvious that we should be held accountable for our actions. We have all been in situations in which we thought we were doing one thing, but were interpreted as doing something else. We cannot be held responsible for how people interpret what we do, the argument continues, and so, at best, we can only be held accountable for what we decide to do—independently of our act and of its effects in the world. What is ethically crucial in this view is not what happens in the world—not even the act of the person, but something about the person who acts.

But if we examine what happens when someone decides to act, we discover much complexity. The person may think through what he or she is doing or not, be motivated by hate or by love in doing the very same thing, act in character or out of character, and so on. A main divide within this complex terrain of a person is between what a person intends to do and the person's character. Even a person with a bad character may intend to do something good, for the right reasons, and the person should get ethical credit for the intention, despite the bad character. So, it may be argued, it is the intention that matters ethically. But, someone may argue, anyone can do something good. It takes real commitment to forge a good character, to make of oneself a person whose very constitution is good and who acts ethically out of a deep, abiding commitment and not some transient intention. On this view, what matters is the character on the basis of which we act.

These disagreements turn on disputes about what kind of world we ought to live in, on competing visions of an ethically ideal world. We can best sketch out the competing theories by imagining ourselves being asked to create an ethical world, a world that we would recognize as an ethical ideal, but a world that *we* could achieve, a realistic possibility given the nature of human beings. There are three main contenders—utilitarianism, deontology, and virtue theories. Each has its strengths, and each has its problems, some of which we shall note.

We shall distinguish these theories in terms of the following different features they bear:

- Competing visions of the kind of world we ought to live in,
- Based on different natural features we have,
- Picking out different facts in a situation as being ethically relevant and important,
- Giving different sets of individuals ethical standing, excluding some kinds of beings from having a say in how they are treated ethically and including others, and
- Providing different ways of justifying what we do or omit doing.

It will help to keep these differences in mind as we go through these theories, marking off one from the other in terms of their competing visions, with all the differences those entail.

We should remark that it is impossible to state these theories in a way that is not contentious. Almost every word and phrase has been subjected to extensive criticism, and one is hard-pressed to find a neutral, natural, and simple way to state the theories without appearing naive. In addition, we are slicing through these theories in a way that is different than the usual because we think that angle of cut best exposes their complexities and differences, opening up the theories for examination and comparison. We think our analysis is particularly helpful for those engaged in using these theories for cases they face in their practice.[38]

Utilitarianism.   Suppose that you are awakened one night, or think you are, by a voice representing itself as from some superior being, and the voice says, "I have chosen you to create a new ethical world. I tried it once before with a flood, but I failed. I want you to tell me what the ideal ethical world should be."

The power to create a whole new world does not come to us, obviously, but we do have the power to help create a different world by what we do, and fail to do, in this world. But without a vision of the kind of world we ought to have, we cannot know the point of our acts and omissions or what we ought to do, and not do, to achieve this new, different ethical world. So this voice we hear one night is asking us a question we all need to ask ourselves in any event, "What kind of world, ideally, ought we to have?"

This is a question about an ethical vision. What kind of world ought we to live in? It is also a question whose answer presupposes something about us, about the kind of world we human beings are capable of having. Whatever ideal we are to strive for, it must be an ideal we can achieve, a realistic possibility, as we have said, given the nature of human beings.

We all share an aversion to pain and a preference for pleasure, for happiness, we may say.[39] And we have the capacity to contribute to the happiness of others—and, unfortunately, to their unhappiness as well. Surely it would be a better world than it is if everyone was happy and no one was unhappy. But that seems impossible given the nature of the world and human nature. As long as resources are scarce and human interests conflict, not everyone can be happy. The triangles of love are not going to disappear, and when things are settled, one (or more) of the lovers will be unhappy. So a more realistic end would be a world in which the greatest number have the greatest amount of happiness they can have. If we cannot make everyone as happy as can be, we can arrange the world so that many more are happy than are now happy. That is an ideal, and it looks achievable.

It is the vision that utilitarians hold up before us as the ethical ideal, the end we all ought to strive for when we act or think about not acting. It is a vision we all presuppose in regard to at least some of what we do. Suppose that on a Friday evening you and six hungry friends each contribute three dollars for a pizza, and you are to call in for it. Suppose as well that you love sausage and that your two best friends love pepperoni and that you have before ordered pepperoni and sausage for the three of you. So you do that again. But four of the group are vegetarians, and you know it. They would rightly have a complaint against you. You took their money for the dinner and spent it on something they will not eat. You might have been so caught up in the idea of having the pizza you and your friends wanted that you just forgot about the others. That would be bad enough. But suppose you remembered what they would not eat and said to yourself, "Well, it's their fault. They should have known better than to let me order."

Your four friends—or former friends—would think you wrong in what you did. Presumably you had a choice of other toppings and a choice to order two or more smaller pizzas, one with pepperoni and sausage and the other vegetarian. But if you knew that four in your group were vegetarians, your last choice ought to be pepperoni and sausage for everyone, even if you love it. That is a choice guaranteed to produce unhappiness for the greater number—four of the seven of you.

You could do worse. It could be that everyone in the group dislikes anchovy, even you, and that an anchovy pizza is delivered without your realizing it. Everyone's money is gone for something no one will eat. That would be a worse situation—more would be unhappy—than choosing a pizza that would at least make three of you happy. That such a choice as anchovy would never have entered your mind is evidence of how powerful the utilitarian vision is. It permeates much of our ethical life.

The judgment your friends would make about you were you to choose pepperoni and sausage is the same judgment everyone would make about someone given the choice to create a new world who chose a world in which as many as possible were as unhappy as possible. We would be almost as upset at someone's choosing a world in which there was less happiness than there could be. We might not conclude the person was evil, only stupid, or careless, but our judgment would have moral weight. Given the choice to create a new ethical world, who would choose anything other than a world in which everyone was as happy as could be? If you chose a world in which everyone was as unhappy as could be, we would think you either evil or crazy. What else could explain your choosing such worlds over a world in which there was the greatest happiness for the greatest number?

The power of the vision of a world where there is the greatest happiness for the greatest number comes in part from our being the kinds of beings who, like all sentient beings—whatever living things can feel—avoid pain and strive for pleasure.[40] Pleasure is a good and pain an evil for all sentient beings, and it is thus ethical, where one has the power, to produce pleasure for sentient beings and mitigate pain. It is thus unethical to kick dogs, and to teach a child to gain pleasure in torturing animals and other children is to go a long way toward creating an ethical monster. Kicking dogs or teaching children to torture helps create a world with less pleasure and more pain than need be—a world that is unethical to the extent that it could have more pleasure and less pain for more beings than it does.

The utilitarian vision is powerful, giving us a view of what could be that is itself attractive and would require immense changes in our world to realize. It provides, that is, an appealing target to aim for in going from where we are to where we ought to be. We live in a contingent world, a world that will change through our actions and inaction, and we can readily imagine living in worlds we would want to change and ought to change—worlds that are less than ideal according to the utilitarian vision.

We could have a world in which a large percentage of the population does not have basic health care. Or a world in which the distribution of wealth is so skewed that some have more money than the gross national products of most countries while others are homeless. Or a world in which children go to bed at night without enough to eat. Or a world in which many die before they need to because of preventable diseases. These are all possible worlds, a kind of world we could live in. But their features are contingent. That is, they can be changed, and to the extent that we are committed to the utilitarian ideal, they ought to be changed so we can live in a world closer to the ethical ideal.

As the examples just given illustrate, it does not take conjuring for us to imagine a world that is less than the best. Our world will do quite well as an example of a world less ethical than it need be. Far too many in our world have far too little chance at happiness. We could distribute what resources we have in an ethically better way, and we ought to do so, utilitarianism tells us, ensuring that we help create a world in which as many people as possible are as happy as possible. Whenever we act or fail to act, our acts and omissions could be, and ought to be, means to realize that end.

The utilitarian vision thus gives us a test for determining what is ethical and what is not. What is ethically relevant—what we should take into consideration in deciding what to do—is what helps or hinders the realization of that end. If an act or omission decreases the likelihood of achieving the greatest good for the greatest number, it is harmful and unethical; if it increases the likelihood, it is beneficial and ethical. Everything else is ethically irrelevant.

So it does not matter what you intended to happen. If your child yells at a sibling, and your ear happens to be next to the yell, it is of no good when your child says "Well, I didn't intend to yell in your ear"when you yelp. Your child did yell in your ear, and it is the effect that counts, not the intention. This is a vision that emphasizes what happens in the world. Good intentions are not enough. Utilitarianism tells us to ignore people's intentions and concentrate instead on how actions affect the participants, determining whether what is done in fact increases or decreases the happiness of the greatest number, whatever the intentions. We need to see results, always acting to maximize the happiness of as many persons as we can.

Because we are concerned with what actually happens in the world, utilitarianism argues, we can have objectivity in our ethical judgments. If intentions were to matter ethically so that the same act could be good or bad, depending upon the intention with which the agent of the act acted, we would have no way of knowing for sure what would be a good act and what would be a bad act. The person who acted might know—although we all act without a clear intent sometimes—but we could not know. But if we judge whether an act is ethical by what we can all see—it and its effects in the world—then objectivity in ethics is possible.

We could also learn to be more ethical. One of the most difficult things to do when we are involved in an ethical problem is to back off and not to let our self-interest dictate or skew the right solution. In deciding what to do, that is, we are not to let our own happiness count for more than anyone else's, and that can be difficult. Nothing in utilitarianism, or in any ethical theory, allows us to be sure that when we judge, we are not biasing our judgments in some way. But because we can see the results of our actions and determine what effects they had on the amount of happiness produced, and for whom and how many, we can at least judge after the fact whether we made the right choice. That will help us make better judgments the next time.

Looking at cases as matters of utilitarian calculation can provide us a handle on how to respond. For instance, Deborah's problem in *The Death of a Baby* can be readily construed as utilitarian. She is faced with telling or not telling what she knows, and the difficulty she has in making that choice turns on the consequences—the additional harm to a family already traumatized by the death, for example, or the risk of harm to the other children. Her intention is to do good and will be the same regardless of what choice she makes. What matters is not her intention, but which alternative she chooses. What utilitarianism tells her is to choose that alternative with the least harmful consequences for the fewest number. Only that choice will help produce more rather than less happiness for the greatest number.

So utilitarian theory gives her guidance, it would seem, about what she ought to do. It sets an end point that is admirable and tells us to look at our actions and omissions as means to that end. So Deborah should ask, "Will doing this or doing that best serve to that end?"

Unfortunately, things are not so simple, and utilitarianism is open to a number of different problems that make it far more difficult to use than we have so far made it appear.

First, the vision is murky. Suppose, when we are going to order pizza, that we discover that the only choices available will make some members of the group unhappy, the different choices producing differing degrees of unhappiness for differing numbers of individuals. One choice is nonvegetarian, and four will be unhappy because they will not be able to eat, but the other three will be extremely happy because that is their favorite meal. Another choice is broccoli, which no one particularly likes, but which all will eat. So the greater number—all seven—will be somewhat happy, but not particularly so. Another choice is a topping that five like fairly well and that the two others will eat, but do not like at all. Which choice is mandated by the end of achieving the greatest happiness for the greatest number?

Are we to work to secure extreme happiness for a few, letting their great happiness outweigh the failure of others to have any happiness? Are we to work to secure some small measure of happiness for as many as we can, letting the numbers provided happiness be the determining factor and ignoring the degree of happiness achieved? Are we to work to secure some higher degree of happiness for the majority of the individuals involved as long as the rest are not unhappy?

All of these options are compatible with the goal of acting to produce the greatest happiness for the greatest number, and so that goal, far from being a clear target we can aim for, is consistent with so many different acts that it gives little guidance at all.

Second, even if the end were clear, utilitarianism tells us that we are not to concern ourselves with the good of each and every individual, but with the greatest good for the greatest number. It tells us that it is ethically permissible, even ethically required at times, to choose an arrangement that will produce unhappiness for some if doing that will provide the greater happiness for more. Some have tried to justify slavery, for instance, by arguing that it made the slave owners particularly happy and that the slaves were better off, too. This view sees slavery as a way of distributing the benefits and burdens of freedom and wealth that uses the slaves for the good of others as though they were simply instruments to provide greater happiness for their owners. But that seems wrong on its face—like lying to people to get them to do what you want them to do.

Third, utilitarian theory draws part of its strength from its vision of the kind of society we ought to live in and part of its strength from our desire for happiness. It seems happily to combine idealism with a realism about what we truly desire. But it fails to be realistic about how we can make decisions about what we ought to do. A pure utilitarian world would have in it only acts and omissions that furthered the utilitarian vision, but we simply cannot calculate the effects of each and every act before we act. Sometimes we must make split-second decisions about what to do—whether to swerve to avoid an animal that darts out between parked cars—without taking the time to calculate out the effects of that act versus any other. Swerving may put us in the path of an on-coming vehicle, for instance, and so cause worse problems.

In response to that problem, among others, a distinction is made between act- and rule-utilitarianism. We have been examining what is known as act-utilitarianism. It tells us that every act or omission ought to be directed toward the vision that utilitarianism holds up before us. But we often act on principle; we act, that is, on such admonitions as "Honesty is the best policy" without stopping to calculate whether acting on honesty in the particular case in question will in fact lead to the greatest happiness for the greatest number. The admonition acts as a rule for our behavior, telling us that we ought to be honest. Following such rules, it is argued by rule-utilitarians, will generally lead to the greatest happiness for the greatest number. So we need not calculate out the effects of every act and omission. We instead act on the basis of rules. One effect of being a rule-utilitarian is that we have a usable guide to action. Another effect is that we will sometimes act in a way that is ethically wrong. Honesty may generally produce the greatest happiness for the greatest number, but sometimes it will not. Lying will and is thus the right thing to do. But we must follow the rule, and it tells us to tell the truth. We thus do what is ethically wrong. So we gain a theory we can use at the cost of countenancing some unethical acts.

Fourth, assessing the full effects of acts or rules seems beyond our capacities. We seem always to be discovering unintended consequences of even what seem to be the best of acts; even the smallest of acts can have enormous and unpredictable consequences far into the future; and we are often surprised by how others respond to what we do. If we are to determine what we ought to do by assessing the consequences of alternative courses of action, that is, it appears we are being asked to do the impossible.

Fifth, even if we could predict the future as well as what would be the future were we to act differently, utilitarianism asks us to make comparative judgments we cannot readily make. When utilitarianism was first introduced as a full-blown theory, the assumption was that pleasure was quantifiable. Having our favorite dessert is more pleasurable than many other things, and on a scale of one to ten, with ten being the most pleasurable, it is closer to ten than one. But when John Stuart Mill articulated the theory, he made a distinction we all make between the quantity and quality of pleasure. Reading a good book can be pleasurable, but it is a far different kind of pleasure than a runner's high. Trying to compare the two by quantifying the pleasures is like trying to compare apples and oranges. They are different kinds of pleasure, qualitatively so different that we do not capture the pleasure of either by treating them both as being of the same kind and quantifiable on a single scale. So the goal of acting so as to produce the greatest amount of happiness for the greatest number is unclear in another way. Are we to choose higher quality pleasures, perhaps less intense, over lower quality pleasures of high intensity, or vice versa?

Sixth, although utilitarianism purports to be objective, whether it includes the quality as well as the quantity of pleasure or not, what pleasure or happiness we get from something depends upon the beliefs we have. If we believe it is wrong to drink coffee, no coffee, no matter how tasteful, will produce pleasure or, if it does, it will produce it along with guilt or shame for having drunk it against our beliefs. But then we cannot determine what is ethically right by appealing to the end that utilitarianism envisages. For that end will itself be determined by our beliefs, some of which may be ethically suspect. If I believed that men and women were fundamentally different and that society ought to be arranged so that each is "in his or her proper place," women in the home, for example, men at work, then I would take no pleasure from a proposal that required equality of opportunity regardless of sex. And if enough people believed that, then a comparison of a social arrangement that guaranteed equality of opportunity with one that put men and women "in their proper places" would tell us that the latter, not the former, produces the most happiness for the greatest number. In short, the utilitarian criterion does not look to be objective and independent of false ethical beliefs, but is itself determinable by beliefs—which may well be unethical.

Seventh, early on in the description of utilitarianism, we wrote about "pleasure, or happiness." The two are not the same, and utilitarian theorists may differ as to which is the proper ethical end. Are we to try to produce pleasure or happiness? Every sentient being—from chipmunks to humans—can experience pleasure and pain. But only some sentient beings—people certainly, perhaps some other animals—can experience happiness. So if we are to provide a world in which the greatest number of beings have the greatest happiness they can have, we leave out of consideration those beings who experience pleasure and pain but not happiness. It is difficult to pick a noncontentious example of such a being. Perhaps chipmunks and cows cannot be happy, but can experience pain and pleasure. But they would not have ethical standing in a world designed to secure happiness. They would not be part of our ethical world and would have no claims against us if we arranged matters in such a way that they were caused pain. What matters ethically in such a world is happiness, and if it furthers the happiness of those beings capable of happiness to cause pain to beings incapable of happiness, so be it. Carnivores may hold this view. Vegetarians may not. In short, the scope of utilitarianism is unclear. Which beings does it cover and which does it not? It matters enormously to such issues how we human beings are to relate to the rest of sentient creation.

So utilitarianism is not without serious problems, but it presents a powerful vision of what kind of world we ought to live in, a vision that, were we to accept it, would obligate us to change much in this world.[41] We can summarize it as follows:

- It tells us that we should hold before us as a vision to create a world in which the greatest number of beings have the greatest pleasure (or happiness).
- It bases its vision on sentient beings having the natural capacity for pleasure and pain (or happiness and unhappiness), wanting to avoid pain (or unhappiness), and wishing pleasure (or happiness).
- What it picks out of a case as being important and ethically relevant are those features of the case that make a difference to creating a world in which the greatest number of beings have the greatest pleasure (or happiness).

- It gives an ethical hearing to all of those beings who are capable of pleasure and pain or, if it is restricted to those beings capable of happiness, to all those beings with that capacity.
- It justifies an act or omission in terms of whether it is the choice most likely to produce the greatest pleasure (or happiness) for the greatest number.

Deontology. *The Death of a Baby* is problematic because Deborah must act in ignorance. That is why she is hesitant. She does not know which alternative is least harmful. She does not have enough evidence to determine the consequences of the alternatives facing her, and even if she knew which was most likely to cause the least harm to the fewest number, her choice may not have the effects she hopes for. Too many factors not in our control can intervene to change the course of events in ways we could never have foreseen.[42]

We cannot even be sure how our best-intended acts will be received. What we mean to be kindness may be construed as meddling. Empathy may be taken as pity. Indeed, we cannot even be sure that what we end up doing will be what we intended to do. We all have made mistakes in which we intended to do one thing (leave the car door unlocked while we check out something) and do something else (e.g., lock ourselves out).

So, the objection goes, why ought we be held responsible for what actually happens because of what we intend to do? What matters, according to deontology, is what we intend to do—what we will to happen, as Immanuel Kant would put it. If what we will is ethical, we ought to get ethical credit, whatever actually happens. Indeed, the argument continues, it is an ethical mistake to consider consequences in deciding what to do.

Suppose a small child comes to a candy store, purchases two lollipops for ten cents apiece, and gives the cashier a quarter.[43] What ought the cashier to do? The answer may seem obvious. Give the child the nickel change. But *why* ought the cashier do that? A utilitarian would consider the consequences of the alternative courses of action—giving the child a nickel, giving the child nothing and saying there is no change, giving the child a penny and saying that is correct, and so on—and choose whatever alternative produces the greatest good for the greatest number. Considering the matter that way, we might choose to give the child a nickel, deciding that the store's reputation for treating customers honestly would be well served by evidence that it treats honestly even those it could easily cheat. Yet deciding what we ought to do by considering the consequences of our act means *using* the child to gain a reputation for honesty. But, deontologists say, the cashier ought to give the child a nickel because the nickel *belongs* to the child. Doing the right thing for the wrong reason is not right. The store may gain a reputation for honest dealing by doing right by the child, but, in this view, the cashier ought to give the child the nickel even if giving the correct change would not produce good results.

In *Doing What the Judge Orders,* John seems to have thought that if Al's test were negative, he would not have to do anything, and if the test were positive, then even if Jane found out that her confidence had been broken, he would not be held responsible. John thus attempted to use Al's being ordered to be tested by the judge as a way to keep himself from being held responsible. Acting that way is like lying to get someone to do what you want them to do. If you are believed and the person does what otherwise he or she would not have done, you will have manipulated the person. Because the information the person was acting upon is false, the person will not have made an informed decision, but will have the illusion of making such a decision. Yet you will have used the person for your own end. The cashier who gives the child the nickel change *so that* the store will gain a reputation for honesty is using the child for the store's own end. The child and everyone else may be happy, but the cashier is not giving the child proper change for the right reason. John has so manipulated things that Al will be tested, without any say, and in doing so, John is using Al's being tested to further his own self-interest. John may have made a decision in which things work out for the best, but how decisions work out is not relevant to whether they are ethical, according to deontology.

The aim of morality, in this view, is not to make people happy, but to accord them the respect and dignity they deserve as persons. Lying to people to get them to do what you want done is not to treat them with respect, but is an attempt to manipulate them—to treat them as instruments for your end and not as persons capable of having ends and capable of deciding for themselves what they ought or ought not to do.

So deontology holds up a very different vision for us from that of utilitarianism. If we try to create the greatest good for the greatest number, and so take consequences into consideration, we treat our acts as means to the end of having a certain kind of world. Deontologists claim we end up treating people as means to that end—using them to produce a world in which they may not be among the greatest number who have the greatest good. We ought instead to work for a world in which everyone is treated with respect, and the way to achieve that end is to treat everyone with respect. We ought to act on principle, that is, regardless of the consequences. We may in fact produce more happiness for more people if we have as our end treating persons with respect, but happiness ought not to be our end.

This is a powerful ethical vision. What matters ethically is that we act out of good will, and "the good will is not good because of what it effects or accomplishes or because of its competence to achieve some intended end; it is good only because. . . it is good in itself."[44] So, as opposed to utilitarianism, the consequences do not matter ethically.

But not just every act of will is good. We might will to kick puppies or to teach children to torture animals and other children, and then we would be acting out of an evil will. So what is it to act out of a good will? Kant's answer is somewhat convoluted, but we do not need to get into it in all of its complications to explain what it is to act from good will. We do, however, need to make a distinction between acting from inclination and acting from duty.

We are all familiar with acting from inclination. We do it all the time. When we are so inclined, we stay in bed longer than we should, indulge ourselves in a large dessert, and so on. We have inclinations relevant to everything we do, and, more importantly, some of our inclinations, at least, are part of our character. Some of us are inclined to help others, inclined to do good whenever we can, inclined to tell the truth, and so on.

We are also familiar with what it is to act from duty. When we were children, our parents often gave us things to do—cleaning our rooms, walking the dog—that we were sometimes not inclined to do, but had to do anyway. Our parents made it our duty. They did not say, "Keep your room clean if you want," but "Keep your room clean." As adults, we all have duties—as parents, as citizens, as professionals. A social worker has a duty to inform needy clients what the welfare system provides, for instance. A social worker has a duty to help clients.

A social worker may be the sort of person who wants to help others and so is inclined to help clients. But, Kant says, we deserve no moral credit for doing what we are inclined to do because we are inclined to do it. We deserve moral credit only for doing our duty, only for doing what ethics tells us we must do, whatever our inclination.

It may be that we are inclined to do what duty tells us we ought to do. It may be that we are inclined to do something other than what duty tells us we ought to do. The latter is the dramatic cases we are likely to notice—the person who wants to kick dogs but, with great force of will, is able to pull back each time. But the person who loves to help others out of an inclination to help deserves no more moral credit, in the view of deontologists, than the person who kicks dogs out of an inclination to do so. Doing good or ill out of inclination has no ethical value. Only acting from duty has ethical value.

So how are we to act from duty? Kant assumes that rational beings like us always ought to have reasons for doing what we choose to do. These reasons can be stated in the form of maxims that provide the reasons for doing whatever it is we do. Someone who eats fruit every day is committed to some maxim like "An apple a day keeps the doctor away," and that maxim provides the reason for the person's eating fruit every day. This maxim is not (in any obvious way) an ethical principle, and in *Dancing a Legal Dance,* the maxim that Mary would have to adopt to justify deceiving Martha is not ethical either. So how are we to tell when we have an ethical principle and when we have something else?

In *Dancing a Legal Dance,* suppose that when Martha asked Mary not to tell anyone about her father's having sexually abused her, Mary said, "No, of course I won't"—while all the time knowing that she would have to inform the authorities. Mary would be committed to an argument roughly like this:

Martha will not tell me what her father is doing unless I promise that I will keep the information confidential.

I cannot help Martha unless she tells me what her father is doing.

But I cannot keep the information confidential.

Yet it is permissible to promise that you will do something you know you will not do when the deception will benefit the person you deceive.

She then concludes, from these premises,

> Therefore, I will deceive Martha by promising I will not tell when I know I will.

The crucial ethical premise is the last one: Is it permissible to promise to do something you know you will not do on the ground that the false promise will produce a benefit to the person deceived? A rule-utilitarian would consider the consequences and judge according to whether acting on that maxim would produce the greatest good for the greatest number. But the proper test, deontology claims, is whether you can *universalize* the maxim. Can you consistently maintain that *everyone* will act on that maxim?

The question asks whether, among other things, *you* would accept others making a promise to you that they know they will not keep because they think it will be in your benefit not to keep it. If everyone can act on that maxim, others can act on it regarding you. Are we willing to be treated as we are contemplating treating someone else? Mary must ask whether she would also approve if Martha deceived her for what Martha thought was Mary's benefit. Universalizing the maxim forces Mary to be objective, to consider how anyone similarly situated ought to act. It especially forces her to look at how she is treating others because it forces her to see her own action from their point of view.

In this case, we cannot consistently maintain that everyone will act on the maxim. It would thus not be rational to adopt that maxim. For to make a promise is to ensure the person you are promising that you intend to do what you have promised. That is the point of promising, and that is why people ask, when in doubt about your intentions, "Do you promise?" But we cannot be promising while intending not to keep our promise. That is not what it is to promise. We can *say*, "I promise. . .," and people may believe us in part because there is a practice of promising in which those words mean that we intend to do what we say we are going to do. But to say the words, without the intention, is to take advantage of the expectation created by the practice and thus to use the practice, and thus all who engage in it, for your own end. You put the practice at jeopardy and so harm others because if others acted on your precedent, no one could ever depend on anyone's saying, "Yes, I really do promise."

So the maxim that we are suggesting Mary may have thought she should act upon is not an ethical principle. She cannot consistently maintain that everyone ought to act upon that maxim. What is ethical is that when we make promises, we intend to keep them. Universalizing a maxim is thus, it is claimed, a test for determining whether a maxim is an ethical principle or not. We can justify a variety of ethical principles by universalization. "Do not lie" is another ethical principle. So is "Do not cause unnecessary harm."

We thus have a vision and a test for ethical principles, and we know what is ethically relevant in a case. It is not what happens, but what is decided and how the decision is made. It is not enough just to intend to do what is right. We might intend to do right for the wrong reason. What is required is that we have the right intention for the right reason. Only then do we decide to do what is right *because* it is right.

Deontology requires that we think through every ethical decision we make to ensure that we are acting on principle. Some people are naturally empathic, for instance, but if they act on empathy, they ought to get no ethical credit for that. We only deserve credit for *choosing* to be empathic. What matters ethically is that we choose to do the right thing for the right reason. Central to Kant's theory is thus what he calls a good will. We must will what is good—will, for instance, that the young child get the nickel change deserved. It is ethically wrong to do anything else.

Making a promise without intending to keep it is ethically wrong even if it should work out that it has good consequences. A wrong has been done regardless and so a person has been harmed, in that the person is wronged, even if the person is benefitted by the consequences of the wrong. So Mary ought to intend to keep any promise she makes because it is ethically wrong to make promises without intending to keep them.

Just as the cashier would be using the little boy if the boy were given the correct change in order to further the store's reputation for honesty, so Mary would be using Martha by lying to her. Martha would be making a decision about what she ought to do based on the false information Mary had given her. Mary would thus be playing with Martha as though she were an intelligent instrument, knowing that if she made Martha believe certain things, Martha would act in the way Mary wanted her to act. That would not be to treat Martha with the respect due another person.

In this vision, each of us is to be treated by every other one of us with the respect due an autonomous person, capable of self-determination. We would thus have a world in which no one uses any other person for his or her own ends, but each of us is treated as what Kant calls an end-in-itself. Were this vision to be realized, we would live in a world of mutual respect, in which each of us would respect all others.

This is a powerful vision, resting on the capacity for rational thought, and it includes among those within its scope all those beings capable of rational thought. We are thus to consider ourselves to be aiming toward a moral universe that we share with any other rational being, but not with all sentient beings. That a being is capable of pleasure and pain is not itself sufficient to make it rational. The scope of deontology—the beings who have primary ethical standing in its universe—is thus significantly different than the scope of utilitarianism.

Deontology is not without its problems, however. Among other things, it is almost impossible for us to know whether we or anyone else have acted ethically. If you have an inclination to be helpful and you are helpful, how can you be sure that you acted from duty and not from inclination? How can the rest of us be sure? Even when you are inclined to be mean, but instead are nice, how can you be sure that it is not your inclination that is operating—an inclination to manipulate, for instance, and trick others into thinking you are nice when you are mean—and how can the rest of us be sure?

Second, if, in Case 1.2, *Dancing a Legal Dance,* we conclude that Mary ought not to promise Martha anything without intending to keep her promise, we have really not done justice to her ethical problems. She cannot just act on one principle, about keeping promises, but must weigh that principle against the principle that she has an obligation to help keep Martha from being sexually and physically abused. The principle that when we make promises, we intend to keep them is thus at best a *prima facie* principle—a principle we ought to keep unless compelling ethical reasons exist not to keep it. It would be wrong for Mary to make a promise without intending to keep it, but it would also be wrong to allow harm to continue when she could prevent it. It is just her problem that she does not know what her maxim of action ought to be because she has no clear way of choosing between the sets of harms. Deontology would help only if we could universalize one, but not both of the contending principles or if we could universalize some compromise between the two competitors. But it seems we can universalize both principles, and it is certainly not obvious what compromise between the two can be universalized. So the theory would seem to give Mary no help.

Third, deontology's vision seems cold. We are to treat everyone as ends-in-themselves, but are we permitted to show more love to one person than to another? To favor one over another by giving that person gifts? How do we avoid making invidious distinctions between individuals while distinguishing between them in ways that reflect our very human capacity for caring and loving? Deontology seems to elevate the rational part of us to the highest ethical level while leaving to one side the sentient and the emotional part that allows us to connect with others as more than simply rational beings.

Fourth, it thus excludes from having an ethical standing those sentient beings who lack the capacity for rational thought. Utilitarianism and deontology stand in stark contrast on this issue.

So, as with utilitarianism, deontology has its problems, but it does present a very different vision of the world.[45] We can summarize it as follows:

- It tells us that we should hold before us as a vision to create a world in which each and every one of us is treated with respect and dignity.
- It bases its vision on rational beings having the capacity to reason about why they do what they do.
- What it picks out of a case as being important and ethically relevant are what those involved have decided to do and what reasons they have for their decisions.
- It gives an ethical hearing to all rational beings and only rational beings. Those other beings who feel pleasure and pain but are not rational cannot be ethical agents and are not to be accorded the respect and dignity we must accord rational beings.
- It justifies a decision about an act or omission in terms of whether it is a principled decision, one based on a maxim which can be universalized.

Virtue Theories.   It is not enough just to decide to do what is right, for the right reason. What happens matters, and being ethical means doing the right thing *in the right way.* Yet the ways in which one may fail to do something right, in the right way, are many. Children asked to apologize to a sibling sometimes yell in anger, "I'm sorry!" They have said what they ought to say, but have not apologized. Just saying the words is not enough. We must feel apologetic and display that feeling with the appropriate behavior. We can fail to apologize by doing it too late, by using the wrong tone of voice or the wrong facial expression, and so on. What virtue theory tells us is that we ought to act virtuously—do the right thing in the right way—and it emphasizes that persons have capacities for kindness, generosity, empathy, and so on and that they can develop and hone these capacities to become ethically better persons. Just as we are born infants and, in growing to adulthood, can affect how we develop physically through exercise, eating well, and so on, so we are born with various capacities that will develop or not, come what may. Virtue theory tells us that we ought to develop those ethical capacities we have to become the very best persons we can be, ethically.

Whereas deontology and utilitarianism concentrate upon particular acts and principles that we follow, virtue theory concentrates upon our character. A person can do what is right without being a good person, and neither deontology nor utilitarianism would allow us to distinguish a bad person who did what was right from a good person who did what was right. What they measure is whether what was done was right. Virtue theory tells us to look not only at our acts and at the principles that animate our behavior, but at our underlying characters—the kinds of persons we are. And it tells us that we should strive to become the very best we can be.

Virtue theory thus provides us with an ethical vision. Because we are born essentially undeveloped and must develop somehow, and because we have the capacity to develop ourselves to become far better persons than many of us do become, we ought to hold up before ourselves the vision of a world in which persons are as fully developed ethically as they can be. We can choose what sort of persons we ought to be in this world, and we ought to become as kind, as generous, as empathic, and, in general, as virtuous as persons are capable of becoming. Morality is best conceived as exercising a *skill,* something we can learn to do better and better.

This is a vision that requires us to take into consideration both the reasons for and the consequences of our actions. Just as we can always make mistakes, no matter how good we are at something, we can always make an ethical mistake, no matter how virtuous we may be. The goal, however, is to strive to become as virtuous as we can be—minimizing the ethical mistakes we make and learning how to handle ethically the consequences of the ethical mistakes we do make. The test for our successes and failures turns on both how we act and why we act as we do. To be truly concerned for Martha's well-being in *Dancing a Legal Dance,* Mary has to feel concerned and act accordingly. And she has to take into consideration how what she does will affect Martha—how deceiving her will mean that Martha will no longer be able to tell, by looking at Mary's face and listening to the tone of voice, whether to believe her or not.

Virtue theory thus tells us what is relevant in any ethical case. Ethical perfection is achieved when someone is so attuned to the specifics of a situation that he or she does exactly what is right, both in the immediacy of the situation and for the long-term. Virtue theory thus gives us as well an ethical vision and a way of testing for what fits that vision.

Some recent work in ethical theory has reinvigorated virtue theory, which long lay dormant, relatively ignored by philosophers. Utilitarianism and deontology are both rule-driven decision procedures. They are decision procedures because they tell us how to go about making decisions about what to do ethically. Utilitarianism, for instance, tells us always to look to see whether our act, or the rule we follow, will or will not produce the greatest happiness for the greatest number. "Do that which provides the greatest happiness for the greatest number!" is a rule, and it tells us to perform those acts or omissions that satisfy it. It thus serves as a guide for telling us what we ought to do. But ethics consists of more than just following rules. In our five-step method of tracking harms, the last step tells us:

5. *Determine how to do what you have determined ought to be done and do it in a way that will itself produce more good than harm.*

The point of this last step is to remind us that making a decision about what to do is not the end of what we have to do ethically. We need to be the kind of persons who, deciding to do the right thing, do it in the right way.

That emphasis on how we are to relate to one another is the emphasis that has been picked up by recent work about what has been called the ethics of caring.[46] This work tells us that the end of ethics is not to follow rules, but to be a caring person. It thus tells us that what matters ethically is what kind of person we are, and it gives us guidance as to which of our characteristics we ought to develop.

But virtue theory, even in its most recent form, has its problems. First, we need an ethical basis for determining what characteristics we ought to cultivate as virtues. A warlike society may think that killing without regret is worth cultivating, and, indeed, different professions in our society value different characteristics. A lawyer must be as tough with a client as any opposing lawyer would be so as to ferret out any weaknesses in the client's story, the better to provide a defense. A social work practitioner who treated a client that way would be acting inappropriately. Compassion is a virtue for social workers, not for lawyers.[47] But it would appear that no version of any virtue theory can tell us why we should develop the characteristics it takes to be of ethical import. If we are to be caring, for instance, what ethical basis can there be for that judgment that does not appeal to the consequences of caring, for instance, and thus to utilitarianism?

Second, even if we could agree on what virtues social workers ought to encourage, for example, virtue theory fails to give us guidance. For instance, it is a virtue of social work that practitioners should *listen* to their clients and try to understand how clients are perceiving their problems. But one practitioner's "listening"—by asking questions, querying responses, testing for consistency—may be another practitioner's understanding of what it is to interrupt. It is not obvious that any one way of listening is ethically preferable to another, and virtue theory gives us no guidance about how to choose between alternative practices of such a virtue.

Third, virtue theory has a more important failing. It gives us no guidance about how to proceed in ethical dilemmas and problematic cases. To be virtuous we must act in virtuous ways, but the problem these kinds of difficult cases presents is that we do not know what it is we ought to do. Whether Deborah tells the physician what she knows or decides to withhold that information, she ought to be so attuned to what she is doing that she does it well—in the right way, with the right tone of voice, at the right time, and so on. But virtue theory gives her no guidance as to which choice is the ethical choice.[48]

We can summarize virtue theory as follows:

- It tells us that we should hold before us as a vision to create a world in which each and every one of us has honed our capacities to become the most virtuous individuals we can be.
- It tells us that what matters ethically is what kind of persons we are, not just whether we act rationally or whether our acts produce the greatest happiness for the greatest number.
- It bases its vision on human beings having various capacities—to be kind, to be generous—that will develop in some way regardless of whether we work to develop them to make ourselves ethically better.
- What it picks out of a case as being important and ethically relevant are what those involved do and feel.
- It gives an ethical hearing to all human beings.
- It justifies a decision about an act or omission in terms of whether it is done in accordance with virtue—whether someone telling the truth honestly feels honest as well as tells the truth, whether a person being apologetic is really apologetic as well as apologizes, and so on.

Comparing Ethical Visions.   Each of these three ethical theories appeals to some essential feature we have and erects a vision for us to achieve, and yet these are visions of distinct ethical worlds with radically different conceptions of what is ethically of value. Utilitarianism emphasizes that we are creatures who desire happiness, and we could have more happiness for more of us. We should thus strive, utilitarianism tells us, to create a world in which the greatest number have the greatest amount of happiness. Virtue theory tells us we have capacities of empathy and kindness, courage and caring, and so on which we can each hone to their fullest expression. Deontology tells us we are rational beings capable of conceiving of and having a world in which everyone is treated with respect and dignity.

If you had to choose among these visions, how could you choose between a world in which there was the greatest happiness for the greatest number, a world in which each of us developed and honed our capacities for such traits as kindness and caring to their fullest, or a world in which we were all accorded dignity and respect without regard to our color, our race, our sex, or any other natural or social characteristic we might have? Each vision is enticing. Yet they compete. Most obviously, what provides the greatest happiness for the greatest number may not only preclude some—the smaller number—from having even a modicum of happiness, but also the sort of respect that deontology emphasizes. One worry about utilitarianism is that, because concerns about the greatest number outweigh concerns about minorities, those minorities—already heavily burdened by a disproportionate share of problems—will find their problems further aggravated by appeals to utilitarianism. They would lose any claim to dignity, along with a chance for happiness.

We can get a sense of how different are the visions these theories hold for us by asking what we ought to do to achieve them. Virtue theory tells us to work on ourselves, to make ourselves better people, letting our relations with others and the structure of our society come to whatever they will, given the changes in us. Utilitarianism requires us to work on the social structures that preclude us from achieving a world in which the greatest number are the happiest. And deontology requires us to ensure that each of us as individuals respects all others as equals and that the social structures do that as well.

That these ethical visions are so different might not be thought to matter if achieving any one of them led to the same practical results. A utilitarian, for instance, might argue that the only way to achieve the greatest happiness for the greatest number is to accord each and every individual dignity and respect. But consider the situation from your point of view if you were denied dignity—by being enslaved, for instance. To claim your freedom, you would have to show that your being a slave *in fact* did not provide the greatest happiness for the greatest number and that some other distribution of freedom and slavery did. This is an empirical claim and hard to prove, especially for someone not well-positioned to prove it because enslaved. So you would have a difficult time obtaining your freedom. But, on deontological grounds, you deserve dignity and thus freedom *as a person*—quite independently of whatever effects the denial has on others.

It matters, practically and ethically, what sort of justification we must give for what we do. Both deontology and utilitarianism may prohibit slavery, but if the reasons for the prohibition differ in the way suggested, the identity of result is not as important ethically as that it is more difficult, under utilitarianism, to justify eradicating slavery. What distinguishes utilitarianism, deontology, and virtue theory is that they have differing visions of the ethical life and, so, differing conceptions of how we ought to justify what we ought to do. A deontologist appeals essentially to the rights of individuals, and if the right of an individual to liberty should happen to cause less happiness for the greatest number, so much the worse for the happiness of the greatest number. For a deontologist, the appeal to rights trumps any appeal to the greatest happiness of the greatest number. For a utilitarian, the opposite is true. We have no rights but what will further the greatest happiness for the greatest number, and should someone claim a right that does not further that end, the claim is denied. The goal of the greatest happiness for the greatest number trumps any other vision of the world. So, for utilitarianism, we ought to encourage only those virtues that further that end. Any other virtue can have only a negative ethical import. Virtue theory, on the other hand, seems not to accept that limitation. What matters is that we strive to become as virtuous as we can be, and we are not to limit ourselves to whatever might happen to provide the greatest happiness for the greatest number.

It thus matters which theory one chooses. But how are we to choose among these ethical visions? The three we have considered are the main contenders, and yet the history of philosophical thought is filled with critiques of them. No criticisms of any one theory have been so devastating as to make it obvious that it is ethically bankrupt, and yet no over-arching ethical theory allows us to choose among these competitors. We thus have no ethical basis for choosing among them.

Yet the theories are ethically different, giving us different answers to the ethical problems we face and opening up ethical situations in different ways, allowing us to see different ethical features. If we do not familiarize ourselves with these different theories, we may find ourselves looking at ethical issues in social work with one vision in mind, not realizing that there are competing ways of perceiving the same situation. That is a recipe for ethical confusion and mistakes. Two or more people may consider the same ethical issue with different visions in mind, without realizing it, and so come to different conclusions about what they ought to do. Or they may consider the issue with the same vision in mind, not realizing that the situation cannot be fully understood unless seen in terms of another ethical vision.

One way to understand the problems with John's decision to have Al tested in *Doing What the Judge Orders* is to ask whether that decision respects Al's right to determine for himself whether he wants to be tested. If you look at the issue as a virtue theorist, you will concentrate upon how skillful or unskillful John was in exercising the capacities to empathize with Al's potential problems or with the problems of Al's mother. And so you may miss the issue of Al's self-determination. If you look at the issue as a utilitarian, concerned only to work things out so that most people involved in the case are as happy as they can be, you may miss seeing the case from Al's point of view. Looking at the case as a deontologist would, and so asking, "Are everyone's rights being respected here?" forces into the open, for examination, the question whether Al should have the right to determine for himself whether or not to have a test.

Even if all theories lead to the same answer, they provide different reasons, and these differing reasons can make an enormous difference in how we think about what we ought to do to prevent recurrences, for instance. Consider lying. It is generally wrong for a utilitarian because it leads to more unhappiness for more people than does telling the truth. It is wrong for a deontologist because it is a form of manipulation, treating the person as an object rather than as a person. It is wrong for a virtue theorist because it runs counter to the virtue of honesty. So all three theories may agree, in a particular case, that we ought not lie. But because the reasons they provide for not lying differ, they direct our concerns in different directions. Virtue theory tells us to work on our capacity for telling the truth. Deontology tells us to treat others as we should treat all persons—and as we would like to be treated ourselves. And utilitarianism directs us to change the system in ways that ensure that lying does not further the happiness for the greatest number.

As the fourth step in our method of tracking harms, we need to:

4. *Back off from the case and judge what is best to do. What will minimize harms?*

We can now see that this question may not produce certainty about what we ought to do. All of the theories agree that we ought to act to minimize harms. They all agree that in making such judgments we need to be sure that each person counts the same as every other person, with no one person's interests being elevated above any other's. But they provide competing interpretations of harm. A harm for a utilitarian is what impedes or at least does not further the creation of the greatest happiness for the greatest number. A harm for a deontologist is a failure to act from duty (and so, for instance, the manipulation of someone by lying). A harm for a virtue theorist is what slows, arrests, or reverses the development of an ethical virtue. With competing conceptions of harm, the fourth step in our method becomes conceptually problematic. We may thus end up with a case in which the competing theories tell us to do different things, and we have no way of choosing, ethically, among the different answers.

True Ethical Premises.   Even though the different theories provide different reasons for not lying, they all agree that it is still generally wrong to lie, whatever the reasons, and as we have seen, we can do a great deal without waiting for philosophers to settle their disputes about which of these ethical theories is ethically best. We have illustrated how much can be done as we have worked through the cases in Chapter 1.

In regard to *Doing What the Judge Orders*, we explored whether John had gained anything by having Al tested. He began the case with the ethical problem of whether he should tell whether Jane had AIDS. He decided to have Al tested, and the consequence was that he caused harm without gaining any leverage on the original problem he had. In giving that analysis, we assumed it ethically wrong to cause harm for no good reason.

In analyzing *Dancing a Legal Dance*, we came to see that, in passing on to the authorities the information Martha gave her, Mary caused harm, but that she had an obligation to pass on the information. We were unsure what Mary had told Martha, if anything, about what she would have to say to the authorities if she were told about abuse. In considering what Mary ought to have told Martha, we were presuming that Mary ought to minimize harms and make sure that Martha understood that any information she gave Mary about abuse would have to be reported to the authorities.

In several cases, we were able to come to conclusions about what ought to be done, and we came to these conclusions in ways we think are noncontentious. Who would think that LaShonda should treat people who are adopted and want information about their parents differently when they make appointments ahead of time with her and when they do not? We also appealed to noncontentious ethical premises in analyzing these cases—that it is ethically wrong to cause harm for no good reason, that we ought to act to minimize harms (when we can), and so on. We will find other such premises as we work through the cases we shall consider in later chapters.

Are such ethical premises true? They are certainly not contentious. No social work practitioner would claim, we can safely assume, that we ought to cause harm for no good reason or that we ought to maximize harms when we can. And each premise is supported by the ethical theories we have examined. A utilitarian would argue that if we are to achieve the greatest happiness for the greatest number, we ought not to cause harm—especially for no good reason. A deontologist would ask whether we could universalize the maxim of causing harm for no good reason and find that we could not. We cannot consistently maintain that everyone ought to act on such a maxim, for, among other things, we would be agreeing that others can harm us for no good reason. And a virtue theorist could not agree that it is a virtue, something we should become skilled at, to cause harm for no good reason.

Some of the premises to which we have appealed are ethical principles, and it may be tempting to think one need only to appeal to them to resolve ethical issues. We can readily draw out of the cases we have discussed so far at least the following principles:

- The principle of self-determination (or autonomy), that a person has the right to decide what to do or omit from doing regarding those matters that affect him or her and so has the right to be fully informed about such matters.
- The principle of nonmaleficence, that one ought not to harm others.
- The principle of beneficence, that one ought to help others, either by mitigating harmful conditions or by providing benefits.
- The formal principle of justice, that we treat like cases alike and unlike cases unalike.

These principles can serve as guideposts for us. First, they give us guidance about the kinds of considerations we need to keep in mind when assessing a case. They remind us of the interests of the various parties involved that we need to consider—an interest we all have in self-determination, an interest in not being harmed, and so on. Second, that we have these interests enshrined in principles reminds us that we shall need very compelling ethical reasons to do something that causes harm to others or denies someone's self-determination, for example. That is the point of these being principles. There is a presumption against breaking them, and the presumption can only be overridden if there are compelling ethical reasons to do so. We might deny someone's self-determination, for instance, if permitting it would cause great harm to others.

But it would be a mistake to think that all we need to do is to appeal to these and other principles to determine what we ought to do. It would be a mistake for three different reasons.

First, consider *Dancing a Legal Dance* again. In deceiving Martha, if that is what Mary did, Mary lied to her and denied her the information she needed to make a decision for herself about what she ought to do. Mary thus broke the ethical principle that we ought not to lie and the principle that we ought to make every effort to foster self-determination on the part of clients. She may have thought she was obtaining information she could use to help Martha, and so she may have been acting on the principle of beneficence. If we conceive of her problem as being a conflict of principles, we must weigh the principle of beneficence against the principles of not lying and fostering self-determination, and it is hard to know where to begin. Is fostering self-determination more important than helping someone? If so, when is it more important, and is *Dancing a Legal Dance* one of those cases in which it is more important or one in which it is not? Does it matter that Martha is so young? In short, we seem not to find a ready resolution of problems when we take them to be conflicts between principles.

Second, even when the principles themselves seem clear, we may disagree on their application. Even an appeal to the formal principle of justice can be contentious. One concern we had about LaShonda in *Adoptive Children* is that she seemed to be treating the young brother and sister differently from the way she treated others because they were not thoughtful enough to call her to make an appointment. She thinks that their not being thoughtful is a relevant difference between them and others in need. We might disagree. We could agree that we should treat them differently if they were relevantly different in their concern for the interests of others, but not think they are really relevantly different. Just appealing to the principle of formal justice will not help.

Third, the ethical principles are contentious because their meaning can vary from theory to theory. Two people might appear to be using the same ethical principle when they have very different sorts of harms in mind. In arranging to have Al tested for HIV, John denied Al his autonomy. Where a deontologist sees a denial of respect that can only be set right by according respect, an utilitarian sees a harm that could be set right if things worked out for the best. They would both appear to be using the same principle, of not causing unnecessary harm, but by concentrating upon it, we obscure the differing kinds of harms that really are at issue in a case. Different ethical theories create different contexts for cases, that is, and approaching a case with principles rather than theories in mind may blind us to different ways of seeing a case.

So we recommend that we range over the ethical theories to understand a case fully, holding a case up first to one theory and then to another to see it in all its aspects. This has the advantage of forcing us, if we are to do a full survey of a case, to lay it out in all the ways conceivable by the competing theories. Just as we can bias our judgment by some feature of ourselves that we bring to a case unawares, so we may bias our understanding of the problems in a case by a particular conception of what counts as an ethically relevant feature.

We do not suppose that holding a case up to survey it in this way will allow us completely to overcome either the personal or social values we bring to the case, but it will help, as will consulting with colleagues, a supervisor, and/or an ethics committee—as long as confidentiality is not broken in the consultations. Bringing another professional's point of view to a difficult case is to bring fresh eyes to the case. Getting his or her views on the case—both on what makes it difficult and on what you might do to resolve it—may help open up the case up so that you can see what it was that made it difficult and help ensure greater objectivity, less reliance, that is, on any personal or social values you may be bringing to the case.

For example, in *Adoptive Children,* someone may be taken by LaShonda's apparent inability to relate well to the brother and sister who came to her. They irritated her, but focusing on that aspect of the case is to concentrate on a feature of the case that virtue theory makes prominent, namely, how properly to relate to others. We may then ignore the issue of whether LaShonda's criteria for breaking the law are adequate or unfairly discriminate—issues we are more likely to notice if we approach the case as a deontologist or a utilitarian. If we approach the case as a utilitarian, we will concentrate upon the consequences of what LaShonda does and so get a better view of the implications of her behavior for her and for others. If we approach the case as a deontologist, we will concentrate upon whether LaShonda lies to those who seek help from her when she does not want to give it. To be sure that we have thoroughly understood the ethical issues in a case, we ought to look at the case from *all* of those perspectives—examining the intentions of those acting, the consequences of the actions, and the virtues displayed in the action.

The procedure we are recommending, as we have seen, can lead to clarity about what is at issue and about what we ought to do. We think that most cases can be resolved by getting clarity on what went wrong and what goals the social worker in the case ought to have. But there is no guarantee that we shall always be able to resolve difficult ethical problems. Among other problems, we cannot always be sure that we have fully analyzed a case and seen all the ethical issues it raises. In addition, we may find that even when we think we have, we cannot resolve the case without making some choice among the competing ethical theories—a choice, as we have claimed, for which you can have no ethical basis. But as with any complex problem, our failure to resolve it does not mean that it is not resolvable by others or by ourselves with more information or a fresh look at it or a different way of thinking about it. We should always presume that cases are resolvable, and when we find ourselves stuck, we should back off and find out new ways of proceeding to untangle the case. We might consult with colleagues, for instance, if that will not breach confidentiality. Only after all available resources have been exhausted are we permitted to say, not that the case cannot be resolved, but that we cannot now resolve it.

QUESTIONS

1. Provide an example from your own experience in which you would have engaged in unethical behavior if you had acted in your self-interest.

2. Provide an example where someone harmed their self-interest in doing what was ethical.

3. Give two examples of when you have acted prudently in your job or in an internship. If you can, give two examples of when you acted imprudently in the same sort of situation or give two examples of when you saw others act in a way you thought imprudent in their job or internship.

4. Examine the acts of prudence you provided for the last question and determine why they are acts of prudence. Are they also ethical? If not, why not? If so, why? Distinguish the reasons for which they are ethical (or unethical) from the reasons for their being prudent.

5. Look back to Case 1.3, *Adoptive Children*, and sort out among all the things LaShonda is doing what is prudent and what is not. You should do this both from her point of view—what must she think is prudent and what not?—and from your point of view—what of the various things she is doing do you think is prudent and what is not?

6. Look back at Case 1.1, *The Death of a Baby*. After sorting out what the law required Deborah to do and not to do, and what she actually did, determine in what ways she acted illegally. Then determine whether she was prudent in breaking the law and whether, given her decision to break the law, she acted prudently to protect herself and/or to protect others.

7. Provide an example, preferably from your professional practice, in which, unsure what to do ethically, you did what was legally required as a way to resolve the issue you faced.

8. Lawyers often put their clients through grueling questions in order to ensure that they know exactly where the weak spots in their clients' cases are so that the lawyers can better defend them. Nothing in their code of ethics specifies the *manner* in which lawyers are to do this and the standard practice varies. Some are nice about it, some are not. Provide a similar sort of example about variations in standard practice from social work.

9. Provide an example, if you can, of someone stepping outside the standard practice. What was the reason for doing this? Did the person not know what the standard practice was? Or did the person have an ethical reason for doing this?

10. Does social work need a code of ethics? Why, or why not?

11. Explain why appealing to a code of ethics does not resolve our problem when we face an ethical dilemma. You may use examples cited in the text.

12. Explain why appealing to a code of ethics does not resolve our problem when we face a problematic case. Again, you may use examples cited in the text.

13. Provide an example, out of your own experience if you can, of how something looked to be one thing but was another—like the example of the woman who killed her boyfriend. What differences did looking at it differently make?

14. In Case 1.2, *Dancing a Legal Dance,* Mary thought that Martha was being defiant in running away from home and staying with friends. She made an inference about *why* Martha was doing what she was doing based on the fact of Martha's staying with friends. We often make such inferences—that the mail carrier has come because we hear our mailbox open and close, that there is orange juice in the refrigerator because we left some the last time we had it, and so on. But these are inferences from facts, and although they may be plausible, they may not be true. Give five examples of plausible inferences from facts in which the inferences are in fact false.

15. Look back at one of the cases we have examined or to one of your own and provide an example of something in that case that turned out to be relevant to its resolution that you did not pick up in your first reading of it.

16. In Case 1.3, *Adoptive Children,* what would LaShonda have had to do to make an objective judgment?

17. Give an example of how you had to discount your biases to render an ethical judgment about a client or a fellow social worker.

18. If it were true that horses have wings and winged creatures fly, what conclusion should we draw? Is the conclusion true? Are the premises true? Can we draw the conclusion even though the premises are false? Ought we to believe the conclusion? If so, why? If not, why not?

19. If we know that someone concluded that he or she had seen a male goldfinch, and when asked, said he or she saw a small, bright, yellow bird with black wings, what premise is he or she assuming?

20. Give an example of a valid argument.

21. What are the two ways in which we can assess an argument?

22. Why do we need to provide reasons for ethical judgments?

23. Give an example of tracking harms in a difficult case in your practice with clients or relations with colleagues. How did you decide which course of action to take?

24. Someone can harm me and my interests by breaking a pencil that I am about to use. He or she can also harm me by shooting me. List five different harms for each situation and rank them by the degree of severity. Make sure that you have listed harms that differ sufficiently in severity that no disagreement seems possible about the ranking you propose.

25. Pick one of the cases we have examined or one of your own and lay out the ethical principles involved.

26. Explain why it is a mistake to rely solely on ethical principles to resolve ethical problems.

27. Pick one of the cases or a case of your own and examine how principles serve as signposts.

28. What are the competing visions of deontological theory, utilitarian theory, and virtue theory? That is, what kind of life does each think we ought to lead?

29. What tests do the competing theories provide to determine what, according to them, is the right thing to do?

30. Suppose that a colleague of yours lies to you regarding something about your job. The colleague thinks that if you knew the truth, you would be upset and thus harmed. Explain how a utilitarian would look at the situation and compare that to how a deontologist and to how a virtue theorist looks at it.

31. In regard to your answer to question 30, explain how a deontologist thinks that one problem with utilitarianism is that it condones using people for ends they may not share.

32. If you were a slave, would you prefer to live in a society of utilitarians or deontologists? Why?

CHAPTER

3 Clients

In explaining the value of the dignity and worth of the person, the Code of Ethics says that "social workers promote clients' socially responsible self-determination,"[49] and later, in laying out social workers' ethical responsibilities to clients, it says:

> Social workers respect and promote the right of clients to self-determination and assist clients in their efforts to identify and clarify their goals (1.02).

Unfortunately, the intervention necessary to promote clients's self-determination can itself raise ethical issues as well as compete with other social work values. We saw a sample of this sort of problem when John denied Al's self-determination in *Doing What the Judge Orders*. We shall consider these issues more thoroughly in the first two sections.

In the third section we shall consider some other ethical issues regarding the relations between social work practitioners and clients and last the question of who the client is, an issue that arose in *Dancing a Legal Dance* in which Mary chose to concentrate her energies on protecting the children when she had been hired to help the children and each of the parents.

The discussion presupposes knowledge of our method of tracking harms, and you should read in Chapter 1 the Introduction, the section on Difficult Ethical Cases, and the subsection on How the Method of Tracking Harms Works (pp. 1–21).

Intervention and Self-Determination

A Difficulty with Understanding the Client

Denying someone's self-determination to further it is not unusual. Parents do it all the time. The aim is to ensure that children will grow up so they can choose for themselves what kind of lives to lead and how to lead them. But though we readily justify intervening in the lives of small children, we find it more problematic to intervene when it is unclear whether those involved are capable of determining for themselves what to do. Consider the following case.

CASE 3.1

Refusing Help

Wilma was in her eighties, had lived in her home for forty-five years, and had lived alone for the eleven years since her husband died. Over the past few years, strangers had moved in with her, who, in several cases, wrote checks from Wilma's checkbook. She had been robbed three or four times. She is forgetful and often seems confused.

Her nephew was called by a multi-service agency for the elderly, and he closed her accounts, removed the unwanted guests, put new locks on the doors and windows, and asked neighbors to keep an eye on things. He felt that Wilma would be better off living in her home than going to a nursing home. He visits her twice a week.

One evening, a neighbor called the police because she had not seen Wilma and was worried. When Wilma answered the door, the police officer found that Wilma's house was unheated. It was winter and very cold, and the officer called an ambulance because Wilma seemed ill. But when it arrived, she refused to go. The officer left and called an agency that provides emergency service. The social worker there called the agency for the elderly, but since no one there could help until the next morning, the social worker went with the officer to Wilma's house with a blanket and small electric heater. Wilma did not answer the door, and, upon forcing entry, they found her dead. Four hours or so had passed since the neighbor had first called.

When we read a case, we may have an intuitive response about what harms there were and what we ought to do about them. It is the point of our method of tracking harms to take us beyond that immediate response so we can be sure we act to minimize harm, but that initial response will sometimes be exactly what we ought to do. That is the more likely the more experienced we become in applying the method. So we need to keep the response in mind as we work through the method. We may also find a case initially puzzling, with questions about the case crowding into our minds.

We can use both our intuitive response and our initial puzzles as checks on our use of the method of tracking harms. We will be using the method properly if we come to understand why we had our initial response about what we ought to do and can then assess that response, understanding why it was right or was mistaken. In addition, we should have answers to the puzzles or at least understand why we raised them.

So we might think of our initial response to a case as the step before the steps of the method—what must precede those steps. Although we will climb to a different place through the steps of the method, we should keep track of where we were initially.

This case, for instance, raises puzzling questions. Why did the house have no heat, and who was responsible for ensuring that it did? Where was the nephew, for instance? Why was the agency for the elderly not set up to help in such emergencies? The elderly have problems at night as well as from eight to five. Why did the social worker and officer not call the local power company to see if the power had been turned off? That would tell them whether the fault lie within the house—perhaps with a broken furnace—and would quickly give them some information about how they might proceed. Some of these questions, as we shall see, we will not be able to answer.

However those questions might be answered, the clearest harm is that Wilma died. If she had gone in the ambulance, she at least would not have died in her house that night. So why did the officer not force her to go in the ambulance? Our intuitive response is that the officer faced a dilemma when Wilma refused to go. He was concerned that she not be harmed by staying in the unheated house, but also concerned not to deny her decision about refusing to go in the ambulance.[50]

That is where we are right after reading the case, without beginning to use the method of tracking harms. The first step of the method tells us to:

1. *Try to understand why the participants are doing what they are doing by constructing arguments that would justify their acts or omissions.*

As we have said, this is a complex step in that it requires asking the following:

- Who are the participants in the case, and who else is affected?
- What is it the participants have or have not done or are or are not doing that they ought to be doing—particularly insofar as they cause harms?
- Why are they doing what they are doing?

The first step in the method is meant to capture these questions while adding another:

- Are the reasons that seem most plausible to attribute to them sufficient to justify what they are doing?

So the method tells us to ask, first, "Who are the participants?" Wilma, the police officer, Wilma's nephew, and the social worker are referred to, and there are others whose presence is implied, those in the ambulance, for instance. Who else is affected? The list of those immediately affected may be long, but if we consider how many in other situations may be affected by any decision that is made, the list of those affected will be significantly longer. For this case may serve as a precedent for how to respond to situations in which those in apparent need refuse assistance. Are officers to be allowed to help people against their will? The answer is not obvious, and in deciding what to do in this case, we will need to keep in mind the precedential implications of the decision.

In proceeding with the first step in the method, we are to determine what the participants have done or not done, and in this case that may seem obvious as far as Wilma is concerned. She has allowed the house to become so cold that staying there risks her life. But saying that Wilma has allowed something to happen implies that she knows what she is doing, and whether she does is a main issue in the case.[51]

The first step in our method tells us that we need to put ourselves in the shoes of the participants, after determining who they are and what they have done or permitted, and then ask:

- Why are they doing what they are doing?

But it is at this step that we—and the officer and social worker—are stymied. We cannot figure out a good reason for Wilma's refusing to take an ambulance. That is, we have trouble putting ourselves in her shoes so that her refusing to come out of the house can make sense to us, and that makes us wonder if she really knows what she is doing. That is, it makes us wonder if she is competent to make a judgment about what she ought to do.

But we do not know. The officer and social worker can leave Wilma in the house or put her in an ambulance. But both sides of the dilemma are factually problematic. They do not know that Wilma would be seriously harmed were she to stay, but can only make a quick assessment of the risk, based on limited information. And they do not know whether Wilma knows what she is doing in deciding to stay. Only a quick assessment can be made based on the conversation with her and on a presumption one way or the other about whether a competent, fully-informed individual would voluntarily choose to stay in such a situation.

The social worker and officer had to make these quick assessments keeping in mind that the harm of someone's dying is worse than the harm of denying that person's self-determination. Harm to the person exercising self-determination can justify denying it—at least temporarily. For if what someone decides to do looks risky, we think it reasonable to intervene—at least to tell the person of the danger. If you see someone about to walk on a bridge you know to be so dangerous that it will fall when anyone walks on it, you should tell the person of the danger.[52] It would be unethical not to.

Yet if we tell the person, who then decides to continue walking, we may have a problem—similar to that the officer and social worker faced. The risk to Wilma that would come from her staying in the house is high. The social worker and officer do not know that she will die if she stays, but have good reason to believe she will be harmed. In asking her to take the ambulance, the officer was effectively informing her that she should leave. The problem arose when she refused and persisted in what appeared to be risky and even irrational behavior.

When Self-Determination Is Possible

To come to grips fully with this case, we need to examine in more detail the conditions that must be satisfied if someone is to be autonomous. Both the situation and the person must be of a certain sort.

The situation—One condition of the situation is that there be real options. If a mugger says, "Your money or your life!" you seem to have options, but if you refuse to hand over your money, the mugger can kill you and take it anyway. The mugger thus gives you no real choice—though you can assess the likelihood of the mugger's killing you anyway and decide to take the chance. The police officer would have no real choice regarding Wilma if, for instance, there were no hospital available that would admit her.

We presume that it was not an option to turn the heat on. If it were, it is hard to understand why the officer left Wilma without heat when heat could be obtained so easily. But we do not know if the furnace could not be restarted, if the power company was contacted to see if it had emergency service available to start the furnace, or even if the social worker and officer considered getting the furnace started. We would need more information than we have to know exactly what options they had and what options they thought about.

The person—When we consider how someone perceives a situation, we are looking at those features of the person making a decision that are essential to self-determination. These features are that a person be:

   a. Mentally competent,
   b. Informed, and
   c. Deciding voluntarily.

We make judgments without full information all the time. We stop at stoplights, for example, without knowing that the driver behind us will stop. Since we do not require *full* information for self-determination, we may ask, "How much information is enough?" We also make decisions often without being fully competent. If you need coffee to wake you up, you may be deciding to get up without being fully competent. So we may ask, "Just how competent does one have to be?"

Yet asking such questions implies that people need to prove themselves when in fact we generally *presume* self-determination. We do not demand evidence that someone old enough to own a house knows what he or she is doing in carrying out the garbage or fixing breakfast. We require evidence only if someone claims that the presumption is mistaken. Rather than ask how much information or competence is enough, we ask:

   a. What presumptions are appropriate for which persons?
   b. When it is appropriate to question a presumption?
   c. What sorts of considerations properly move us to override a presumption?

None of these questions is easy to answer, and yet how we answer them matters.

Anyone who has had a teacher or a parent, or a boss or colleague, who thought he or she was not good at something knows how hard it is to prove oneself when someone presumes that proof is needed. Doing something right once is not enough. That may be luck. We must instead do the right thing time and again—enough to outweigh the presumption. So making a presumption one way or the other matters enormously.

Some cases pose no difficulty. We presume that infants are unable to determine for themselves what is in their best interests. We maintain that presumption for children up to a certain age even though, as any parent can attest, the age at which that presumption ceases to be appropriate can be the subject of much dispute, especially with the children. We even presume someone capable of self-determination sometimes when it is not clear the person is capable. We do this for children as they grow older, saying to a child, for instance, "You are old enough to think about how someone else might feel who was treated that way!" Presuming the capacity for self-determination encourages responsibility, and so we sometimes presume it in unclear cases. Of course, such cases can present ethical issues if the presumption is inappropriate.

Sometimes the person we presume capable of self-determination does something that does not seem right for the situation. We question the presumption because of there not being something right about the situation. Wilma did something—refused to ride in the ambulance—that did not seem right for the situation, and so the police officer had to consider whether she was really competent. The form of what does not look right will suggest to us what condition is at issue—whether the person was uninformed, incompetent, or acting involuntarily.

These three conditions work in concert with one another. If someone is competent and informed and yet does something we think a reasonable person would not do, we presume the action was involuntary in some way and try to figure out whether the person was coerced or is acting under some internal compulsion. If someone competent is acting voluntarily but does something we think a reasonable person would not do, we presume the person is not properly informed. Lack of the relevant information would explain, we think, why someone who is competent would voluntarily do something unwise. And if someone is fully informed and acting voluntarily, but does something odd, we presume lack of competence. Nothing else would explain, we think, the mistake. The three conditions so work together that when two are satisfied, and yet we have some failure, we presume that the third is not satisfied.

We also presume that someone cannot be properly informed if incompetent. The officer may have explained to Wilma what the situation was—that she was likely to die if she did not get warm—to try to ensure that she was fully informed, but she may have been so cold that she could no longer think clearly. Then she would not be competent enough to become informed.

When someone does something that does not seem right for the situation, we can, to summarize, raise a question about the presumption we make, whatever it is. The form of failure suggests what condition of self-determination is at issue. The person may not have had appropriate information. Or the person may do something, we discover, that he or she had no choice but to do. The choice would then be competent, but involuntary. Unfortunately, there are both practical and conceptual problems in determining whether someone is capable of self-determination—knowing that someone had appropriate information, or had no choice, or was competent.

Problems with These Criteria

The most obvious practical problem arises because we often are unable to find out enough about a person to make an assessment of his or her competence. A person may seem to exhibit all the traits of competence and yet, for all that, still be incompetent. Part of Deborah's problem in *The Death of a Baby* is that she does not know enough about Hal to know whether he could have intentionally chosen to suffocate his son. She might have found out more with more time, but we often do not have time to gather relevant evidence. The officer could at most ask a few questions to get a sense of whether Wilma understood, and could not be sure that any hesitation or apparent false steps in Wilma's responses were not caused, for instance, by being questioned by a police officer who had come unbidden to her door.

Besides these practical problems, we can find ourselves unclear about what we would be willing to count as competent, or appropriately informed, or properly voluntary. We may be plagued with conceptual unclarity. We may find ourselves unsure what we would be willing to count as instances of the thing in question. Consider incompetence, for example. People may choose to do things that others find incredible, for example. They choose to go over Niagara Falls in a barrel or to climb hundreds of feet up sheer rock faces covered with ice. Some of us would judge them incompetent because they decide to do such things; others would not. Determining competence by *what* people decide to do can be problematic. If we question what they do, should we then examine their mental capacities—their capacity to reason, to assess risks properly, and so on? But some persons with mental illness may be perfectly good at logic. They reason well from irrational premises.

One factor that matters in what we presume about others is the degree of risk to which they subject themselves. We are not concerned with whether someone is really competent, informed, and acting voluntarily when the stakes are low and the presumption thus carries little risk. Presuming that a child is competent is easier when the child is in a sandbox than up a tree. Wilma appears to be in a life-threatening situation and presuming competence puts her at great risk. We generally require less evidence to override the normal presumption of competence when the presumption puts someone at great risk than we would in a less risky situation.

We also generally agree upon what makes a difference to someone's being competent. The police officer thought Wilma was ill, and being ill can make one less competent—easily confused or too tired to pay attention. Being too cold can make a person think less clearly. In addition, Wilma is in her eighties and so, arguably, is more likely than those who are younger to have some physical condition, such as Alzheimer's, that would make her confused. The police officer thus has *some* reason for thinking that Wilma was not competent in refusing to ride in the ambulance.

But being sometimes confused does not mean being incompetent. Even being sometimes incompetent does not mean being always incompetent or incompetent in the situation in question. Even if the officer knew that Wilma would die if she did not leave the house, that may not be enough, even with hesitations about her competence, to override the normal presumption we make. Wilma might have decided that she was going to die and that she preferred dying that way, in her own house, without the hassle and expense and indignities of hospitals. That someone might disagree with that decision, even that most might disagree, is not evidence that it is mistaken or that the person who makes it is incompetent.

It is her life at risk, some may argue, and anyone is entitled to as much respect as possible for a decision about something so vitally important. We are properly reluctant to override someone's decision about something so vital—especially when it is expressive of the person. Thus, we are reluctant to override a decision not to seek medical help when it is made on religious grounds because we presume that the decision is more firmly founded on beliefs deemed vital, by that person, to the person's sense of who he or she is. What we do not know is whether Wilma's decision not to go in an ambulance is expressive of something of concern to her.

We thus find ourselves with an ethical problem at the very first step in our method, namely, in presuming Wilma's competence in making a judgment about not going in the ambulance. The case is factually problematic, that is, because we cannot be sure, from the information we have, whether Wilma is competent. So a judgment about what to do will have to be made considering both possibilities, namely, that she is incompetent so that some others (e.g., a police officer) can appropriately decide for her, and that she is not incompetent, so that if others do decide for her, they are denying her self-determination (and so may be liable for a legal suit, for instance).

Choosing Harm

The Code of Ethics tells us that we may "limit clients" rights to self-determination when, in the social workers' professional judgment, clients' actions or potential actions pose a serious, foreseeable, and imminent risk to themselves or others," but it also tells us that we are to "promote clients'. . . self-determination" (1.02). Wilma risks a serious, foreseeable, and imminent risk to herself, but she may be choosing that. She may be like the person who is about to walk across a dangerous bridge who, upon being told that, says, "I want to anyway." Is her decision itself a sign that she is incompetent? Or can individuals competently do things others of us would not do?

In this regard, consider the situation a medical social worker faced:

CASE **3.2**

Depressed and Ready to Die

Juanita was diagnosed as having rectal cancer while she was also going through a nasty divorce. She had radiation treatment, but became very depressed and suicidal. She was diagnosed as schizophrenic, but was functional. She had her own apartment and car and cared for her two-year-old daughter. She came back into the medical hospital with inoperable cancer of the liver, but tried to sign herself out and stopped taking medication. She was sent to a psychiatric hospital.

The psychiatrist wanted her to have chemotherapy, but Juanita refused. "I don't want to do it. If I go through that again, I may prolong my life six months at most." She wanted to go back to her apartment. She had lived there with her cancer before, but the psychiatrist refused to release her from the hospital unless she had chemotherapy, and even then would only release her to foster care.

The other members of the multidisciplinary treatment team agreed with Juanita that she should be allowed to go home. They had explained the options to her and talked with her at some length. They agreed that "she could talk quite clearly about all of this and about what she wanted." When she had chemotherapy before, she became very ill physically, and she saw no point in such pain to prolong her life for so short a time.

But the psychiatrist told Juanita, "If you do not agree to accept chemotherapy, I will have to consider you suicidal, and I can't release a suicidal patient." The other members of the team attributed this response to the psychiatrist's having been trained as a pediatrician and to her having come to this country as an adult. "She has different cultural values and wants to save people in spite of themselves. So she treats them like children, which she finds easy to do."[53]

The other members of the team thought about going to the director because the psychiatrist was essentially holding the patient for a medical condition, and that was inappropriate under the mental health code. But whenever they pressed the psychiatrist about this, she fell back on the claim that the patient was suicidal, and when staff members had gone to the director before, the director always backed the doctors, and they just got a reputation for causing trouble.

So they wrote up in their reports what they thought should have been done so that, whatever happened, they would be covered.

Juanita's psychiatrist takes her decision to forgo treatment as evidence that she is not competent to make such a decision. Choosing to forgo treatment is tantamount to choosing to die sooner rather than later, and so what Juanita decides is enough, the psychiatrist thinks, to prove her incompetent.

The story is complicated by the psychiatrist's having come to the United States as an adult and having been trained as a pediatrician. The other team members question whether the psychiatrist's judgment is really based on an objective consideration of the patient.[54]

But what concerns us about this case is that Juanita provides reasons for refusing chemotherapy. Her argument is straightforward:

> I have inoperable liver cancer and will suffer great physical and emotional harm if I have chemotherapy for it.
>
> The suffering is not worth the short additional time I can reasonably expect to live with chemotherapy.
>
> Therefore, I do not want chemotherapy.

We may disagree with how she weighs the suffering of chemotherapy against living longer, and we may think she is mistaken in how much she thinks she will suffer. But it is she who has to suffer and her life that will be prolonged. She has thought about what she wants to do and why, made her judgment, and made her position clear.[55]

If we return to *Refusing Help*, we can see the striking difference between these two cases. Whereas Juanita's decision may be thought of as being expressive of her views of the relative values of life and suffering, we have no understanding of Wilma's refusal. Her refusing the ambulance not only does not seem right for the situation, but also seems to have no clear, plausible basis.

The most difficult ethical problems occur when we must choose between competing harms. The social worker and officer are faced with this sort of problem—risking harm to Wilma's autonomy or her life. The evidence does not make it obvious which choice is the best, but some action is required. If the social worker and officer knew Wilma would not die if she did not go in the ambulance, there would be no ethical problem; and if Wilma were known to know what she was doing in rejecting the ambulance, there might be regret, but no ethical problem. The ethical problem arises because the social worker and officer do not have enough evidence either to force her to go or to leave her alone, but do have enough concerns that doing nothing is not an option. So what ought they do?

2. *Determine what goals the participants had and what means they thought would achieve those goals; then determine what goals ought to be achieved and determine what means are best for achieving those goals.*

The goal seems clear enough. Try to minimize the harm to Wilma. The problem the participants face is to determine which alternative causes minimal harm. Since Wilma is in a life-threatening situation so that the risk to her of great harm is high, we require less evidence to override a presumption about her being competent, informed, and acting voluntarily. Yet though we have doubts about the appropriateness of that presumption, we also have doubts about those doubts. She may be perfectly competent. One way we handle such unclarity, when we see harm occurring if we do not intervene, is to moderate the form of our intervention. We try to determine a way to respect a person as much as we can while minimizing the possibility of the harm that may occur.

One way to respect Wilma, and still act to protect her life, is to provide her with the ability to warm herself. Only if it were not possible to do that, relatively quickly, would the officer be faced with forcing her to go to the hospital or leaving her in the unheated house. Seeing the neighbor who called about the problem was an option since Wilma might have been willing to stay with the neighbor. Tracking down the nephew was another option. Calling the power company to see if the problem was with a loss of power was another one. What the officer did was contact a social worker, and they tried to allow Wilma to warm herself by bringing a blanket and heater to the house. We can understand why they did what they did—even if it was too late to be of help.

Understanding, however, is not justification. Since time was of the essence, it is arguable that the officer ought to have pursued the other options to see if something could be done more quickly. It is also arguable that if no alternative was available to allow Wilma to warm herself quickly, the officer ought to have made her take the ambulance. The justification would be that that was the best way to minimize the harm to her. First, it would be more harmful to Wilma to die than to be forced to go to the hospital. And, second, there would be time enough, after she was treated and warmed up, for her to go back to her house if she wished and do what she wished to do.

We have considered only the ethical issues here, and relevant laws may have made it difficult, if not impossible, for the officer to put her in an ambulance—or made it mandatory for the officer to do so.

In summary, if a person's decision does not seem right for a situation, we question the presumption we make, whatever it is, about self-determination. We hunt for evidence of lack of information, or of incompetence, or of less than voluntary choice so we can understand why the person would have made the decision. When the case is factually problematic, as with Wilma, we try to find some form of intervention that respects the person involved, as much as possible—though we need less evidence to overturn a presumption of self-determination when the situation is life-threatening than otherwise.

Impaired Self-Determination

It is an issue regarding Wilma and Juanita whether they have full self-determination. Let us consider briefly a case in which there is no doubt that the capacity for self-determination is impaired. The issue for Bianca, the social work practitioner, is how to respond to a concern that a boy, Rob, be placed in a foster home.

CASE 3.3

Low-Functioning Parents

"The parents met in the state hospital," Bianca said. "They're not psychotic. Their main problem is that they are low-functioning. Rob is ten, and he's smarter than they are. He's hyperactive. He's on medications. He's got sexual identity problems. He's a behavior problem. He tells his parents what to do."

"The school and a private agency want us to place him in foster care because the parents seem unable to handle him. The parents are like pack rats, collecting everything. So the house is filled with stuff, but it is not filthy. They were dressing him like a little girl and letting his hair grow into bangs, but once I explained to them what they needed to do, and provided them with funds to get a haircut and new clothes, they did what was needed. They clearly love their son. When he refuses to do his homework the mother calls me, worried that he will fail. They're not abusing their son, and they're not neglecting him. So I have no good reason to justify taking him out of the home."

"Besides, he would be a difficult placement, with all his problems, and I've seen the difficulties children have experienced in foster care—adjustment problems, attachment separation issues, and also abuse.

"The real issue is that this family is always going to need someone from the community to assist them in parenting the child. They are doing the best job they can."

Rob's parents are not fully competent, and Bianca thus has a dilemma, brought on by the insistence of the school and a private agency that Rob be taken from his home and placed in foster care. But, she argues, he is not being abused or neglected. There is thus no reason to take him out of his home. And trying to find a good placement for him would be difficult. She is tracking the harms in the case, following the third step in our method:

   3. *Determine what the harms are of various courses of action. To whom would they occur, what kinds are they, and what are their magnitudes?*

Bianca's judgment about what is best to do—how best to achieve the goal of minimizing harms to Rob—is that he should stay at home.

This case raises a variety of issues, but we note the case here only to see how, in trying to minimize the harms to Rob, Bianca respects what capacities for self-determination Rob's parents possess. Bianca's decision in part reflects the view that it is usually better to keep a child in his or her natural family, but it also reflects the judgment that Rob's parents are competent enough, given proper guidance and help.[56] They are not fully functioning, but they do function and can parent Rob—with help. The case is thus a good object lesson to remind us that maintaining someone's capacity for self-determination is a paramount aim, even if that capacity is less than perfect.

Conflicts with Self-Determination

Self-determination is not an absolute value. We recognize restrictions on someone's right of self-determination for all sorts of ethical reasons. My right to swing my fist stops where your nose begins, and the reason is that each of us has a right not to be harmed that is at least as weighty as the right to self-determination. The right to self-determination is a *prima facie* right—a right that ought to be respected and thus can be denied only for ethical reasons more weighty than the reasons supporting the right to be denied. As we have said, "weighty" is a metaphor that needs filling out in terms of the extent and kinds of harms that would occur were such a right not denied, and as we have seen, determining what reasons are more weighty in a particular case can be difficult.

In *Refusing Help,* the officer needs a good, ethical reason to override Wilma's decision not to ride in the ambulance. The threat of harm to her would arguably be weighty enough only if no other form of intervention were available. In *Depressed and Ready to Die,* Juanita's decision not to have chemotherapy ought to be respected unless very good ethical reasons exist for overriding it.

Wilma and Juanita were exercising their self-determination in ways that could harm themselves, but self-determination can also conflict with other values in social work practice. Indeed, there are as many possible conflicts with self-determination as there are social work values. Self-determination can harm others, for instance, by causing bodily harm, as when I swing where your nose is, or by denying someone's right to confidentiality, as when a social work practitioner tells someone something given in confidence. We cannot determine ahead-of-time, as the Code emphasizes, "which values, principles, and standards are most important and ought to outweigh others in instances when they conflict" (Purpose of NASW Code of Ethics).

In *Doing What the Judge Orders,* John thought Al might be putting others at risk of getting AIDS. But because John received in confidence the information that Al might be HIV-positive, he got his supervisor to go with him to get the judge to order a physical, including a test for AIDS, without telling Al. When we were following through the first step in our method to try to make sense of what John was doing, we attributed to him something like the following reasoning:

> I ought to minimize the amount of harm that may be caused.
>
> Al may cause harm to his foster family and his girlfriend.
>
> If he is tested for being HIV-positive, we will find out whether he may cause harm to his foster family and girlfriend.
>
> So he ought to be tested to determine if he is HIV-positive.

In analyzing this case, we decided that the third premise was false. The test may not give us the information we need.

But if we are to understand why John had Al tested without telling him, we also need to attribute to him something like the following:

> If I tell him he is to be tested, I risk his mother finding out that his mother's social worker has told what was given in confidence.
>
> He is fifteen years old and so not entitled to much self-determination.
>
> The possible harm to others if he is HIV-positive and the loss of confidentiality if he is told are more weighty than whatever right of self-determination he may have as a fifteen-year-old.
>
> So I can arrange to have him tested without asking him.

These arguments allow us to see how the values of maintaining confidentiality and not harming others operate for John in *Doing What the Judge Orders.* John thought the risk to others to be substantial enough to have Al tested, and he thought the concern not to breach confidentiality was weighty enough to deny Al's self-determination.[57]

We might disagree with the ways in which John weighed these values against one another. As the Code makes clear, "Reasonable differences of opinion can and do exist among social workers with respect to the ways in which values, ethical principles, and ethical standards should be rank ordered when they conflict" (Purpose of the NASW Code of Ethics). But we did not need to get so far as to try to assess the weight of these values in this case. For when we asked what goals John had in mind in testing Al, we realized that whatever he found out, he would have to inform Al, and so we did not need to weigh these values one against another to determine if John had acted correctly.

Consider another case in which the issues of self-determination, confidentiality, and harm to others are intertwined for a clinical social worker, Mohammed:

CASE **3.4**

Lying to Save a Marriage

"A married woman came to me. She is running around. I am also counseling her husband, and she asks me, 'Do you think my husband is running around?' I told her no. And he isn't. He's a good man. I wouldn't tell the husband that the wife is running around if he asks me, but I know damn well she is running around. I have to lie to the husband because if I say, 'I don't know' or 'I can't tell you,' or if I refuse to answer on the ground that I have a professional and confidential relationship with the wife, he will believe his wife is running around.

"Since I am a professional person, I will be believed if I say the wife is not cheating. I am patching up a relationship then. In our culture if you tell a lie with a straight face, it will be believed. Arab culture is a face-saving culture; American culture is a guilt-ridden culture. I will not feel guilt at lying. I would feel shame if someone found out that I was lying, but I will act to protect myself from being found out. I sometimes feel I shouldn't send an Arab client to an American social worker if there is an issue in which guilt and shame are involved."

Mohammed is considering what he would do were the husband to ask about his wife. He is thus beginning the third step of our method:

   3. *Determine what the harms are of various courses of action. To whom would they occur, what kinds are they, and what are their magnitudes?*

What follows is an object lesson in how to work with step 3 of our method. We shall consider only one possible course of action, namely, what Mohammed says he would do—lie. But, to put it briefly, that would not just prevent the husband from being informed about what his wife is doing. It would *mis*inform him. The harms of doing this are many, are of different kinds, and of very different magnitudes.

a. When we lie to someone, we prevent that person from acting with self-determination to the extent that the person acts without the information we fail to provide or on the misinformation we do provide. Suppose I want you to do something for me, but I know that if you knew the truth, you would not do it. So I lie to you, and you, believing me because you think I am your friend, act on that false information.

    The harm is not just that I get you to do what you might not otherwise do, but that I get you to do it by treating you as an object—an intelligent object, with a mind to be manipulated by false information, but an object nonetheless. I deny your capacity for self-determination even more effectively than I would by grabbing your arm and moving it—since you would then know you are being manipulated—and I deny it in a particularly devious way because I make it seem to you that you are making the decision with full self-determination.

    I thus harm you in a special way. As we saw in Chapter 1, I have wronged you, and I wrong you by denying your self-determination, whatever good may happen to come from what I have done. And I have not just wronged you, I am poisoning our relationship. I am not treating you as a friend if I treat you as an object.

    Mohammed says he is giving the husband false information for the good of both the husband and the wife. He says he is "saving the relationship." But even if he were saving the relationship, we should have to weigh his saving it against his wronging the husband by treating him as an object.

b. If Mohammed thought the husband, if he knew, would choose to save the marriage, he could tell the husband. But Mohammed says he is keeping the information from the husband to save the marriage. So he must be deciding not as the husband would decide, but as he thinks the husband *ought* to decide. One test that we use for making decisions for people who are incompetent is to ask whether, if they were competent, they would choose what we choose for them. If we can answer with good evidence that they would, then we know we have chosen rightly. By this test, Mohammed is harming the husband doubly—by treating him as though he were incompetent, and choosing for him what he might not choose if he were informed.

c. The wife's self-determination will be harmed. She is now a party to a deceit that she must maintain, and so she must be careful not to say or do anything that would reveal what she has told Mohammed. Every time she acts, every time she speaks, she must think about whether what she does or says will reveal the secret she and Mohammed are now a party to. Her self-determination is limited to the extent such hesitation enters into her actions and words.

d. The marriage will be harmed. On the one hand, the way the wife relates to her husband will be conditioned by the possibility that he will come to know, and that will harm her capacity to be spontaneous, open, and intimate with him. On the other hand, the longer her husband does not know, the more she is in a position of power over him, having deceived him once without any bad consequences, and that will prevent their being in a relationship of mutual trust and respect. Were the relationship to continue, that is, it would be based on a lie, a false understanding. That is harmful in itself, and the falseness may reverberate through the relationship and affect other aspects of it. It is certainly not obviously better that their relationship continue, based on such a lie, than whatever comes about if the husband comes to know.

e. The relations between Mohammed and the husband and wife will change no matter what happens. If Mohammed tells the husband, he will have broken the confidential relationship that ought to exist between a social worker and a client, for he will have told something the wife told him in confidence. But if he does not tell the husband, he will be a party to the deceit the wife is practicing on the husband. In addition, not telling the husband puts the wife in Mohammed's power. She knows that he knows, and he is always in a position to tell.

Much immediate harm thus comes from Mohammed's lying to the husband. Mohammed says he would be believed if he lied because he is a professional and because in his culture, lies said with a straight face are believed. But, however that may be, at least one other person knows the wife is fooling around, and so this information may get back to the husband. If it does, he may discover that he has been deceived by his social worker as well as his wife. That will change his relationship with the social worker—as well as, presumably, with his wife.

In short, if we weigh the possible benefit of saving the marriage against the known and likely harms, it is no contest. The supposed benefit is not worth the harms to everyone involved. But the social worker has the information about the wife because he is seeing both professionally. If he were to tell the husband that his wife is running around, he would be divulging confidential information. So there is another issue here. Ought he to give the husband such confidential information? How are we to weigh the harms that will come from that against the harms that come from lying to the husband?

Mohammed is not in the best position to make this decision. His telling would harm his professional relationship with the wife, and he would likely be held responsible, justly or not, for any subsequent problems with the marriage. Not telling misleads the husband, but the husband may never come to know that. So the social worker is protecting himself from harm by not divulging the information.

Acting in a way that protects one's self-interest is not wrong if it is the right thing to do, but we have another reason to be concerned about Mohammed's objectivity. He would not be in a position to consider passing on such information if he were not individually counseling both the husband and wife. The difficulty with divulging confidential information would never have arisen, that is, had he followed the practice of never taking on as individual clients people whose interests are so intertwined, like spouses, that knowing about one may cause a change in the relationship with the other.

Mohammed got himself into such a difficult situation because he made a bad decision about whom to take on as clients or because, having made that decision, he failed to follow standard procedure. Before he begins, he should, as the Code puts it:

> Seek agreement among the parties involved concerning each individual's right to confidentiality and obligation to preserve the confidentiality of information shared by others (1.07[f]).

He should also inform his clients that he "cannot guarantee that all participants will honor such agreements" (1.07[f]) and that when he does disclose confidential information, he will inform the clients (1.07[g]). *Lying to Save a Marriage* is an example of how what seems to be a simple mistake can later produce a difficult ethical problem. But because Mohammed has made the mistake, what ought he do now? What are his options?

It might seem that his only options are to keep the confidence, and so lie to the husband and cause harm to him, the wife, and their relationship, or break the confidence, and so cause other harms. But it helps here to consider the second step in our method:

> **2.** *Determine what goals the participants had and what means they thought would achieve those goals; then determine what goals ought to be achieved and determine what means are best for achieving those goals.*

Mohammed says his goal for the marriage is to save it, but if he is denying the husband's self-determination by lying to him, it is at the price of both spouses being in a relationship in which they have less than full self-determination. Neither spouse will be able to be fully self-determined. The husband will be acting without full knowledge; the wife will be acting while trying to keep up the deceit. Is saving such a marriage, at such a price, a worthy goal? What is so valuable about a relationship in which the self-determination of both parties is so harmed?

In addition, Mohammed would be in a therapeutic relationship with both the husband and the wife that would be less than fully open—because deception is necessary to maintain one relation and denial is necessary for the other. Is any potential gain from counseling the husband or the wife worth such costs in such circumstances?

If Mohammed's goal were to encourage self-determination, he would encourage the wife to tell her husband and not lie to him. Instead of taking upon himself the decision whether to break the confidence of the wife or lie to the husband, he could encourage the self-determination of both by encouraging the wife to take responsibility for her actions. It is unclear what the result would be, but Mohammed would at least not be causing harm to produce a harm. He would be encouraging self-determination to encourage relationships in which self-determination would have a chance to flourish.

Being clear about our goals is thus helpful in determining how to weigh one ethical value against another. Self-determination is not always the most important value, but in this case, when we consider what Mohammed's goals ought to be, encouraging self-determination is the best way of achieving them.

Of course, the wife may refuse to tell her husband, and then Mohammed would have to determine what to do. His options are limited then, and each causes harm. For instance, he could tell the wife that if she does not tell, he will have to tell. But that is a form of coercion and is counter to the trust that ought to exist in a therapeutic relationship, and counter to the goal Mohammed ought to have of encouraging self-determination. He could also respond to the husband's question, should he ask, by saying that the information is confidential. Because, he thinks, the husband would then assume his wife was playing around, that answer would presumably encourage the husband to confront the wife. That could have terribly harmful effects—and certainly should never be taken lightly—but it also could force the wife to take responsibility for her actions. In short, having agreed to see each person individually, Mohammed has few options, and no good ones.

One of Mohammed's arguments in favor of lying to the husband is that, in the culture he and his clients share, he will supposedly be able to succeed in lying. If this is true, the husband will never find out—from Mohammed at least. But he may find out from some other person, and, in any event, the other harms we have laid out remain.

It is important that social workers have an understanding of different cultural values, and the Code of Ethics speaks to this obligation at 1.05(a) and (b). However, whether Mohammed is right that there is a different cultural norm makes no difference in our understanding of what Mohammed ought to do.[58] Assured success at being deceptive does not justify deceiving.

Of course, that conclusion rests upon some premises about ethical relativism that would need to be defended thoroughly if we were to fully justify it. Briefly, there appear to be three ways of understanding differing judgments about what ought to be done that appear to differ because of the different cultures of those making the judgments:

- Accept that no one in one culture has a right to make an ethical judgment about anyone's acts or omissions in another culture.

- Argue that although those in different cultures appear to make differing judgments about what ought to be done, there is a core set of ethical judgments that are identical. Lying is lying, that is, and is always wrong, but what looks like a lie to someone from another culture may be the truth, appearing to be a lie only because of the different cultures.

- Argue that someone from a different culture has no ethical right within another culture to use the cultural norms of his or her own culture.

Each of these responses to ethical relativism has its problems. The first response, for instance, would seem to imply that if we are not German, we cannot make the ethical judgment that the Nazis were wrong to kill Jews. But we are not going to explore here the various reasons for and against these three kinds of responses. It suffices to note them and to note that the second and third will have the same outcome for at least the core set of ethical beliefs that will generally be at issue in social work practice.[59]

Relations with Clients

Dual Relationships

A physician who giggled when examining you would be acting unprofessionally, no matter how funny you might look. A social worker who made friends with clients would have crossed the same sort of boundary. These boundaries can be difficult to draw or maintain, but both parties to the relationship have obligations that come from being in a professional relationship.[60] A lawyer who fails to file legal papers on time has failed a professional obligation, and if you fail to show for an appointment, you have not fulfilled an obligation to the lawyer.

The third step in our method says that we should:

3. *Determine what the harms are of various courses of action. To whom would they occur, what kinds are they, and what are their magnitudes?*

As we work through this step when we come to different cases, we shall find that many of the harms we uncover will concern the relationships between social workers and their clients. Yet how unclear the boundaries of these relationships may be is illustrated by the following case.

CASE **3.5**

Friends and Professional Relations

Raul was a recovering substance abuser who regularly attended meetings of Alcoholics Anonymous. He was also a social work therapist who worked with substance abusers. He encouraged Mark, one of his clients, to attend AA meetings. He had himself been attending meetings, but AA encourages those who come to the meetings to rely on each other, to call if they need help, for instance. Mark needed help and called Raul regularly.

Raul felt that he was doing therapy at Mark's beck and call rather than during their scheduled sessions. He confronted Mark, and Mark, feeling very rejected, stopped seeing Raul, dropped out of AA and out of treatment, and had a relapse.

In going to AA, Raul put himself in a situation in which he had obligations to help the other members of his group, including Mark—just as they had obligations to him should he call on any of them for help. He also had a professional obligation to help Mark because Mark was his client. It might appear that far from competing, these two obligations of Raul's would reinforce each other. After all, they are both obligations to help.

But Raul's professional obligation to help Mark was an obligation with clear, temporal boundaries. The two met at a certain time, for a certain length of time, and that was the end of the relationship until the next time—unless Mark had some emergency. The obligation that Raul had from being in AA was to help whenever any other member of his group needed help. Of course, Raul could refuse to help if it was two A.M., say. But far from reinforcing each other, the obligations conflict because the one from AA is relatively open-ended while the one from the professional relationship is relatively restricted. The former encourages, while the latter does not, extra help whenever in need.

More importantly, the relationship a therapist has with a client is marked by power of the therapist over the client, and that power relationship does not fit well with the form of collegial relationship encouraged in AA. Raul must be both therapist and confidant to Mark, and although a person may function in both capacities without any conflicts arising, there is always the possibility for a conflict of interests.

The Code puts up a red flag regarding conflicts of interest:

> Social workers should be alert to and avoid conflicts of interest that interfere with the exercise of professional discretion and impartial judgment.

The Code goes on to say that social workers should inform clients of "a real or potential conflict of interest" and then "take reasonable steps to resolve the issue in a manner that makes the clients' interests primary." It notes that sometimes such conflicts may "require termination of the professional relationship with proper referral of the client" (1.06[a]).

Raul has competing interests—an interest in helping Mark because both are in AA and an interest in seeing Mark professionally. In helping Mark through AA, Raul is providing what other members of their AA group presumably cannot provide, namely, help from a professional skilled in working with substance abusers, and he is doing it for free. The relationship Mark has with Raul through AA at the least allows Mark to overstep what ought to be the normal professional boundaries that generally preclude a client from calling a therapist regularly.

Mark also knows personal matters about Raul that clients would usually not know about their therapists. He knows that Raul has himself enough of a problem with alcohol to feel the need for going to AA. So Raul's seeing Mark professionally as well as in AA changes Mark's relationship with Raul as well as Raul's relationship with Mark.

This case concerns both the obligations and the proper boundaries in a relationship between a social worker and clients. Does Raul have an obligation to cease going to AA because he has an obligation to refer his clients there when they need it? The answer depends in part upon how many AA chapters there are around, upon whether Raul can go to one that is not too inconvenient for him where he is not likely to meet his clients, and upon whether, if he cannot, he has an obligation to go significantly out of his way so as to avoid his clients. Is it proper for Raul to have a relationship with a client, Mark, that is independent of his professional relationship? And, in regard to this last question, if he has any such relationship, does it matter that it is about the same issue that Mark is seeing him for professionally? Would it matter if they sat on a community board together?

These questions are not easy to answer, and, were we to continue to examine this case, in accordance with the method we propose, we might well discover, as the Code makes clear, that "There are many instances in social work where simple answers are not available to resolve complex ethical issues" (Purpose of NASW Code). These kinds of cases can be notoriously difficult to resolve satisfactorily.

Further Kinds of Dual Relationships

We are not concerned to provide answers to the cases we examine here, but to raise the kinds of problems that social workers can face in regard to clients. In this regard, consider the following case, which pursues the issue raised in Case 3.5, *Friends and Professional Relations*, of what kind of relationships a social worker may have with a client, or a former client, outside of their professional relationship.

CASE **3.6**

Can You Help Me Now?

Angela had an alcoholic client who responded well to therapy. Although eventually the therapy ended, the client stayed in AA, still feeling the need for support.

Angela had liked the client as a person in the therapeutic relationship. The client was a massage therapist, and so, after a period of time had passed, Angela went to her to get massages.

The woman later relapsed, but did not come back to Angela. Angela later discovered that the woman had wanted to come back, especially in those shaky stages before the relapse, but felt that because they now had a different relationship, she could not.

Angela may have thought that the client was effectively cured. But her choosing to see her former client raises an issue about what sorts of relations are permissible between professionals and clients. We need to distinguish at least three different kinds of cases. As we shall see in examining these cases, what is at issue is the potential for harm that occurs for a professional relationship when some other kind of relationship comes to exist as well.[61] As the Code of Ethics states:

> Social workers should not engage in dual or multiple relationships with clients or former clients in which there is a risk of exploitation or potential harm to the client. In instances where dual or multiple relationships are unavoidable, social workers should take steps to protect clients and are responsible for setting clear, appropriate, and culturally sensitive boundaries (1.06[c]).

As we noted, we shall be marking the kinds of harms that can occur because of the professional relationship between a social worker and a client.

First, it is sometimes difficult not to have some sort of nonprofessional relationship with clients even though having such a relationship may interfere in some ways with the professional relationship. A therapist who refused to help anyone he or she saw socially would ill-serve a community if no other such care were available. In any event, we often get thrown into relationships with others. You and a client may both have children on the same sports team and find you must juggle driving schedules together. We could hardly fault a psychiatrist who called the only available plumber to help with a flooded basement even if the plumber were seeing the psychiatrist professionally. Yet these further relationships may well mar the professional relationship. The plumber might respond to the request to come at an odd hour by reciprocating and asking for therapy at odd hours, or the psychiatrist might find the plumber incompetent and be faced with all of the harm that making an issue of the incompetence could do to the client's self-esteem (and perhaps the client's reason for being in therapy) and to their professional relationship.

Second, you may come to have a relationship with a former client voluntarily, and you may seek that relationship innocent of any bad intent. Angela's case seems to fall into this category. She chose to become her former client's client, reversing the former professional relationship. We may fault her for having sought out a relationship with her former client, but whether we fault her, and how much, will depend upon such factors as the risk of harm to her client, whether others besides her former client were available, and how badly she needed to see someone to give her a massage—for medical reasons, perhaps? How long must you wait to have any other sort of relationships with your clients, or should you try never to have such relationships?

Third, other relationships with clients can put into question the intent of the professional involved. These cases raise serious questions about whether the client's interests in obtaining the best professional service possible have been harmed. Consider the following case.

CASE **3.7**

Having Sex

Theresa came to see a therapist, Aubrey, in a family counseling agency. It came out over a number of sessions that Theresa had been in therapy before and had an affair with her previous counselor that began several months after the therapy ceased. She was married and was struggling with the affair's having ended and with her guilt at having had an affair.

Aubrey suggested that the counselor had crossed the proper boundaries between therapist and client in having a sexual relationship, even though the therapy had ended several months before the affair began. Theresa had not thought about that, but, as she did, she began to think that perhaps the initial stages of the affair started before the sessions with her therapist had ended, and she wondered if, as she said, "I somehow perhaps may have led him on."[62]

Despite Aubrey's urging, Theresa decided not to press charges—partly because she did not want the publicity, which she thought would harm her relationship with her husband, and partly because she was not convinced that the affair was wholly the therapist's fault.

So Aubrey investigated on her own.[63] She discovered that the therapist, who lived in a nearby community, was referred to as a licensed psychologist although the law required a Ph.D. for that title and the therapist did not have a Ph.D. Aubrey called a university where the therapist was to lecture, informing the university that the therapist was not a psychologist (it had advertised that he was), and she let it be known in the community that he was operating under false credentials.

One factual unclarity concerns what relationship Theresa and her therapist had in the professional relationship. It may look as though he had acted professionally because he had not pursued his romantic interest in her until after their professional relationship had ended. But, thinking back, Theresa thought perhaps the therapy had been unsuccessful just because the therapist had a romantic interest in her.

The reason Theresa has to wonder about whether her therapist provided her with proper therapy is that the therapist has competing interests sufficient to make her unsure that he did all he ought to do professionally. The same sort of problem arose in *Friends and Professional Relations.* Since both Raul and Mark belonged to AA, Raul was obligated to help Mark when Mark needed it—just as Mark was obligated to help Raul. But the professional role and the role within AA can get easily mixed so that Mark may have some reason to wonder whether, in calling Raul because of their AA connection, he would be getting the best help that Raul was capable of giving. After all, Raul is likely to resent being at Mark's beck and call when they already had an established relationship, with set times for appointments. Just so, we must wonder whether Theresa's therapist really did the best job he could do for Theresa. If his romantic interest blossomed before the therapy ended, then he would presumably be acting in that interest to ensure that, whatever else happened, she be available for him. That might cause him to end the professional relationship prematurely, for instance. If Theresa was seeing him because of problems with her husband, his romantic interest in her may have caused him not to help her as much as he could to sustain her marriage. We do not know, but we do know that the therapist put himself in a position in which Theresa had to wonder about such possibilities and about his commitment to helping her.

A similar sort of problem could hold in *Can You Help Me Now?*—although the difficulty can best be seen from the client's point of view. The client needs help and would have gone to Angela except that Angela was now her client, seeing her for massages. So the client might have been concerned that if they reestablished their old professional relationship, she would not be able to keep the new one because Angela would be unwilling to see her as a client while still getting massages from her. Her interest in retaining her former therapist as a client—perhaps just because she needs the money—is at odds with her interest in seeking help from the therapist. In addition, she will again be in a dependent position vis-a-vis her therapist after having been the expert in giving massages.

Conflicts of Interest

These last three cases, Case 3.5, *Friends and Professional Relations,* Case 3.6, *Can You Help Me Now?,* and Case 3.7, *Having Sex*—have in common that the relationships in which the professionals are in have produced potential conflicts of interest that put at risk their capacity to perform their professional obligations. People often have more than one reason for doing something. The only concern we have is whether harm occurs if one interest comes to predominate and causes unnecessary harm to the client. If Raul prolonged Mark's therapy only to get more money, refusing to see him for free through their AA connection, that would conflict with the interest Mark has as a client in having Raul help him work through his problems expeditiously and with the least expense possible.

In *Friends and Professional Relations,* Mark and Raul have a situation in which conflicts of interests can occur, and that is also what happened in the other two cases. In *Can You Help Me Now?,* Angela created a situation in which her interest in receiving a massage from her former client conflicted with an interest she ought to have in being available in case her client needed her again. This latter interest arises because once a professional has seen someone as a client, that professional is usually better positioned than anyone else to help the client again. The professional has presumably earned the client's trust and knows what problems the client had and may continue to have, what has been done to help, how the client has responded, and how the client is likely to respond to new treatment. By initiating a new kind of relation with the client, the professional may make it difficult, if not impossible, for the client to seek the best help available should help be needed again.

Theresa is unable to go back to the therapist whom she first saw. By initiating a romantic relationship with Theresa, the therapist should make Theresa wonder if she got the best treatment possible while in his care. In addition, Theresa is now unable to go back to him for help because of the loss of trust in the relationship as well as her feelings of guilt and shame associated with the therapist. Her inability to return to the therapeutic relationship with him harms her because he may be the one best positioned to help her. He saw her through the initial stages of treatment and so is presumably better able to understand her problems than someone might be who would begin completely ignorant of her past. The relationship of implicit trust that ought to mark a professional relationship has been lost—as it was in each of the three cases we have just examined.

Cases like that involving the therapist in which a professional and a client have a sexual relationship, either during or after their professional involvement, pose a special sort of ethical problem. But as the case involving Angela makes clear, being vulnerable in a power relationship arises even when sex is not involved. A therapist who calls a plumber to help with a flooded basement may be taking advantage of a professional position if the plumber is a client. The plumber is right to be concerned that the quality of the therapy may be affected if the work is not done to the therapist's satisfaction. Social workers may terminate services or withhold benefits, and their power to affect their clients in those ways may cause clients to be timid, fearing loss of benefits if thought too assertive of their rights. Professionals have immense power over clients, and clients are thus especially vulnerable.

The cases we have just considered are object lessons in how that power may affect vulnerable clients. In therapeutic relationships, for instance, the quality of care received may well depend upon the *perceptions* the client has of the professional's concern. If the client thinks the professional is interested in the client for other than professional reasons, then the care received, even if it was appropriate, may not be taken to be appropriate and so may fail to achieve its end. Even if you as a professional do what you ought to do, others may question whether you did as much as you ought to have done or whether you did it as well as you should have. Appearances themselves can cause harm, that is, especially in therapeutic relationships.

The Obligation to Serve a Client Competently

A professional has an obligation to ensure that a client is competently served. A professional mapmaker, for instance, has an obligation to draw a map correctly so that those using it are not led astray, turning left when they should be turning right, for instance. Such obligations to be competent are the minimal obligations of a profession. The professional is a professional only because he or she has special knowledge—of how to draw maps accurately, or of how to help substance abusers. Clients have a right to expect that that knowledge will be used to help them.

As we have seen, the harm that occurs when that minimal obligation to help is not fulfilled can be enormous. In *Friends and Professional Relations*, Mark found himself unable to turn to Raul for help when he needed it. The Code of Ethics states that:

> Social workers should take reasonable steps to avoid abandoning clients who are still in need of services (1.16[b]).

With nowhere else to turn, Mark had a relapse. In *Can You Help Me Now?*, Angela's client felt that she could not return to Angela for help because their relationship had changed in a way that, the client apparently thought, prevented Angela from having a proper professional relationship with her. And in *Having Sex*, Theresa had to wonder whether the therapy she received failed because the therapist was more interested in pursuing her than in pursuing her therapy. In each case, it can be questioned whether the professional fulfilled the minimal professional obligation to help and to promote the client's well-being.

Since the appearance of a conflict of interest can itself cause harm, professionals have a special obligation not to put themselves in situations in which there are potential conflicts of interest. In *Friends and Professional Relations*, Raul had a special obligation, before sending Mark off to an AA chapter that he himself went to, to work out something with Mark that would have allowed Mark the help he needed. Even at the end of a professional relationship, a professional cannot know whether a client will have need of the professional again. Because that professional is usually best positioned to provide help if it is needed again, special care needs to be taken to ensure that such care can be available. Raul and Angela had obligations, that is, to anticipate the kinds of concerns their clients would have given the potential conflict of interest. It is this same concern that ought to make us uncomfortable even if Theresa's therapist were only to have sought her out for friendship several months after the therapy ended.

Reciprocity and Obligations in a Professional Relationship

In tracking the kinds of harms that can occur in having more than just a professional relationship with clients, we have concentrated on the minimal obligation that social work practitioners have to use their special knowledge to help clients. Our aim has been to illustrate the complex and various ways in which we can fail in fulfilling even that minimal condition. That is, even if we thought social workers had few ethical obligations to clients, they could still face complex and varied ethical problems. For even the simplest of ethical obligations can give rise to difficult ethical issues.

But there are other obligations that are also minimal conditions for proper practice—to tell the truth, to treat one's clients fairly, to encourage self-determination, and so on.[64] We have examined some of these in the various cases we have so far discussed. For instance, in *Doing What the Judge Orders*, John manipulated the situation so that, he thought, he would not have to inform his client, Al, of what he was doing, thus denying Al his autonomy. And in *Adoptive Children*, LaShonda did not tell the brother and sister what she knew about their natural parents, and one issue was thus whether she was treating them in the same way she treated other adoptees.

In each of these cases, as in the cases we have just examined, what is at issue is what harm is being done, and what these cases tell us is that social work practitioners have a set of *prima facie* obligations they ought to fulfill, obligations, that is, they ought to fulfill unless weighty moral reasons obligate them not to fulfill them. For the failure to act on a professional obligation will cause harm. In short, the ethical life of a social worker is even richer—and so more complicated—than we have so far suggested. Each obligation that social workers have—to encourage autonomy, not to cause harm, to treat clients fairly, and so on—can give rise to ethical problems as complex and varied as those we have been considering in regard to the minimal obligation of social workers to use their special knowledge and skills to help their clients.

Drawing Boundaries

Every relationship brings with it reciprocity. If you are discourteous to me, you make it that much harder for me to be courteous to you. Just so, clients have obligations to those professionals who are committed to helping them. Mark is obligated not to call Raul late at night except under very special circumstances, and Raul may rightly object to Mark's calling provided they began their relationship by Raul setting boundaries for their relationship that excluded such behavior.

Drawing clear boundaries can be difficult, however, and a therapist, for instance, can be faced with a need to make a delicate judgment. Consider the following case.

CASE 3.8

Gift for Services

Jacinda is in therapy with Marie and has been diagnosed as having Post Traumatic Stress Syndrome. She is thirty-five and has a history of sexual and emotional abuse by her father and her stepfather. After her grandmother died, she became extremely agitated because she was emotionally close to her. She told Marie that she would like to give Marie a gift from among her grandmother's belongings.

Marie told Jacinda that she does not accept gifts. Jacinda was upset, and after some cajoling by Jacinda, Marie told her that she would accept a gift only in exchange for the time spent in calls with Jacinda between therapy sessions.

Jacinda came in the next week with seven of her grandmother's belongings and put them on the desk. Marie told her that she could not take all seven and asked Jacinda to pick one. Jacinda insisted that Marie pick out what she wanted, but Marie told Jacinda that Jacinda had to select one gift.

Jacinda picked out a vase, and Marie displayed it in her office. Jacinda looked at the vase when she came in for her next session and expressed pride at seeing it there. Marie does not know the vase's value and is afraid it may be very expensive. She is thinking of having it appraised and if it is expensive, crediting Jacinda for a number of therapy sessions.

If we take the first step in our model and try to understand why Jacinda is doing what she is doing, we find that we need not get too deeply into psychoanalytic theory to sense that Jacinda is trying to transfer affection from her grandmother to Marie. It appears that Marie may no longer be just a therapist for Jacinda, but someone who will be for Jacinda what her grandmother was. The gift then becomes symbolic, a way of associating Marie with the grandmother. Marie has a responsibility to discuss the meaning of the gift with Jacinda.

That this may be the correct reading of what Jacinda is doing puts Marie in an especially awkward position ethically. On the one hand, if she refuses the gift and the gift is symbolic, rejecting it would be construed by Jacinda as rejecting her. Jacinda may think she is only valued when she gives something, and so refusing the gift may harm Marie's capacity to help Jacinda. On the other hand, accepting the gift may encourage Jacinda to think she is valued only when she gives a gift. It also may encourage her in thinking Marie is to take the place of her grandmother. Yet transference is sometimes a good thing, helpful to both therapist and client. So Marie has a dilemma, with unclear and perhaps harmful consequences no matter what she does. Her goal, presumably, is to help Jacinda without having to take the place of Jacinda's grandmother, and she does two things to further that goal.

First, she insists that Jacinda pick out what she wishes her to have. If Jacinda gave Marie something that Marie wanted, Jacinda might think that Marie owed her in some way. Marie is trying to maintain the proper professional relationship by insisting that Jacinda pick out the gift.

Second, Marie refuses to accept the gift *as* a gift, but insists that she will take it as payment for the time spent in calls with Jacinda between sessions. That insistence tells Jacinda that whatever she may wish to think, the gift is not symbolic and will not change their professional relationship. It also tells Jacinda that the time between sessions is marked by their professional relationship. Marie is telling Jacinda that despite the loss of Jacinda's grandmother, the relationship is to remain what it was. Marie's deciding to have the gift appraised and to credit Jacinda with a number of therapy sessions if it turns out to be particularly valuable is a further indication of Marie's concern to maintain professional boundaries.[65]

But Marie broke her rule about not accepting gifts. In breaking that rule, she may have encouraged Jacinda to think the relationship was more than professional. Without more details, we cannot be sure whether Marie made the proper judgment in breaking her rule, but we can see how drawing the lines she ends up drawing will further her goal of helping Jacinda without being drawn in by Jacinda's desire to have Marie take her grandmother's place. It looks, at least, as though Marie has succeeded in drawing a line that will minimize potential harms—although we would have to find out what happens afterwards to see if that is really the case.

Sometimes drawing lines seems as though it should be no problem at all. Consider the following case.

CASE **3.9**
A Social Visit

Tineka was a thirteen-year-old in therapy with Diane. She had been sexually abused by her father and was diagnosed as having Post Traumatic Stress Disorder. Diane had heard that Tineka had gone out socially both with her Protective Services worker and with the prosecutor of the case against her father.

Therapy terminated when Tineka had a baby and moved out of town. She came back in a year with a second baby and called Diane, asking to see her at Tineka's mother's house. She said she especially wanted Diane to see the babies. Diane tried to arrange to see Tineka at the office, but that did not work out and Diane went to visit her at her mother's.

Diane happened to mention that she would be driving to Florida for a vacation in a few days, and Tineka begged her to drive her to Georgia on her way so she could visit the father of one of the babies. Diane refused, and the situation became extremely uncomfortable.

Diane has not heard from Tineka again.

Individuals with Post Traumatic Stress Disorder have a tendency to encroach on boundaries,[66] and Diane's going to Tineka's mother's made it easier for Tineka to ask for a ride—a clear violation of boundaries. Tineka was apparently reaching out for Diane in some way, and Diane's refusal to help in the way that Tineka wanted help apparently cut off a chance to continue a professional relationship that Tineka may need. But this is a case in which the former client was taking advantage of the professional relationship, and Diane should have insisted on seeing Tineka in her office.

Virtues

We have concentrated in these past few cases on ways in which a relationship between a social work practitioner and a client can go wrong, but in doing that, we are relying on an understanding of what makes the relationship right. But determining what such a relationship ought to be is a complex, ethical undertaking. At a minimum, a practitioner ought to be fair, honest, dependable, competent, trustworthy, and attentive.[67] These are *virtues*, character traits that social work practitioners ought to display in their relations with clients as well as with colleagues and others with whom they have professional relations. We can thus readily imagine ways in which practitioners could fail to do what we all presume they ought to do just in the normal course of their work—by failing to meet some of these criteria for their professional relationships. They can fail to listen carefully to what clients are saying, spread around what was told in confidence, neglect to do what they told clients they would do, fail to establish boundaries, fail to provide needed information for some social service, treat some colleagues differently from others for no good reason, and so on.

Yet even if practitioners display the appropriate virtue, they may fail to display it in the right way. It is not easy doing what we ought to do in just the right way, at the right time, with the appropriate manner, and with all the other features that make things go well.[68] The ways in which we can fail to attend just to what a client is saying are too numerous and diverse to list. Leafing through papers while a client is trying to talk, or looking constantly at your watch, are obvious ways to be inattentive, but it is equally inappropriate to concentrate so hard on what your client is saying that the client becomes uncomfortable with the intensity of your concern. That would be as inappropriate as giving all of your time to a client, no matter what the client had to say, to the detriment of your other concerns. Being virtuous is a skill, and we must find the right way to be virtuous. We must learn how to listen appropriately, how to provide information that a client can and will make use of, how to set appropriate, clear, and culturally sensitive boundaries, how to seek guidance from colleagues without breaking a confidence, how, in short, to do just what is right.

The situation that practitioners face can be complicated because clients can fail to meet the criteria for a professional relationship. We do not often think about the ways in which a client can fail to live up to the demands of a professional relationship, but patients who refuse to take the medicine their physicians prescribe can cause enormous problems for the physicians as well as for themselves. The same is true for a social work practitioner's client who encroaches on the practitioner's boundaries or fails to do what needs to be done—by not coming to meetings when scheduled or by failing to fill out forms properly.

The inexperience and failures of clients put additional pressures on social work practitioners. Because they are in the position of power, and presumably have experience about how relationships can go wrong, they have a special obligation to ensure that the relationship goes well, taking special care to encourage the right sorts of responses and to empower clients to act in their own self-interest. Some general features of the system, or some feature of the social work practitioner, may have discouraged a client, and the practitioner then has a special obligation to change whatever it is that is causing a client not to get done what is needed. After all, if the goal is to help a client, and the client is not doing what needs to be done to get help, the social work practitioner's goal has not changed. Achieving it has just become more complicated.

"Recalcitrant" Clients

Special problems arise when a social work practitioner thinks a client is making a mistake and, despite the practitioner's urging, refuses to do what the practitioner recommends. In *Having Sex*, Theresa refused to bring charges. What ought a professional do when the client declines to act on a matter the professional thinks requires action? Is it appropriate for the professional to act on behalf of the client? Or, as in *Having Sex*, is it appropriate for the therapist, Aubrey, to take action if the client does not? Aubrey is apparently assuming that if Theresa were to bring charges, Theresa would not be harmed by any backlash that might result from attacking the therapist, or that any backlash that may result is worth risking to prevent potential harm to other clients from this therapist. What we need to do is to apply our method and ask what Aubrey's goals are and what they ought to be.

Aubrey seems to have the goal of ensuring that the therapist is in some way punished for his behavior with Theresa. She may be right that Theresa will not be harmed by bringing charges. It may even be that Theresa will benefit by doing that. But it is notoriously difficult to predict the consequences of any particular course of action, and Aubrey cannot be sure that harm will not occur to Theresa if Theresa brings charges. Indeed, harm would occur because Theresa has made it clear that she wants to put the issue behind her. In pursuing it, Aubrey is denying Theresa's expressed wishes and so denying her self-determination. In addition, Theresa does not want her husband to know about the affair, and it is difficult to see how he would not find out about it were she to bring charges.[69]

Aubrey's goal ought to be to help Theresa and to ensure her well-being. She thus has an obligation to assist Theresa in coming to understand that it was her therapist's obligations to set boundaries, not hers, and an obligation to help her heal from the trauma of the affair. For Aubrey to pursue the therapist is for her to pursue her own agenda. It certainly would not further Theresa's self-determination, and it may cause further harm to Theresa. That clearly does not further what ought to be Aubrey's goal of helping Theresa.

Having Sex is marked by the social work practitioner trying to convince the client to do something that the client does not want to do. The same sorts of ethical problems can obviously arise when a client wants to do something that the practitioner thinks the client ought not to do. Consider the following case in which the therapist tries to discourage a client from testifying, in part, the therapist claims, for the client's own good.

CASE 3.10
Hurting Oneself

Annette had been seduced by her former therapist. She is mentally ill and prone to extreme shifts in mood, but is consistently angry about her former therapist. She wants to pursue the case, take him to court, and see that he does not harm anyone else.

Her new therapist is concerned that Annette will hurt herself by pursuing the matter, that she is fragile emotionally, and will regress psychologically. Such cases are notoriously difficult to prosecute, and pursuing it will put a great stress on Annette when she is already very unstable. Besides, the therapist is not convinced that Annette will be believed, but thinks she will lose the case and lose what progress she has already made. So the therapist encourages her to drop the case.

The therapist is judging, rightly or wrongly, what is in Annette's best interests and is trying to convince her not to do what she had clearly said she wants to do. A professional's concern that a client become capable of self-determination sometimes requires that the professional make judgments he or she thinks the client ought to make. But these judgments are justified only if they arguably make the client more capable of self-determination. The therapist's advice is just advice, that is, and we must determine whether it is good or bad advice by determining what is in the best interests of Annette.

Our model tells us that we need to weigh the alternative courses of action. In this case, we are weighing them to see what course of action will best enhance the self-determination of a client. Will Annette be better or worse off, in the long run, to pursue the case against her former therapist? What is at issue here is how to weigh the goods involved. On the one hand, good may come to Annette in fighting the case so that she will feel she has not been completely passive in response to what happened, and if she wins, she will gain a feeling of power and accomplishment. On the other hand, good may come from putting that part of her life behind her and getting on with the rest of it.

Her present therapist urges her not to pursue the case because such cases are hard to win even with clear evidence and a clearly competent victim, and they put great stress on those pursuing it, even if they are emotionally strong. Even in the best of situations, someone seduced by a therapist would have a hard time making the case, and he thus thinks Annette would have a hard time—too hard a time, given her emotional state, to make it worthwhile. To come to that advice, he ought to weigh all of that against the presumed advantages of success—Annette's need to express her anger and the feeling of accomplishment that a successful prosecution would bring. He ought also weigh the possibility of a compromise position, bringing the suit with Annette's understanding that it is not likely to succeed, because it does not often succeed in the best of cases, but that it is worth pursuing so that she can feel she has accomplished something in regard to her former therapist.

Unfortunately, this is a problematic case, one in which we simply cannot know, ahead of time, which is the best course of action for Annette. The therapist is judging that it is better for her not to pursue the case, and we should give his voice significant weight because he must be presumed to be in a better position to judge than we are. He knows Annette better than we can and is better positioned to assess how well she would handle the stress of bringing the case and the emotional loss should she lose it. But the decision is Annette's, presuming that she is competent enough to make a decision, and so the therapist ought to realize that he is in an awkward position ethically—encouraging her to do something she has said she does not want to do, and thus, at the least, failing to encourage her self-determination, when he cannot be completely sure of what will happen whatever she does.

Of course, Annette may not be competent to make a judgment about what is in her best interests. What the therapist should not do, certainly, is to declare Annette incompetent to pursue the case because he does not think she should.

What he should do is try to determine independently whether she is. The fact that she wants to pursue the case is no more evidence of her incompetence than Juanita's refusal to seek treatment for her rectal cancer was evidence of her incompetence to make such a judgment in *Depressed and Ready to Die.*

His goal must be to do good for Annette, and so, when we do not have enough evidence to know quite what judgment to make, or when, as in *Refusing Help,* we do not have enough time to gather evidence, we must make reasonable presumptions. Just as, in that case, what we thought appropriate was dependent upon what presumptions we thought appropriate, in the same way, making judgments in this case is dependent upon presumptions we make—about Annette's mental state, about what is more or less likely to produce good or to cause harm, and so on. If we presume that she is able to bounce back readily from adversity, we will be far less likely to discourage her suing her former therapist than we would be if we presumed her on the edge of a further breakdown, unlikely to survive failure. The issue is what presumptions ethics requires us to make, and the general stance must be that we should presume whatever will cause the least harm and the most good. Unfortunately, we do not have enough information to know whether there is a clear answer in this case.

Who Is the Client?

The first step in our method requires that we:

> **1.** *Try to understand why the participants are doing what they are doing by constructing arguments that would justify their acts or omissions.*

We have been using this step as though it were straightforward what roles the various participants have in the case—who the client is, who the social worker is, and so on. But, in fact, it can be difficult in some cases to determine who is in what role, and ethical issues turn on making those determinations. We shall consider here the sorts of problems that can arise in identifying who the client is.

Choosing One's Client

The problem of identifying who the client is runs through many of the cases we have considered so far. In *Dancing a Legal Dance,* for example, Aubrey had all four members of the family as her clients, but she was concerned to protect the young girls and was being pressed by co-workers to get the father to confess to sexual abuse. Because her clients had competing interests, they should have had different social workers, but Aubrey never realized that she had an ethical problem about who her client was. That problem is harder to miss in the following case.

CASE **3.11**

Co-dependents

In an alcoholic's family, the spouse and children often need therapy as well. The need is severe enough that, without treatment for the other members of the family, the alcoholic is unlikely to cease using alcohol because the family members are unable to give support for the new forms of behavior necessary to remain off alcohol and, by their habitual practices, reinforce the alcoholic behavior.

But Rosemary cannot bill the company paying for treatment for treating anyone but the person who is abusing. "So sometimes," Rosemary says, "we put down 'family session' for the substance abuser when the focus was really on treating another family member. Other times we do not charge and see other family members for free."

Treating all of the members of a family may not seem to raise any ethical problem about who the client is because no obvious conflict may seem to exist. Treating the alcoholic, Rosemary claims, requires treating members of the family, and presumably treating them means that she is helping the client as well. So the choice that Rosemary faces—treat the alcoholic or treat the family of the alcoholic and the alcoholic—may seem only a strategic choice of treatment, and not an ethical choice, because no obvious harm is done no matter which choice is made. But, in fact, making that choice requires making a series of ethical judgments. We can see this by applying the third step in our method:

   3. *Determine what the harms are of various courses of action. To whom would they occur, what kinds are they, and what are their magnitudes?*

So what are the harms?

First, the choice raises an issue of justice because unless there was much free time and not enough demand for services, every family member seen free may take the place of an alcoholic who could have been seen and needed help. Rosemary decided to serve some alcoholics by seeing them individually as well as with their families rather than to serve more alcoholics individually in what she judged to be a less effective way. So her choice means that some who need help will get no help at all when they would have gotten some help otherwise. She may have made the correct ethical choice, but it is a choice that needs ethical justification because it causes harm to some.

Second, she has no money to pay for treating the family members, and so there is an issue about how to bill the companies paying for treatment. Are they fairly billed when they have agreed to pay for treating a substance abuser but are sometimes billed for treating other members of the family as well?[70] There are two different ethical issues here because Rosemary is not only billing the companies for treatment they have not agreed to pay, but she is also putting down false information on the billing form so that they are deceived into thinking they are paying for what they agreed to pay.[71]

Third, the focus of concern of the therapy is different given the different choices. If Rosemary were to treat only the alcoholic, the focus of her concern would be the alcoholic—the alcoholic's behavior, beliefs, and role in relations with others. But if the alcoholic is treated as part of a family, Rosemary will focus on how the alcoholic and the other members of the family interact. The concern will be to change the behavior of all, with the focus on changing the behavior of the family members so they do not continue to enable the alcoholic in the behavior that produces alcoholism. But changing the focus of concern raises an ethical issue. It was itself produced in part by an ethical commitment to the client. Treating only the alcoholic was thought to be harmful to the alcoholic because, by not treating the family, the therapist is unable to change the behaviors of those who enabled an alcoholic to remain an alcoholic even after treatment. But treating the family means that the alcoholic may receive less concentrated treatment than needed given the limited time that can be spent on any treatment. Choosing between treating the alcoholic alone and treating the alcoholic as a member of an enabling family is not an ethically neutral choice, that is, whichever is the right choice to make.

Either choice that Rosemary makes may harm someone—those not being treated, those who pay for treatment, or the alcoholic or the alcoholic's family. In short, choosing who is the client can be an ethical issue, and we must do whatever we ought to do when faced with an ethical choice. We must track the harms and choose the alternative that causes the minimal amount of harm, if we can determine what that is.

No Choice

Often an ethical problem with determining clients does not present itself as a choice. Consider this case in which Tamara finds herself with a problem about who her client is.

CASE 3.12
Automatic Assignments

In one agency, social workers are assigned cases in the order in which they arrive. "If it is Monday, and I'm at the top of the list, I get the first case," Tamara said, and so she was assigned a case in which she was to do individual therapy for five children plus family therapy for the father and for the mother. The case was complicated by the various relations among the different members of the family, with some of the children having different fathers and some different mothers.

One day somewhat later Tamara was assigned another case—two young girls who had allegedly been sexually abused by their father, Marvin, who was no longer living with them, but was visiting them and seeking custody. She became close to the children, and especially to one child, and continued to see them for over six months.

Tamara then discovered that the boyfriend of the mother in the first family was Marvin, the father of the two girls in the second. She was concerned about sexual abuse in the new family setting and so told the woman there to be careful with her children around Marvin. She didn't tell the woman why, but the woman must have told Marvin that she was to be careful with him around the children and he was upset.

Tamara was asked to write a report for Friend of the Court, which was considering custody, and she wrote about the reports of sexual abuse that the two girls gave her. Friend of the Court put her name and position on the report, and since Marvin was acting as his own lawyer, he read it, put two and two together, and came into her office, angry and upset.

Tamara felt she had to choose between the two families, and she stopped seeing the little girls from the second family. She tried to have the one girl see another therapist, but the girl refused and stopped coming to the clinic. She apparently felt rejected, and although Tamara tried to explain to her that she was not being rejected, Tamara could not give the complete explanation.

Tamara's relationship with the first family was changed because of what Tamara came to know about Marvin from her relation with his two girls. She had access to information she would not have had but for the assignment of cases that gave her two that overlapped. Having this information created two ethical problems for her. That is, although she had no choice in coming to this information, having the information has created a set of choices for her in which she can readily cause or permit great harm.

First, Tamara had to determine whether it is ethically permissible, or even obligatory, for her to use the information she had about Marvin to protect the children of the first family. Tamara decided that rather than give the girlfriend the information, she would tell the woman to be careful with the children around Marvin. Telling the woman to be careful around Marvin seems to have been a compromise to help protect the children without breaching confidentiality. But it was a compromise that denied the woman full information, thus preventing her from acting with full self-determination.

To put as positive a face as we can on what Tamara did, she chose a course of action to provide as much protection and self-determination as she could, consistent with protecting confidentiality. But to put as negative a face as we can on what she did, she pointed a finger at Marvin, without explaining why, and left the children at risk by not telling the woman why she had to be careful with the children around Marvin. Why should the woman take Tamara's remarks seriously without any reasons for taking such care?

Second, having the information alters Tamara's relationship with the original family. She knows the children are at risk. Having the information also alters her relationship with the second family. She does not make clear why she felt she had to choose between the two sets of clients, the original family and the new one, but she may think that if she were to pursue the case of sexual abuse raised in the new family, she would find herself at odds with Marvin and would not be able to work well with the first family.

This case seems to present a painful choice for Tamara. She felt that she could not give therapy to a child who really needed it and yet continue to maintain her contacts with the original family.[72] It is an essential part of the third step of our method that we brainstorm alternative courses of action:

   3. *Determine what the harms are of various courses of action. To whom would they occur, what kinds are they, and what are their magnitudes?*

What could Tamara do, and what are the harms of these various courses of action? To determine whether she made the right choice, we need to consider her choices and weigh them ethically—considering, as the second step in our model tells us, what her goals ought to be and then laying out her options, determining how well they achieve those goals and what harms result to those involved. Tamara seems to have thought she had two options—though, in fact, there are at least three.

   a. She could continue to see the first family and drop contact with the second. This is the choice she made, and one reason for it is that although Marvin's children were as much at risk as the children in the first family, the mother there knew about the charges and so could herself act to protect the children. If a new social worker was assigned to that case, he or she would find out about the charges. The mother in the first family did not find out about the charges, and it is not clear whether a social worker assigned to the case would be able to find out about them. That would depend upon whether the information about the court case was public and upon whether, if it was, it was somehow brought to the new social worker's attention. So it is reasonable to think that Tamara was more needed with the first family than with the second.

One problem with this decision is that Tamara has already had a confrontation with the mother's boyfriend, Marvin. The likelihood of her working well with the family is much diminished because of what she knows about Marvin and what Marvin knows about what she knows. So she may not be an effective therapist there especially because, although she can warn the mother to be careful of the children around Marvin, she cannot tell the mother how she knows Marvin is an object of concern—unless the court case becomes a matter of public record. Then she would have to decide whether to bring that to the attention of the mother.
   An additional problem with this decision is that Tamara was assigned to do both individual therapy with five children and family therapy with the mother and father. So choosing to work with the first family is not itself a simple matter. It may not be easy to look after the interests of the children while providing family therapy to the mother and father knowing that the mother's boyfriend may be putting the children at risk. If Tamara's reason for choosing the first family is to protect the children, she has not simply made a choice between helping the children there and the children in the second family, but also between helping the children there and providing family therapy. The interests of the children may conflict with those of the mother and the father.

On the other hand, if she turned the original family over to another therapist, it is not obvious that she could tell that person the information she accidentally came to know. Maintaining the confidentiality of the information she had is a value she needs to consider in deciding what to do. A new therapist would not be in a position to protect the children if Tamara did not say anything and if the information about the court proceedings were not public and somehow part of the social work case involving Marvin.

    b. The second option would be to drop contact with the first family and continue to see the second. The children's interests in the second family would be better served by Tamara continuing therapy with them. Because one of the girls had become quite attached to her, as Tamara makes clear, cutting the tie means a loss. The girl felt rejected and stopped coming for therapy. But, as we have seen, dropping contact with the first family means putting the girls there at risk, at least in the short term, or perhaps means breaking confidentiality to inform a new therapist of the problem.

    c. Choosing either option risks harm to the children involved, and so that raises the issue of whether Tamara could not do something that would allow her to continue to see both families or, at least, the original family and the girls in the second family. She could give therapy to the girls in the second family and look out for the girls in the first family without breaking confidentiality. This choice has all of the problems of the first choice, including the problem of working with Marvin, but there is no reason to think others would be better able to work with Marvin if they know of the abuse. Besides, it is difficult to see how not working with the girls of the second family would allow Tamara to work *better* with Marvin in regard to the first family.

So why did Tamara feel she had to choose between the two families? She may have thought that the children in the second family would "take" to a new therapist after awhile. Tamara may also have thought that she was best able to handle the problems of knowing about Marvin but not being able to tell the mother. She was wrong about one of the children, and her being wrong changes the whole equation. Given the goal of helping the children, laying out Tamara's options and tracking the alternative harms make it clear that if we add in the harm to the child of being deprived of therapy, it is better for both sets of children that Tamara continue working on both cases.

The Family as Client

In this next case, as in many of the cases we have examined so far, the social workers find themselves with identifiable individual clients. But the case with which we began this section, Case 3.11, *Co-dependents,* raised the issue of whether the social worker's client ought to be the family rather than, in that case, the alcoholic within the family, and the following case presents this issue even more dramatically.

CASE **3.13**

Caring for the Family

A mother of low intelligence loves her three children, does well for them with what she has ("dresses the girls beautifully, irons their clothes"), and keeps in constant touch with the school and social workers. There has been a history of sexual abuse—the father first abusing the two girls when they were in the first and third grades and then a boyfriend abusing them. So Carrie, the social worker assigned to the family, allows the mother to stay with the children provided that certain rules are followed, which, it is hoped, will protect them from child abuse.

As it stands now, the family is entrenched in the social services system. "If we were not here for her, the family would not stay intact," Carrie says. The system cannot afford the time and resources to make that family a continual object of concern. So the family is likely to disintegrate, and, by law, the children must then be placed in foster care. When that happens, the mother will fall apart, Carrie thinks, and the children will be separated since no foster home is likely to take three children. The children will certainly be worse off in terms of losing a mother who truly loves them and in no longer being members of a family.

The family is so fragile that it is dependent upon the social services system. "What is needed," Carrie says, "is a foster home *for the entire family*." But that is not presently an option. The only option is to continue to treat the family until it is decided that too much has been spent on it and each of the children is then put into foster homes.

Who is the client here—the mother? The children? The family? All of the evidence would suggest that the family—the mother and her three children—ought to be the client. As Carrie puts it, paradoxically, the family needs foster care. But the current system cannot treat the family as a unit to be put, as it were, in a foster home. Or, put another way, the system forces certain categories of clients onto social workers even if using those categories causes more harm than using other categories. If social workers have families as their clients, it is either because the families can be kept intact with minimal resources or because short-term intervention, even with intensive resources, is likely to solve whatever the problem is. They cannot have as their clients entire families that are to be kept intact by providing continual resources. After all, caring for a family for the rest of its life is an enormous drain on the resources of any social services system. So when a social worker gets a family like this, the pressure is enormous to split the family into individual clients—the mother and the three children—and to treat them individually.[73]

From Carrie's point of view, the current categories are counterproductive. They ensure that families that cannot remain intact without much supervision and many resources will not be saved. This case squarely raises the issue of whether the institutional setting is *itself* at fault. It forces us to distinguish between ethical issues that arise about individual actions within an existing institutional setting and ethical issues that arise about the setting itself. What seems to be needed is some change in the system if Carrie is to have a good option, for the system precludes her choosing the best solution and makes it unlikely that she will be able to keep the family together.

In *Dancing a Legal Dance,* Mary found herself facing a problem because the judge said that the children were legally not abused, and it is certainly not obvious that a legal system that permits that sort of judgment is a fair one. Mary's problems arise in part because of the judgment, and Mary may have a moral obligation as a social worker to try to change the system that creates such difficulties for her.

It is arguable that in *Adoptive Children,* LaShonda had the same obligation about the state law that she thought was unfair to natural parents and adoptive children. It is the perceived unfairness of the law that she thinks justifies her giving information illegally to those seeking it, and so it is the setting itself that causes the ethical dilemma she faces.

Similarly, this case raises an issue about the policy our society has of either choosing to keep families together, if it does not cost much, or breaking them apart to save the children—the policy, that is, of not spending enough to do what is needed to keep families intact. Carrie faces a problem that arises within the framework of that policy, and it is that policy that forces her to choose between trying to hold the family together, without adequate resources, or pulling it apart by putting the children in foster care. So it is arguable that she has an ethical obligation to change the existing policy. That does not help her in the present case, because existing policy is not going to change in time to ease the difficulty she has with that family, but it indicates how a social worker's responsibilities can go beyond individual cases.

Diversity among Clients

Finding oneself unable to refuse a potential client without causing great harm is a common sort of problem. Consider the following case in which this common problem is complicated by another.

CASE 3.14

Self-Identity

Joanna had a client, Vicky, who was having difficulties with the consequences of her divorce. Joanna was black, Vicky was white, and Vicky's ex-spouse is black. In the course of Joanna's work with Vicky, Vicky brought in her oldest son, Tommy, who was six and having trouble in school primarily, the school thought, because his parents were going through a divorce. But when Joanna talked with him, she found out that he was upset because the school officials had called him black.

Tommy was staying with his mother, who identified Tommy and the other two children as being white. When Joanna spoke with her, Vicky said she thought "her children would have a very hard time if they were identified as being black." She said she had told them that if you mix vanilla and chocolate, you get a combination, but "not black," something "closer to white."

But the children cannot pass for white. "They do not even have the features to pass for white," Joanna told Vicky. "Society is always going to see them as black, and the children need to feel good about that. You can't say he's brown. You can't say he's mulatto. You can't use those terms. You have to say he is a beautiful black child and you accept him. You have to validate that for the child."

Vicky said she couldn't tell Tommy that, that it would mean giving up her son. So Joanna was concerned that Vicky would stop coming in for therapy and particularly concerned that she would not talk to Tommy and tell him what Joanna thought he needed to hear. The situation was complicated by Tommy's fear that his mother would be upset with him—for not being white, Joanna surmised.

But Joanna persuaded the mother to go in and talk with Tommy and tell him that he is black, that she loves him, and that it is good to be black. The mother didn't believe any of that, but she did it. Afterwards, Tommy said, "I knew I was black all along."

If we consider the third step of our method and consider the potential harms the case raises, we will find at least four different problems:

a. Joanna feared Vicky would think it was only because Joanna was black that she wanted Vicky's son to think of himself as being black. Joanna thought Vicky would think that she was imposing her own values on Vicky and Tommy. She was afraid that Vicky would not think of her as being objective, so that she would be ineffective as a social worker.

b. We have carefully retained the words used by those in the case, "black" and "white," because one difficulty the case presents concerns the categorization of persons in terms of color and/or race. We did not want to beg the issues by using the categories of "Black" and "Caucasian" as though these were clear and unproblematic. This is not a single difficulty, but a nest of them.

Until very recently in the United States, "biracial" had no official meaning. Officially, Tommy was either black or white. In other societies, and in the United States now, a person can be biracial. When this case occurred, the law made Tommy either black or white, and, in any event, one issue the case raises concerns the categories that society imposes upon individuals and the social consequences of being in one category rather than another. Those of mixed ancestry must decide whether to accept or reject the categories that society imposes. Rejecting them is difficult for anyone, let alone a six-year-old, and we may see Vicky's explanation to her children—"a combination"—as an attempt to resist society's categories. We may also see Joanna's insistence that Tommy is black as acquiescence in those categories or as a realistic appraisal, given Tommy's physical appearance, of how he is going to be judged.

There is also a problem regarding self-identity. Our sense of ourselves is tied up to the way others perceive us and so relate to us. It is difficult to change those perceptions and difficult to act in ways that are contrary to the way others expect us to act, and so act toward us. Others will tend to take us to be acting in certain ways because of their perception of us, despite our attempts to act in different ways. If Tommy is treated as a black person by others in society, it will be difficult for him to resist seeing himself as black—no matter how hard he may try.

There is an ethical issue here. People's sense of who they are is arguably the most important ethical aspect of their lives. Everything people do and can do hinges on their conception of themselves. Yet if that conception depends upon the beliefs of others, and those beliefs are false, people's sense of who they are will be affected.

Put another way, if one of the highest values in any social system is the capacity of those within it to dream for themselves what kind of life they wish to lead and to choose to pursue that dream or not, that capacity will be affected by a person's understanding of what it is possible for them to dream and what it is possible for them to realize. The plans you have for your life may be limited by someone else's perception of who you are, and your chances of putting your life plan into effect may be thwarted by someone else's perceptions of what you are capable of achieving. So Tommy's being perceived as black is not just a factual matter—a matter of how he looks—but an ethical matter, a matter in this society of what his prospects are.

Tommy's mother was correct in her understanding of how different his prospects would be if he were perceived as black. But if he looks black, pretending that he is not will not help him. In a racist society, being the wrong race will diminish our life prospects no matter how we try to protect ourselves.[74]

c. Vicky stated that she thought her son would be better off as a white person. She thought she was acting in the best interests of her family. Joanna did not change Vicky's mind, but somehow got her to talk to her son. So there is an issue of self-determination here. What are the proper limits for a social worker in persuading others to act in ways they do not choose to act? Joanna might be thought of as being too pushy. Some might think she has no right to intervene in the way she did to get Vicky to tell her son he is black.[75]

d. Who is the client? Joanna's initial client was the mother, Vicky, who was having troubles because of her divorce. When Vicky brought Tommy in, Joanna could have refused to see him, and so refused him as a client. When she did not, Tommy became her client, but he would have been affected in any event. For in trying to help Vicky, Joanna would have had to deal with what Vicky told Tommy and so would have had to concern herself with what was best for Tommy as well as Vicky.

From Joanna's perspective, the two had competing interests because Vicky wanted Tommy to think of himself as being white, whereas Joanna thought he would be better thinking of himself as being black. The conflict between these two sets of interests was such that Joanna thought she might lose Vicky as a client, and thus lose Tommy as a client too, if she pushed Vicky to tell Tommy he was black.

If we now brainstorm and consider Vicky's options, as the third step in our method tells us to do, we find that she had three: (1) back off from confronting Vicky about her son's problems, and so not help the son; (2) confront the mother about her son's problem and so risk losing both the mother and the son as clients and not resolving the difficulty; or (3) talk to the son herself and so risk alienating Vicky and losing her, and perhaps her son, as clients.

What are the harms attached to each of these options? Choosing (1) would mean not helping the boy. That is a harm. Choosing (3) would mean not helping Vicky come to grips with the problem. That is a harm. It is also less likely to be effective to tell the son and not have the mother's support. He would then be getting mixed messages, being told on the one hand that he is black and on the other hand that he is white. Option (2) is the only choice that does not in itself cause harm—if we assume, and it is a big assumption, that it would be better for Tommy not to be told he is biracial.

Yet Joanna risks losing Vicky as a client and thus risks losing contact with Tommy if she chooses (2). If, however, she confronts Vicky and Vicky is unwilling to tell her son, Joanna will at least have explained the problem to Vicky, and she still has the options both of telling or not telling the boy and of urging that he get counseling from another social worker. In addition, choosing (2) is to treat Vicky with respect. It is to presume that Vicky is mature enough to come to grips with the problem, however emotionally upsetting it may be for her, and to resolve it in Tommy's best interests.

QUESTIONS

1. Provide an example, out of your own experience, of you or someone else having done something that was less than voluntary, then something less than fully informed, and then something less than fully competent.

2. In Case 1.2 *Dancing a Legal Dance,* compare Mary's explanation for why Martha was running away from home with the alternative we provided. Do any of the differences turn upon a judgment that Mary is uninformed about something, or acting involuntarily in some way, or is incompetent in some regard? In answering this question, remember the first step in the method of tracking harms. Did Mary try to understand why Martha was running away from home?

3. In Case 1.4, *Doing What the Judge Orders,* was John fully informed when he decided to go to his supervisor to get Al tested? If he was not, what more did he need to know, or did he know enough even if he was not fully informed? If he was fully informed, was he acting voluntarily or was he in some way coerced by, say, Al's mother threatening her social worker if Al found out she was HIV-positive?

4. What is wrong with lying? Suppose no one ever finds out. What is wrong with it then, if anything? Suppose it does some good for the person to whom you are lying. What is wrong with it then, if anything? Are there circumstances in which it may be ethical to lie? Give reasons for your answer, one way or the other.

5. By telling the wife that in order for the husband and wife to be in a mutually respectful marriage, he would tell the husband about her infidelity if she does not, Mohammed would be encouraging self-determination by denying it. Discuss whether that is always wrong.

6. Give two examples of how self-determination conflicts with other social work values besides those used as examples in this section. Examine each conflict and assess how it is to be resolved ethically.

7. What are some obligations that social workers owe to their clients? Give four and provide examples of each drawn from the cases we have examined and your own cases.

8. A client that someone might think is recalcitrant may be exercising self-determination. All of the issues that arise regarding clients who do what others may consider signs or even proof of lack of self-determination—as, for instance, Juanita in Case 3.2, *Depressed and Ready to Die*—arise regarding so-called recalcitrant clients. Give an example from your own experience of someone you thought was recalcitrant and explain why you found him or her recalcitrant. Was the person incompetent? Ill-informed? Acting involuntarily? What would need to be true about the person for him or her to be exercising self-determination but making a decision you would not have made? (You should apply the first step in the method here.)

9. Pick one of the virtues of social workers and explain what it requires a social worker to do regarding clients and colleagues.

10. Drawing boundaries is difficult in any relationship. Give an example of a problem you have had with a friend or relation regarding boundaries. Discuss the pros and cons of how the problem was settled or ought to have been settled.

11. What interests are in conflict in Case 3.5, *Friends and Professional Relations*? Whose interests are they? What could be done to prevent the conflict? Would it be enough for Raul simply to follow the Code and inform Mark of the potential conflict? If so, why? If not, why not and what else should Raul—or Mark—do?

12. Deciding to provide "a foster home for the entire family," as Carrie says in Case 3.14, *Caring for the Family*, would require significant changes in existing policy. Discuss the pros and cons of making such a change. In doing this, you should consider whether it is always good to keep a family together, whether concentrating upon a family may mean losing sight of individuals, and so on.

13. We sometimes come to have information we would have preferred not to have. That was Tamara's situation in Case 3.12, *Automatic Assignments*. Look back over previous cases that we have examined and pick one in which the social worker also is privy to information that creates ethical problems. Discuss.

14. Having more than one client in a single case can create problems because the clients' interests may compete with one another. This sort of situation is not unusual, however. Every parent with more than one child faces this kind of problem regularly. Give an example from your own experience in which you have had responsibility for two or more individuals whose interests have competed. Consider how one is to settle such matters in a way that causes the least harm.

CHAPTER

4 Relations among Social Workers

As anyone who works knows, those who work together can cause problems for each other. Social work practitioners are not immune from this general truth, and ethical issues can arise because of the relations among colleagues or between them and their social work supervisors. As in any profession, social work practitioners work with others in their profession, and when they have differing judgments about practice, conflict may result. We shall consider this issue in the first section and then, in the second , we examine other ethical problems that can arise among colleagues.

Social work practitioners may have professional relations with such professionals as physicians, lawyers, and teachers as well as with other social work practitioners. In the last section we shall consider the sorts of ethical issues that can arise in relations between social work practitioners and other professionals.

Our concern is to articulate the ideals that ought to regulate relations among social work practitioners and between them and other professionals.

Difficulties among Colleagues

The method of tracking harms requires that we come to understand why the participants are doing what they are doing, and one of the best ways to achieve that end is to ask them. But although the method thus works best when those involved in a case talk with one another, communication can fail for a variety of different reasons. We shall explore first the ideal and then ways in which that ideal can fail to be achieved. We are thus not using the method here, but are exploring one of the conditions for its best use.

The Ideal

Differences in status, in gender, in experience, and in educational background, among others, can make a difference as to how one is perceived by others in the profession, and such different perceptions can create ethical problems. Consider the following case.

CASE **4.1**

Peers?

A male social worker seduced and molested one of his clients, an adolescent male, who then molested his younger sister. The boy is now with his father and step-mother, but his present social worker, Malik, is pushing to reunite the boy with his mother and sister.

The girl's social worker, Margaret, is uncomfortable with this. She thinks the child needs more therapy, and that will end if the family is reunited. But most importantly, she is not sure the girl will be protected if the boy returns to the family.

Yet she says she is unwilling to "confront" the boy's therapist, as she puts it. "He has a Ph.D., and I don't; he's established, and I'm new to this community."

Margaret thinks her client is at risk of being molested again if the brother goes back into the family without more therapy.

The boy is Malik's client, not hers, and in judging that he needs more therapy, Margaret is also judging that Malik is mistaken in thinking the boy should be reunited with his family. Yet she says she is unwilling to "confront" Malik. If we follow the first step of our method so we can understand why Margaret is unwilling to confront Malik, we can attribute to her something like the following reasoning:

> To protect my client, I need to tell Malik that he is mistaken in his judgment.
>
> But Malik is superior to me both in terms of his credentials and his experience in the community.
>
> Therefore, I will not confront Malik.

This reasoning is faulty in a variety of ways, as we shall see. But one additional reason that Margaret may have for being hesitant in "confronting" Malik is that he has been providing therapy for the boy and so is presumably better positioned to make a judgment about the need for further therapy than is Margaret. So Margaret not only has a natural and understandable reluctance to query a fellow professional about a professional judgment, especially when she thinks he is more experienced and better qualified than she, but she may have a reluctance to query him about a judgment that he is better positioned to make than she.

Yet since Margaret thinks the boy needs further therapy, she presumably thinks that failing to tell Malik means not protecting her client. Because she has an ethical duty to protect her client, she would seem to have an ethical duty to tell Malik because telling Malik appears to be the only way that she can protect her client (see the Code of Ethics 2.01[c] and 2.05[a]). But she says she is unwilling to confront Malik. We thus have two issues:

- Why does Margaret think that it is only by confronting Malik that she can tell him of her concerns?
- Even if she must confront him, is she not obligated to do that to protect her client?

Margaret must think that she has very good ethical reasons for not confronting Malik if she thinks not doing so puts her client at greater risk. She says it is because he is more experienced and educated than she and because he is established in the community and she is not. But neither are relevant reasons for not acting to protect her client.

We know that education and experience count. They put a person in a better position to know what to do in any particular situation, but someone's having education and experience does not guarantee that a correct decision has been made in any particular case. What matters is what is in the children's best interests. For all we, or Malik, or Margaret can know, Margaret may be in a better position than Malik to make the proper determination because, perhaps, she knows something about the details of the case that Malik does not know. She will not be able to find out whether his judgment is well-reasoned until she talks with him, and if she fails to do so, she will never know why he is making the judgment he is making and thus will never herself be in a position to judge whether she or he is correct.

What matters in coming to a decision about what we ought to do are the reasons for the decision. The reasons must be relevant, and where there is an ethical issue, the reasons must themselves be ethical and weighty enough to determine the conclusion. In appealing to Malik's being established in the community and better educated than she, Margaret is not appealing to any reasons why Malik's client ought or ought not have more therapy. By not talking with him, Margaret guarantees that she will never know whether he had good reasons for his judgment.

We are not in a position to judge whether she will harm her relationship with Malik if she talks with him any more than we are in a position to judge whether the boy needs more therapy. But whether or not any harm may come from her talking to Malik, Margaret does not have an ethical dilemma. An ethical dilemma only arises when we have two or more incompatible options, one of which we must choose, but both of which will cause harm (or produce good). Margaret cannot both do what she feels she ought to do for her client and not talk with Malik. So her options are incompatible. But although she has good ethical reasons for trying to help her client, she gives no ethical reasons not to talk with Malik.

Indeed, as a general rule, in situations where cases impinge upon one another so that what happens in one case can affect what happens in another, practitioners have an obligation to talk to one another (see the Code of Ethics 2.05[a]). In the first step of our method, we ask, "Who are the participants in this case, and who else is affected?" Whether Margaret likes it or not, her case and Malik's are intertwined, a decision in one affecting the other, and she thus has an obligation to try to understand why Malik is making the decision he is making—just as Malik has an obligation to talk with Margaret so he can understand her concerns.

One problem with the reasoning we attributed to Margaret is that it needs another premise. She must be thinking that:

> I can only tell Malik about my concerns by confronting him.

Malik may be the sort of person one cannot talk to without confronting, but that seems unlikely. He may be better positioned than she to know what to do in this case, but what is the harm in asking him for his reasons? If her primary concern is to ensure that her client is not put at risk of being molested again, she has good reason to talk with Malik and no good reason not to.

Indeed, she has an obligation to talk with Malik if that is the best way to protect her client. She would need an ethical reason for not talking with him, and an ethical reason weighty enough to justify putting her client at risk, but all she says is that she would have to confront Malik. That does not provide an ethical reason.

But she also has other reasons for explaining to Malik her concerns. Allowing him to proceed, despite her misgivings, may harm Malik's client. If Margaret is right that the boy is not yet capable of handling the pressures of being back with his mother and sister, Malik causes him harm.

And Margaret may cause Malik harm as well. If someone is about to make a mistake—like walking on a bridge that will collapse with the slightest impact—you have an obligation to inform the person of the difficulty so that the person can reconsider what to do in the light of this new information. And if that mistake will harm you or your interests—because the hillside you are on will collapse as well—then that person has an obligation to talk with you although, until you inform the person of the problem, the person may not realize he or she has such an obligation. Perhaps Malik should take the initiative, but if he does not realize how what he is doing affects Margaret's client, her failure to talk with him means that he will not fulfil his obligation to talk with her. Margaret thus harms Malik by not allowing him to do his duty.

In addition, deferring to Malik's judgment without talking with him means he has no chance to hear her concerns and no chance to assess his judgment in the light of those concerns. No one is immune from error, and he may have made a mistake. By not talking with him, she fails to treat him as a reasonable person—someone with the capacity for learning in light of new information (see the Code of Ethics 2.01[a]). She also encourages Malik to make the same kind of mistake the next time and so harm a new client. So Margaret has an obligation to talk with, and listen to, Malik.

Similarly, Malik has an obligation to talk with and listen to Margaret's reasons why the boy should not be placed in his family and, if he thinks Margaret is mistaken, an obligation to explain to her why he thinks she is mistaken. This is an especially pressing obligation when harm may result to the client of a colleague because of our actions. Professionals are obligated to explain their actions when those actions impinge upon the legitimate concerns of other professionals. This is not merely a matter of professional courtesy, though it is that, but a matter of ethical concern because of the harm done if the obligations of Margaret and Malik to their clients are not fulfilled.

Ideally, a social work practitioner should not be hesitant in talking about a case of mutual interest with another social worker. How Margaret talks with Malik will do much to determine their working relationship, and if she begins by confronting him, she may irreparably harm that relationship. Ideally she ought to be able to talk with Malik, a colleague, about what is best for her client, as well as for his, without any concerns about differences in status, in educational background, or any other feature that is irrelevant to her doing her best by her client. She ought to be able to talk with him presuming that he has reasons for doing something she thinks unreasonable and, presuming that because he is competent, he will respond to the reasons she has for thinking he is making a mistake. Indeed, morality requires this for two different reasons.

First, justice requires that we treat like cases alike and unlike cases unalike. When we are trying to decide what to do in a particular case, this means we ought to make the same decisions for the same sorts of cases and different decisions for different sorts of cases. If we are to be just, we must consider only relevant reasons. It would be unjust to treat one person one way and another person another way if the only difference between the two is their race, for instance. Just so, it would be unjust for Margaret to decide what to do in regard to her client by taking into consideration Malik's educational status and standing in the community. These features of Malik are not relevant to whether Malik's client ought or ought not to have more therapy. If decisions were determined by anything that anyone happened to consider, we would have no assurance that like cases would be treated alike and unlike cases unalike. It might turn out that if Margaret does not talk with Malik, for the reason she gives, and the boy is placed back in the family, everything will turn out all right. But that would be luck, and Margaret will not have done her duty to do what she can to help her client. Ethics requires her to take into account only what is relevant in deciding what to do.

Second, any social work practitioner has an obligation to find the best ethical solution for a case. In situations in which the cases of two or more practitioners overlap, so that a decision in one case can affect what happens in another, there is, as we saw, an obligation for the practitioners to talk to one another. But we ought always try to seek help in making a decision about a difficult case if we can do so without breaching confidentiality or causing any other serious ethical harm.

    a. It can help enormously to talk a case through with another professional, including a supervisor, who understands the sorts of issues involved. In discussing it with another professional, we are forced to articulate the case's important features to explain the problem we are having with it. That helps us get clear on the essentials of the case. We also gain the power of another mind who can help us get clear on why those in the case are doing what they are doing, what our goals ought to be, what our options are, and what the various harms are of alternative courses of action. It is always an advantage to brainstorm about various options. As possible ways of resolving the problem are floated, we can more readily come to understand better what features of the case are causing the main problems and why certain proposed solutions will not work and others might.

b. One problem we have when we are part of a case is that because we are inside it, as it were, we may find it hard to back off to judge what is best to do. It is difficult to be a participant and a judge simultaneously. Our self-interest as a participant can conflict with making an objective decision. Another professional provides another point of view, one that is likely to be more objective than ours.

c. We can get advice about how to do what we have decided we ought to do. Margaret thinks of herself as having to confront Malik, but one piece of advice to her may be that she should not think of talking to him in that way. She apparently thinks she must accuse him of making the wrong decision. But she might just tell him of her concerns and ask him to explain to her more clearly why he thinks she should not have the concerns she does. She seems so enmeshed in the case that she does not realize how irrelevant it is to concern herself with Malik's educational status and length of service in the community. Getting her to see her way clear of those irrelevancies does not yet solve her problem, however, if she still thinks of herself as having to confront Malik. So she also needs to figure out how to talk with Malik, and talking to another professional can help provide her with the kind of distance from her problem that will allow her to see how to proceed.

Dialogue can always help, that is, in working through the method of tracking harms, and we have been engaging in dialogue about each of the cases we have considered so far. We have thus suggested ways of looking at them that may not have been clear to those practitioners whose cases they are, and we have suggested goals and alternative solutions that have often opened up the case so we now have much more clarity about what we ought to do than we had when we first encountered the case.

Questions of Competence

For instance, we have decided that Margaret ought to talk with Malik if for no other reason than that she thinks his judgment about his client adversely affects her client. To talk with him is not to question his general competence, but sometimes we may question the reasons that a colleague gives often enough about a wide enough variety and large enough number of judgments that we do put in doubt his or her professional competence.[76] Consider the following case.

CASE 4.2

Family Therapy

Jessica was a member of a family service agency that had brought in a person from outside to teach the agency personnel about structural family-centered therapy. Peer review was instituted, and the seven social workers would meet regularly, view videotapes, and talk about their cases.

Jessica was having a very hard time learning to use the new form of therapy. It requires that the social workers align themselves with a particular family member, but only for strategic purposes. One is never to form permanent alignments. But Jessica would form relationships with particular family members, the woman or a female adolescent, and not be able to break them. But that is harmful to the clients. Rather than achieving independence, they end up with a different form of dependence, unable to achieve a new balance of relationships within their family because of their attachment to the social worker.

When this was pointed out to Jessica, she became extremely frustrated, threw up her hands and said, "Well!" She cried another time, upset because, as she put it, "I was doing everything right, and yet you tell me it's all wrong."

The other social workers all agreed that she was not competent using this particular approach. "She was operating off a psychodynamic individual model, which is very different from a structural or strategic model." They all felt that Jessica was harming her clients, but although they had the evidence of their own eyes and could talk about how she failed to respond to suggestions, they said they could not prove her incompetence to the supervisor. Besides, she had been with the agency for almost 20 years and so had seniority over the other six.

This case raises the issue of whether Jessica is competent using the structural model (see the Code of Ethics 1.04[a]). An incompetent social worker can badly harm the interests of a client, and so ethics requires that judgments of competence be made. Yet making such general judgments is a delicate task, and at least three questions need to be asked.

a. Who is to decide? Just as Malik seemed better positioned than Margaret to make a judgment in *Peers?*, so Jessica's colleagues seem better positioned than any outsider to judge what she is doing. But because they are in the case, and most affected by what they think she is doing, they may not be the best judges. In addition, being good at something, like social work, does not in itself mean being good at making judgments about who else is good at it and who is not. The competence to make judgments of competence requires special knowledge and skills and attitudes—an understanding of the various ways in which to practice in the profession; an ability to back off from your own preferred method of practice to assess another method of practice that may not mesh at all well with yours; a capacity to withhold judgment while you listen to all those involved, aiming for a full hearing of a case's ins and outs; and so on (see the Code of Ethics 1.04[b]). So we should not presume that because Jessica's colleagues are social work practitioners, and know a great deal of information about the case, they thereby are competent to make a judgment about Jessica's competence.

b. We should not presume competence especially because another issue makes a difference to judgments of competence even when we have the best of evidence. By what standards are we to judge? People can disagree about what it is to be a competent social worker. This is particularly so in regard to therapy in which different techniques have their advocates. The level of disagreement may be so high that some who use one technique think that those who use another technique flirt with incompetent practice.

Even when there is agreement about what model to use, we may have disagreement within a model about what is acceptable and what is not. Practitioners using the structural model may agree that alliances with certain members in a family should be terminated, but disagree with when to terminate them. Some may think that the sooner the better, before the alliances are firmed up and the risk of dependence becomes too great. Others may think that the later the better, after the alliances are firmed up and independence from the family is achieved, even at the risk of dependence upon the therapist.

The difficulties that Jessica's colleagues now face become clearer. They must not only have evidence of incompetence, but also essential agreement about what would make a social worker competent. Because they are themselves presumably new at using the model, they must realize that others may think they lack experience about its features and particularly about when to terminate alliances adopted for strategic purposes. Even those adept and seasoned at using the model may disagree in a particular case on this issue. In short, Jessica's colleagues must be prepared to be clear not only about what Jessica is doing wrong, but also about what she would have to do to be doing things right, and being clear about that may be harder than it might seem.

c. Jessica's colleagues are well positioned to respond to the third question that must be answered whenever we make a judgment of competence. On what evidence are we to make a judgment? Evidence of incompetence can be difficult to achieve in many professions, social work included, for two different sorts of reasons.

First, we are rarely able to observe the field practice of our colleagues. One of the marks of being a professional is having autonomy—the capacity, among other things, to make decisions about what is or is not in a client's best interests independent of the oversight of others. But our having autonomy means that most of our work is done with clients in such a way that others have few ways to judge whether we are competent or not.

Second, the sorts of decisions we make as professionals are complicated enough, and can go wrong in so many different ways we cannot be responsible for, that our competence or incompetence may be hard to discern. Too many other factors in a case may be responsible for failure.

In *Family Therapy*, Jessica's colleagues have more than most colleagues would have on which to base a judgment. They have videotapes of her in therapy with clients, and they have the dialogues they all engaged in about all their cases.[77] So they could see how Jessica interacted with her clients, and they know how she interacted with them when she talked about her cases and about theirs. So in answering the question, "What's your evidence?", they had as much as anyone could reasonably expect anyone to have in such a case.

So what ought they to do? In regard to *Peers?*, we argued that when social worker practitioners have a conflict about a case, they have an ethical obligation to talk with each other, each beginning by presuming the other competent and concerned to help their clients. Talking is required by the method of tracking harms because if your colleague is impinging on your case by what is being done, you must understand the reasons for the colleague's actions before proceeding (see the Code of Ethics 2.01[a]) & [b]). You ought to presume that your job is to find out why your colleagues are doing something you think is unreasonable. If, after talking with them, you think their reasons are not good ones, you are to try to convince them that what they are doing is not the right thing to do.

But a judgment that someone is incompetent is very different from a judgment that the person has made a mistake. When we think colleagues have made mistakes, we presume competence on their part in talking with them to understand the reasons for their actions. But when we judge them incompetent, we talk with them not to convince them to act differently, but to see how we may help them become competent. The Code of Ethics requires this:

> Social workers who have direct knowledge of a social work colleague's incompetence should consult with that colleague when feasible and assist the colleague in taking remedial action (2.10[a]).

It was in talking with Jessica about what she was doing with her clients that her colleagues became convinced that she was incompetent using the structural model. She was unable, it seems, to see why others might think what she was doing was not right. So talking with her about remedial help does not seem to be a serious option. If she is unwilling or unable to understand why others might see that what she is doing is wrong, she would presumably be less willing to admit that she needs remedial help so she could do things right.

Whatever her colleagues's solution, it ought to be necessitated by what must be their primary concern—the well-being of the agency's clients.[78] The obvious next step would be to go to the supervisor and explain what they thought was happening, but they say they do not think they could prove her incompetence. We have provided some reasons for their thinking that, even with the best sort of evidence anyone can get.

So what are they to do? Their options seem to be limited. They must do something to try to protect the clients from harm, and they cannot do anything without talking with the supervisor. This is the sort of situation in which brainstorming possible alternatives and assessing their consequences would help, but initially, at least, there appear to be two options.

First, they can try to convince the supervisor that Jessica is incompetent or, as the Code of Ethics says, they can "take action through (other) appropriate channels established by employers, agencies, NASW, licensing and regulatory bodies, and other professional organizations" (2.10[b]).

Second, if they think that sort of move is ineffective and likely to cause harm to the agency and perhaps to them, they can point out to their supervisor that they are unable to work with Jessica. They may truly say that Jessica and they are unable to work through cases to the satisfaction of all concerned. The consequence is that the sessions are not working well, they are dissatisfied, Jessica is dissatisfied, and the clients are being harmed, if for no other reason than that the social workers cannot reach consensus about how to treat them. They might then suggest that because the set of them can reach agreement about how to proceed, and because Jessica is the one who does not agree, it might be best for all concerned if Jessica were reassigned to do something else.

Jessica's colleagues should be prepared for one effect of their judgment. It is not an easy thing to have your colleagues judge you incompetent, and Jessica's colleagues ought to be prepared for what is a quite normal set of reactions to the judgment they are making about Jessica—anger, indignation, countercharges.

It is because anyone can be presumed to take such criticism amiss that those making the judgment should carefully consider how they should talk with the person about the problem. The last step in the method of tracking harms requires that you:

5. *Determine how to do what you have determined ought to be done and do it in a way that will itself produce more good than harm.*

We do not know what transpired in their meetings together, but, given Jessica's reaction, we can surmise that she did not perceive the criticisms as helpful suggestions about how she might improve. But given the natural defensive reactions to having one's competence questioned, we have an ethical obligation not to raise the issue without a full understanding that questions about one's competence put one's entire professional life at risk. Indeed, having judged that she is incompetent in this area, Jessica's colleagues must wonder whether she is competent in other areas in which they have not been able to witness her practice, and they cannot assume that the inference will be lost on her.

That her colleagues will make this judgment about her general competence is all the more likely given the breakdown of communication. The case might have been different had Jessica been able to say, "The reason I'm not breaking off the alliances I am forming with the female members of the families I'm working with is that I think it is better to risk their dependence on me than to risk abandoning them too soon in the therapy. Could we talk about how we tell when is the appropriate time to leave them?" She might ask a colleague, "How do you know when to let go?" With that beginning, dialogue is possible. It was Jessica's apparent inability to communicate anything except her frustration at being criticized that seemed to cause the impasse she had with her colleagues and cause them to consider other options, such as going to the supervisor. Her frustration may have been justified by the ways in which her colleagues criticized her, but we do not know that.

We can obviously fail to meet a complex ideal in a variety of ways, to a lesser or greater degree. Some people listen very well; some do not. Some speak very well; some do not. We can all think of ways in which we could improve how we communicate in our relationships. But Jessica's problem is not that she needs to learn to communicate better. What has gone wrong is not that communication has failed to reach the ideal, but that it has broken down completely between Jessica and her colleagues. We have the opposite of what we ought to be striving to achieve among social work colleagues.

Failures to Communicate

The following two cases raise a different, but connected, set of issues. We are often in situations in which we seem to be communicating, but nothing happens that ought to happen. We may tell someone of a bad performance and explain that this or that must be done if the performance is to be improved. The person appears to understand what needs to be done, but, in the end, does not change. Consider the following case.

CASE **4.3**

Relapsing

Cynthia had been having problems with her work, but before her supervisor, Corliss, was able to talk with her about them, a client of hers who knew she was a recovering alcoholic reported that she had seen Cynthia drinking in a bar. A colleague also told Corliss that he thought Cynthia had begun drinking again. He had gone in to talk with her and saw that she was leaving little, empty whisky bottles in her wastebasket. Corliss then discovered that Cynthia had had periodic problems for some time before she had transferred to Corliss's department. "There is a history here," Corliss thought.

Corliss talked to Cynthia and explained that if her colleagues could see the empty bottles, her clients could too. Corliss and Cynthia agreed that she would have a month of residential treatment.

Cynthia did that, but although she was O.K. for awhile, after she came back, she relapsed. Corliss discovered that Cynthia had not followed through on her appointments, and, in addition, she was not doing her job well. So Corliss fired her.

Cynthia committed suicide, leaving a note blaming the colleague who had told Corliss that he thought she had begun drinking again. Corliss had told Cynthia that although she was fired, she could return if she "went into treatment and was sober for six months." So "she knew," Corliss added. "She had that option."

One potential source of difficulties in any professional organization is that although each member is a professional, some have power over others. Because each member of the organization is a professional and so is presumed competent to make proper professional judgments, difficulties can arise if other professionals, in positions of power, overrule the members' professional judgments. In addition, those professionals with power over others are wearing several different hats, as the standard metaphor has it, and their wearing several hats can be a source of ethical problems.

So, although Corliss arranged for Cynthia to have treatment, she did not do that just because she is a social worker. She also did it because she was concerned about her and because, without the treatment, Cynthia could not be an effective employee. So Corliss was acting both as a concerned colleague and as a supervisor. She did not cease being Cynthia's supervisor in dealing with her, even as she tried to help her, as though she were a client. It was thus not a "suggestion" that Cynthia get treatment for a month, but an order, with the threat of being fired if she did not go into treatment and remain "sober for six months." The ethical situation was thus different from what it would have been had Cynthia just been Corliss's client. If she were to keep her job, Cynthia had no choice but to do what Corliss recommended she do.[79]

Corliss could not have taken off her supervisor hat even if she wanted to, and in that way, the metaphor of wearing several hats is misleading since it implies one can wear first one and then another. So even if Corliss had not directly threatened Cynthia with the loss of her job, Cynthia would know that the same person who was telling her what she needed to do to become well enough to keep her job was the person who could fire her if she did not do it.

When those who hold supervisory positions are social workers as well as supervisors, their relationship with their employees is complex. They are, as social workers, peers of their employees. Yet as supervisors, they can no longer relate to them just as peers. They must relate to them both as peers and as supervisors.

But though it changes the relationship between social work practitioners when one is the supervisor of another, it should not change the ideals that we articulated regarding *Peers?* (see Code of Ethics 2.09[a]). We ought to presume that social workers have the same ends in mind and that the best way for them to achieve those ends when there is disagreement is for them to talk the problems through to determine the ethically best thing to do. A crucial difference one of them being a supervisor adds is that the supervisor can fire the employee. So when Corliss and Cynthia talk things through, Cynthia may find she may have to do what she does not want to do. As the case makes clear, the outcome was that Cynthia was fired and that she subsequently committed suicide. In asking whether Corliss did the right thing in firing her, we need to consider both results.[80]

What preceded the firing was a *pattern* of problems. Cynthia's repeated failures were interfering with her effectiveness as a social worker and harming her clients. Corliss did not fire Cynthia because she relapsed, but because she formerly had problems that had not been resolved and because she was not doing what she was supposed to do in order to resolve those problems. First, there is the pattern of repeated drinking. She drank before, and she is drinking again. Second, there is the pattern of failure to solve that problem. Cynthia did not solve it before, and she is not now doing all she can to solve it because she is not following through on the appointments she was supposed to have made and kept when she came out of her treatment.[81]

We have here the same sort of justification that was needed in *Family Therapy*. It would not be enough for Jessica to have one or two problems using the new form of family intervention. What was necessary to justify her colleagues judging her incompetent was a pattern of failure with the new form of intervention, a pattern that continued even after talking about her problems with her. Similarly, what is necessary to justify terminating Cynthia is a pattern of behavior that repeats itself despite treatment.

Such patterns are not always necessary to justify action. We can readily imagine single acts, such as an assault, which would justify termination, and it is not just any pattern of behavior that would justify termination, but one destructive of people's capacity to do their work properly without harming clients. Having been given several chances to change, and having been given another chance when she was told she could come back if she went to therapy and remained sober for six months, Cynthia has no good reason to complain of bad treatment in being fired.

Similarly, she has no good reason to blame Corliss or anyone else at the agency for her being fired, and so neither Corliss nor the other social workers ought to feel any guilt about Cynthia committing suicide. A failure to understand on the part of someone, despite numerous attempts at trying to communicate in a variety of different ways, is not the fault of the person trying to communicate. If what we do is the right thing to do, then we are not generally responsible for how someone responds to that action.

Unfortunately, even when communication is successful and, we want to say, the person must surely understand, other factors may intervene to prevent the person from acting on the communication. We then have a new ethical problem. This can be especially troublesome when there are patterns of behavior that would justify firing someone. Consider the following case.

CASE **4.4**

Bending over Backwards

Betsey had known of Jonathan for a long time and had met him as a colleague. He had been very successful working with clients and was well regarded in the community. She needed someone for a supervisory position and hired him after going through "the regular routine of references." Although Jonathan's director at his former agency complained and said he hated to see Jonathan go, he said he would prefer that he remain in the community.

The staff really liked Jonathan, but after a half-year or so, things began to go wrong. Jonathan did not handle his routine business well, failing to answer phone calls or respond to letters. He was writing letters for the agency even though those had to be approved by Betsey. And he was confused a great deal of the time, testifying in court, for instance, about a case but mixing up the details with some other case.

After documenting the difficulties, Betsey told him that "things are not going right" and would have to be corrected. The following Monday Jonathan's wife called and said he had been readmitted to an alcohol unit. Betsey had not known that Jonathan had problems with alcohol. He was off for six weeks, came back, did well for awhile, but then began to have problems again. It turned out that he needed a heart bypass operation.

Betsey was getting a lot of pressure to fire Jonathan from some of the staff and from the Board (see the Code of Ethics 2.09[a] & [b]). The agency was short-staffed anyway, and Jonathan's comings and goings over such a period of time, combined with the state of his papers and memos because of his confused state of mind, were creating extra work for everyone. In fact, the agency was audited seven times because of the problems Jonathan created and was beginning to get a bad reputation. But some of the staff were adamant that he be kept, and, as Betsey said, "I didn't feel I could fire someone who was going in for heart surgery."

But when Jonathan came back, he was no better. Betsey made him "a line worker" even though he was being paid as a supervisor, but he could not handle that either. Betsey suggested that Jonathan resign with disability, coming in to work on a contract basis whenever he felt able, but he refused, and after trying to get him to quit, she finally had to fire him. Jonathan was black, and he claimed racism on Betsey's part.

When she later talked to the director of the agency that Jonathan had worked at before, the director said that he had tried to warn her, but also that he didn't want Jonathan in his agency. Betsey thought that she had gotten anything but a warning from the director and that he had given her good recommendations in order to get rid of Jonathan.

This case raises a variety of issues, including whether it is appropriate to provide misleading or false recommendations.[82] We are concerned here only with the features of Jonathan's condition that led Betsey to fire him and with the difficulties she had in communicating and getting the kinds of changes needed from him. Her argument for firing him is not complicated, but it is instructive about how best to proceed in such cases.[83]

First, it was not enough, Betsey thought, for there to be a single incident or even several in which Jonathan did not do what he was supposed to do or got confused enough to cause problems for the agency. Although she did not articulate this, she must have thought she needed a pattern of problems in order to proceed and that she needed to be able to prove that there was a pattern by citing time and place and problem. The presumption must be that it is only with a pattern that we have evidence of some underlying difficulty, something that will continue to cause problems if action is not taken. As with Jessica in *Family Therapy*, it is not enough for there to be a single mistake; what is needed is a pattern of mistakes that suggests an underlying incompetence.

Second, Betsey documented the problems that Jonathan was having. First you find a pattern, and then you write it down. The presumption is, appropriately, that only with documentation of such a pattern of behavior can a clear case be made, one that does not rely on contestable memories.

Third, Betsey raised the issue with Jonathan so that he could know what she thought the problem was with his behavior. She told him both what he was doing and that what he was doing was unacceptable.

Fourth, Betsey tried to ensure that Jonathan got treatment for the underlying difficulties without being penalized. He was given leave to get treatment for alcoholism and then leave to have bypass surgery. Betsey acted on the assumption that the pattern of behavior that needed correcting was caused by alcoholism, or by the physical problem, or both. If Jonathan needed bypass surgery, his heart may not have been pumping enough oxygen to his brain, and that might account for his being confused.

The ethical reason for ensuring that he got treatment is that it would be wrong to penalize people for something that is not their fault or for something that may be their fault, but may be correctable within a reasonable period of time. Having heart problems was not Jonathan's fault, and although some may hold him accountable for being an alcoholic, giving him a chance to change means, at a minimum, that he has no right to complain if he does not change and the problems attributable to his being an alcoholic continue.[84]

Fifth, when the problem continued, Betsey lowered the expectations of what was required of Jonathan, but without penalizing him, giving him a line position while paying him as though he were a supervisor.

Sixth, when that did not help, and the problems continued, she gave him the option of retiring, with disability, working on contract whenever he wanted to and was able. Only when Jonathan refused, and the problems persisted, did she fire him.

What Betsey did very nicely captures the steps we all ought to try to follow in such situations if we can. It represents, in fact, the ideal—the best that we could be expected to do for our colleagues in one of the worst of situations between colleagues. So it is worth laying out in a more orderly fashion. Communication can fail in many ways, and when the stakes of successful communication are high— as they are when someone's career is on the line—we ought to be as sure as we can be that we have communicated as best we can.

1. Gather evidence of the supposed pattern of misconduct and document it. That will show what the basis of the concerns are. It is wrong to discipline anyone without clear and documented evidence of a sustained pattern of misconduct in regard to the ordinary course of one's professional activities. Of course, as we have said, about some matters no pattern is needed. One assault is enough to justify disciplinary action.

2. When you have such a written statement, you should talk with the person accused of the problem. It is wrong to discipline someone without the person's knowing what he or she is accused of doing. So that person needs to be informed. This is part of what one owes to colleagues because they are colleagues. It is a matter of professional courtesy, but it is also required so that you can be sure you understand what the source of the problem is. You not only need to inform the person of what you think, but you also need to be informed by the colleague. What looks wrong given what you know may turn out to have an innocent explanation. It would also be imprudent, in this age of lawsuits, to discipline anyone without a written statement of a pattern of misconduct.

The situation we examined in Chapter 2 in which the woman killed her lover with a butcher knife while he was being held by the police is an object lesson in how something can appear one way and be another. She looked stupid to do such a thing in front of what are presumed the best witnesses a court could ask for, and yet she may have done it because she thought it was the smartest thing she could do.

In any event, we ought to inform those about whom we have evidence of misconduct because, for one thing, he or she may simply not be aware of the problem, odd as that may sound. Busy people often become overloaded and simply do not realize, for instance, how many phone calls they have failed to return. Or there may be another simple explanation—the person accused may be overextended because he or she is covering for someone else. Without talking to the person, we cannot be sure we know what we seem to have solid evidence for.

3. When the person is willing, we should try to help by changing the underlying conditions that are producing the problem. In some cases, it may be a simple matter of providing additional support—additional secretarial help, for instance. In others, it may require more substantial intervention. This was the case for Jonathan, who was first given leave to get treatment for his alcoholism and then to have bypass surgery.

In some situations, giving someone a chance to change is not always wise or ethically right. If Jonathan were engaged in a pattern of sexual harassment against other employees, Betsey's giving him a chance to change would subject those employees to the continued risk of harassment. She would have to ask whether taking the chance that Jonathan would change was worth the risk of further harm to other employees—and the lawsuits that subjecting them to such a risk would itself risk.

4. Where it is possible, provide an alternative for the employee that solves the original problem. Betsey did this by making Jonathan "a line worker"—a position that he had successfully held before. Unfortunately, in this case, that did not solve the problem. Jonathan was as unable to handle the obligations of this position as he had been unable to handle those of being supervisor, and the agency's clients were at risk of harm.

But we can understand Betsey's motivations. On the one hand, she was trying to retain someone who had been an asset to the agency, and she was trying to retain him in the position in which he had worked well. On the other hand, she was trying to provide some alternative for Jonathan short of firing him, something that would allow him to continue. Her underlying aim was presumably to cause as little harm as she could either to the agency's clients or to Jonathan, given that she could not let him continue to work in his supervisory position.

5. If a person must be fired, try to provide another option if possible. Betsey did that when she suggested that Jonathan retire with disability, coming in to consult when he could. Her concern was presumably to minimize the harm—both to Jonathan and to the agency.

If we go through the steps in this process, we find that two ethical concerns animate them. On the one hand, we need to minimize the harm to those concerned—to Jonathan, to the agency's clients, and to the agency and its staff, some of whom found Jonathan's comings and goings on leave disruptive. We may question whether Betsey acted to minimize those harms as much as she could, whether, for instance, her continuing efforts to help Jonathan may have harmed the agency's clients while he muddled through, but there is no doubt that she ought to act to minimize the harms. On the other hand, we need to provide as much respect to those involved as we can. Betsey did this for Jonathan. She gave him choices where that was possible, for instance, as in the last step where she gave him the option of resigning.

We might question whether Betsey found just the right combination of these two ethical concerns—whether she weighed the potential harm to Jonathan more heavily than she should have since one consequence of the delay in firing him was that the agency was audited seven times. But our concern here is not with the details of how Betsey handled the case, but with the principles she utilized and the procedure she adopted.

Betsey needed to be concerned about firing Jonathan because he claimed racism, he was ill, and the staff was split over whether he should stay or leave. So one way to assess whether what she did was right is to ask whether, at the end, the clients, Jonathan, or any of the staff had any right to complain of how he was treated. Was he informed of what was expected of him and what he was doing that was wrong? Was the evidence of what he was doing wrong correct? Was a good-faith effort made to help him change what needed changing? Was an alternative provided so he could stay on without causing difficulties for the agency and its clients? Was he provided a graceful way out of the situation? We can work through the case asking each of these questions and determine how well it matches up to the ideal procedure for handling such situations.

Less than the Ideal

As we have argued, social work colleagues ideally ought to respect and talk to one another about common problems without any other concern than that of trying to achieve their common goals. In *Peers?*, Margaret was overly concerned with how Malik would react to her talking to him about her client, but even when we communicate well with our colleagues, achieving among ourselves the ideal that ought to mark our professional relations with one another, we may still fail to reach agreement or, reaching agreement, find ourselves stymied by some feature of the situation we cannot talk through:

- We may find a disparity regarding goals. We may disagree about what the proper goals ought to be, or agree but fail to realize that we do, or realize that we do but fail to coordinate our activities well enough to achieve our goals, and so on.
- We may agree about our goals, but disagree about how best to achieve them, one colleague thinking we must do one thing, and another thinking the best way to proceed is to do something quite different and incompatible.
- Even if we agree on our goals and the means to achieve them, we may find ourselves unable to work well with a colleague.
- We may find ourselves at odds with colleagues even though we agree on our common goals, and on the means to achieve them, and respect the colleagues and can talk well together. For someone else may have created a situation that puts us at odds with our colleagues in a way that we as colleagues cannot repair, even with the best of intentions and the best of relationships. Such a situation may arise when, for instance, employees are paid differently for the same work.

When colleagues are working together, we should always ask:

a. Is there agreement in goals?
b. Is there agreement in means?
c. Even when there is agreement in goals and in means, do other difficulties get in the way of their working well with each other?
d. Even if they can work together well and agree on goals and means, are external factors producing problems between them?

We shall consider each of these issues in turn as we look at new cases and reexamine others (see the Code of Ethics 2.05[b]).

a. *Is there agreement in goals?*—In *Having Sex*, the social worker, Aubrey, thought Theresa's previous social worker had been wrong to have a sexual relationship with Theresa, and she wanted Theresa to press charges. When Theresa refused, Aubrey pursued the matter on her own. Aubrey's goal was to "get the former therapist" while Theresa's was to get on with her life. We can readily imagine two social workers disagreeing and communicating their disagreement to each other—as Aubrey and Theresa do.

b. *Is there agreement in means?*—In *Hurting Oneself*, Annette wanted to take her previous therapist to court, but her new therapist tried to persuade her that it was not in her best interests to do that. This case illustrates how difficult it can be to determine, when there is disagreement, whether the disagreement is about the goals themselves or about the means to achieve them. Although Annette and her therapist are at odds about what she ought to do regarding her former therapist, they agree that she should do what will raise her self-esteem and increase her sense of personal power. Annette thinks she will be better off standing up to someone who has hurt her and winning, and her new therapist thinks the likelihood of losing is so high that it will harm Annette more to pursue the matter. So they seem to agree about the goal—doing what is best for Annette—but disagree about the best way to achieve that goal.

Working out such disagreements can be a difficult matter, and the normal difficulties of resolving such disputes can be complicated when each party to the dispute thinks his or her position is ethically best. Consider, in this regard, the following case.

CASE **4.5**

Value Judgments

Jane works in private practice in a clinic that specializes in feminist therapy, with a strong emphasis on holistic health and "a general understanding of the mind-body connection." She works with several other social workers, one of whom, Daniela, she found naive about the risks involved in working with battered wives.

Daniela was encouraging one of her battered clients to confront her husband. Daniela thought that confrontation would help to resolve the problems between the couple. But it did not seem to help, and Jane thought Daniela was unable to cope with the husband of the woman she was counseling. The man kept coming to the clinic, threatening Daniela and other social workers, and putting all of them "in grave danger."

The group met without Daniela to talk about the problem and then spoke to Daniela about the harm they thought she was causing her client and the danger she was putting them all in, but Daniela refused to change her focus on this client. She thought it had to do with the client's right of self-determination. The client really wanted to stay in the relationship.

Jane disagreed with Daniela's understanding of the situation. As she put it, "If a woman's getting hit, and it could escalate to something worse, and she's telling you about it, but is not willing to leave, how long do you remain a part of that situation?" Battered women often have trouble leaving those who batter them, and Jane thought that Daniela's client was not really exercising self-determination and that Daniela was failing to intervene appropriately.

Daniela ended up leaving the group "under pressure." She did not want to leave, but the group was not willing to risk the danger to themselves or to the battered woman.

Daniela thinks she is doing the right thing in urging her client to confront her husband, and Jane thinks she is doing the wrong thing. This case raises the ante over that in *Peers?*, for instance. It involves the issue of what social work practitioners ought to do when they disagree with what another social worker is doing and, after talking with the social worker, find that the disagreement reflects differing conceptions of how to handle what are admittedly difficult cases. It is one thing to judge a colleague wrong when the colleague seems genuinely unable to understand what is at issue, as in *Family Therapy,* and it is quite another to judge a colleague wrong when the colleague has clearly articulated ethical reasons for acting in a way you think is wrong.

At least one of you must be wrong when you disagree in this way, and perhaps you both are, but when you both make ethical cases for doing what you think is right, and you disagree, working out what is right can be difficult. After all, you each think that if you were to do what the other is suggesting, you would be doing what is ethically wrong, and it can be difficult backing off and making an objective judgment in such a situation.

The first step is to:

1. *Try to understand why the participants are doing what they are doing by constructing arguments that would justify their acts or omissions.*

We need to try to get clear on why the client wants to do what she wants to do, on why Daniela is so sure she is right about how to help the client, and then on why Jane is so sure she is right (see the Code of Ethics 2.05[b]).

If we are a participant in the case, it means suspending for awhile our own reaction to the case and trying to construct the argument we think justifies our actions and would justify what we want to do. We have not yet emphasized this turning of the method upon ourselves, but participants in the case are not to make themselves immune from the requirements of trying to be objective about why they themselves are doing what they are doing.

But let us take the client first. She wants to stay in the relationship, she says, and even though she is being battered, she may think that her leaving might preclude forever the couple's resolving their difficulties. The wife must think she has a terrible dilemma. If she stays, she sustains a relationship with her husband, but risks being battered more. If she leaves, she risks losing the relationship she says she wants, but presumably protects herself against the harm she incurs in the relationship. What she wants, it seems, is a new kind of relationship with her husband, one not harmful to her. The problem she thinks she faces is how she can both protect herself and forge that relationship.

If we follow the first step in our method in regard to Daniela, we must ask why she thinks the woman should confront her husband. The possibilities are many, but one likely reason is that she thinks the very act of the woman's confronting her husband will force a new relationship between them, that his wife's standing up to him will require him to recognize her as a person.

The Code of Ethics tells us that we ought to encourage self-determination, but in this situation, encouraging the wife to stay, and particularly to confront her spouse, may encourage further battering and not further self-determination. So if Daniela encourages the woman to stay and confront her husband, she bears a heavy burden. She must have very good reasons for encouraging something that may be so harmful. What could explain her thinking that she is doing what is right?

Is there an argument we can plausibly attribute to her that would make sense of what she is doing? We will need to remember that in trying to figure out why she is doing what she is doing, we are not justifying what she is doing. No matter how plausible we can make her position sound, its sounding plausible does not make the premises true.

So what could Daniela say? She could concede that the wife is at risk of being harmed further, but insist that a proper respect for the principle of self-determination requires that a social worker do what can be done to further what the client perceives to be in the client's best interests, not what the social worker or anyone else believes the client ought to do. Of course, Daniela cannot argue that she is helping the client further her self-determination unless she has provided the client with all of the relevant information about domestic assault shelters, batterers, victims, and the cycle of violence—how research shows, for example, that couples cannot resolve their differences staying in the relationship, how the prognosis for the husband is poor even if he gets counseling, and so on. Daniela cannot argue that she is acting to further the woman's self-determination unless she has provided the woman with the means for proper self-determination.

If she has done that, then, she can argue, she has an obligation to respect the woman's judgment, even if she thinks it is mistaken. Just as in *Ready to Die* it was a mistake for the psychiatrist to argue that the woman was incompetent because she did not want chemotherapy, so here it would be a mistake to argue that the woman is incompetent because she has decided to stay in the relationship. If she has made that decision after a full examination of all the relevant information, and if she is competent, and if she is not being coerced or threatened (as she might be if her spouse said, for instance, that he would kill her if she left him), then we have to accede that whatever decision she makes is her decision and that we must live with it, however irrational or harmful we think it may be.

Daniela could also argue that because the woman has said she wants to remain in a relationship in which she is likely to be battered, the only way for

Daniela to help her is to try to change the relationship so that the husband will not beat her. And that would explain why she encourages the woman, if she is to stay in the relationship, to confront her husband. For Daniela may think, as we said, that the act of confronting the husband will force a new relationship, as the woman stands up for herself and the husband is forced to see her as someone who can stand up for herself. She thus can give an ethical argument for encouraging the woman to confront her husband—despite the risk of further battering.

She has no choice, Daniela can argue, if she is to respect the woman's decision and try to prevent her from being harmed. We ought not to substitute our judgments for that of our clients, Daniela could say, for clients need to be encouraged to act with self-determination, and, anyway, it is hard to get people to do what they do not perceive to be in their self-interest. So sometimes, Daniela could concede, we need to support clients who are not doing what we think they ought to do.

Again, none of this is to suggest that Daniela's understanding is correct. She has other options that she apparently did not explore, for instance. She could encourage the woman to see another social worker—Jane, for example—on the assumption that perhaps a new voice could begin to change the way the woman is thinking about the problem (see the Code of Ethics 2.06[a]). She could tell the woman that her husband ought to seek treatment. She could teach the woman skills that do not require confrontation to help her handle her problems. She could teach the woman that love does not require being a victim. But we are at this stage only trying to figure out why Daniela may be doing what she is doing, not assessing whether her position is correct.

Now let us see if we can understand Jane's position. Hers is that Daniela's encouraging the wife to confront her husband not only risks harm to the wife, but also puts the members of the clinic at risk. Battered women often have trouble leaving those who batter them. So Daniela may be wrong in thinking she is furthering the woman's self-determination. We ought not always do what clients want us to do. Clients can be badly mistaken about their best interests, and as the Code of Ethics states, social workers have an obligation to be concerned about clients' exercise of their self-determination when that poses "a serious, foreseeable, and imminent risk to themselves or others" (1.02). In saying she wants to remain in the relationship, the woman may not be expressing her self-determination at all, Jane suggests, but expressing a desire determined by the relationship in which she is battered. We should no more let her do what she says she wants than we should let a sleepwalker drive who says she wants to go out. The woman's desire to remain in the relationship should not be a decisive factor in determining what ought to be done, Jane is saying, given the harms that do and may result.

So where are we now? We can understand why the issue between Daniela and Jane is so contentious that it led to Daniela's leaving the group "under pressure." Either the woman ought to go back into the relationship or she ought not. Daniela cannot agree to the latter because she thinks that denies the woman's self-determination, and Jane cannot agree to the former because she thinks doing that will harm the woman.

Daniela and Jane have directly opposite views about what ought to be done, each founded on their ethical judgments about the right thing to do, and it is difficult to figure out how either could compromise in any way.

We also are not well positioned to assess who is right. The weight of research about spousal abuse is against Daniela, and the potential harm to the staff must be weighed in as well. But the primary focus ought not to be who is right, but what will happen to the client. Will Daniela continue to help the wife, even though she is no longer associated with the group? Will some member of the group take over? Or is the woman to be an innocent victim of this dispute? We ought to take special precautions to ensure that the person being abused is not subject to further harm, and so, whoever is right, the primary consideration must be to ensure that the client is served (see the Code of Ethics 1.16[a], [b], [e] & [f].

But putting the matter that way makes clear just how the form of the dispute is part of the difficulty. Daniela and Jane share a common goal, the self-determination of the woman, but disagree on the best means to achieve it. So how the client is to be helped after Daniela leaves the group will be as contentious as how she is to be helped while Daniela is in the group. And even the judgment that it is not clear who is right without further information (about, for instance, what Daniela has told the woman about spousal abuse) is likely to be contentious to those who hold either position.

We should note one other issue before leaving this case. It is essential to the members of a group working together and achieving what success they can that the members respect the other members of the team. If the members do not respect each other's capacity to be good professionals, they cannot well achieve their common goals (see the Code of Ethics 2.01[a]). The clinic was organized to specialize in feminist therapy, for instance, and presumably anyone not committed to that basis for organization would not fit in well.[85] So one issue that emerges in this case is what degree of agreement in judgments is required by those in the clinic. How much agreement is required for social work colleagues to work together as a team?

Having everyone agree about what ought to be done may mean that nothing decided ever gets challenged and mistakes get repeated. So there are good reasons for encouraging diversity in a group. Differences can enrich a team. But they also can cause difficulties, as in this case and in *Family Therapy*. The danger when faced with someone in a team who does not readily fit in is that we will too quickly make the issue into one of competence without good reason. It can be easier to exclude someone from a group for being incompetent than it is to accept the sorts of disagreements that we see between Daniela and Jane. That is not to suggest that Daniela had good reasons for her position, but it is to suggest that the ideal is a dialogue that encourages the diversity in judgment that each person brings to a group.

What this case illustrates is that agreement on the goals may be accompanied by significant disagreement on the means to achieve the goals. This has much to do with the way goals are usually framed. We say that we want the client to exercise self-determination, but that is a vague phrase, consistent with a variety of different understandings of when a client actually exercises self-determination. So we may have verbal agreement without substantive agreement, and, unfortunately, there is no magic formula for handling disagreements in goals or in the means by which to achieve agreed-upon goals.

Some cases that raise issues about goals can be relatively easy. But *Value Judgments* is not an easy case. The principle to follow in all cases, but especially when there is doubt about what to do, is that one should do that which causes the least harm, consistent with helping one's client. Unfortunately, this principle gives us little leverage in *Value Judgments*. Both parties to the dispute argue that their solutions cause the least harm, consistent with helping the client. They disagree on what is most helpful to the client.

Perhaps the best advice we can give in such a situation is to remind everyone involved that the client's interests are paramount and that unless there is compelling evidence otherwise, they should presume that their colleagues are working in what they believe to be the client's best interests. At least then, when there is disagreement about the ends or the means chosen, it need not escalate into confrontation, and colleagues can still continue, despite the disagreement, to treat each other with the respect and good will that ought to mark ideal collegial relations.

    c. *Even when there is agreement in goals and in means, are there other difficulties that get in the way of their working well with each other?*—In *Bending over Backwards*, Betsey's colleague at the agency at which Jonathan had previously worked told her that he hated to lose Jonathan and was at least happy that Jonathan would stay in the community. Betsey liked Jonathan's work and presumably shared the goal of keeping him in the community. Hiring him was a way to do that. But the head of the other agency then claimed, after Jonathan had left his agency and the harm was done in Betsey's, both that he tried to warn her and that he wanted to get rid of Jonathan. It is difficult not to believe that he lied to Betsey to get rid of an employee he did not want.

We do not have his side of the story, but it is easy enough to construct the dilemma that those who make such recommendations typically face. On the one hand, they have an employee who is not doing a good job whom they either do not wish to, or cannot readily, fire. If they give a bad recommendation, they do not solve their problem. They might decide not to give a bad recommendation, just saying that the person worked here and describing the duties of the position. But that is to risk questions about the evaluation. So they might agree to give the employee a good recommendation if the person resigns. They have a prudential reason for giving a good recommendation. But they have other reasons as well. If they do not give a good recommendation, they risk being sued by the employee, who will complain of someone's recommending that he or she not be hired when that person is employing them. If the employee is doing such a bad job that he or she cannot be commended in a recommendation, he or she can ask, why is he or she still employed?

In addition, employers may be convinced, or want to be convinced, that while the employee is not working out for them, he or she may work out much better in a different setting. Writing a bad recommendation means judging that the person is beyond hope, and things have not yet reached that point, presumably, or the person would have been fired. So it is ethically wrong to write a bad recommendation, the argument would go, for an employee who is not working out. It would be to limit his or her options without good reason.

Of course, to the person receiving the recommendation, all this is likely to seem, after the fact, like so much self-deception and self-interest on the part of the person making the recommendation. Not remarking on serious problems with an employee when asked for a recommendation is, at a minimum, to mislead a colleague. Surely Betsey should wonder about whether her colleague in the other agency is going to tell her the truth about any other difficult matter they may need to work out together, and she will now think twice about relying on anything he might say that makes a difference to her or her agency and its employees. His misleading her about Jonathan does not just have an effect for her regarding Jonathan, but has implications for any future relationship with him. She now knows she cannot rely on the other agency's director to tell her the truth if her knowing the truth could hurt his interests.

Those who must recommend people they would prefer not recommending know how difficult it can be to craft a statement that is honest, but does not invite a lawsuit. The way out of the dilemma that Jonathan's former employer may have faced was to be honest, letting Betsey know of the problems they were having with Jonathan and letting her decide, on the basis of accurate information about his bad and his good points, whether to hire him or not (see the Code of Ethics 4.04). As it was, Jonathan's former employee simply passed his problems with Jonathan on to Betsey, unremarked, and so the two failed to reach the level of honesty that ought to mark relations between colleagues—through no fault of Betsey's.

Sometimes, however, the difficulties that colleagues may have cut so deeply against the ideal that it becomes ludicrous to suggest that they guide themselves by that ideal in trying to resolve the difficulties. This sort of situation can be aggravated when one colleague has power over another. Consider in this regard the following case.

CASE 4.6

Harassment

Amy works in an agency associated with a hospital. She had been hired by her supervisor's boss, not by the supervisor, Don. Both Amy and the boss are African Americans; the supervisor is white. Both the supervisor and his boss are males. Amy was at the agency before Don came, and he told her that he resented her being there and did not want her there. He then proceeded to harass her, she says, for over two years in a variety of ways.

Don had the secretaries keep records of when Amy was on the phone and of how long she was gone from her office. Such records were not kept for other employees. He would pin memos to her door about what he thought she was doing wrong. He created a new schedule for her one day when she was gone to work on a case at the hospital and then, when she came to work at her normal time the next day, he said, "I've gotcha. Where were you?" He would not let her look in her personnel file (although she wanted to see the memos there). When she took leave to attend a funeral, he suggested she really was using that as an excuse to have lunch with a friend because she did have lunch with the friend before the funeral.

Don enforced a policy against Amy about not taking more than three sick or personal times in ninety days. She had to leave to take her sick child home from school, then to have minor surgery the next week, again to have the stitches taken out a week later, and then for something else for one other short period of time. He said, "I'm writing you up for dismissal because you've violated policy." But the policy had never been enforced before, and he did not enforce it against anyone else at the agency.

Don continually harassed Amy verbally, she said. He would call her into his office and find fault with her work, always taking her to task for not doing something right and saying how good he was compared with her and always complaining that she was getting selected for this or for that when he was the manager. He had, Amy said, "taunted" two African American secretaries until they finally left, and she was convinced that he was out to make the agency as white as could be.

Amy eventually filed a grievance, and when she went before the grievance board, she fully documented what she could of what Don had done. The board found no grounds for harassment, and Amy was told afterwards that the hospital's lawyer told the board that if they did find grounds, Amy would have had good grounds for a lawsuit. The board did find that there was "a gross misunderstanding" between Amy and Don, and, Amy learned, the whole agency was later to be reorganized, with Don's managerial responsibilities taken from him. She felt vindicated, but meanwhile the harassment continued.

In a situation where there is harassment, we seem as far removed from the ideal relationship between colleagues as we can get, and all of the features that go to make up the ideal are in question. There is no respect for the other's professional abilities, no willingness to listen and try to understand the other's point of view when there is disagreement, no willingness to work together to solve common problems, and so on. There is a loss of all of the features that mark the ideal.

Don's motive is unclear. Perhaps he is a racist. He is accused of having harassed the two African American secretaries so that they would leave, and Amy is the only African American among the other employees of the agency.[86] Perhaps he is sexist. Amy is apparently one of the few females among the staff who is not a secretary. Perhaps he revels in power. His complaining that she was selected for various things when he is manager suggests professional jealousy. Or perhaps, and it seems highly unlikely, he was concerned about the budget and chose an inappropriate means to try to balance it by forcing Amy out.

Don's motive matters if we are concerned to try to change his attitude so he no longer engages in such behavior. But his motive makes no difference to assessing the harm he has caused. And he clearly has caused great harm (assuming that what Amy asserts is true).

First, he has engaged not just in a single act, but in a sustained pattern of acts. Consider the application of the rule that no more than three leaves may be taken in a ninety-day period. It is not enough to say, in objection, that the rule has never been applied before. Don's response can be that it ought to have been applied before and that he is now beginning what he should long ago have begun. The objection to what he is doing must rather be that he is not applying it to others, and so is in that way unfair, or that he is not applying it fairly to Amy, and so is in that way unfair. She could properly object if she later discovers that others have also been absent for more than the rule allows and have not been disciplined. Or she might properly object that the rule is meant to be used when there are *inexcusable* absences, not when the absences are minor and necessary.

Yet even if her objections are well-taken, Don might say, "Oh, sorry. My mistake." He may or may not have made a mistake, but everybody accused of doing what is wrong can get themselves off the ethical hook by claiming that they made a mistake—conceding, that is, that they were wrong, but suggesting that we all make mistakes and so should not be penalized if we do and admit it.

But a pattern of unethical behavior implies a sustained campaign. We are less willing to let someone off the ethical hook if there is such a pattern because there are far fewer ways to explain how one could have made a mistake that produced such a pattern of inappropriate behavior.

Second, it is thus important that there be acts or omissions of different sorts—applying rules, tacking memos to Amy's door, berating her, and so on. For it is then much harder to justify what one is doing as the result of some sort of simple mistake.

In *Harassment*, there is not just a variety of acts, but, and this is a third feature to note about this case, a pattern of *harmful* and varied acts. It is possible, and sometimes seems diabolical, to harass someone by engaging in acts, over and over again, that are in themselves perfectly harmless. Siblings seem to have a knack for figuring out just what they can do that in itself seems harmless but, when done over and over, harasses a brother or sister, sometimes to the point of tears. But in *Harassment*, some of Don's actions are in themselves harmful to Amy. We might be able to provide an explanation for his applying the ninety-day rule to her, but it would be significantly harder to explain why he would berate her professional skills. That seems unnecessary and harmful in itself.

As is obvious, this pattern of harmful and varied acts that constitutes Don's behavior is as far removed as can be from that necessary for the ideal relationship between professionals that we have argued ought to regulate relations between colleagues. If Don is having trouble with how Amy is doing her job, his job, as her supervisor, is to speak with her, try to get her to see what she is doing wrong, and work with her to see that what needs changing is changed. But harassment is ethically wrong, whatever the motivation for it, and it is far worse ethically when the person doing the harassing is a superior to the person being harassed (see the Code of Ethics 3.01[d] & 3.03). In addition, as this case makes clear, harassing is risky because the person being harassed may file a grievance, and it is an inefficient way to change a person's behavior, if that is the point. So it is not only ethically wrong, but ineffective.

Yet people engage in harassment, for whatever reason, and its existence creates some serious practical problems. Even bringing it to a supervisor's attention can cause difficulties—and especially so if the supervisor is the one accused of harassing. It can be difficult to prove, and even if it can be proved, other factors may intervene to prevent an appropriate remedy. Amy says she was told that the reason the Board did not find for her is that the lawyer for the hospital told the Board that she would then have a good case if she sued. Documenting harassment so that one can present a compelling case can be difficult, especially if the person doing the harassment is careful not to leave a paper trail. And just bringing a grievance means that the professional relationship between the two parties involved is severely damaged.

These practical problems are all accentuated if the person accused is one's superior. The powers that be may be more reluctant to remove someone from a supervisory position if only because they will then be admitting they made a mistake in giving power to such a person. Again, supervisors must take a critical attitude toward the behavior of employees, in order to ensure that the work is done properly. So they can always defend themselves against a charge of harassment by saying that perhaps they were just a little overzealous in administrating—or that their attempts to help a recalcitrant employee were misinterpreted or that the employee is peculiarly sensitive to helpful suggestions. No matter what happens as the result of a grievance procedure, the employee and the supervisor are going to have a strained relationship, and the employee may have a difficult time getting good recommendations to go elsewhere—unless, as in *Bending over Backwards*, the supervisor is willing to lie to prospective employers to get rid of the employee. This prospect is a good example of how one bad ethical situation can beget another.

  d. *Even if colleagues can work together well and agree on goals and means, are there external factors that produce problems between them?*—In the cases we have considered so far regarding the relations of social work professionals, the focus has been on problems created by the professionals themselves. But many ethical problems between practitioners do not arise because of anything one practitioner or set of practitioners does regarding another practitioner, but because of some feature of the situation they find themselves in. They may not do anything to each other, that is, but may find that something has been done to them that creates ethical issues between them. Consider, in this regard, the following case.

CASE **4.7**

Lying about Salaries

In an agency of about twelve employees, several who have been there for some years are earning significantly less than others more recently hired. The agency has such a good reputation that many were willing to work for it even though their starting salary was lower than what was then the normal going rate, but, as inflation has outstripped raises, their salaries have become significantly less competitive. As the agency's director puts it, "There are staff members who really have low salaries."

The director has pushed for increases, and was able to get an increase for one employee who pushed hard, but the agency has always been able to obtain very good employees at lower salaries. So the director has not been able to obtain a general increase for all employees.

One consequence is that some are not getting what they deserve. Another is that some who are equally situated are getting different salaries. As the director says, "The present situation supports dishonesty." If the news gets out that one employee has gotten an increase, then others, equally deserving, will demand increases as well. The agency does not have the money for that, and so the director has to be less than forthcoming with his staff about their salaries. Indeed, he told those employees who received raises not to tell the other employees.

This case raises a variety of ethical questions—about what is just, about what ethical reasons an agency might have for not doing what looks to be the right thing by its employees, and so on.[87] Our only concern here is with the relationship among employees that is created by their being treated differently by the agency and by the director's being less than forthcoming.

One issue is that different employees, equally deserving, are getting different salaries—through no fault of their own. First, a person cannot be held responsible for having been hired in at a higher salary than someone else in the agency. Prospective employees are not likely to know what others make and would probably not be told if they asked. Second, we can hardly blame a person who succeeds in getting an increase to get what he or she deserves. So, we can presume, the differences between the salaries of the employees are not the fault of any of the employees.

Yet those differences create a set of ethical problems, as we can see by using the third step in our method and tracking the harms, determining what they are and who is harmed:

1. The situation is unfair in two different ways. First, some are not getting what they deserve, quite independently of what is happening to others within the agency. Even if all were underpaid, each would not be getting what he or she deserves. Second, the situation is more complicated ethically because some are getting what they deserve and some are not. So those who are not getting what they deserve are being doubly harmed—by not getting what they deserve *and* by being treated differently from the way others similarly situated are being treated. It is a matter of justice that those in the same position ought to get the same treatment, and here they are not. So some of the employees are being harmed significantly more than others because they are having a double injustice inflicted upon them.

2. Many employees know that they were hired in at a low salary and know that they are not now getting what they deserve. They may not know that others are getting what they deserve, and so may not know about the disparities in

treatment, but certainly the agency director knows. Were word to get out, his employees would then know that he knows. That would cause the director, and the agency, great harm.

It would cause the director great harm because the employees would then know both that he had hired them in at different salaries, despite their similar positions, and that he had kept from them information they would need if they were to press for increases to make things fair. In short, the director's position as a fair employer would be compromised. His employees would know that he is the sort of person who will take advantage of them if he can and that they cannot trust him to inform them about matters vital to their interests as employees. Good evidence for this judgment of him is that he told the employees to whom he gave raises not to tell the others (see the Code of Ethics 4.04).

3. The director is keeping information from the employees. The phrase used, "being less than forthcoming," is a euphemism that may cover a wide variety of sins—from not saying anything at all about something the director knows to be wrong, to lying to those employees who ask. The employees are harmed by this, as we all are who must make decisions affecting our lives without full information. Their capacity for self-determination is being harmed. The agency and its mission are harmed as well. It would be amazing if, were word to leak out, the employees were not very angry at both the injustice of it all and the deception used to try to ensure that the injustices never came to light. Having angry employees in a social work agency is not likely to do the agency or its clients any good.

4. In addition, the director is harmed. If we presume that he has the best of intentions and would much prefer his employees being paid what they deserve, the situation he is in has created a significant ethical problem for him. It is never good ethically when someone with good intent is put in a position in which he or she must either lie or risk great harm, and the director has at least the apparent dilemma of either lying to his employees, directly or indirectly by not telling them what they ought to know, or risking the sort of commotion to the agency and to the relations of those within it that the truth would bring. Those who are making what they deserve to make ought to feel that their colleagues are being unfairly treated, and those who are not making what they deserve to make ought to feel that they are being unfairly treated.

Of course, the argument that the director may make is that he has no choice but to treat his employees unjustly. Funding for the agency, he would argue, is not sufficient to provide what each person deserves. So when he hires, he must try to hire someone for as little as he can because he must make the money he has go as far as he can, and yet he will sometimes have to hire at market value, so to speak, paying as much as someone deserves. Disparities will inevitably arise through the hiring process because of the pressure that insufficient funding produces.[88] The situation in the agency is no different, he could argue, than that faced by any other agency or any business.

In addition, once employees are hired, the lack of funding means either that he cannot make up differences in salaries or that he cannot do that without taking funds from essential services and so harming the agency's mission. So differential hiring will produce differential results that will not be rectified and will, as time goes on, become worse and worse as those newly hired make or approach the market rates and those hired earlier cannot be compensated sufficiently to make up the growing differences. Again, the director could argue, this is no different than what one finds in any agency or business as those already on board are presumably not going to leave unless the differences in salary become so great as to be intolerable and employment beckons elsewhere.

Whatever the virtues of the director's arguments, the situation produces another harmful result:

5. The employees' interests are at odds with each other. If only a limited amount of money is available, and if many deserve more than they are getting and, more importantly, more than they could get if all of the money available was distributed, then any gain by one employee is a loss by another. It is an ethical loss as well as a financial loss because each employee is ethically entitled to what he or she deserves, and someone else's getting some of the little that is available means that every other unpaid employee will get less than he or she deserves. Whether the employees wish it or not, their interests conflict, and so the situation puts the employees' interests at odds with one another—through no fault of their own.

One result—one wants to say, "the natural result"—of the employees being put into that sort of situation is that they will have less than the ideal collegial relation with one another—through no fault of their own. After all, some of the employees have been asked to keep from the others how much they are making, and so, if anyone asks, they must at least consider not telling the truth. And if they do tell the truth, they will have less than the ideal collegial relation with the director.

Keeping information from one's colleagues, particularly about matters that are often kept private, does not inevitably lead to other failures, but everyone's knowing that such information is off-limits puts everyone on notice that decisions are being made about some matters affecting the agency without everyone's having full information. And some knowing that they have been asked not to tell the truth puts them on notice at least that others may have been asked not to tell the truth about other matters. Suspicion cannot help but be engendered in such circumstances, and with suspicion comes a loss of a sense of self-determination. To the extent that we cannot know that we are acting on full and accurate information, but suspect that we are making decisions based on inaccurate or incomplete information, we must feel that we are not making fully informed decisions—independently of the status of the decisions themselves. Our decisions may be fully informed, but the history taints what follows it, and so we cannot be sure that we are acting with complete self-determination. That is a harm when colleagues must trust each other to be forthcoming in trying to work through common problems.

Although conflict among employees is often the outcome of such situations, it need not be. Even though they have competing interests, they do, after all, have common interests. They have been deceived and put in an unjust situation—those who are being paid what they deserve as well as those who are not. It is less harmful to be paid what one deserves in a situation where others similarly situated are paid less, but it is still harmful. Those in that situation have more than their fair share of the common resources, and if the disparities become public, they know that in getting what they deserve, they are getting more than each in the group deserves because of the limited resources available, and they ought to feel angry. So there is no reason why the employees need be at odds with each other.

They could band together and press for justice for all of them, arguing for a more equitable distribution of the common resources until the situation can be rectified so all will get what they deserve. They would need a real sense of community to be able to do that, of course, and it would help if the director was willing to fight for their interests.

Of course, the director need not have kept all this a secret. He could have made it clear, from the outset, that he was committed to fairness in pay and that only the budget problems prevented him from providing fairness. And he could have committed himself, publicly, to working to try to increase the budget to ensure fair treatment of all of the employees (see the Code of Ethics 3.07[d] & 3.09[c] & [e]). The ethical problems he has are, to some extent, self-inflicted.[89]

Our goal is not to work through this problem, however, but rather to point out that a great many problems that arise among colleagues may be systemic in this way, not caused by one colleague directly harming another, but by a situation being created in which colleagues have competing interests, and so are at odds with each other, through no fault of their own. We would fail to understand the ethical complexities of such a situation if we looked merely at the conflicts among the colleagues. We rather need to look at what produced those conflicts, as in this case. We are then better able to see what produced the conflicts, and thus what needs to be changed. We can also see that what the colleagues share is that they are in a situation that produced such conflicts and that they can build upon that knowledge to help resolve their common problems.

Relations with Other Professionals

We have examined a number of cases in which social workers have worked with other professionals and have had some difficulties in those relationships because of perceived differences in the weights of their professional judgments. In *Depressed and Ready to Die*, the psychiatrist thought that the patient who did not want chemotherapy was therefore suicidal, and the psychiatrist's judgment was given significantly greater weight than the judgments of the other professionals, including social workers, concerned about the patient. The psychiatrist presumably took the judgment to be one about the patient's mental state, something she thought she was particularly well-qualified to judge. The social workers thought the patient's not wanting chemotherapy was reasonable, given how little it would prolong her life, how painful it would be, and how it would require her to stay in the hospital when she could be home in a more familiar setting as she died. But there was no discussion between the psychiatrist and the social workers. The psychiatrist thought she was right and saw no need, apparently, to try to understand why the social workers thought she might be wrong or to explain to them why she thought she was right.

This case illustrates rather nicely the reasons why professionals in different areas ought to talk with one another, with mutual respect. The social workers were at least as well-positioned as the psychiatrist to judge what would be in the client's best interests, and so their understanding of the client's problems is relevant to deciding what to do. The psychiatrist ought to ask them for their opinion if only because they have information relevant to the client's decision. But the woman was also their client, and because the psychiatrist's decision would make a difference to what they would need to do for the woman, the psychiatrist ought to consult with the social workers out of professional courtesy (see the Code of Ethics 2.03[a]). Their role with the woman would be far different were she forced to have chemotherapy, against her will, than if she were to go home to die in peace.

The case also illustrates rather nicely the two sorts of problems that can arise when the concerns of professionals in different fields overlap.

First, the social workers in this setting do not have the power to overrule the decision of another professional, to ensure that the professional consider their concerns in making a decision, or even to encourage the other professional to talk with them. The structure of the hospital setting was such that the psychiatrist could ignore them completely and make a decision that would stick, whatever the social workers might think. So one problem that arises when professional concerns overlap is that sometimes nothing about the situation requires that the one professional communicate with the other. Or, to put it from the perspective of the social workers in this case, the psychiatrist had complete control over what happened to their client in a situation where, once the psychiatrist's decision was made, their relationship to the client changed. The psychiatrist had power, and they thought they had little, if any (see the Code of Ethics 2.03[b]).

Second, the competencies overlap. Judging what is in the client's best interests is not exclusively a matter for the psychiatrist because social workers are also trained to assess both what a client wants and what is in a client's best interests. Indeed, the social workers may be better positioned than a psychiatrist to determine what is in the client's best interests because they were able to take in far more relevant information and have a much better feel for the life of the client outside the hospital. The psychiatrist may not wish to accept this claimed overlapping of competencies, but if she does not, the social workers are equally entitled to claim they are competent and the psychiatrist is not. What this case sadly illustrates is that sometimes different sorts of professionals working together on a single case do not work together for their single client's best interests.

Consider the following very similar sort of case.

CASE **4.8**

Attention Deficit Disorder

Mark is an eighth grader with an attention deficit disorder. He has a high I.Q., and when he is on medication, he is extremely well-behaved and productive. But he does not now take his medication regularly. He is doing this as a form of rebellion, it seems, and that is what those his age are likely to do. So he is sometimes inattentive and disruptive in class.

His teacher hits Mark on the head with a folded-up paper when he is acting up, and it is not just harmful to him, but embarrassing and ineffective.

Mark told his school social worker, Janet, who is new to the job. She is unsure what to do. She can tell Children's Protective Services, or the principal, or talk to the teacher. Anything she does must be done carefully. She cannot be in the classroom all the time, and "when the door is closed to the classroom, the teacher has the power." But it is clear that the method the teacher has adopted to "control" Mark's behavior is counterproductive.

Janet faces a delicate problem here. As a school social worker, she can only work with students through teachers, and she is not able to be in the classroom all the time to monitor the teacher's behavior. In addition, whatever she does in this case will have an impact on future cases regarding other teachers. As she said in further explaining her problem, "If you alienate teachers, it becomes a very difficult thing to be able to work things through." In addition, as she goes on to point out, "There are a lot of different ways you can abuse a kid without actually being able to be reported on." So she is concerned that trying to help Mark by approaching the teacher may backfire. The teacher may stop hitting Mark, but continue to abuse him in more subtle ways.

All of this suggests that Janet ought to talk to the teacher first and do so very carefully—so as not to antagonize her (see the Code of Ethics 2.03[a]). And we should emphasize Janet's problem. She has to tell another professional that what that professional is doing, as a professional, in her own classroom, is not right.

This case illustrates more clearly than any other we have examined the importance of the fifth step in our method for resolving ethical problems:

> **5.** *Determine how to do what ought to be done in a way that will itself produce more good than harm.*

For it is *how* Jane now proceeds, having decided she ought to talk with the teacher, that will make all of the difference both to how Mark is treated and to how other students Janet may be concerned about will be treated.

Talking with other professionals is always a delicate matter, as we pointed out in *Peers?*, and whenever there are problems in a case involving more than one professional, from the same discipline or from several, we should look to determine if one issue concerns how the professionals approached one another. In *Depressed and Ready to Die*, for instance, it may be that the social work professionals did not proceed to talk with the psychiatrist in a way that would help them with their position. We cannot know from the facts we have.

In this next case, this general issue of how to talk with another professional is even more complicated.

CASE **4.9**

First Grader

Jerry was referred to the school social workers on the second day of school by a teacher who "knew his older brother and had had run-ins with the child's mother and didn't like the way they came out." Mike was the social worker assigned to assess the boy, and although he decided that the boy was a kinesthetic learner, having to touch everything to learn anything, he also decided that with some effort, the boy could be taught to behave as the teacher wanted.

Mike put together a program for the teacher with a check sheet where Jerry would receive points for behaving in certain ways and not behaving in other ways. The teacher filled it in, and he took it home every day. His mother signed off on it, and Jerry's behavior began to come under control.

But the teacher still was not happy because, although Jerry was improving, he was not one-hundred percent better. She wanted him to be certified as emotionally impaired. That would mean that he would then be removed from her classroom.

Mike interviewed the parents, the teacher, and Jerry again, and he found that Jerry was able to develop and maintain relationships, and he did not act out outside the classroom. So he was not emotionally impaired. "Actually," Mike said, "he's a pretty happy little kid."

The teacher was upset. She dropped the program that Mike had developed, and she put Jerry "in a box"—behind a set of room dividers so that he was screened off from the rest of the children. She had the support of the principal, and so finally Mike certified Jerry as emotionally impaired to get him out of the bad situation.

Labeling a child as emotionally impaired is not anything one ought to do lightly. The labeling will stick with him for the rest of his school days—and beyond. So Mike wanted to avoid labeling Jerry if he could. One option would have been to go over the teacher's head to the principal, but that was foreclosed by the principal's siding with the teacher. Another option would be to go over the principal's head to the school district's administration.

Appealing to the administration is not likely to be effective because, just as the principal backed the teacher, so the administration is likely to back the principal. After all, those in the administration can say, "Those best able to know whether this student can be taught in class with the rest of the children are the teacher and the principal, not a social worker who is not in the classroom all the time. So we must stand by their professional judgments." Besides, appealing beyond the principal would likely poison the relations between Mike and the teacher and the principal for any other work with Jerry or other students.

The problem Mike faced was that he either had to work it out with the teacher or label Jerry as emotionally impaired. His failure to work it out with the teacher left him with no good option. What is sad about the case is that although Mike has the expertise to determine what is in Jerry's best interests, he ends up making a judgment about Jerry that he does not agree with. He feels he has no option because the teacher is the one who has the power to determine what to do for, or to, the child, and the teacher will not do what is necessary to further what Mike thinks is in Jerry's best interests (see the Code of Ethics 2.03[b]).

The case illustrates that when things go awry between professionals, there may be no good solution. This seems particularly so when one sort of professional has power and the other has the relevant competence. But the case also illustrates how important it is to work to achieve the ideal of communication that we have set out in this chapter.

The same sort of relation we would want to hold between social work practitioners should hold between professionals from different fields who ought to be working together for a client's benefit. Professionals ought to explain their actions when what they do affects the legitimate concerns of other professionals. They ought to listen to the concerns of those other professionals. And they all ought to strive to work out with each other what is best for their client, giving due weight to all professional judgments.

QUESTIONS

1. The fifth step of the method of tracking harms requires that we consider how it is that we are going to do what we have decided we ought to do. The issue it raises of the manner of our doing what we ought to do applies to the process of reaching a decision as well as to doing what we have decided, through that process, we ought to do. When that process best involves communicating with another person, we need to consider how to speak to the other person. Confronting someone is not the same as inquiring of someone. Examine the ethical aspects of an example from your own experience of a good conversation. How did you each treat the other person? For instance, did you listen? Did you interrupt? Etc.

2. What deference, if any, ought we—ethically—to give education and experience in coming to a decision about what we ought to do? Consider what appears to be the two extremes regarding how Margaret might respond to the boy's therapist in Case 4.1, *Peers?*. She might do exactly what the therapist says, or she might ignore him completely. Could either response be correct? If so, why; if not, why not? What response would be ethically correct? Why?

3. Why ought we to talk a case through with others when we can?

4. Judging whether someone is competent at something can be difficult to do. Take what may seem a simple example such as throwing a ball. Should we judge competence in terms of the effect—the ball gets where it had to go? In terms of manner—the ball is thrown gracefully? In terms of how well the thrower understands what it is to throw a ball—and so is self-conscious about how to improve a throw? Now apply the same model to social work practice. Are we to judge social workers in terms of the results they obtain? The manner in which they go about proceeding with their work? Their capacity to understand why they are doing what they are doing and why things go wrong when they go wrong? Or some combination of all three? And if it is the latter, what counts the most ethically—and why?

5. Someone who was competent may become incompetent through failing to learn new skills, or by becoming too jaded in the use of old skills, and so on. Suggest ways to ensure that social workers are competent and remain competent. It might help here to compare the situation of social workers with that of teachers. How are we to ensure that they are competent and remain competent?

6. In regard to question 5, how are we to ensure that social workers are competent and remain competent without intruding on the privacy of their relationships with their clients? Without insulting them by presuming that they have become incompetent and must prove their competence?

7. A single failure can be explained away as a lapse, but we take a pattern of failures as a sign of a deeper problem. With this in mind, examine Mary's reaction to the judge's decision in Case 1.2, *Dancing a Legal Dance*. Would she be justified in trying to change the system? If so, why? If not, why not?

8. When we are faced with a problematic colleague or employee, as Betsey was in Case 4.4, *Bending over Backwards,* we need to follow a set procedure to ensure that we are treating the colleague or employee fairly. Lay out the steps of the procedure and explain for each of them why they are essential if we are to be ethical.

9. Lay out the four ways in which we can fail to reach agreement even when we communicate well with colleagues. Taking each of the four ways, use cases from the book or from your own experience in which a failure to reach agreement occurred and show how agreement could have been reached. In other words, how do we rectify such failures to reach agreement?

10. As Case 4.5, *Value Judgments*, illustrates, cases of spousal abuse can be particularly difficult for social work colleagues. These are the sorts of cases in which there is likely to be much disagreement about the means to achieving an acceptable end. Lay out the alternative ways we might proceed to handle a case of spousal abuse and then lay out and assess their strengths and weaknesses.

11. One of the problems Betsey had in *Bending over Backwards* was that her counterpart at Jonathan's former agency was not open with her about Jonathan's problems. How can someone like Betsey ensure either that such a situation does not arise or that, if it does, she can double-check? In other words, what procedures might we put in place to ensure that such a consequence as hiring a problematic employee because of a former supervisor's recommendation does not occur?

12. What is harassment? Explain why a single act is sometimes sufficient to justify harassment and sometimes not.

13. Case 4.7, *Lying about Salaries*, illustrates well the problems created by keeping private information about such an agency matter as salaries. But making public such information has its downsides too. Explain what the problems are and then consider ways to prevent or mitigate the problems that arise from disclosure or from confidentiality. For instance, would it help for the director to turn this problem over to the employees, asking for their solution as to how to mitigate the harms arising from the inequities?

14. We have considered cases in which a social worker has had professional relations with a psychiatrist and with teachers. Describe a case—real or imagined—that could arise between a social worker and some other kind of professional and then consider whether the nature of the other professional makes a difference as to how the social worker ought to work to resolve the problem. Does it make any difference, for instance, whether the other professional is a psychiatrist or a teacher? If so, why? If not, why not? What does make a difference, that is, if anything?

5 Agencies

Social work agencies are organizations—like General Motors, or the Red Cross—and they are subject to all of the difficulties and ills that all such organizations are subject to. They differ from most such organizations in that they should have an ethical vision of their role in society and thus an ethical mission to further that vision. They are thus more like the Red Cross than like General Motors. But having an ethical vision and, thus, an ethical mission does not immunize a social work agency from having all of the problems such corporations have, from not being nimble enough to respond well to changing social conditions, to having to downsize in times of financial stress, from being plagued with internal disorders when its practitioners disagree about how to proceed, to having its practitioners badly treated by the director or others in power.

Just as ethical problems arise for those in business when corporations are buffeted by external forces and internal tensions, in other words, ethical problems arise for social work practitioners within agencies for the same reasons. An agency may not have enough funding to support its mission, or those within the agency may disagree about how best to support its mission even when there is enough money, or the agency may be ill-equipped to handle new programs it has come to have, or the director may be unable to work well with the employees, or competing agencies may be tapping the same community resources to support their programs, and so on. The problems that may arise, that is, are numerous.[90]

We have already examined some cases that raise some of the issues of this chapter. Social workers generally work for an agency or in group practices. We examined at length one case of a group practice when we looked at Case 4.5, *Value Judgments*. Although we did not make much of how its being a group practice made a difference to the problem, the case illustrates well how complicated things can become among peers, trying to work together. Case 4.7, *Lying about Salaries*, involved the director of an agency hiring workers of similar skills and experience at different salaries, and although our primary concern there was with the relations among the participants as social workers in those settings, those cases flirted with our primary concern in this chapter, namely, to examine the kinds of ethical problems that arise for social workers because of difficulties in the relations between social workers and the agencies for which they work. The field is so broad, and the issues raised so diverse and complicated, that we can, at best, examine only some representative samples of the kinds of problems that can arise.

One feature of social work agencies that distinguishes them from many other organizations is that social workers are not just employees, but also professionals. Professionals are supposed to have self-determination to make professional decisions. But employees have obligations, and when professionals are employees, conflicts can arise between what they are supposed to do as professionals and what they are obligated to do, or empowered to do, as employees (see the Code of Ethics 3.09[a] & [d]). In the first two sections, we examine some of the ethical issues that arise because of these competing obligations within agencies. As we shall see, this conflict gives rise to issues about social workers' self-determination and integrity.

In the last two sections, we consider some other ethical issues that arise because agencies are organizations. We first consider some of the issues that can arise when an agency's aims are at odds with its capacities. We then consider conflicts that can occur between agencies. Just as corporations may vie for the same customers, agencies may vie for the limited resources a community may offer.

As in previous chapters, we shall make use of the method of tracking harms, with the discussion organized around the method, but two cautions are necessary. First, using the method ought to become second nature, with the steps of the method clicking in when faced with an ethical problem. For instance, we should habitually ask what the goals are before proceeding to determine what harms will result from various courses of action. We have thus begun in this chapter to use the method as though it were a habit, not always explicitly drawing attention to what step is at issue. Second, as we have indicated, each step in the method has its own complications. What it means to *harm* someone, for example, is the subject of many a book and article. We will focus in this chapter on some of the kinds of issues that arise around goals—the subject of the second step in the method.

Maintaining Autonomy

In Case 4.1, *Peers?*, we emphasized how important it is that social work practitioners treat one another professionally, with the courtesy and respect due to one another. Such mutual respect can be difficult enough to attain when the practitioners are peers, but when one is an employee and one the administrator, complications seem almost inevitable.

Professional Autonomy

Any professional working with other professionals must sometimes face the problem of compromising his or her autonomy, or self-determination. Even when all are peers, all professionals working together on a team to further a common end, compromises may have to be made that run counter to what one of the team members might think ought to be done. But this difficulty of compromising autonomy arises most acutely when the professional is ordered to do something by a supervisor that is directly contrary to what would be done if the professional were acting on his or her own. Consider the following case.

CASE **5.1**

Skimming

Nina had been working at an agency for four years when she wrote a grant proposal that was approved and funded. It was one of four given out in the country.

After the grant money began to come in, the director of the agency, her boss, changed his salary in the grant, taking more. He also took part of the money from the grant to pay his secretary, who was not doing work on the grant, put Nina to work on other projects even though, by the grant, she was to work full-time on the grant, and skimmed off, or was about to skim off, part of the money to run the main office.

When Nina complained, she was put on probation and told, "If you do not do what I want here, you will be fired." When she complained to the federal representative for the project, her boss told her not to talk to that person, even though she had to in order to administer the grant and report on it.

The grant had an eight percent leeway built in so that some of what her boss had done could be hidden and perhaps even justified. Nina was not sure. At any rate, apparently as a consequence of her complaint, some governmental officials came and met with her director and local "heavies," as she called them. When they came out, they told her not to worry, that this happens all the time.

Nina and the grant were moved to another agency.

One issue raised by this case concerns who is responsible for the funds. If Nina was incompetent, or had failed to follow the granting agency rules, or had herself skimmed off money for her own purposes, the director of the agency would presumably be legally responsible, as the director of the agency to which the grant had been given. In any event, he would be ethically responsible. The money is to help those the agency is charged with helping, and he has an obligation to ensure that the money is used for the purposes for which it was granted. If Nina had skimmed off money for herself, and the director had done nothing about it, even though he knew about it, we would think he would have failed his ethical duties—to the agency's clients, who are supposed to be served by the money, and to the government, who granted the money in the expectation that it would be properly spent. It is wrong to make someone responsible for something without any control over it, and so Nina's director must have some say over the use of the grant money.

In addition, without further details, we do not know what reasons the director had for diverting money or whether features of the grant proposal might have made that acceptable. Grants usually pay for overhead, and perhaps some of the money was to be used for that purpose. For all of the information we have about the case, Nina may think she is entitled to determine all of the details of how the grant money is spent, and her director may simply be fulfilling his obligation to ensure that the conditions of the grant are fulfilled.

That seems unlikely, but concentrating on that aspect of the case will make us miss the more immediate problem, namely, that he has told her not to talk to the federal representative responsible for the grant. Because Nina has a legal obligation in administering the grant to report to that official, the director's order creates a dilemma for her. Nina cannot both follow the order not to speak to the representative and do what federal law requires her to do in administering the grant. So she has to either talk to the representative, thus not following a direct order of her director, or follow the direct order of her director, thus not fulfilling her legal obligation as the person in charge of the grant.

It is easy enough to track what harms will occur from whichever choice she makes. If she talks to the federal representative, she could be fired, but given that she wrote the grant and presumably best knows how to administer it, the representative is unlikely to let the agency have the grant in her absence. In addition, the director is unlikely to follow through on his threat to fire her. The order he is giving her is an order she cannot follow under federal law. To fire her on such grounds would thus subject him to a lawsuit and, perhaps, to federal penalties.

Of course, he is likely to make her life unhappy in a variety of ways if she talks to the representative for the grant, but not talking to the representative is not a real option for her. She has a legal obligation to report to the representative and will subject herself to legal penalties if she refuses to communicate. She also has an ethical obligation. She has at least some responsibility to make sure that the money she is primarily charged with administering is spent as the grant requires, and so if it were not spent to help the agency's clients, as it is supposed to be spent, she would fail in her ethical obligation if she failed to report that to those providing the funding.[91]

But she not only has legal and ethical obligations to report. She has no practical way not to talk to the federal administrator. The federal representative is bound to ask about the progress of the grant and to ask for a final report, if not intermediate ones, and if Nina fails to respond, the representative will seek her out. Failing to return telephone calls, or saying, "My supervisor says I cannot talk with you," will force the situation out into the open, making it clear to the representative what the director has done. So not talking to the representative is not a real option, and in such a situation, she has to refuse to obey her director's order. Her dilemma is not a difficult one to resolve.

The case raises other issues—about, for instance, whether the federal officials who came to visit properly handled the situation by simply allowing Nina and the grant to move elsewhere, or whether they should have done something more regarding the director—but our concern in this case is that although one can face even the loss of one's position by refusing to do what one's director demands, one is sometimes obligated to do that. Nina is thus obligated to disobey her director's direct order because, among other reasons, she has an obligation to the clients for whom she wrote the grant (see the Code of Ethics 3.09[d]).

This case illustrates how, in an agency setting, social workers are sometimes obligated to do something other than what they may be ordered to do. When one is a professional, being an employee does not mean doing whatever one is told. For one may be told to do something unprofessional, and although one then always has a dilemma, and so, depending upon the circumstances, may have a difficult decision to make, the dilemma is created just because one is a professional and an employee and therefore may have conflicting obligations.

We have considered cases already where such conflicts arise. In Case 1.2, *Dancing a Legal Dance*, it was suggested to Mary that she drop the case of the two abused children. She was told, "You're spending a great deal of time and getting nowhere. We've got other people to serve." In our discussion of the case, we did not pursue what Mary ought to do if that suggestion were to turn into an order, but it is clear that if it did, she would have a dilemma, one complicated by her seeming to be "getting nowhere."

It should not be a surprise that hovering in the background of one of the first cases we considered is this issue of a conflict between what social workers are required to do as employees and what they ought to do as professionals (see the Code of Ethics 309[c]). An agency's interests are not always best served by allowing its employees to do what they feel they are professionally obligated to do. As the spokesperson for the agency in *Dancing a Legal Dance* made clear, the agency has an obligation to serve a number of individuals, even if serving others means giving up on serving those Mary is currently trying to serve.

Wearing Different Hats

Skimming looks at the difficulties that may arise for an employee of an agency because he or she is a professional. But ethical problems can also arise for those who are in supervisory or management positions in an agency, and these problems may not be as obvious as those that occur when a supervisor or administrator tells you to do something that you think you ought not to do as a professional.

Consider the following case in which the director of an agency has ethical problems. These do not arise because her director is telling her to do something that she thinks is professionally wrong. She is the person in charge.

CASE **5.2**

Buying Friendship

June is the director of a local agency and was called by a man, Don, who volunteered to give the agency money to help the needy. She arranged to meet him at a local cafeteria, where they met and had a long conversation about what the agency did, what more money could do, and what he was willing to provide.

June was struck by the man's appearance when he came up to her and, later, by his conversation. He did not look like someone who could afford to give money. "He looked like one of the people we try to help." In conversation, Don seemed somewhat confused, and June thought that he might be somehow mentally impaired, though in a minor way.

After the conversation, June received a check for several hundred dollars in the mail from a local bank, with a note that the contribution was from Don and that a like amount would be provided every month, "in perpetuity."

June was concerned that Don could not afford such a gift and called the bank to check. She was told that the information she requested about his financial status was private and that she would have to ask Don.

Don called June several days later and asked to meet her for lunch. She went to explain to him her concerns. She did, and he brushed them off, saying that he had enough money and that he wanted her to have it.

That lunch was followed by more invitations to lunch and by phone calls, in which Don called June his girlfriend. June went to several lunches with him, explaining that she felt that she owed that to him, but got more and more uncomfortable with going to lunch and with what he apparently expected from the relationship. At the same time, June felt that Don, like one of her clients, seemed to need help and that she might be able to help him.

June is wearing three different hats. She is the head of the agency, collecting money for its operations when she can; she is a social work practitioner, wanting to help Don; and she is being asked to be his friend. She seems not free just to act as the head of the agency, thank him, and leave. Her training and her obligations as a social worker prevent her from doing that, and, besides, it looks as though Don is trying to attach strings to his gift. This last feature of the case would complicate matters for June even if she were not concerned about whether Don was competent to make decisions about giving money to the agency and about whether he could afford as much as he has committed himself to give.

June thus has a complex set of ethical problems. As head of the agency, she is concerned to ensure that it has sufficient funding to fulfil its mission, and any gift is presumably welcome (see the Code of Ethics 3.07[a]). So she has an interest in obtaining the funding Don has promised. But Don looks "like one of the people we try to help," and he wants more than a donor/recipient relationship with June. Each of these concerns raises the issue of whether Don is competent, and so let us begin by exploring how June can explore that issue.

How Don looks is irrelevant except insofar as it raises issues about whether he is competent to make decisions about how to spend whatever money he has and whether he has enough money to be able to afford to give away as much as he has promised. The first issue raises a question about whether June should accept any money from him; the second issue raises a question about whether she should accept as much from him as he has promised. These are distinct questions. Even if June should accept some money from Don, it may be that she should not accept as much as he wants to give or accept that amount "in perpetuity." But even though this second question is distinct from the first, it cannot be answered without first determining whether Don is competent to make any decision about money.

Should June be asking this question? If she had not met Don, there would be no difficulty. Those collecting donations for an agency usually have no obligation to check on whether the person giving money is competent. First, it would be too expensive and time-consuming to do that for everyone who gives money. Second, having a practice of checking would not presume competence, and so would insult some potential donors, who would then be less likely to give money. So such a practice would be counterproductive. It would also be ineffective because those concerned about having their competence checked would soon learn to send in money anonymously. Indeed, if Don had sent a check for the total amount he was going to give, and had not made any other contact, June would have had no reason not to cash it. So getting the money is not the cause of any problems for her.

The problem about competence arises because Don appears to be as needy as those for whom he is giving money to help. But he may be giving precisely for that reason. Knowing what it is like to be in need, he is willing to give what he has to help others who do not have as much. Or he may be wealthy and prefers dressing the way he does. June cannot know without further checking, and what checking she has done indicates that Don has enough money to give away what he has committed to the agency and that the decision to give it away was competently made.

First, although the bank said it could not tell June Don's financial status, it did do as Don had directed it to do, indicating that he had enough money to give the agency several hundred dollars a month in perpetuity. Second, he made a commitment, and he made sure that it would be kept, whatever his mental state may be or may come to be, for he authorized his bank to handle the transaction. So everything he has done regarding the gift indicates competence.

Knowing all that, June may still wonder whether, in giving that amount away, he has left himself enough. Has he made the right judgment in determining how much he can afford? One reason she asks that question is that he wants to be more than a donor. Don has made the wrong judgment about having a relationship with her, calling her his girlfriend, without any encouragement on June's part. That is some sign that he does not understand fully what it is he is doing.

Of course, nothing is wrong with being friends with those you get money from. If a fundraiser were unable to raise money from friends, that would make it hard to raise money for charitable causes. But just as it would be wrong to become friends with people in order to obtain money from them, so it would be wrong to give money to become friends. In the former case, you would be using friendship to gain money, and in the latter case, you would be using money to gain friendship. Both are equally wrong. Friendship is not the kind of relationship that can be bought or sold.

So what is June to do? If we apply the second step in our model and ask about her goals, we find that she seems to have two different goals—the short-term goal of setting boundaries for Don that make it clear to him that she is not his girlfriend, and the long-term goal of obtaining funding for her agency. It is helpful here to apply the third step in our model:

3. *Determine what the harms are of various courses of action. To whom would they occur, what kinds are they, and what are their magnitudes?*

What are June's options, and what are the harms that are likely to flow from each option? It appears that her options are to pursue the former goal or the latter, but perhaps not both. For one issue she seems to face is that pursuing the former goal may set back the latter. If she sets boundaries for Don, he may rescind his gift. He may have no interest in the agency, just an interest in June.

Putting matters that way makes it clearer what June ought to do. It would be ethically wrong for her to maintain a relationship with Don that encourages him to think she is his girlfriend so that he will continue to give the agency money. That would be using Don, treating him as an intelligent instrument for her own ends, to use the phrase we used in Chapter 2 when we examined deontology, not as a person with the capacity for self-determination.

As a social worker, June ought to want to encourage self-determination in general, even among those who are not her clients. In addition, she has no interest in being Don's girlfriend. She thus has good ethical reasons for making it clear to him that she is not his girlfriend. So the first thing she ought to do is to sit down with him and lay out what are to be the boundaries of their relationship.

This may not be as easy as it sounds, of course. Besides the problem that Don may not respond well to whatever she may say, June has the problem of determining what the boundaries ought to be between the agency and a donor. Whatever she tells Don ought to be a general policy, the general way in which relationships are maintained, not a position tailored specifically to Don. The latter would be unfair. But June may not have ever thought through the issue before, and thinking it through may raise some issues that may cause particular problems because of this case. For instance, should it be general policy to keep donors informed of how the agency is doing and how donations are spent? June might hesitate to have such a policy because that would mean she must continue to have contact with Don, but such a policy might encourage additional donations, and she should not design a policy for the agency that is responsive to the problems she is having with Don, but that is harmful to the agency's long-term goals. She has to be careful not to let her short-term goals undermine her long-term goals for the agency.

In sitting down with Don and talking through the boundaries of the donor/recipient relationship, June not only risks losing the money he has promised to give the agency. She risks losing contact with Don, and because she is concerned about him, she may hesitate in trying to clarify their relationship. But June is the wrong person to be helping him. She cannot both take his money and treat him as a client whom the agency is helping. She cannot wear both of those hats at the same time because doing that creates just the sort of problem she now has.

Because June is concerned about Don, she might arrange some way to help him that does not involve her. She might suggest that he do volunteer work with the elderly, for instance, perhaps with some other agency (in which case she should inform the head of that agency of the problems she is having). She might tell him that one way he might give would be to give of himself, and she could then direct him to a number of different voluntary activities.

If she sets boundaries for Don and encourages him to make contact with someone else (who would presumably help him if it turns out he needs help), June risks losing the funding, but will have done all she can do ethically.

Buying Friendship illustrates how complicated even taking money can be from someone willing to give it. Just as employees readily have ethical problems because they are professionals who may have competing obligations, so managers and agency directors readily have ethical problems because they often wear more than one hat. What it seems someone ought to do as the director of an agency may conflict with what he or she ought to do as a social work practitioner. It is not easy being the head of an agency.

We saw that at the end of the last chapter when we examined Case 4.7, *Lying about Salaries*. Both that case and *Buying Friendship* raise issues about the appropriate roles that directors and others in supervisory positions ought to play in agencies. *Buying Friendship* points out that a source of ethical problems can occur when the professional obligations one has as a social work practitioner conflict with the obligations of one's role as a director within an agency.

Integrity and Agency Policies

Internal Ethical Problems

Along with most of the cases we have considered so far, *Skimming* and *Buying Friendship* illustrate that it is not easy being a social work practitioner. The very nature of the position guarantees conflicts that may not be possible to resolve. June's problems are what we may call *internal to the profession* (see the Code of Ethics 1.06[a] & [b]). She has these problems because, given the position she holds, some cases will create conflicts of interest, and she will have such conflicts as long as she remains in that position. They are built into it. Such conflicts can sometimes be intractable, incapable, that is, of being resolved in any satisfactory way.

A comparison may help. Physicians are obligated to care for their patients, but they also must learn to look at bodies without becoming embarrassed or giggling. They must look at them as objects. The last thing we would want is that we disrobe for an examination and have our physician giggle at the sight of us. We want what we call a professional demeanor in our physician, and that means that our physician is to view us as a mechanism, like a bicycle that seems not to be working properly. But caring for us requires not looking at us as objects, but as persons who suffer and need sympathy and care. These two requirements—that we be looked upon as objects and that we be treated as persons who suffer—are both imposed on physicians, and so are internal to the profession, but are in tension with each other. It is not easy, and perhaps not possible, to look at people as objects while also being sympathetic to their plight as suffering individuals.

Just so, the very nature of the position that social workers are in can create ethical tensions, seeming to require that the practitioner act in incompatible ways at the same time. Nina's problem in *Skimming* is that she is both an employee of the agency and a recipient of a grant, and that position creates the possibility of ethical problems because, as we saw, her director may order her to do something she cannot do as a grant recipient (see the Code of Ethics 3.09[a], [c] & [d] & 4.04).

Many of the cases we have examined raise ethical issues that are internal in this way to the profession. In Case 1.1, *The Death of a Baby*, Deborah had an obligation to report what she knew about the causes of the baby's death because she was obligated, as a social work practitioner, to report suspected child abuse. But she also had an obligation, as a social work practitioner, to provide care and support for the family of the baby. They were her clients, had suffered greatly already, and would suffer even more were she to report what she knew.

External Ethical Problems

Such internal ethical issues are difficult enough, but, unfortunately, professionals have other kinds of ethical problems as well. Social workers are persons, with beliefs and commitments, and they may find that what they are sometimes obligated to do as social workers is in conflict with what they believe, as individuals, they ought to do. We call these conflicts *external ethical problems* because they are not dependent upon what it is to be a social worker, but upon a conflict between what being a social worker requires and what the particular individual who is a social worker believes.[92]

Another comparison may help. If physicians who work with pregnant women were obligated to provide all legally permissible medical procedures, then those who believe that abortion is wrong would have external ethical problems. For they would be obligated to provide abortions because abortions are permissible medical procedures. They would thus be obligated to do what they believe is ethically wrong. This is not an ethical problem internal to medicine because nothing about being a physician requires that one must believe that abortion is ethically wrong. A physician who came to believe that abortions are ethically permissible would cease to have this ethical problem and yet would not be any less a physician. This sort of ethical problem is thus what we call external to the profession.

As this example makes clear, some external ethical problems may be extremely difficult for practitioners. We need only imagine a physician deeply opposed to abortions who is required to provide them. Such a problem can be especially difficult because it seems that practitioners are forced to choose between their careers and their integrity as ethical persons. Consider the following case.

CASE **5.3**

A Pacifist

Helen works for an agency that has a contract with a company with significant defense contracts. She is a pacifist, but she was asked to coordinate the agency's work with the company. When Helen told her supervisor she did not want to have anything to do with this company, her supervisor told her that if she were serious in this, there was a real possibility she would be out of work. Besides, the supervisor added, it is not the company she is helping, but its employees.

The agency's general mission is to help workers who are too poor to afford purchasing help on their own, but the workers of this company are very well paid. So the contract departs from the agency's mission. On the other hand, the contract is lucrative, and, Helen tells herself, the profits allow the agency to further its mission. It is "taking from the rich to give to the poor." Besides, she thinks, if anyone needs help, those working in the military-industrial complex do.

Yet, Helen realizes, if she is successful in counseling them, she may make them more productive and thus herself be supporting the military-industrial complex. On the other hand, she thinks she may be counseling those who are having difficulty with the system at the company to leave the company. In addition, although the agency is taking from this particular corporation to help the poor, she thinks that, in general, the support we give the military-industrial complex takes away from what we could do for the poor.

Helen and her supervisor worked out a compromise in which she works with the employees, but is not the coordinator for the agency and the company.

The issues in this case could be raised in a variety of ways. The agency you work for might have a contract with a waste management firm not known for its commitment to the environment when you are deeply committed to cleaning it up, or with a governmental agency whose policies you disagree with, or with a private, nonprofit public interest group that is pushing for regulatory changes that you judge would harm those your agency is committed to helping. We need to sort out two different issues that such cases raise.

First, ought you to help those who may harm your interests as a social worker? Working for a public interest group opposed to any form of welfare would seem to raise this issue most sharply because it seems that part of what it is to be a social worker is that one is committed to advocating for a social safety net and to assisting the poor and oppressed to have their basic needs met (see the Code of Ethics 6.01).

Second, ought you to help those whose policies you oppose, not as a social worker, but as an individual? Some social workers may think it is essential that we have a strong defense and others may oppose war. It is not necessary, however, in order to be a social worker, that one be a pacifist any more than it is necessary that one think abortions are wrong to be a physician.[93]

Neither of these two questions is easy, but they are different questions. The first raises an issue about what it is to be a social worker. To determine what one ought to do, one would have to determine, among other things, whether it is an essential commitment of social work, and thus of social workers, that they support the social welfare system and serve the poor and oppressed. And then one would have to determine whether it is essential, to be a social worker, that one help others—such as those opposed to any form of welfare—irrespective of what you may believe about what you are doing. This first question is about something internal to the profession, that is.

The second question concerns a personal belief of the social worker, one a person need not hold to be a social worker. So that question is about something external to the profession. Ought one to do something as a professional that one would not do as an individual?[94]

We shall concentrate on this second question here, but it is no easier than the first, and neither is made easier for someone, such as Helen, who risks being fired if she does not answer it the way her agency wants her to. Unlike Nina in *Skimming*, who had no good reason to fear that she would be fired despite being told she would be fired if she disobeyed orders, Helen may be fired if she does not work with the company. So she has a good practical reason to work with the company. But that does not settle the ethical issue of whether she ought to work with the company, despite her personal beliefs.

As she recognizes, that issue is not simply one of good versus evil. There are benefits of working with the company. She is helping the employees, and she is earning money for the agency that can be spent on others the agency is charged to help and would have difficulty helping without the lucrative contract with the company. Whatever her personal beliefs, these benefits would occur.

On the other hand, she is not sure, as she admits, that she would be completely unbiased in the way she would help those employees who are having trouble in the company (see the Code of Ethics 1.06[a]). She says she is inclined to counsel them to get out of the system. Her ethical belief may make her less effective as a social work practitioner, that is, being less objective about what those she is counseling really need. So that is a reason for not helping, even if she became convinced she ought to.

So what ought she to do? She chose to compromise, agreeing to work with the company's employees without serving as the agency's coordinator with the company. Presumably she thought that being the official representative of the agency to the company would compromise her commitment to pacifism too much, and her agency agreed that she need not be the coordinator. So the dilemma she faced was not as stark as it could have been. She was not faced with either working with the company or being fired. She and her director found a way for her to work with the company in working with the employees.

But this choice is not without its downside. She is working with the company, and so to some degree she is supporting the military-industrial complex she opposes. She may help the workers become more productive, and by helping the workers, she may help the company make a better showing and justify even more governmental spending on the military rather than for the poor. So, someone might object, she cannot be a real pacifist and still work with employees of the military-industrial complex. She has rather compromised her moral integrity, it might be claimed.

A second problem arises because it is difficult for any institution, even if it is a social work agency, to let its employees pick and choose which contracts to work on and which ones to refuse. Besides the complications of monitoring such a policy to ensure that the objections to working on a contract are based on conscience, and not convenience, the agency would be giving its employees a veto over what those in charge of the agency have judged is in its best interests. Organizing an agency to allow for this sort of conscientious objection on the part of employees may work, but as in all structures that require consultation and agreement, it would take more time and energy than the usual hierarchical arrangements in which workers are assigned responsibilities. Helen was able to reach a compromise, that is, because her agency permitted it, but such a compromise is not always possible.

It is clear that Helen is herself torn about what to do, recognizing, on the one hand, that if she works at all with the company or its employees, she will harm the ethical purity of her position and, on the other, that the agency has good reasons for its contract with the company and that some of its employees do need the help that she is able to give. The compromise she chose is one way through these conflicts.

Such compromises tend to be the norm when we are faced with competing ethical demands that are so evenly matched, with the harms and benefits so balanced, that no one option seems obviously better than the other. We choose a way to satisfy as many of the demands as we can, without undue harm.

If Helen's problem were internal to the profession, we could say more about whether she did the right thing. We could ask whether the competing ethical demands are both essential to social work, whether one or the other better realizes social work ideals, and so on. But because Helen's problem is an external ethical problem, arising because of a belief she has about pacifism that need not be shared by other social workers, the ultimate decision must be hers. This is not the trivial claim that those who face ethical problems must make the moral choice, but the claim that the person affected is best positioned to put the proper ethical weight on personal moral beliefs.

It is *Helen's* ethical integrity that may be denied, or compromised, or upheld—depending upon whether she decides to act as the agency's coordinator with the company, decides to work with the employees without being coordinator, or refuses to have anything to do with the company or its employees. It is not her ethical integrity as a social worker that is at issue, but her ethical integrity as a person who happens to be a social worker. Determining what she ought to do does not mean, as with a problem internal to social work, balancing competing social work demands, but rather balancing what a social worker ought to do with what Helen ought to do. And so, even with more understanding of the case, an outsider may not be able to assess well her choice. Although we may be able to determine what a social worker ought to do, if we had an ethical problem internal to social work, we may not be able to determine what Helen ought to do. The best we can do is to try to do what the first step of our method tells us we ought to do, namely, reconstruct what would justify one of her choices rather than another. It may turn out, as we do that, that we can see that some choices are not good choices, but it also may turn out, as it seems to have turned out in this case, that we cannot be sure whether the right choice was made or not.

So one difference we can discover between the sorts of ethical problems we have looked at so far and the external ethical problems we are examining in this section is that in regard to the latter sort of cases, we cannot as readily assess the decisions that practitioners make. This is a significant difference if only because some believe that no one can ever tell what someone else ought to do. What they say is truer of *A Pacifist* and other such cases than it is of the sorts of cases that raise internal ethical problems.

To take the simplest such cases, the ones that cause no problems, social workers ought not to lie to their clients, for instance, or cheat their colleagues, or steal from their agencies. That is, they ought not to do these things without an overwhelming ethical reason, something that could ethically justify doing what is prima facie so wrong. Thus, to take a clear case, a practitioner might justify lying to a client to protect the client's life. The harm caused by the lie would be offset by the greater good caused by it.

Even in harder cases, where there is an ethical dilemma, or when the case is problematic in some way, we can often determine what a social worker ought or ought not to do. We have seen this in case after case. Thus, in *Doing What the Judge Orders*, whatever else John ought to have done, he ought to have talked with Al about the risks of unprotected sex when one may be HIV-positive. Even in cases where it is not clear what the social worker ought to do, we can go a long way toward getting clarity—laying out what being a social worker ethically requires, getting clear on what the options really are, and understanding more clearly why a decision is not clear.

What we discover in *A Pacifist*, however, is that we cannot be sure what Helen ought to do. The reason for that is that we cannot put an ethical weight on the moral values she holds. We cannot be sure how deeply she is committed to pacifism or what sorts of compromises she can make and still maintain her integrity. For they are compromises she must make not as a social worker, but as a person.

Such external ethical problems are shared by all of the professions, as the example from medicine with which we began this section makes clear. For it is always the case that the demands of our profession or our employer may run counter to what we believe we ought to do as individuals. A lawyer may feel sympathetic to a client's plight, but good legal practice requires hard questioning, the sort of unsympathetic querying that an opposing lawyer is likely to dish out when the client is on the witness stand. A lawyer's job requires knowing a client's answers to such queries, the better to defend against them, and being sympathetic may harm the client rather than help because the lawyer, and the client, may be less prepared to respond to unsympathetic questions of the opposing lawyer. So what is required of lawyers in preparing for a case may run directly counter to what they feel they ought to do as individuals.

Thus, to summarize, this sort of conflict raises two different ethical problems for a professional. The first problem is that the professional may be obligated to do something he or she would not do as an individual. This obligation may arise either from what it is that social workers, as social workers, are required to do or from what a social worker, as an employee, is required to do. The latter is Helen's problem in *A Pacifist*. The other problem is that being a professional may require a character and an attitude that run counter, or are at least in tension with, what one thinks one ought to be as an ethical individual.

Having an Ethical Character

The character we display, the attitude we have, and the emotions we feel are as important as what it is we do. Indeed, to be accurate, they are part and parcel of what we do. If a person were to run down a child, by accident, as the child darted between parked cars, we would be aghast if all he or she did was say to the family, "Oh, I'm sorry." What is ethically required in such a situation is that one *be* sorry and so evince all of the emotions, and the appropriate attitude, of someone who is truly sorry.[95] Sometimes, indeed, the emotional response one gives is far more important ethically than whatever it is one says. Someone in deep pain may not hear you well, but can feel the sympathetic hug.

This concern about how we ought to do what we have determined we ought to do runs throughout the cases we have examined. The guide to ethical decision making is divided into two parts, with parts 1 through 4 telling us how we are to determine what to do, while part 5 says:

> **5.** *Determine how to do what you have determined ought to be done and do it in a way that will itself produce more good than harm.*

The point of step 5 is that it is not enough to determine what to do. We also need to determine how to do what we have decided we ought to do.

But how we act is reflective of our character, and in *A Pacifist*, Helen has an ethical problem because her agency is asking her to act against her character. It is, as we said, her ethical integrity that may be denied, or compromised, or upheld—depending upon what she decides to do and how she decides to do it. She must not only decide what to do, but both go about deciding what to do and then do it in ways that reflect her sense of herself. For instance, threatening her manager for putting her in such a situation would not seem to be the right response for someone committed to pacifism.

We have seen this sort of issue before. In *Peers?*, for example, what Margaret ought to do is to talk with Malik, the social worker for the boy who sexually abused his sister. Malik wants to put the boy back into the family; Margaret thinks that is a mistake. In describing how she would meet Malik, Margaret said she would have to "confront" him, but if she were to confront him, then she and he are not likely to be able to talk through the problem they have of determining what is in the best interests of her client and his. What turns out to be crucial in that case is not just Margaret's deciding what to do, but determining *how* to do what she ought to do. Going about talking to Malik in the wrong way is likely to set back the interests of her client, not advance them. One of the disturbing aspects of the case is that Margaret thinks she must confront Malik. That she thinks that is her only choice tells us more about her than anything about the situation. It looks to be a character flaw that she seems unable to see other less harmful alternatives.

In both *Peers?* and *A Pacifist*, as well as in the other cases we have examined, it is essential to have the right emotional response and the right attitude. We do not mean to suggest that one ought to fake these aspects, as though one could take on one character or another as the situation warrants, or that one ought to work to tailor one's emotional response and attitude to the situation at hand. The point is rather that one ought to strive to be an ethical person and that being an ethical person requires more than deciding what is right. It requires doing what is right, and doing what is right requires having the right emotional response and the right attitude, both of which come from having the appropriate character. We ought to strive to have an ethical character, that is, and then doing what is right will come from our character, with the appropriate emotions and the right attitude.[96]

Professional Character Traits

Striving to become ethical is a lifelong pursuit, and one feature we need to attend to if we are fully to appreciate how difficult it can be to be an ethical professional is that the sort of character one has to develop, or comes to develop, as a professional may be at odds with the sort of character one ought to develop as an ethical person. The alternatives in that statement—has to develop, or comes to develop—are important. The problems may arise because of some character traits the profession itself either requires or encourages. Let us briefly consider each of these in turn.

  a. As we saw, empathy may get in a lawyer's way of seeing the kinds of problems with the case that an opposing lawyer would exploit. A lawyer has a professional obligation not to be too empathic or kind-hearted. But a lawyer's manner, honed in an office and in court, ill serves the lawyer with family and friends. A person may find it difficult to integrate the professional attitude necessary to be successful as a lawyer with the sorts of attitudes appropriate for friendship and intimacy. The traits one has to develop to be successful in a particular profession, in other words, may be just the traits one does not want in other, nonprofessional relations.[97]

Social work practitioners might seem not to have this problem. After all, the traits we most value in our personal lives are just the traits that social workers must hone in their professional lives into skills—the ability to listen well to what others are saying, the capacity to empathize with the problems others have, the ability to understand individuals in their social contexts, and so on. As the Code of Ethics says, social workers' "primary goal is to help people in need and to address social problems," and they are obligated to "increase their professional knowledge and skills and to apply them in practice" (Code, Ethical Principles). But, as it turns out, social workers are not immune from this common professional problem of integrating their professional and personal lives. It is just that they generally seem to have the opposite sort of problem that lawyers, for instance, seem to have.

In Case 5.2, *Buying Friendship,* June felt that she could not just take the money that Don offered and leave. Her difficulties arose in part because she seemed unable to act only as the director of an agency concerned with raising money. She wanted to help Don, and it was her wanting to help him, along with wanting to obtain his donation, that caused her problems. Of course, helping Don may have been the right thing to do. But June would not have had such an obvious problem if she had not been committed to helping others. Similarly, in *Relapsing,* we will fail to understand Corliss's problems in trying to help Cynthia if we do not see that Corliss thought Cynthia needed tough love to help her overcome her problems with alcohol and that being tough in that way, even for a good end, can be difficult for someone whose natural response may be to be empathic and caring. Being empathic and caring while setting clear limits is a real skill that can be difficult to achieve.

b. Professionals may also come to develop character traits in their profession that make it difficult for them to be as fully professional as they ought to be. It is a common problem some nurses have who must care for those who are terminally ill. It is difficult to lose patients, and giving a full commitment of love and caring for patient after patient, all of whom die, can carry a heavy toll. A nurse quite predictably may become less willing to give so much when so much is lost, and yet that response, however natural it may be, makes the nurse less able as a nurse. Terminally ill patients certainly need at least as much as those who are going to recover and perhaps more, and the hundredth terminally ill patient is in as much need as the first. It sounds paradoxical, but it is true that the very practice of the traits that most mark a professional may, in certain circumstances, make the professional less able to practice those traits.

Social workers may become as burnt out as nurses become as they try to maneuver through the bureaucracy or as they listen to more complaints from clients. They may find it difficult to maintain the capacity for optimism in the face of what often appear to be intractable bureaucratic hurdles over which they have little control, and they may find it hard to listen empathically to the same client who has failed, yet again, to do what he or she was told they had to do in order to continue to get support. The very nature of the position that social workers find themselves in will often complicate, and may well compromise, their capacity to realize the ideals of the profession. We see, once again, that it is not easy being a social worker.

Agency Goals

Unfortunately, although we have illustrated this truth about how difficult it is to be a social worker in many different ways, we have not exhausted the possibilities. In the second step of our method, we are to:

> **2.** *Determine what goals the participants had and what means they thought would achieve those goals; then determine what goals ought to be achieved and determine what means are best for achieving those goals.*

This admonition turns out to be far more complicated than it may appear. When we examined Case 1.4, *Doing What the Judge Orders,* we were concerned with whether what the social worker, John, did made sense, given what his goals were. We decided that John's convincing a judge to have Al tested for HIV made no sense if John was concerned to ensure the safety of the family Al was living with and Al's alleged girlfriend. We were looking in that case only at the goals of one person, but limiting ourselves to determining the consistency and sense of the goals of one person can become even more complicated when, as we saw in Case 5.2, *Buying Friendship,* that person has one set of goals wearing one hat and another set wearing another.

We can readily see the progression up the ladder of complications. When we examine the goals of all of the participants to an ethical problem, we then not only have to examine the consistency and sense of each participant's goals, but also the consistency and sense of the set of goals of all the participants. And when one of the participants to an ethical problem is the agency for which one works, or an external agency or company whose policies and goals directly affect one's work, so that we are not just weighing against one another the competing goals of relatively equally situated participants, things get even more complicated. We shall consider some of those complications in this section.

Discretion and Benign Neglect

As we have seen, an agency's need for funding can cause problems for its director, but it can also cause problems for its employees. Consider in this regard the following case.

CASE **5.4**

Money or Care?

The state permits up to six children per foster home. The agency that places the children gets administrative money for each child placed—over $50,000 per foster home if the home takes in as many children as the state permits.

José is head of an agency charged, among other things, with placing children in foster homes. The money the agency makes from the placement that is not used for the placement itself or for training the foster parents is used to support other agency activities. Because the agency places a great many children, it makes a great deal of money that way and is able to support a wide variety of other programs for the poor.

The problems that the foster parents face with the children can be remedied if they are the result of lack of proper training, and in the worst of cases, children are taken from the home. But there are alway going to be marginal cases, "gray areas," José says, and the agency has a new problem because the kinds of kids it is now getting have more serious problems and are more difficult to care for.

The agency has solved that problem of what to do with cases that fall into the "gray areas" through "benign neglect," preferring to assume that the problems are not serious enough for the child to be taken out of the home. But this has caused problems for the social work practitioners who must work with the families. These problems cannot be resolved through training, and the practitioner can only tell the families that they must deal with them somehow.

The difficulty that some kids have more problems now is more serious, and the agency has responded by cutting the number of children it places in a foster home from six to four. That is better for the children, and better for the foster family too—except that the family is getting less funding and so is the agency. Indeed, the agency's program is now losing money because of the way it feels it must handle this new difficulty.

José certainly has a problem because he is the director of the agency and the agency should at least break even in the program. But those who work for the agency in the homes have problems too. They are to judge whether the situation is clear or gray, and so the agency's policy gives them discretion. And when they judge that extra training of the parents will be helpful in alleviating the problem, they are permitted to give that. But when the problem is in a gray area, where it is not clear quite what would work, if anything, they are to do nothing, neglecting it, with the hope that the neglect will cause no harm. They are not permitted to explore alternative ways of solving the problem such as changing the mix of children, or working more with the children, or providing therapy for the family, the children, and the parents together. Such exploration can be expensive, as can such potential remedies, and the agency has decided, as a matter of policy, not to spend the money for that. Presumably if a practitioner were always to judge that situations need correcting, he or she would be told to intervene less or would be put into some other program. The clear intent of the policy is to save money, consistent with the agency's mission of helping those children it can clearly determine need help.[98]

Such situations are typical for any agency. An agency must choose to maximize funding while providing the best service it can to those it is supposed to help. It would be as inappropriate for an agency to provide the best service it can without regard to any funding problems as it would be for it to try to maximize its funding without any regard to the service it provides (see the Code of Ethics 3.07[a] & [b]). Making either choice would cause harm to the agency's mission of helping those in need.

Because there are always going to be problems in placing children in foster homes, there will always be occasions for spending more money. The agency is likely to run out of money if it responds to every minor problem, and, in any event, it will be spending money for marginal gains in that program when it could be spending those funds for clearer victories in other programs. Yet if the agency decides to maximize its funding by not responding to *any* such problems, even clear ones, it will countenance and encourage situations in which real harm will occur to those in its charge (see the Code of Ethics 3.07[b]). In *Money or Care?*, the agency's policy of "benign neglect" in gray areas is presumably meant to be a middle ground, one that minimizes the harms while maximizing the benefits to those the agency is supposed to help (see the Code of Ethics 6.04[a]).

But this policy will cause difficulties for the agency's practitioners working with the foster homes. It gives them discretion without guidance about how to respond to some hard cases. They may thus be unsure what to do in some cases, and may make the wrong judgment, and the entire program may end up running in an inconsistent manner because the individual practitioners respond in different ways to the same sort of unclear problem.

For instance, what is a practitioner to do in a gray area if the likelihood of any harm occurring seems small, but the kind of harm, or the amount of harm, that could occur is great? We had such a situation in *Doing What the Judge Orders.* Al's foster family was potentially at risk of getting AIDS since Al may have been HIV-positive. The likelihood of getting AIDS in such a situation is small, but the harm caused is immense, especially when it is multiplied by the number of people in the foster family. Since the likelihood of such harm occurring may be small, a practitioner may presume that nothing need be done, but because the magnitude of the harm that could occur is great, another practitioner may presume that something should be done. A policy giving discretion in such a gray area gives no guidance.

Someone may respond to the problem in *Money or Care?* by arguing that given its charge to provide care for the children, the agency has an obligation to ensure that they are not harmed in any serious way and so has an obligation to intervene when the potential harm is great or the kind of harm is serious, even if the likelihood of such harm occurring is small. For the same reason, the argument would continue, it has an obligation to try to ensure that the families not be harmed in the same sort of situation. Minimizing the potential harm to the children and families is presumably one consideration in the agency's reducing the number of children it places in a home to four, but it should also be a stated consideration in its policy of benign neglect.

Of course, that would cost more money. Indeed, whatever policy is adopted will reflect a tradeoff between financial considerations and the potential benefits and harms to the agency's clients. Put another way, the agency's mission requires that it maximize both its financial resources and the help it gives to those in need, and these two goals are always in tension, given the limited resources that any social work agency has.

Clarity of Goals and Professional Discretion

If the agency comes to have a clearer policy, that may not solve a social worker's problems. It may even be the source of problems. Consider the following case in which the relevant institution—a hospital in this case—has adopted a clear policy, but one that provides for no discretion on the part of its social work practitioners and one that also may cause great harm:

CASE **5.5**

Limited Number of Visits

Pat is a social work practitioner in a hospital who helps clients with alcohol and drug problems. Most of her clients are covered by health insurance, but the insurance companies are demanding full records—partly in order to be sure that its clients are being served by properly accredited professionals and partly because, Pat thinks, "if they can find any little thing that doesn't look right to them, they can disallow the claim. So they are going to try to get as much information as possible."

But it is not in Pat's clients' best interests to have information that they are being treated for drug dependency or alcoholism getting back to their employers or even to the insurance companies. She had a client who gave permission for his insurance company to look at his files, but was later denied life insurance by the company because, it said, alcoholics die younger. The insurance company found out from the records the client released that he was in treatment for alcoholism. In addition, an employer can make life difficult for those of its employees it knows have been in treatment for drug dependency or alcoholism.

So one of Pat's problems is that she is caught in the middle, especially if the client refuses to give permission for her to reveal the complete record. She also thinks it is a mistake for clients to give her permission to reveal their records. She thinks that information ought to remain confidential. But if clients do ask her to send their records on to their health insurance companies and a company then refuses payment, the hospital will have to pick up the cost for those clients who cannot pay for the therapy themselves.

One consequence of this problem is that the hospital has dropped its outpatient program. Too many of the clients in that program were being supported by the hospital. It also limited the number of sessions for those in therapy in the hospital to ten unless the hospital can determine ahead-of-time that they will be covered by insurance or are able to pay their own way.

If Pat's analysis is correct that the insurance companies are seeking as much information as they can so as to find something that allows them to disallow an otherwise acceptable claim, they are acting unethically—though we may understand, and lament, the economic imperatives that are driving their attempts to disallow claims.[99] Insurance companies are for-profit organizations, and with nothing to constrain their seeking profits wherever profits can be found, increasing the bottom line is the primary aim, driving everything the company does. Managed care is under the same economic imperative, and we are witnessing the same driving force and its consequences for the sick and poor.[100]

The hospital's response to the problem seems driven in part by that aim as well. After all, it closed the outpatient program, and it has put a limit on the number of visits a client is permitted when the hospital must pick up the bill. But that the hospital is willing to pay for ten visits means that it is also not acting just to increase its profits. It is giving away up to ten visits and so, to that extent, is acting as a charitable organization, a not-for-profit institution that is willing to take a loss to provide a needed service. It has chosen ten presumably as a compromise to provide a service while keeping its losses down.

Both the insurance company's activities and the hospital's policy cause Pat problems, and they are connected in at least one way. Were she to encourage her clients not to give the insurance companies what they want, then (a) those who were unable to afford to pay for the sessions themselves would cost the hospital, and (b) they would only be entitled to ten sessions. Each of these consequences causes problems.

   a. Pat works for the hospital, and so, if she were to suggest that her clients not have their insurance companies pay, she is costing her employer money—putting at risk, among other things, its ability to serve other clients she is committed to serve, as the hospital's dropping its outpatient program makes clear. So the advice she thinks she ought to give her clients about how to handle the insurance companies is not cost-free. Either the clients will be asked to pay, or the hospital will pay for some sessions if the clients cannot, or, as she discovered, she will not be able to serve any of those who could only use the outpatient service. Besides harming her professional concerns, advising her clients not to give the information requested by the insurance companies also may harm her personal interests because the hospital is not likely to be pleased with her advising clients not to have their bills paid. Even her own position may be at risk because as the hospital's costs mount, it will need to cut back, perhaps by cutting staff.

   b. The hospital's limiting the number of visits to ten when there is no funding, however charitable that may be, constrains what Pat may judge to be the right treatment for particular clients. Some clients may need fewer than ten sessions, but others may need significantly more. Setting a limit of ten may seem to be a compromise between the hospital's imperatives of obtaining sufficient funding to provide services and providing free services when the need is great, but it draws a line that appears relatively arbitrary—why not twelve, or eight? More importantly, the policy prevents Pat and other social work practitioners in the hospital from providing for particular clients what they may judge is in the clients' best interests. Drawing a line limits Pat's autonomy as a social work professional (see the Code of Ethics 1.01 & 6.04). The hospital is saying that given its overarching need to cut costs, it wants to ensure that Pat's judgments about what is in the best interests of her clients are also consistent with the hospital's interests.

So the insurance companies' insistence on complete information from her clients creates a complex set of difficult ethical dilemmas for Pat. On the one hand, if she counsels her clients not to provide that information, they will be harmed, she may be harmed, the hospital will be harmed, and unclear numbers of other needy individuals will be harmed because they will not be served. On the other hand, if she counsels her clients to provide the information, they may be harmed. She could provide no advice, letting her clients do as they wish, but her choice is not ethically neutral. It is a choice between competing ethical demands. She knows what harm can come from either choice, and not giving advice means not informing her clients (see Code 107[d]). She would then be responsible for their making decisions that may vitally affect their interests without full information, without, that is, informed consent.

Of course, part of Pat's problem arises because of the hospital's response to the situation. In the interests of economy, it has decided on a clear policy—a limit of ten visits per client—that both constrains her professional judgment as a social work practitioner and may cause harm to some of her clients because ten visits may not be sufficient to help them with their problems. That such a policy is the usual way in which hospitals, for example, handle these sorts of situations does not make Pat's problem any less difficult.[101]

An additional source of problems for Pat is that she is the one in the middle, acting as a go-between for the insurance companies. She is to ask the clients for permission to release the information, and she is then to send it on to the insurance companies.

Pat's options to try to resolve these problems are relatively limited. She can try to change the policy of the insurance companies (see the Code of Ethics 6.04[a]). That would presumably mean working at the state level to change the relevant legislation. She can try to change the hospital's policy. The Code of Ethics obligates social workers not to "allow an employing organization's policies, procedures, regulations, or administrative orders to interfere with their ethical practice of social work" (3.09[d]). Pat thus has an obligation to work within her organization to convince it either that it is not going to cost any more to give the social work practitioners the power to make judgments about how many visits are needed for each client or that, if it is going to cost more, the cost is worth it to serve clients well. Obviously, what ought to matter in setting a policy is not just cost, but what is ethical.

Or she might try to change her position between the insurance companies and the clients. In acting as a go-between, she is effectively working for the insurance companies. She could set up a process whereby she routinely sends on to insurance companies the information she thinks is appropriate and sufficient to justify payment, having obtained the clients' informed consent to do that, and she could deflect all further inquiries by telling the companies they will have to contact the clients directly to get their permission. Obtaining that permission from the clients, without her help, may cost the insurance companies enough that they will be deterred from seeking more information, at least in every case. But she would still be sharing private information with the insurance companies, and she would still be caught in the middle with the additional problem of having no clear way to determine what information to send and what to keep and how private the information she sends will remain.

   Another option might be to provide the hospital administration and the insurance companies any research that provides evidence for the number of sessions needed for particular problems (see the Code of Ethics 5.02[c]). Or, if Pat thinks the policy cannot be changed, she might advocate on a case-by-case basis for each client—a time-consuming task.

   How successful any of these initiatives may be is unclear. But there seem to be no other ways out of the complex ethical dilemmas that Pat faces, and yet, as we have just seen, those solutions are as constrained by external forces, not within her control, as her professional judgment is constrained by the hospital's rule of limiting visits to no more than ten. Unlike *Skimming*, where Nina could do something to salvage her autonomy, it seems that unless Pat works to change the external factors causing her difficulties, she can do little to change the complex ethical dilemmas she finds herself in and, in particular, little to regain control over what ought to be professional judgments about how long particular individuals need care. What *Limited Number of Visits* shows, that is, is that social workers sometimes must work for change in the system that creates the ethical problems they face (see the Code of Ethics 6.04[a] & [b]).

Lack of Clarity about Goals

This case and *Money or Care?* both concern the problems created for social work practitioners by the institutions they work for needing funding to sustain or further their missions. But such institutions may act altruistically, and such an institution's acting in this way may cause as many ethical problems for its practitioners as its striving to maintain or increase its bottom line. In the following case, an agency considers whether to expand its mission to meet a new need and it becomes unclear what its goals are.

CASE **5.6**

Taking On More Than It Can Chew

When crack cocaine hit the streets, its quick spread wrought social havoc, and, except for the police, human service agencies were the only institutions with any kind of experience in dealing with drug use and the harm it causes families and other social institutions. The crack epidemic spread so quickly, and so overwhelmed the agencies that traditionally dealt with drug dependency, that Aurelio's agency was asked to take on a new role to help with the problem.

   The agency had no serious financial difficulties, and it was successful in its other programs. That was one reason it had been asked to take on this new problem. But it also had no experience in drug dependency programs and taking on a new program would stretch it resources. There was no promise yet of any new money, and so the main problem, as Aurelio put it, was that he and the board "had to balance the long-term financial stability of the agency with the mission of responding to emerging social problems."

Aurelio was extremely reluctant to have the agency take on the new cause, but some members of the board argued that the problem was so overwhelming that they had no ethical choice but to help, despite the problems that might cause. They felt they could not just sit back and hope that the crack epidemic would run its course without significant harm to the community it was their mission to serve. They were also concerned that the problem might harm some of the activities the agency was currently engaged in and that they would end up having to take on the new mission in any event. "We might as well do it at the beginning," they said.

Aurelio agreed that taking on the new cause would further the agency's mission, but, he worried, unlike practitioners in other agencies whose mission had included working with drug dependency, the agency's employees had no special training or particular experience in working with drug dependency. They would need to be trained, and the new program and the need for training would take them away from the agency's regular programs and leave those programs underfunded as well as understaffed. Aurelio was thus concerned that the agency's practitioners were not the best ones for the job and that the agency's other programs would be jeopardized by the transfer of money and personnel to the new program.

No agency can do everything. However important an agency's mission, and however deeply committed to it the agency may be, no mission can be so powerful as to overwhelm all other considerations such as whether an agency is competent to take on a new program, even one that furthers the agency's mission. Even deep ethical commitment should not preclude practical questions. But, then again, some agencies must respond to new social problems that arise. Agencies cannot rest content to till the same field over and over. Otherwise, no one would respond to the new social problems that strike us all too frequently.

In considering such problems, therefore, the questions to ask are whether a new program is a good fit, a natural extension of programs an agency is already involved in, or whether, if it is not, the problem is so important that the agency must take it on in any event and train its workers to handle the problem. The crack cocaine problem is not a natural fit for Aurelio's agency.

One consideration in deciding what to do is, as Aurelio put it, whether taking on the new social problem is consistent with "the long-term financial stability of the agency." Clearly the answer to that question is contentious, given the different responses of Aurelio and the board, and without more information, we cannot take one side or the other. The answer is not obvious, that is, given what we know.

What is obvious is that any answer ought to consider the impact on the agency's practitioners, for when an agency takes on a problem it is ill-equipped to handle, its practitioners will face special problems that they would not face otherwise, and both the old programs and the new program will face special problems.

Any arguments for or against taking on the new problem must thus have as premises claims about the following:

a. With money and personnel going from the old programs into new ones, and the old programs thus being shorthanded and not as well funded as they have been, what harms will occur? This question in turn has two parts. First, if the old programs become shorthanded and underfunded, will either of those shortages cause harms for those whom the programs are designed to help? Second, will those working in the programs face any kind of special problems because they do not have enough personnel to help them or enough money? There is likely to be an impact for the worse both on the beneficiaries of the existing programs and on those administering the program.
b. With money short and with practitioners who are inexperienced in the new field the agency is to take on, what harms will occur? Just as there will be an impact on the old programs and on those working in the programs, so there will be an impact on the new program and on those working in it.

First, the new program is likely to be as underfunded as are the old programs. With enough money to cover its existing programs, and not enough to cover an expansion of services, the agency will need to take money from all of its programs to fund the expansion. It is not likely to fund the new program to its fullest. Or, more accurately, any judgment to do that must be weighed against the greater harm that would then occur to its existing programs. So one question that must be considered and answered in order to decide whether to take on the new program is how to distribute the harms that will occur to the old and the new programs by the subsequent shortfall of money.[102]

Second, Aurelio would no doubt check among the agency's employees to see if any happened to have any training or experience in drug dependency, and those employees would presumably be first in line for the new program if they can be spared from the other programs. But if there are not enough of them, or if not enough employees can be spared, employees will have to be trained, which will cost the agency funds, and then they will need to be put to work in the new program with no experience. Just as the new program is as likely to be as underfunded as the old programs, given the shortfall of money, so the new program is as likely to be understaffed as the old programs. The harms that occur from understaffing are many—from the staff being overworked to their being overwhelmed—and so one question that must be answered to decide whether the agency should take on the new program is how best to distribute the harms that will occur from understaffing. Would it be better to put a lot of employees to work in the new program, to get a jump on the problem, even though that decision will leave the other programs more severely understaffed, or would be it best to spread the harms more evenly (see the Code of Ethics 3.07[b])?

Again, we cannot know the answer to this question, or the other questions we have raised, without more information. We cannot be sure what kinds of problems the practitioners will face in this new area. In *Money or Care?*, those working in the foster homes were not given adequate guidance about what to do, and in *Limited Number of Visits,* Pat was given a guideline that was clear, but seemed arbitrary and unresponsive to the real problems she faced in tailoring therapy to particular clients. In those cases, the institutions in question were operating well-established programs. But if there can be those kinds of problems for the practitioners in those sorts of programs, it is unreasonable to assume that the practitioners in Aurelio's agency will not have any serious problems in taking on a wholly new project, in an area in which they have little or no experience.

Some might argue that no one could be prepared to tackle the problems created by the crack epidemic, especially given its magnitude and the persistence of the dependency, but at least those practitioners with previous work in substance abuse programs would have some idea how to proceed with this new variety of addiction. In deciding whether the agency ought to respond to the new cause, Aurelio and the board will thus certainly need to consider not only how well taking on the new problems fits with its existing mission and with its existing programs, but also what new problems the practitioners of the agency may have. They have a large stake in the answer that Aurelio and the board give. It is, of course, as difficult to anticipate what kinds of problems those in the new program will face as it is to anticipate what kinds of problems those in the existing programs will face because of fewer resources. But these are problems that will matter in making the right choice.

What is missing so far in this discussion of the various harms that may occur given one choice rather than another is what ought to be guiding the discussion. As the second step of our model tells us, we need always to be clear why we are doing whatever it is we decide to do. What do we intend to accomplish? We cannot begin to determine which sets of harms and benefits the agency ought to choose without first understanding what goal or goals the agency is committed to achieving. For instance, one issue the case raises is why this agency was asked to take on this problem. Why was not an agency with experience in substance abuse approached? It might be that this agency has some special goals that fit well with handling the new social problem, or it may be that the agencies that handle substance abuse have special problems that make them inappropriate choices to handle this problem. We do not have enough information to know one way or the other, but we will need to know what the agency's goals are before we can determine what the agency ought to do.

We may find, were we to investigate this issue, that other agencies in the community are better prepared than this one, but that discovery leads into the questions we shall examine in the next section.

Conflicts between Agencies

In any community with two or more social work agencies, overlapping services may exist, and the agencies involved may cooperate or compete. Cooperation can raise as many ethical issues as competition, and the issues can become very complicated when other ethical issues are involved as well.

Agencies in Competition

Consider the following case in which a director misrepresents her agency and misleads both the community and the agency's clients, causing difficulties for the agency's social work practitioners and for other agencies and their practitioners.

CASE **5.7**

Agency Misrepresentation

An agency advertises itself as taking care of the homeless. Its big promotion under its new popular director, Delores, who is a minister, is that it provides "A Home for the Homeless." Because of this campaign, and the way it has advertised itself, the agency under Delores has been able to raise significant funds in the community from foundations and from private citizens, and it now receives support from the county government.

But the agency provides only drop-in support for the homeless, and only in the day time. Delores went to the local motels and hotels asking for donations of small pieces of soap because, she said, "the homeless need to travel light on the street." There is no intent on the part of the agency to provide homes for the homeless.

In addition, the agency prides itself on providing help "no questions asked," and so is unable to direct those who need housing to other agencies that could help. It refuses to question those who drop in because, it argues, that would be an invasion of privacy, but that policy is also part of a campaign to attract those who need help. The agency tells them, "We don't ask; we just give."

Janet is the director of an agency that does provide homes for the homeless. She coordinated the original agreement among the various agencies in the area about how best to help the homeless, but Delores's aggressive advertising and fundraising have caused funds that would have gone to provide housing for the homeless to go instead to Delores's agency. In fact, county money that is earmarked for the county shelter to provide housing for the homeless is being sent to this agency on the mistaken assumption that it provides housing. The checks are made out to the agency, and Delores is using the money for the agency's programs. The agency's advertising has clearly caused confusion about what the agency does. The agency's accountant, who also works part-time for Janet, has told her of the misdirected funds and is unsure what to do.

Janet's agency has not only lost funding, but it has had to spend additional money for "outreach therapy" at the agency. "We have to go in there," Janet says, to assess the needs of the clients so it can try to provide homes for those who need them. The agency was unwilling initially to provide office space for that, and, although it now does that, it charges them eight cents for each phone call and makes it difficult in other ways for Janet's agency to do its job.

This is a complex case, raising many different problems, not the least of which is that the agency Delores is in charge of is taking public money that does not rightfully belong to it and using it for purposes other than what it is supposed to be used for. It may be using that money for some good purposes, but it is not spending it for the purpose it was given. It is not a difficult ethical judgment that this situation is wrong.

The accountant has a professional obligation to inform the county that it is making a mistake, but now, because Janet knows about the problem, she has an obligation as well. How Janet can best fulfil that obligation is another issue (see the Code of Ethics 2.11[a]–[d]). If she cannot convince the accountant to act, she may need to write to the county authority informing him or her that, somehow, the money is mistakenly not being sent to the agencies that provide housing for the homeless.

The source of the accountant's professional obligation is that the money is being misappropriated and the accountant knows it. Janet's obligations are more complicated. She has an obligation to allow the accountant to act before she acts because, if she acts first, the accountant will be in difficulty. But she also has an obligation to act—either by allowing the accountant to act or, if the accountant will not act, by acting herself. The source of that obligation is that she knows that the homeless are being harmed and she now knows how they are being harmed.[103] She has the obligation that any of us would have to help those who are being harmed, through no fault of their own, when we can help them. She has an additional reason for acting because she and her agency are trying to help provide housing for the homeless and are having a more difficult time of it because of the misallocated funds.

How Janet should act is another question. It is always important to try to talk through the issues with those involved, and so her first obligation is to talk with Delores, explain what she thinks the problem is, and then listen to what Delores has to say (see the Code of Ethics 2.11[c]). Janet will then be far better positioned to determine whether she needs to do anything else or whether, somehow, she may have misunderstood something about the situation.

It is a situation that, as Janet now understands it, clearly needs to be turned around. Among the other problems are these:

a. Delores's agency is misrepresenting what it does. That is itself a harm because it is taking money from the public under false pretenses, but Janet's worry ought to be that harm will come to the other social work agencies in town when the truth comes out. People who have given to Delores's agency and then discover that they have been taken may be less likely to give in the future to any such agency, not knowing which agencies are misrepresenting what they do. After all, if one cannot trust a minister in charge of an agency, why should one trust others who claim their agencies will help?

b. Delores's agency is giving the homeless a Band-aid when major surgery is needed. What the homeless need, it may be argued, is a long-term solution that provides them with housing, not just small bars of soap so they can "travel light." That Janet's agency has had to create an "outreach" program to go into the community to reach the homeless to determine what their needs are and try to meet them is a rather obvious sign that the homeless need more help than the agency is giving them—help with filling out forms, for instance, so that they can get other aid that they are entitled to from other agencies.

c. Because the homeless are not being housed, they are presumably still in the neighborhood at night, sleeping in lobbies of businesses and on the streets, causing resentment among business owners and the public in general who are then less willing to give since the dollars they think they have been giving for the homeless are not solving the problem.

d. The agency has turned what ought to be a cooperative endeavor among the various agencies in the community into a competitive enterprise, harming the interests of the homeless in the process, obviously, but also making it significantly harder for the other agencies to provide the aid the homeless need.

If Janet, or the accountant, do what they are obligated to do regarding the county checks, that may in itself set in motion a train of changes sufficient to turn the situation around. Taking on Delores may be difficult, given her popularity, but her popularity is bound to fall once it is known that she has been using money for one purpose that was allocated for another.

But a long-term solution requires a concerted community effort, one in which various agencies do not find themselves in competition for the limited funds that are going to be available. Since Janet coordinated the original agreement among the agencies about how to help the homeless, she has a special obligation now to try to reinvigorate that agreement, perhaps bringing in the county or other governmental agencies not only to ensure that any public funding goes to solve the long-term problems, but also to provide a check against the "Lone Ranger" mentality of the agency in question. What is needed is oversight as well as a long-range solution, and only through a coordinated effort with the other social work agencies and with governmental bodies can Janet hope to deal with the various problems this agency has created.

Cooperative Endeavors?

Agency Misrepresentation presents a particularly complicated set of ethical issues. These are caused in part because of the agency's misrepresentation, but, rather obviously, conflicts may occur between agencies even where there is no misrepresentation and when the agencies involved are both committed to the same ethical goal. The free-market system encourages that, and when a not-for-profit agency has the same goal as a for-profit company, the conflicts may be particularly difficult to resolve.[104] Consider the following case.

CASE **5.8**

An Adoption Agency

Adoption agencies are licensed by the state, and the state restrictions are all designed to ensure that the best homes are found for adoptive children. One agency, which we shall call "Homes for Babies," is advertising that "it will get you a baby," according to Joan, the director of another adoption agency. The advertisement also says that Homes for Babies does not always get "the cream of the crop," or, as Joan puts it, "a baby of Caucasian parents, with excellent medical backgrounds, no mental illness, prenatal care, a healthy attitude toward adoption, a willing father." So they are "tagging babies," Joan thinks, making distinctions among them that are inappropriate.

Joan has had several cases in which she or one of her social work practitioners has been working with a client for several months, only to go to the hospital to discover a representative of the other agency there. In most cases, the birth mother has said that she wants to work with the other agency.

Joan is concerned that such agencies are being licensed. They charge a great deal of money for an adoption, and the adoptive families pay the medical and other expenses. Her agency and the other nonprofit adoptive agencies charge their expenses and do not let the adoptive families pay any of the medical or other expenses. One former client told Joan that the Homes for Babies would allow her to meet with the adoptive parents when Joan's agency would not allow that, and Joan is concerned that the agency may be paying the birth mother, which is illegal.

Joan is even more concerned that the agency is not doing right by the children. One concern is that the home studies are not as thorough as they should be. The agency has an incentive to keep its costs as low as it can and so may not pay enough to provide a sufficient check on the adopting families. But the main problem for Joan is that while her agency starts with the children and tries to find the right home for them, Homes for Babies starts with those who want to adopt and makes a profit only if it finds a baby for them. It thus has a financial incentive to place children in homes that may not be best for them.

We have some problems in this case similar to those we had with the agency in *Agency Misrepresentation*. For one thing, the relationship between the two adoption agencies is more uncooperative than Joan's agency thinks relations ought to be between agencies providing the same sort of service. If she thought that the other agency's primary concern was for the welfare of the children, Joan might call this new agency if her agency had a child it could not place well. Yet her concerns about what Homes for Babies is doing means that she must hold back in order to ensure that the child's best interests are met. And Homes for Babies is not likely to call her should it run across a baby it cannot place right away. To maintain its profits, it is more likely to keep that knowledge to itself until it can find a set of adoptive parents for the child.

This noncooperative attitude also extends to the services the two agencies provide for the birth mother because, as Joan's experience in several cases makes clear, Homes for Babies is aggressively recruiting birth mothers whom Joan's agency had worked with right up to the birth date.

Homes for Babies is apparently not misrepresenting what it does. Indeed, its advertising that it does not always get "the cream of the crop" may be thought to be like a product warning label: "Look before you buy!" But, of course, that warning may also be a defense against potential lawsuits from any parents who end up being dissatisfied with the adoption. The agency can always say, "We told you so."

But the agency's concentration on finding babies for adoptive parents rather than finding homes for children may cause harm in at least the following ways:

a. Rather obviously, that concern to find babies rather than homes for babies may mean, at a minimum, that it will not provide the best home environment for the babies that is possible and, at the worst, that it will provide a bad home environment for them. If its primary incentive is to increase its bottom line, it is more likely to overlook potential problems than to proceed as cautiously as it should were its concern only with the baby's well-being.

b. A second area of concern is that it will not do the best that can be done for the birth mothers. They need prenatal care, but they also need extensive support. It is not easy giving up one's baby, and the sort of counseling needed both before and after the birth is time consuming and so expensive. Homes for Babies has some incentive to ensure that a birth mother obtains good prenatal care because it presumably wants to ensure that the adoptive parents have a baby that is healthy enough to satisfy them, and it has some incentive to provide counseling before the birth because it does not want a prospective mother to change her mind. But counseling that encourages a prospective mother to give up her baby is not neutral and, rather obviously, may not be in the prospective mother's best interests—or the baby's, for that matter (see the Code of Ethics 1.06[b]).

In addition, the agency has little incentive to ensure the extensive support a birth mother needs after giving up a baby. The agency will want to keep its expenses low so that it can be competitive with other for-profit agencies and so that it can earn more without charging so much as to discourage potential adoptive parents. So the agency has an incentive that the woman not change her mind, and so an incentive to counsel her after the birth, but, again, not with a neutral frame of mind.

c. Another source of harm is that nonprofit agencies will have fewer babies to offer adoptive parents. Indeed, Joan may object that, as its name suggests, Homes for Babies does get the cream of the crop since its aim is to find adoptive homes for babies, not for all children who need them. Since most adoptive parents prefer babies to older children, they are more likely to work with that agency than agencies like Joan's, which will come to have fewer babies and more older children, the more successful Homes for Babies is. Potential adoptive parents will become more and more likely to work with for-profit agencies than with nonprofit agencies, who will have fewer and fewer babies to offer. Potential parents who might have come to consider adopting older children may not come to the agencies that would have given them that opportunity.

    d. In addition, the agency's primary concern to increase its profits may cause it to overstep the bounds for placement. For instance, it may have paid the expenses of the birth mother, getting the money from the prospective adoptive parents and providing a real incentive for the birth mother to give her child up and to give it up to that agency rather than to Joan's. Joan suspects Homes for Babies of providing funding for the birth mothers because that seems the most reasonable explanation for why that agency is able to take over birth mothers that Joan's agency has been working with. But that financial inducement makes it seem to Joan as though the agency were buying babies.

    e. Another source of harm is that if the agency is failing to match well the needs of the babies it places with the families that adopt them, not only will the babies be harmed, but the families and society at large may have to pay heavy prices for the consequences.

    f. Any failures of such agencies as Homes for Babies will harm the reputation of all adoption agencies among those who fail to distinguish, or are unable to distinguish, between the ones that operate for profit and those that do not. So, just as in *Agency Misrepresentation,* the long-term consequences of one agency's failures may harm innocent agencies engaged in the same sort of activity and so harm their fund-raising capacity and thus the services they are trying to provide.

    Of course, all of these harms—real, likely, and possible—must be balanced, as our method tells us, against the good that such agencies as Homes for Babies do. In advertising that it does not always get "the cream of the crop," it is saying that it is willing to place infants whom other agencies may have trouble placing. So some babies who would not get homes, or who would not get homes until they were older, will get homes. And that is a benefit. In addition, some couples who would like to adopt children will no doubt get them through such agencies when they might have had a long wait with nonprofit agencies, and that is a benefit— provided, of course, that they ought to be parents and that they ought to be parents to the particular baby they have adopted.

    So what ought Joan to do, if anything, to mitigate the harms she thinks are occurring, or are likely to occur, given the entry of for-profit adoption agencies like Homes for Babies into the adoption market? She faces the same sort of problem that Janet faced. There is little she can do within the system to mitigate the harms.

    In fact, it is striking what potential remedies will not work in either case. The sort of consultative process that ought to be the norm for how social work practitioners work out problems is likely to be ineffective in either case. Homes for Babies has no incentive to change its way of operating, except perhaps in regard to some features it might be called to account for legally, and although Janet has an obligation to talk with Delores about the problems her agency is causing, the problem is that there is a need for a long-term, community-wide program for the homeless. Whatever Delores may agree to do, what is required to achieve the needed end is a broader consensus among the interested parties than Janet can achieve just by talking with Delores. For one thing, other agencies will have to be brought into the process. What they will need to do, to achieve their ends, is to change the structure of the systems that are producing the problems they have.

In other words, as we work through the harms in the existing system and ask ourselves what Janet or Joan might do to mitigate those harms, we find ourselves turning, once again, to ask what goals are in question. If Janet's goal is to ensure that the county spends its money properly, she could go to the county to complain about Delores's misrepresentation. There may be no other way of getting the county to reconsider what it is doing with that money. But if Janet's goal is to find long-term housing for the homeless, the problems Delores is causing are minor irritants—an occasion for remedial action to change the system. Of course, Janet has an obligation, in any event, to hold Delores accountable to the Code of Ethics, and, if Delores is not willing to stop the misrepresentation, to file a complaint with NASW or with the state licensing bureau.

The same is true of Joan. Ticking off the harms that Home for Babies causes could initiate an inquiry that would consume a great deal of the for-profit agency's time and thus a great deal of its profits. But the most likely way to prevent the multitude of harms that Joan thinks such agencies cause would seem to be for the state to make such agencies illegal or to regulate them so that they operate for the benefit of the babies being placed. To achieve either of those ends, Joan would undoubtedly have to work together with other nonprofit agencies to lobby the state legislature to change the existing laws and licensing requirements.

The problems that Janet and Joan face are no different in kind from those faced by other organizations. We sometimes expect fierce competition between corporations like General Motors and Chrysler, but even nonprofit organizations can clash. The Red Cross might seem a paragon of disinterested benevolence, but it controls the nation's blood supply, and when it increased prices to its customers and a variety of competitors sprung up in response, it played economic hardball to retain its customer base. One lesson of the cases we have examined is thus that governmental or nonprofit social work agencies are as subject to the collision of competing interests as are for-profit organizations.

We may think it should make some difference when the clash is between social work agencies when they have a common mission, for that ought to make it easier to set up cooperative arrangements to settle the sorts of jurisdictional disputes raised by *Agency Misrepresentation*. And when organizations are working for the same end, as in *An Adoption Agency*, it might seem easier to create the kind of collaborative programs that Joan would like. But as those two cases illustrate, agencies can come into conflict with one another or with other organizations, like Homes for Babies, for a variety of reasons, and one or both of those organizations having an ethical mission neither prevents such conflicts nor allows for easy resolutions.

QUESTIONS

1. How can not-for-profit human service agencies profit from adopting features of corporations like General Motors?

2. Expand on the following statement: "What's good for social welfare agencies is good for the country."

3. How do social welfare agencies differ from such groups as the Red Cross? What would it help or hurt for social welfare agencies to be more like the Red Cross? Remember that we are examining the "corporate" structure, as it were, of social welfare agencies and such groups as the Red Cross. Even General Motors employs social workers, but that does not make it like a social welfare agency.

4. In an age of increasing privatization, ought governmental social welfare agencies be privatized? What would be the gains? What would be the losses?

5. Law firms and accounting firms are like human service agencies in that their members are professionals. What similarities and differences are there between human service agencies and other such groups of professionals? It will help in pursuing this question to ask what changes would need to be made in law firms and in lawyers' conceptions of their role in society for them to operate like not-for-profit human service agencies.

6. Would social work be better or worse off moving toward a model of organization more like that of law firms? In responding to this question, discuss the goals of social work practice as they differ from those of legal practice.

7. Define autonomy. What makes autonomy professional? What is the difference, if any, that is, between the autonomy of clients and the autonomy of social workers?

8. Assess the truth of the claim that a social work practitioner has autonomy about everything except what makes a difference to his or her supervisor.

9. A social work practitioner working in an agency is an employee, and the goals of an agency may differ from those of a social work professional. We saw that difference in Case 1.2, *Dancing a Legal Dance*, when the agency suggested that Mary was putting too much effort into the case while she thought she needed to spend more time on the case. Is there some procedure that agencies could introduce, besides appealing to a supervisor, to handle these sorts of problems in which one thing should happen in the professional judgment of the caseworker while the agency's decision is that something else could happen? Explore the advantages and disadvantages of alternative ways of handling such conflicts.

10. The problems that can arise from wearing different hats can happen to any of us in almost any situation. A vote on school taxes requires that we consider ourselves both as parents and as citizens concerned about the educational well-being of children. There need be no incompatibility between what we do under one hat and what we do under another, but when there is, we have ethical problems. Give three examples from your experience or from the cases in this book of ethical problems that arise from wearing two hats.

11. One analysis of what went wrong during the launch of the *Challenger* space shuttle is that the chief engineer at Morton Thiokol was asked at a crucial junction to wear his "management hat." As an engineer, he was risk averse, arguing that it was too risky to launch the *Challenger* when the temperature was to be so low at launch. But as a manager, he was to do a risk/benefit analysis in which the chance of a disaster was a risk, but one that had to be balanced against the risks to the shuttle program of another delay and other such matters. That is, wearing two hats sometimes means that we change the very way in which we make decisions. In managed care, one complaint of professionals is that decisions are being determined by economic factors that ought not to make a difference in assessing what, professionally, ought to be done. Discuss how we as a society ought to resolve such problems as the conflicts that occur when professional judgments are beholden to other considerations such as cost.

12. What is an internal ethical problem? What makes such a problem internal?

13. Different professions can be distinguished from one another by examining the differing internal ethical problems that mark out their boundaries. For instance, we expect a nurse, as a nurse, to care for the well-being of his or her patients. A sales clerk who cared for his or her customers' well-being rather than, say, the profits to the store would not last long. Distinguish the internal ethical problems of social work practitioners from those of sales clerks, from lawyers, and from physicians.

14. What is an external ethical problem? What makes such a problem external?

15. The Catholic Council of Bishops has voted that those in political office are to support life in all ways. That means, they say, that a politician cannot be a good Catholic and also support abortion rights. So a Catholic politician who supports abortion rights—Senator Kennedy, for instance—has an external ethical problem. What is that problem? Find a similar sort of problem for social work practitioners.

16. An employer cannot easily let employees pick and choose what they want to do and not do. But it seems wrong to require employees to do something they think is ethically wrong. Suppose you are the head of a human service agency faced with the kind of problem examined in Case 5.3, *A Pacifist*. What principles should your agency adopt to handle such problems—given that the agency cannot always let its employees decide for themselves what to do and not to do?

17. Deontological theory seems to require that each time we are faced with a decision about what we ought to do, we are to consider the maxim of our action and determine whether it is ethical. But if we have an ethical character—we are honest, for instance—we do not take time to decide to answer honestly. Being honest is just part of who we are, and we just do it. Indeed, mulling the matter over seems itself unethical. If being honest is the right thing to do, why would you need to think about it for any period of time? So if we ought to develop an ethical character, then, it seems, deontological theory is a mistake. Discuss.

18. Aristotle has said that there is only one way to do what is right, but many ways to do what is wrong. We can say we are sorry in the wrong way, at the wrong time, for too long a time (saying it over and over, in many different ways), for too short a time ("Sorry"), and so on. We display a character trait in a variety of different

ways, that is, by the tilt of our head, by our concerned expression, by whether we lean forward or back when expressing sympathy, and so on. Lay out in detail the various ways in which we can express our character when, for instance, we want to express sympathy. How can an expression of sympathy go wrong? Consider how it can go wrong regarding each way in which we are to express sympathy.

19. Some of us have irritating little habits that indicate a lack of character in certain ways—looking off in the distance while talking to people so that we are not looking at them and it looks as though we are not concerned about talking to them, looking at our watch constantly while talking with someone, and so on. List a set of five "little habits" that some professionals you know have and explain why they are character defects. What harms do they cause?

20. What is a professional character trait?

21. What are several of the character traits that social workers need if they are to be successful?

22. What are several of the character traits that social work students are trained into during their social work education?

23. In your lists in the previous two questions, which characteristics are good for social workers to have and which are not? Explain each.

24. What are the goals of the agency for which you work or the kind of agency you would like to work for? Are they consistent with one another? Would achieving them produce a good agency? Are they consistent with the self-determination of the agency's employees? Are they in any way harmful to clients? The public good? Be specific.

25. We often talk of "gray areas." What does that phrase mean? Give an example from among the cases we have discussed and explain why it is an example. How ought we to decide what to do in a gray area?

26. We will sometimes have ethical dilemmas in which the reasons for doing any of a number of things are equally weighty so that it is difficult to know how to determine what to do. How is that kind of situation different from our being in a gray area?

27. What is discretion? Do police have discretion about whether to issue tickets? What does that mean? Do medical practitioners have discretion about whether to report someone with an infectious disease to the authorities? Do social work practitioners ever have discretion? When? What are the pros and cons of a social work practitioner's having discretion? Should Mary have had discretion in Case 1.2, *Dancing a Legal Dance,* about whether to report that Martha's father had sexually abused Martha?

28. With the increasing privatization of various social and medical services, it has been claimed, the discretion of professionals is being eroded. A physician no longer has discretion to require certain medical procedures, for instance, but must obtain permission first. How would or could the privatization of social services affect the discretion of social work practitioners?

29. Assess the advantages and disadvantages of privatizing social work services in regard to professionalism.

30. When the court system took on the burden of regulating desegregation, and some courts ended up running the school systems, as in Boston, one objection was that the courts are institutionally ill-designed for such a task. They lack the administrative oversight necessary for running a large bureaucracy, for instance. Similarly, some may argue that human service agencies are well-designed for some tasks and ill-designed for others. Examine the general form of human service agencies and lay out, in regard to two or three activities, what they are well-designed and ill-designed to do. Show in regard to at least one of those activities how the design of the agency can have ethical implications because of its ability to perform one sort of task well and badly.

31. One way to resolve the problems introduced when agencies compete would be to have an overarching, centralized agency of agencies, as it were, to ensure that agencies help rather than harm each other. Another solution would be to allow competition full rein so that inefficient agencies do not survive. Discuss the merits and demerits of both proposals. Determine which is the best solution, if either is, and justify on ethical grounds the determination you make.

CHAPTER

6 Justice

In Case 1.2, *Dancing a Legal Dance*, Mary Todd was upset because she thought that by declaring that the twelve-year-old was not sexually abused, the Juvenile Court judge invited more sexual abuse. The girl had accused her father of sexual abuse and taken it back in open court, in front of her father. Mary thought that if the judge had looked at the child's situation in and of itself, he would have investigated further. She thought it was only because the judge required that the girl's story match her sister's that he made the legal finding he did. She thought it "so unfair that the twelve-year-old should be treated differently because she has a sister." Mary thought the twelve-year-old was not being treated justly because any other child in such a situation, but without a sister, would have been treated differently.

We all know that hearings in Juvenile Court are imperfect. The proceedings may fail to protect someone who is being abused or may penalize someone who is not abusing. Mary thinks that the judge made a mistake and that the judicial system is wrong because it allows such a finding. The procedure, she thinks, should err on the side of protecting the innocent when the innocent are abused children, not on the side of protecting the guilty. So, she thinks, the procedure is unjust.

Mary thus has at least two complaints about injustice in *Dancing a Legal Dance*. First, she thinks the judge has not treated like cases alike because he has treated the twelve-year-old in a different way than he would have if she not had a sister. He has failed to be just even if the system as a whole is just. Second, she thinks the system itself is unjust because it allows for such a judgment, forcing the child to be abused again to get justice rather than protecting her in case she had been abused. Mary is in effect applying our method of tracking harms and asking of the judge, "Why didn't he consider the consequences of what he decided? If he had, he would have realized that he is setting up a situation in which the younger daughter will have to be abused—harmed—again in order to restrain the father." Laying out the alternatives, in other words, and assessing their consequences makes it obvious, Mary thinks, that the judge ought not to have acted as he did.

But Mary also objects to the judge and the system not supporting the family well, but letting it drift apart. She thinks this is happening because the mother was developmentally disabled and the family was African American and poor. Mary thought that the mother did not know how to make use of the system to help herself or her children, but, more important, she thinks that the nature of the system makes those in it less willing to help because it was "a family of that nature." It is an unjust system, she thinks, when those in need of help are not helped as much because they belong to a particular class, or a particular race, or have particular personal characteristics (see the Code of Ethics 6.04[d]).

So Mary thought the legal procedure was unjust and the social system in which it is embedded was unjust as well. It was in response to these difficulties that she decided to work against the judge's reelection. Her hope, presumably, was that replacing him would produce a judge who was more just.[105]

Almost every case we have examined raises issues of justice, and we shall need to sort out and examine at least two questions:

1. Is the system as a whole just or unjust?

Apartheid in South Africa is a good example of an entire system that was unjust. But there is a second issue:

2. Is a particular act (or omission) within a system just or unjust?

When Mary complained about the judgment made by the judge, she was objecting to a particular judgment, saying that it was unjust. But when she complained about the racism she thought was motivating those who failed to act, she was complaining not just about the acts of individuals within the system, but about the injustice of the system itself.

A particular act or practice may be unjust without the whole system in which it occurs being unjust, and, vice versa, a whole system may be unjust but still have within it just acts and practices. So we need to distinguish questions of social justice, concerning the system as a whole, from questions of particular justice.

For both we must distinguish between formal and substantive principles of justice and between various forms of procedural justice. These distinctions will be made as we work our way through a case that raises an issue of particular justice.

Particular Justice

Consider the following case.

CASE 6.1
Still Waiting after All This Time

An agency had the opportunity to provide an Employee Assistance Program (EAP) for a number of local businesses. In such programs, businesses contract with agencies to provide such services as substance abuse or mental health counseling for their employees.

When asked whether the agency struggled with the issue of its serving fewer clients if it took on EAP clients, the director, Abe, responded by saying that without EAP clients, the agency would be serving fewer clients. With EAP clients, the agency has the potential to see more clients at "full-cost reimbursement". "In fact," he said, "we're treating all of the clients exactly the same. The clients we had are still on the waiting list, *and* we are seeing the EAP clients. Those who pay up-front get quick service, and those who cannot continue to wait, just like before. It's just like the health-care system."

Abe does not see any ethical issue in his agency's providing an EAP. He says that when his agency takes on EAP clients, nothing has changed and so no injustice has been done to the agency's other clients. He says, "We're treating all of the clients exactly the same."

If adding an EAP does not change the way that anyone is being treated, and allows the agency to serve more clients, and to get paid fully for doing so, who could be harmed? What could be unjust? Such a combination seems too good to be true, and it is. But if we are to understand fully Abe's response, we must distinguish between *formal* and *substantive* principles of justice.

The Formal Principle of Justice

We all remember cases in which we felt that we were being treated unjustly because we were being treated differently than someone else when we thought we should be treated the same. A colleague has a larger office, or better equipment, for instance. We can also empathize with the experience of having others being treated the same way we are treated when we think they should be treated differently. A new employee for the agency is getting paid just what you are getting even though you have been there for a number of years. We all are familiar with such feelings. Lying behind them is what is called the formal principle of justice, namely, that like cases ought to be treated alike and unlike cases ought to be treated unalike.

Any attempt to justify what appears to be unjust treatment always appeals to the formal principle of justice. When you complain that your case is unlike someone else's who is being treated the same way you are, or is like someone else's who is being treated differently, the form of response is always the same. Those you are complaining to will claim that the case you think is different is not (really) different, or the case you think is the same is not (really) the same. So your supervisor argues that the office of your colleague just looks larger, but is not really, or that it is larger, but that more has to go into it and the colleague really has no more room than you do, or that the colleague's situation is different from yours because the colleague has a different kind of work, requiring meeting with more people at a time than you do, say, and so requiring a larger office. We are all familiar with such responses, having given and received similar ones ourselves, and, in each case, an implicit appeal is made to the formal principle of justice.

Yet this principle only tells us that like cases should be treated alike and unlike cases, unalike.[106] It does not say which are like cases and which cases are unalike. This principle demands that we be consistent, but we can be consistent and still be unethical.

For instance, if some colleagues were consistently treating clients differently because of their skin color, they would satisfy the formal principle of justice. They would be treating like cases alike and unlike cases unalike because, in their racist view, persons of the same color are alike and persons of different color are different.

We may ask what good the formal principle of justice can be when it is consistent with such injustice. How can the formal principle be important for justice if we can satisfy it and still have racism, for instance? The answer is that treating like cases alike and unlike cases unalike is necessary for justice, but not sufficient. We need to add a substantive principle of justice to tell us what we are to count as like and unlike.

But the formal principle of justice has an ethical bite even without the addition of a substantive principle of justice. Thus, one implication of it is that whenever you make a decision, you have to worry not simply about making the right decision in the particular case you are concerned with, but also in all relevantly similar cases. So if you grant an exception to a client, saying, for instance, that the client does not need to list all resources for a particular form, you have to worry, first, about what has happened in the past in similar cases and, second, about what will happen in the future in similar cases.

The first worry is that those who were treated differently in the past will have a right to complain. Is the present case different enough to justify having treated past clients one way while treating the present client a different way? If not, the past clients have an ethical claim against you, and unless you have some additional ethical reason for treating the present case differently, you are ethically wrong to make an exception.

The second worry is that those whom you will see in the future, and those who will see other caseworkers in similar organizations under the same laws, will have a just claim that they also should be granted an exception. Individual practice creates precedents. So whenever you are working with an individual client, you need consider past practice in relevantly similar cases and consider that you are setting a precedent for the future.

The formal principle of justice has an ethical bite, that is. It requires consistency and thus implies that if we treat similar cases differently, or treat dissimilar cases the same, we are prima facie ethically wrong. That is, we must have a very compelling ethical reason or set of reasons for denying what seems to contravene the formal principle of justice.

Substantive Principles of Justice

But to be just, it is not sufficient only to treat like cases alike and unlike cases unalike. The formal principle of justice needs to be supplemented with a substantive principle of justice. A substantive principle tells us which cases to count as like and which as unlike, and there are as many substantive principles, for as many kinds of things as can be distributed, as there are ways of sorting people out. So when someone claims to be treating like cases alike and unlike cases unalike, we need to ask a series of questions:

a. Because anything that can be distributed can be distributed justly or unjustly, we need to ask, "What are you distributing?"
b. Because what is being distributed can be distributed to some people and not to others, we need to ask, "Who is getting what?"
c. And because what matters in determining whether a distribution is just or unjust is the reason for the distribution, we need to ask, "What is your reason for treating those people in that way and others differently?"

These questions force out the basis the person has for distinguishing people and thus force out the substantive principle of justice being assumed so that it can be assessed.

We can see how these questions operate in the simplest of cases—ones in which we might not think justice is an issue. Anything that can be distributed is subject to some substantive principle. If you give yourself the best seat in your office, the one with the best view, for instance, you are committing yourself to distributing the seating in your office in a way that benefits you in respect to having the best view and so burdens your clients with less than the best view. So the answer to question a is that you are distributing seats in your office and, so, views in your office. The answer to question b is that you are distributing views to you and to your clients, and the answer to question c might be that because you must sit in your office all day and your clients only sit there for short periods of time, you deserve having the best view. The substantive principle of justice is what is called a principle of desert. Who gets what depends on who deserves it, and you are claiming that you deserve the best view and your clients do not.

It is another question whether you are ethically right in distributing views in your office in that way. Some may think that it matters ethically how we distribute views in our offices; others may think it not important. But because anything that can be distributed can be distributed justly or unjustly, we are committed to some substantive principle of justice for any benefit or burden we distribute—some basis for distribution—whether we are self-conscious about that or not. We might not think about views in our offices as being something we distribute, and it may not matter ethically, but we distribute smiles, we distribute irritation, we may distribute welfare payments and eligibility for other benefits, and so on. In each case, there is a basis for our distribution, whether we are conscious of it or not. To determine what that basis is, to determine if we are acting ethically, we need to ask the questions we have identified.

What we shall discover is a wide variety of substantive principles that people have used, and that people argue ought to be used, to distribute benefits and burdens. Because any distinction can be used as a reason for distributing benefits and burdens, the range of substantive principles is as wide as the range of distinctions among people—gender, race, height, or whatever. Most of these substantive principles will not withstand ethical scrutiny, even for views in your office, but among all of the possible substantive principles, there are some strong contenders, even for such major social goods as liberty, wealth, and income.

Some—Marxists—argue that benefits and burdens ought to be distributed "from each according to their ability, to each according to their needs." Others argue that the distribution should be on the basis of merit. Others argue that it should be on the basis of intrinsic worth as an individual. We shall examine two of these substantive principles, one that emphasizes individual liberty but accepts wide disparities in how individuals are to be treated in society, and another that emphasizes the essential equality of individuals and ensures that each will be benefitted by any gains of society as a whole, with one consequence being that everyone's basic needs will be met. We shall not examine all of the main contenders among substantive principles, but the two we shall examine articulate incompatible ideals that arguably lie behind all other substantive principles—except, perhaps, the Marxist view, which we will examine briefly at the end of this chapter.

Using Principles of Justice

If we return now to *Still Waiting after All This Time,* with questions a through c in hand, we can get a better understanding of the ethical situation the agency's taking on EAP clients has produced. We are able to see where the harms lie.

Abe is distributing places in line among EAP clients and the agency's traditional clients. He claims that with the EAP everyone is treated the same way as before. We need to ask, "In what respect are they being treated the same? What, in short, is being distributed?" Abe says that if the traditional clients were on a waiting list, if they were in line, that is, they still are.

Yet EAP clients go to the head of the line, in front of those who may have been waiting for some time for help. If a client who is not an EAP client is tenth in line, he or she might expect to be served after the nine in front are served. But at any time any number of EAP clients may jump in front. So although Abe is right that the former clients are on a waiting list, as they were before, he is wrong in implying that they are not being harmed by the agency's taking on EAP clients. They are being harmed in two ways. First, they may have to wait much longer for service, and, second, they are not being served in the order in which they have lined up. They are being treated as second-class clients, pushed aside if a "full-cost reimbursement" client shows up. So the agency's clients are being treated the same way they were before in respect to waiting in line, but they are being treated differently in respect to being served, in a timely way, in turn (see the Code of Ethics 6.04[a] & [b] & 3.07[b]).

The agency's original clients have been harmed by the agency's taking on EAP clients, and the agency thus faces an ethical problem. Ought it to take on EAP clients, which provide assured funding for the agency, or ought it to refuse to do so and make sure that its former clients are served in a timely way in their proper turn? Or ought they to try to ensure somehow that EAP clients—despite presumably paying for preferential treatment—take their turn in line?

The Agency's Role

However we answer that question, taking on an EAP client raises another issue about the agency's role. Taking on EAP clients and putting them at the head of the line means that of the two groups of clients the agency now serves—those employees from businesses that have contracted with the agency and the traditional clients of the agency—those likely to have the most resources are being served first. The agency's traditional clients are low-income people with limited access to the sort of counseling the agency provides, but they are being treated as second-class clients because the agency is taking on EAP clients who are employed and would normally, but for their employers' contracts with the agency, seek private help.

So by taking on EAP clients, the agency is helping those less needy than its traditional clients and in helping them and, indeed, helping them before it helps its traditional clients, it is shifting somewhat the focus of the agency away from its traditional role of providing help for the needy who are unable to seek outside help because of limited resources (see the Code of Ethics 6.04[b]). That the agency has made no clear decision to change its focus does not mean that the focus is not changing. Indeed, taking on EAP clients may require the agency to provide such services as stress-management and retirement management, thus shifting the focus of its resources from mental health problems to issues of more immediate concern to businesses.

What ethical justification could there be for the agency's taking on EAP clients, given the harms to its traditional clients and this worrisome shift in the agency's focus? It may be that the agency is so underfunded that it needs to take on an EAP to continue to provide service to its existing clients. We cannot know without further information, but if that is the case, we have a question of trade-offs. Justice is not the only value, and Abe would need to argue that the agency must compromise what it takes to be its mission in order to continue its mission.

As usual, trying to understand a particular issue in a case has revealed other issues—including an issue of what is called procedural justice.

Procedural Justice

Let us look at a case that raises the issue of how those in line should be considered for help.

CASE 6.2
The Waiting List

There is a waiting list for service in a mental health agency. The list never gets shorter, only longer, and people stay on it "just in case." People are taken by priority of need, not by the time they spend on the waiting list, and poriority of need is determined by, for example, whether a person needs hospitalization.

Some of those on the list injure themselves to get services, act out, "or do whatever" to be sure they are hospitalized, and Michael, the person at the agency in charge of taking cases, must sort out those who are in real need from those who are not.

By the time a decision must be made because of an overdose, for instance, Michael has met with the prospective clients three or four times and so has some basis for judging whether they are a danger to themselves or others. In addition, he asks questions to determine the seriousness of the situation.

The most diffucult cases are those in which the patient is borderline—enough of a problem to risk harm to those around and to themselves, but not enough to get hospitalized. Michael says he "puts those through their paces." If they want treatment, for example, they must come to therapy, three days a week for six months. If someone will follow through, then Michael will let him or her in.

He says he is right sixty percent of the time, and the rest of the time "we won't know what they will do." The decisions are complicated because the patients are very sophisticated in manipulation. One patient, Martha, wrote letters every three months asking for treatment, and Michael's assessment is that she wants to form more dependency-type roles.

A waiting list implies that one's entry into the system is determined by a wait. So if you were on such a list, you would presume that you would get treatment and that your getting it will be determined by your position on the list.

But the "waiting list" does not serve that function at this agency. Some on the list will never get service because it has been determined that they do not need it, and some not on the list will get service ahead of those on the list because it has been decided they need it right away.

In *Still Waiting after All This Time,* the procedure adopted by the agency for serving its clients appeared to be first-come, first-served when it was not. The agency really had two lines—one for the EAP clients and one for its regular clients—and a rule that said EAP clients get served first, regardless. So the agency knew what it wanted and devised a procedure to get it.

The agency thus followed what is called perfect procedural justice. Perfect procedural justice occurs when, for instance, each of two children should get half the dozen cookies one has. We simply divide the dozen in half—"one for you, and one for you," and so on. The procedure is simple and effective. Similarly, if we are concerned that those who get to a store or a bus stop are served in the order in which they arrive, having a line is a simple and effective procedure to guarantee that—provided no one crashes the line and no one in line lets another in who came later.

What marks perfect procedural justice is that one knows ahead of time what a just distribution would be and can figure out how to achieve it. The difficulty with *Still Waiting after All This Time,* as we noted, is that the director was mistaken in thinking he knew ahead of time what was just.

In *The Waiting List,* the situation is different. The "waiting list" does not line clients up for service in the order of their arrival. It does not line them up in any way because the agency takes whichever client it judges is most in need, regardless of where that person is on the list and even whether that person is on the list. What the agency wants is to serve those clients most in need and to rank clients in a way that matches up to their need for the agency's services. Having a waiting list is no help to that end. First, new, more needy cases can occur at any time and will not go to the end of the list. And, second, being on the list is no guarantee that the agency will agree that the person truly needs the agency's services.

The agency would like to select out from all who apply for its services all who truly need help and only those who need help. If it fails to help some who need help, or helps some who do not truly need it, it will have failed in obtaining its end. But the best it can do is to devise an imperfect procedure and then, as the agency sees how the procedure works in practice, fine-tune it to get closer and closer, if possible, to achieve the end of sorting out all and only those who need help.

The agency has a set of problems that make that end difficult to achieve. On the one hand, even if everyone with a borderline personality disorder needs help, the agency must sort out those with a borderline personality from those who do not have a borderline personality disorder, but, as it were, who border on it or are just faking it. On the other hand, the agency will not be able to help all those who clearly have a borderline personality disorder, but distinguishing within the group with a borderline personality disorder those who are most in need is itself difficult, requiring, if one is to be sure, just the sort of intensive examination received by those who are judged most in need and are taken on by the agency. In short, the agency cannot be sure it is making the right judgments about who is most in need and who is not unless it takes on everyone, and it cannot do that.

The agency is thus faced with designing a procedure that will be imperfect—just as are the judicial hearings that so concerned Mary in Case 1.2, *Dancing a Legal Dance.* The agency knows that what would be just would be a procedure that sorts out for help all and only those who truly need help, but it cannot design a procedure that will ensure that result. So it must draw a line somehow, and it can weigh its line either toward helping those who need it or keeping out those who do not. It can devise a procedure, that is, which, though not perfect, is generous and attempts to help all who need help, but will also help some who do not. Or it can devise a procedure that keeps out those who do not truly need help, but risks keeping out some who do need help. Either way, the procedure will be imperfect. Either some who do not truly need help will get it or some who do truly need help will not get it.

Even if money were no object, drawing a line would not be easy. If money were no object, we might think we ought to be generous and make sure to help all who need help even though that will mean that some who do not need help will get it anyway. But giving help to those who do not need it may create just the kind of dependency that help is designed to eradicate. The best help for some prospective clients may be no help. So there are harms no matter where the line is drawn.

We have just made a distinction between two kinds of procedural justice, and it is worth making the distinction clearer.[107] We often commit ourselves to a procedure to determine what is just and what is not. For instance, we might be committed to a substantive principle of justice that says that everyone gets a certain benefit if they deserve it, but then, because it is not obvious who is deserving and who is not, we might devise a procedure to make that determination. The procedure might consist of hearings before an impartial panel giving evidence for and against someone's deserving the benefit. Our criminal justice system is based on the substantive principle that those who commit crimes deserve punishment and those who do not do not, but because it is not obvious who has committed crimes and who has not, we have a procedure—a criminal trial is part of that procedure—to make that determination.

A procedure is perfect if we know ahead of time what is just and can devise a procedure that ensures that result. If we know that each of two persons deserves half of what is available, for instance, then we can have perfect procedural justice if we can divide the benefit in half. Unfortunately, the situations in which we know what is just and know how to achieve it are rarer than we might like. We are far more likely to find ourselves having to devise a procedure that is imperfect. We have such a procedure when, as with perfect procedural justice, we know ahead of time what is just, but cannot devise a procedure that ensures that result. The criminal justice system is one example. *The Waiting List* provides another. The welfare system itself provides yet another.

We would like welfare benefits to go to all of those who need help and only those who need help, but we cannot design a procedure that will pick out all and only those persons. The consequence is that in drawing a line, we need to make a value judgment about which way to weigh the benefits—to help all who need help and thus help some who do not, or to keep out those who do not need help and risk not helping some of those who need help.

In either case, we will find examples of persons who need help and do not receive it and of persons who do not need help and do receive it. It is the nature of imperfect procedural justice that there will be such examples. So one cannot properly argue that the welfare system is bad because of those who take advantage of the system for their own benefit when they do not need aid. Similarly, however, one cannot properly argue that the system is bad just because some who need help do not obtain it. To make an ethically proper argument about the welfare system, we need to begin with an examination of the relevant percentages. Of all those who need help, how many do not obtain it, and of those who do not, how many do obtain it? Then we need to examine whether the disparities can be remedied or lessened by fine-tuning the procedure in any way. Only if too large a percentage of those in need are not being helped or too large a percentage of those not in need are being helped can we proceed to object to the procedure, and, of course, people will disagree about how much is "too large." And only if the procedure can be fine-tuned to be more discriminating can our objections have any fruitful outcome.

Discretion

A last issue to examine in this section concerns discretion.[108] In *The Waiting List*, those "in need" get served first, but, however clearly in need some persons may be, subtle judgment is often necessary to pick out others. In any situation in which there are standards for judging, someone must do the judging, and two sorts of ethical issues can arise. On the one hand, even if the rules by which to judge are clear, the person doing the judging may not apply them correctly. Or the rules may be unclear so that their application is unsteady even when applied by the most fair-minded of persons.

In *Adoptive Children*, LaShonda was giving some adoptive children information about their natural parents. One issue that case raised concerned whether it is ever ethical to break the law, and another concerned how we decide who gets the illegal information and who does not. LaShonda was making exceptions to the general prohibition against providing information. Even if we agree with her that some sort of exceptions needed to be made, we might wonder about some of the particular judgments she made. In one instance she mentioned, she did not provide information to a brother and sister who came twice, unannounced, asking for help. She preferred, she said, that people make appointments so she could do a better job of preparing, and these two were demanding.

She is engaged in risky, illegal behavior and so needs to do careful screening. She needs to judge who is likely to talk and who is not. She also has concerns about the well-being of the natural parents. Who is likely to be concerned about their interests and who is not? So she might be likely to think demanding persons put her and the natural parents at risk.

Exercising discretion raises ethical issues. Because LaShonda is making exceptions to a general prohibition, and she is making her own rules to guide herself, she has to be especially sensitive that she may be unjust—either in making up the rules she applies or in applying them. They seem unclear. What does it mean to be "undemanding," for instance? And her application of these rules seems unclear—how is one to determine who will not talk because they are extremely happy, or will talk because they are angry at having to go through the complicated ritual that LaShonda seems to be demanding?

Social Justice

Social work has been called the altruistic profession.[109] As their professional calling, social workers help others. But we can help individual clients by changing the society within which they live as well as by concerning ourselves with the personal difficulties they have, and social workers have a professional obligation to work for social justice.[110] The Code of Ethics says that social workers "should advocate for living conditions conducive to the fulfillment of basic human needs and should promote social, economic, political, and cultural values and institutions that are compatible with the realization of social justice" (6.01; see 6.04).

Even if social workers were not committed to this end as professionals, it takes little examination of what it is like to be working within the profession to understand why they would be motivated to achieve this end. A caseworker soon discovers, first, that many clients' particular problems are social problems—lack of educational opportunity, lack of a stable and adequate source of income, lack of child-care facilities, and so on—and, second, that what the caseworker can do for these clients within the system is little compared to what could be done by changing the system.[111]

We shall first examine what are called the conditions of justice, what must be true in order for issues of justice to arise. We will then examine two competing visions of justice. One emphasizes individual liberty, but accepts wide disparities in how individuals are to be treated in society. The other emphasizes the essential equality of individuals and ensures that each will be benefitted by any gains of society as a whole. These are not the only contenders among substantive principles, but they represent incompatible ideals that will allow us to see how we might agree on the end of achieving social justice and yet have such completely different visions of justice that we would disagree on everything else.

But however incompatible the ideals of these two visions of justice, at least one other vision—that of Marxism—requires a radically different understanding of what is essential for justice. We shall consider this alternative when we have finished briefly sketching the other two.

Conditions of Justice

It is a condition of any question of justice that what is being distributed be moderately scarce.[112] If what was being distributed was not scarce at all, everyone could have as much as they wanted, and there would be no need to concern ourselves with how to distribute the thing justly. If it were very scarce—like a single glass of water on a life boat with twenty passengers—then justice is not possible. So we are only concerned about questions of justice when there are some of the goods in question, but not enough for everyone to have as much as they might want or need.

Social workers are committed by the Code of Ethics to "promote the right of clients to self-determination and assist clients in their efforts to identity and clarify their goals" (1.02). That commitment assumes that each of us can have a particular vision of a life for ourselves and that each of us has a right to the general means to realize that vision—equality of opportunity, for instance, sufficient income or wealth to satisfy at least our basic needs, and so on.

Such goods as opportunity and income are basic goods—extremely valuable to us as means to an end, namely, achieving our particular vision of the good life for ourselves. But, unfortunately, it is true of everything of value to us in achieving our particular visions for ourselves that it is at least moderately scarce. And so, in determining how to distribute such basic goods, we need to agree on a principle of distribution, a substantive principle of justice. As we shall see, that turns out to be much harder than it might at first appear. Let us begin with a view articulated best by the philosopher Robert Nozick.[113]

Justice as Free Transactions

Whenever we go shopping, we take money (or a credit card), and when we decide to buy something, we give the merchant the money, and the merchant gives us the goods—milk, clothes—we have purchased. This exchange redistributes the goods of the world. You had some money that the merchant now has, and the merchant has some goods that you now have. If this redistribution of goods is to be just, there must be a substantive principle of justice underlying it and it must be justifiable. We can best see that principle and understand how it works by pursuing an analogy.[114]

Monopoly is a game in which money and property are distributed. At the end of the game, if the game is played to the end, one player is likely to have most, if not all, of the wealth of the game—all of the money and all of the property. The players begin even. Each is given the same amount of money, $1500, and no one begins with any property. They are all subject to the same rules, and as the game proceeds, money and property are redistributed. A player gets $200 for going around GO; so $200 goes from the bank to the player who passed Go. Another collects $6 rent; so $6 goes from one player to another. Each play in the game not only shifts one's position on the board, but also holds the potential for shifting one's fortunes. Will one land on Boardwalk? Will one land on Parking—diagonally across from GO and sometimes filled with the money from fines and assessments?

We all know what can go wrong in such games. If someone cheats by taking money from the bank without permission, or by turning over mortgaged cards without paying off the mortgage, or by refusing to pay Community Chest by burying the tax card in the deck without admitting that it was the tax card, then the game is unfair, and the outcome of the game is unfair to the extent that it reflects the unfairness in the game. If the final distribution of winners and losers depends upon someone having unmortgaged Boardwalk without really paying off the mortgage, for instance, then the winner did not really win and the losers did not really lose.

Similarly, if there is no cheating, but there is coercion, the game is unjust. An older sibling may tell a younger, "You better not buy B & O; that's mine!" To the extent that the final result of the game reflects that earlier coercion, it is as unjust as if the person stole the B & O.

Yet if all the transactions of the game are uncoerced and if there is no cheating, the final results, whatever they may be, seem just. No one who plays seems to have any proper grounds of complaint even if everything is lost. Or, at least, that is the way we think about the game and about similar situations in which people start out with equal shares and, through a series of transactions, end up with unequal shares.

For instance, no one complains about races in which there are winners and losers. As long as everyone started at the same mark, the result is deemed just provided that there was no cheating or coercion. In competition in the marketplace, no one seems entitled to complain when, at the end of the day, the farmer ends up with less fruit and produce and more money and various customers have less money, but some fruit or produce. As long as they were not cheated, and no one was coerced, the exchanges of money for fruit and produce seem just. The final distribution at the end of the day is as just as the distribution at the beginning.

Such examples are convincing because, it is claimed, any distribution that is achieved through free and uncoerced transactions from an originally equal distribution is just. What matters in this view is not what shares of any distribution anyone has, whether one has more or less than another, but how the distribution was achieved. If it was achieved in a just way, then it is just—even if the final distribution is very unequal, as in *Monopoly.* One person has everything, and the rest have nothing. But, on the theory of justice being articulated here, that distribution is just provided it was achieved in a just way.

One implication of this theory is that the apparent, vast disparities in our social system may in fact be just. We cannot tell just by looking at how things are now. We shall instead have to determine how the disparities were achieved. What matters is that people within society are allowed to engage in free and uncoerced transactions. If government interferes with their capacity to engage in such transactions, the end result of such transactions is unjust to the extent the result reflects the interference. In this view, taxes are a form of interference because money is redistributed not through free and uncoerced transactions, but through the government's demanding a share. Regulations regarding buying and selling would be a form of interference because they prevent people from freely doing what they wish to do. The vision is of a society unfettered by governmental regulations, in which persons engage in exchanges with each other, buying and selling what they wish as they wish. Whatever happens as a result of such transactions is just provided the original distribution was just and provided there is no coercion or cheating.

This can be a powerful vision, especially when we view it as explaining our everyday commercial transactions and their results—whether, for instance, our having our house and furniture is just when others have neither. It surely resonates with the system of capitalism in which we live. Justice has been called "the first virtue of social institutions" because, among other things, it sets the normative relations among citizens.[115] Justice as free transactions tells us that it is just to buy and sell and trade and that we are not being unjust in having more than others have provided only that we achieved what we have through free transactions. Cheating and coercion are the great sins in such a social system, for they impede justice.

The Implications for Social Work

This vision sets a view before any social worker about where this society ought to be heading if it is to become a just society, and it is a view that has implications for how a social worker ought to respond to the problems faced by individual clients. That is, if we have this view of justice, we will think that our clients can face only two sorts of problems. Either (a) the system is somehow preventing them from realizing their full potential by restricting, in some way, their transactions with their fellow citizens, or (b) the clients are themselves not taking advantage of what the system allows.

If the problem is (a), a social worker ought to work to remove governmental regulations that hamper free enterprise, must work to prevent cheating in the system, and must work to purify the system of any coercive elements that may harm clients in pursuing their aims.

If the problem is (b), a social worker must meet a client's problems by offering options and encouraging the client. "You ought to be more self-confident of your capacities to succeed" or "You have a number of personal assets, and you need to develop those if you are going to succeed in this society" or "You seem to have difficulty in competitive situations. Let's work on that by practicing competitive games."

In short, the vision of justice has implications for a social worker's practice. If a social worker accepts this vision, then he or she will be obligated to tell clients to strive to succeed within the system to the extent the system satisfies the theory of justice. That is, failures of a client become the personal responsibility of a client in this theory of justice if a client does not compete well within the social system, and a social worker would have the obligation to tell a client that and to try to help the client compete better.

One virtue of this theory of justice is that it attempts to maximize the liberty of those within the system. They are free to do whatever they wish with whatever assets they have, provided that they do not coerce or cheat others in making transactions. But the theory has its problems. We can best bring these out by examining what we might call "the lottery of life."

Natural Features and Social Circumstance

One cause of injustice is that persons are born into social circumstances that make a profound difference to the kinds of lives they are able to lead. It is no fault of their own that they are born into such circumstances, and by the time they become responsible enough to make decisions, the circumstances may already have worked such harm as to stunt forever the person's life chances. This impediment of being born into social circumstances that are less than optimal is compounded when one is born with a natural feature that is a deficit in the social system in which one must live.[116]

Consider the following case.

CASE 6.3

Differing Social Circumstances

The social worker, Amena, is visiting a client in the city. The client has a son, Thomas, who is four years old. The woman lives generally by herself in a small, ramshackle house. She has a scar down her arm, put there by her occasional boyfriend who blowtorched it one night when he was angry. Her son has a hearing defect, and although he is intensely curious and talkative, Amena has a difficult time understanding him. He repeats what he hears, and what he hears is not clear.

Amena has finally found public housing for the woman and her son and explains the conditions. It costs, but her welfare payments will be increased to pay for it. Her boyfriend cannot live with her however.

They talk, and after pointing out that living in public housing will finally put Thomas in a position where his hearing impairment can be helped, Amena says, "It will also give you a reason for not seeing that man again. So he won't be able to hurt you."

The woman says, after a slight delay, and in tears, "You don't understand. He's my man, and any man is better than none." She refuses to move.

One may regret the woman's decision, thinking it a manifestation of a fatalism she could try to overcome. But the plight of her son is more dramatic. He is bright and inquisitive, but having been born with a hearing defect, and living in such social conditions that he is unable to obtain help, he will not be able to make himself understood readily and will have difficulties in school and in his social life. A natural defect, perhaps readily remedied, condemns him to less than a full life because, through no fault of his own, he was born in a system that left his well-being up to a mother who, for whatever reason, was unable to provide for proper medical aid at the time when it would do the most good.

What we might call natural assets and deficits are distributed at birth. Some are born with features that will aid them in seeking their own conception of the good life; others—like Thomas—are born with features that will impede their seeking the good life for themselves. We are all born into certain social circumstances. Our parents are poor or rich, upper-class or lower-class, educated or not, and so on. Our prospects for life are to some extent determined by these circumstances. Those parents who presume that their children will go to college, for instance, are more likely to have children who go to college.

Thomas has been hit by bad luck twice in the lottery of life. He was born with a hearing defect, and he was born into social circumstances that make help difficult to obtain. It seems unjust that matters should be so arranged in a society that children should be harmed so much because of something that is not their fault. It is one thing to condemn people to less than a full life for something they choose to do. That is how we justify sending those who commit crimes to jail. It is quite another thing to put people at risk of living less than a full life because they are born with a defect in social circumstances that make it difficult to correct. They are not responsible for having been born with a defect that will substantially alter their life prospects, and they are not responsible for being born into social circumstances that make correcting that defect in a timely way unlikely. It thus seems unfair that they should be penalized in trying to achieve their life prospects.

It seems particularly so because we live in a capitalist society. Some natural features are thus obviously more valuable than others because wealth and income are distributed in large measure on the part of one's capacity to achieve the good life for oneself. Native intelligence and a willingness to work count for more than a natural sense of cooperation in a society in which one acquires goods through competitive practices. Thomas was born into a system, that is, that values articulate individuals who can make themselves clear.

What counts as natural assets and natural deficits are themselves socially determined. Any particular society is an artifact, a creation of human beings, and it can be changed if human beings wish to change it. In one sort of society, some natural features may be assets that are deficits in another sort of society. For instance, in Eskimo cultures, a willingness to share everything has survival value while, in other cultures, such altruism might count as naivete.

That natural assets and deficits are social artifacts is important to keep in mind because it is arguable that societies ought to be arranged so as to compensate those who are not well-endowed from birth with the natural features that make for success within a particular society. Those persons who are born mentally handicapped in some severe way are unable to compete in society, through no fault of their own, and it is not just, it may be argued, to have a social system so arranged as to deny them the benefits that the social system arranges for others who are born with what the system makes natural assets. Those who are born with natural features that are assets within such a society should get no credit for being born that way anymore than those who are born with what are considered deficits should be held responsible.

We should look carefully at a theory of justice that fails to compensate those who lose out in a social system because they lack the natural features the system defines as assets, and we should look equally carefully at a theory that rewards those who win out because they are born with natural features the system considers assets.

We are, in effect, here making use of the fourth step in our method of tracking harms. For we are here asking what harms will be unmitigated, produced, or entrenched by the particular arrangement Nozick argues is just.[117]

Difficulties with Justice as Free Transactions

The theory of justice as free transactions does nothing to nullify the conditions of social circumstance. If one is born into a social position that makes it difficult to utilize one's natural assets, the theory does not compensate in any way for that problem. We start off a game of *Monopoly* even with others, and it is that even start that explains in part why no one complains of uneven results.[118] Any eventual unevenness is the result of the participants' own play and luck, good or bad. But if the distribution of money at the beginning of the game had been uneven, so that some were, as it were, born into different starting positions, with significantly different assets, then it is not obvious that the outcome of the game would be thought just, even if the transactions were uncoerced and free of cheating. If someone begins with $5,000 and another with $10, then no matter how good the luck of the latter, it will be difficult to purchase enough property early on to make a run at winning the game.

Taken as an analogy of a society, *Monopoly* fails because it supposes people start out equally situated while, in real life, they start out in different social circumstances, some so advantaged by the successes of their parents that it is difficult for them to fail and some so disadvantaged that it is difficult for them to succeed. *Monopoly* presupposes an even playing field, as it were, while the game of life is marked by the unevenness that societies impose in discrimination—against women and certain ethnic groups, for instance.

Monopoly also fails, like the theory, to compensate for natural deficits. If one is born with low intelligence, or some other feature that harms one's capacity to engage in transactions, or if the system is biased against women, for example, a person with the "wrong" natural characteristics may be disadvantaged in a system that emphasizes such transactions. Again, it is no fault of one's own to be born with such features, and yet the system is so designed that someone with such features is less likely to achieve success than someone who is born with natural assets.

Of course, the assets and deficits are "natural" only in the sense that they are natural features of people. That such features are deficits or assets is a result of having a social system that makes them deficits or assets. *Monopoly* makes competitive features assets and makes deficits of such cooperative or charitable behavior as letting someone get all four railroads so he or she can have a complete set. A different game, or different social system, might make competitive features deficits and cooperative features assets.

So the vision of justice at issue is doubly at fault, it may be argued. For it first defines what counts as assets and deficits, making justice depend upon them, and then fails to compensate those who, through no fault of their own, fail to have those natural features the social system deems assets.

The vision is thus open to the objection that it distributes the goods of society on the basis of characteristics that are themselves socially determined and that are not distributed justly. For it is arguable that because no one deserves the natural features they have or the social circumstances they are born into, it is unjust to distribute the goods of society, like opportunity and income, on the basis of any natural features or social circumstances.

The theory picks out some natural features as crucial, namely, those helpful to engaging in transactions. It picks those features, it is claimed, because they encourage the liberty of individuals and, when emphasized, produce the most efficient system. The argument is that when people are free to do whatever they wish, without interference, they will produce more than when a governmental agency is telling them what to do or restricting their actions.

But one additional problem the theory faces is that in attempting to encourage liberty, it may undermine it. In the game of *Monopoly,* those who lose out lose out completely. Unless one modifies the game to allow for bank loans, some players will slowly or quickly lose all their assets through bad luck or bad play. The implication is that if we were to adopt this vision of justice for our society, some would not make it. They will simply not have enough natural talent to make it or to overcome bad luck or a poor inheritance, in a society that values the capacity to engage in transactions. So they will lose their liberty because they will lose the capacity to engage in any transactions at all. In the worst case, they will die, and in cases less worse, they will have nothing to sell. Similarly, those who win in the game will have their liberty diminished because there will be fewer and fewer individuals with whom they can engage in transactions. They are, of course, not likely to notice that because, unlike *Monopoly*, real societies produce new wealth and new players all the time, but the point is that the liberty of individuals depends upon the choices available to them, and if the choices are diminished, so is their liberty. Those who succeed in such a system are impoverished by the loss of liberty of those who fail, and that is some evidence that a just society cannot be arranged the way *Monopoly* is. Even the winners lose something if matters are so arranged that there are winners and losers.

But justice as free transactions is not the only substantive principle of justice we could adopt as our vision of a justice society. John Rawls has articulated a very different theory.[119]

Justice as Fairness

It is wrong to punish people for something they did not do. It is thus wrong to send people to jail when they committed no crime, and it is equally wrong that people should be penalized in any way for things they are not responsible for. But you are not responsible for having been born into a particular social position, and you are not responsible for having been born with whatever natural features you may have, some of which may be assets in our society and some of which may be deficits. So, one might argue, a just world would be one in which people are not penalized in their quest for the good life for themselves by natural and social contingencies for which they are not responsible.

We might imagine modifying a society modeled after *Monopoly* in a series of stages, each modification responding to a harm done in such a society and all the modifications leading to a very different kind of society, articulating a very different vision of justice. For, first, as we saw, those who are born into poor social circumstances are harmed by their birth in those positions through no fault of their own. In a real society, unlike *Monopoly*, individuals do not start out equally situated. One way to compensate for the inequality is to ensure that everyone has an equal chance to be a success in the society.

But we must distinguish between different ways of understanding what it means to have an equal chance. What is called *formal equality of opportunity* guarantees that when we all compete for positions, each person is judged wholly on merit. The person who most merits the position wins it. But individuals with equal natural talents will not compete on a level playing field if all that is required is formal equality of opportunity. For those born into poor social circumstances have that much further to go to catch up with those who have equal natural talents, born into the best social circumstances. The latter will generally win the best positions not because their natural talents are better, but because their social circumstances allow them to develop better the natural talents they do have.

Requiring formal equality of opportunity after people have been affected by their social positions comes too late, it can be argued, to help those harmed by being born into less fortunate social positions. What is needed is *real equality of opportunity.* That means that society must be arranged so that those with equal natural talents rise, or fall, to the same level no matter where they may be placed by birth in the social scale. Providing real equality of opportunity requires a fundamental change in the way in which we educate our children, guaranteeing real equality of opportunity throughout the educational system. It would require fundamental changes in the ways in which we rear and support our children, making sure that some are not harmed by their family circumstances.

But even providing real equality of opportunity will not help those who are born without the natural features the society values. Those who cannot make it in a competitive system will not be helped by a system that guarantees that natural talents rise to their natural levels regardless of the social position in which one was born, for they lack the natural talents to make it. Yet it is not just, it is claimed, for those people to suffer for being born with whatever natural features preclude their making it in a competitive system. It is not their fault they lack those features, and it is unjust, it is claimed, to arrange a social system in which they are penalized for having the features they have.

What is needed, the argument continues, is some floor below which people are not allowed to fall, a floor high enough so that they can live a decent life. Society should compensate them for having made valuable natural features that they do not have.

With real equality of opportunity, and with a floor below which citizens are not allowed to fall, a society can compensate those who would otherwise be harmed in a social system arranged like *Monopoly.* But such modifications leave untouched those who are born with natural features the system designates as valuable and who are born into such good social circumstances that they can parlay their position into great gains for themselves. Yet, it is argued, they deserve their success as little as those without the favored natural features deserve their failures. We should look at the distribution of natural features as a lottery, with no one deserving whatever features they have. Because society determines which features are valuable and which are not, rewarding some for having those valuable features is as unjust as penalizing those who lack those features. Society should not be arranged so that the distribution of income and wealth and other social goods depends upon natural characteristics for which no one can properly claim credit.

Instead, it is argued, it should be arranged so that benefits accrue to those with natural talents only if they are to the benefit of everyone. This arrangement effectively puts a cap on everyone's income and wealth as well as a floor. Indeed, any difference between the cap and the floor can occur only if those making more help those on the floor. If any rise, all rise. Injustice, in this view, is an inequality that is not to the benefit of all.

The Implications for Social Work

We can envision the social structure that would occur under this theory of justice by imagining a situation in which persons are normally competitive—students in a classroom, for instance, vying for grades. What the theory requires is that those with natural assets that would normally allow them to rise to the top use those assets only for the benefit of all. Natural assets become public assets and natural deficits become public deficits. Each member of the class would get the grade of the person who gets the lowest grade unless getting a higher grade advantages everyone. So each member of the class would try to raise the lowest grade as high as possible. The students thus do not compete, but cooperate for grades. Altruism becomes a social virtue and competitive self-interest becomes a social vice.

As with the view of justice as free transactions, this view sets before a social worker a vision of society for which we can aim. To the extent that we let individuals fall through the social net, we are unjust; to the extent that we fail to have real equality of opportunity, we are unjust; and to the extent that we allow some individuals to amass income and wealth that is not to the benefit of all, we are unjust. Social activism means working for a deep egalitarianism, in this view, and this view has implications for practice in particular cases as well.

For many of the cases that come before social workers will reflect injustices within the system. Individuals will find that they are not getting ahead, even with natural talent, and will find that some impediment to real equality of opportunity is blocking them. Or they will have fallen through the floor and discover that there is no support for them within the system. The need for social workers would diminish considerably were the theory of justice as fairness realized, for many of the individuals put at risk by our current system would be taken care of in a system with real equality of opportunity and with a floor. But, also, the concerns of social workers would change. In justice as free transactions, a social worker's job would be to make sure the system does not prevent individuals from achieving their true potential and to encourage clients to take advantage of what the system offers them. But in justice as fairness, a primary concern would be those who are so self-interested as to attempt to gain advantages for themselves that do not benefit all. Bill Gates would become an object of concern rather than a role model.

Difficulties with Justice as Fairness

This vision of a just society is deeply egalitarian, and it has some significant disadvantages. For one thing, it is not at all clear how one could institute it without a heavy loss of liberty. The advantage of justice as free transactions is that once the system begins, everyone is free to do what they want to do, consistent with allowing everyone else freedom. Anything that interferes with freedom creates injustice. Normally, individuals in a society come to occupy different positions, with different assets and deficits, through their own individual efforts and through luck, both bad and good. A storm that demolishes your house puts you at a disadvantage vis-a-vis others through no fault of yours, and a deal that you make at a flea market puts you at an advantage although it harms no one else. Individuals become differentiated one from another through their own acts and acts of nature, and yet, in a society in which justice as fairness operates, continual tinkering is required to make sure that any significant differentials are to the benefit of all. Individuals would not be free to do whatever they wished, and significant transfers of income and wealth would be required to create a floor below which people cannot fall and to make sure that those who would otherwise rise high within the system gain only when the gains are for the benefit of others. Justice as fairness requires a loss of liberty. We trade liberty for what the theory claims is fairness.

Tied to this concern about a loss of freedom is that the theory would make a society just only at the price of great inefficiency. The more egalitarianism is required, the more transfers from one to another are required and, it seems, the more individual incentives for using one's talents are reduced. One may respond that we are socialized into a competitive system and that we may just as well be socialized into a cooperative one. But it needs to be argued on independent grounds that competitive appetites are not natural features of individuals. The concern is that if they are natural features, the system is at odds with what humans will do in any event and that this creates friction and thus, in that form as well, a source of inefficiency in the system.

Besides, it may be argued, though it is just to provide for those who, through no fault of their own, have natural features that disadvantage them in society, the argument for a high floor is less plausible when one considers those who have the natural features that are assets in a society, but fail to develop them, through no fault of society. Someone who fails to develop his or her talents is still supported by the system and thus by other individuals within the system who are effectively working for that person as well as for themselves. That seems unjust. Why would some provide for others who are perfectly capable of providing for themselves, but refuse to? The incentive to develop one's talents for the benefit of all is reduced if others could develop theirs as well, but do not wish to and yet still are supported by the system.

Besides, some may object, those who do have what society recognizes as assets can develop them for their own benefit only if others benefit as well. So the features that make them distinct individuals become public property, as it were, to be used to benefit all if used to benefit any. Individuals are not allowed to choose any sort of life they wish, to develop their talents any way they wish, but only for the benefit of all. That may be good, but the price may be too high. We lose individuality as well as liberty.

Alternative Theories of Justice

We may compensate for both natural and social differences or not. Justice as fairness compensates fully for both; justice as free transactions compensates for neither. If there are no other differences that a system of social justice arguably needs to compensate for, these theories represent the limits. But, obviously, there are alternatives.

We might compensate for natural differences, providing a floor, for example, but not compensate for social differences. Or we may compensate for social differences, providing real equality of opportunity, but not compensate for natural differences. Or we may compensate for some natural differences and not for others or for some social differences and not for others. Or we may compensate for all social differences and some natural differences, and so on. Each of these alternatives would need to be explored for its harms and benefits if we are not convinced that either of the two visions we have examined properly captures a just society.

In exploring these various alternatives as well as the two visions we have examined, however briefly, we would be exploring differing forms of social organization. A society organized so that it would be just in Nozick's justice as free transactions would differ in significant ways from one organized so that it would be just according to Rawls's justice as fairness.

Not only would the wealth and income generated by those within the society be distributed in different ways, but what would count as social virtues—as a "good person"—would differ too. Someone who takes advantage of every competitive opportunity to increase his or her wealth is an entrepreneur in a society organized to express justice as free transactions. Entrepreneurs are generally to be praised. Helping the least advantaged would be not an act of justice, but of kindness—not required, but nice to have. We would praise such acts, but we would not think them expressions of a just individual, but of an individual who is, besides being just—neither cheating nor coercing—also kind.

But in a society organized to express Rawls's justice as fairness, helping the least advantaged is an act of justice, provided that everyone benefits. It is not kindness to help those in need of help. Rather, they have a claim upon us. We shall be living in an unjust society if there exist inequalities not to the benefit of all.

We need only imagine a society "writ small"—a group of social work professionals working together, a classroom of students—to appreciate the significance of how the differing visions of justice can make a difference to the ways in which those within the society interact and to the structure of the society as a whole. A classroom in which inequalities in grades are unjust unless they are to the benefit of all means that the very best students will need to work together to help those least advantaged—or everyone will achieve the grade to be achieved by the least advantaged. On the other hand, a classroom in which only ten percent are to obtain an A, twenty percent a B, thirty percent a C, and so on does not encourage cooperation. Each act of helping that may advantage another student may disadvantage the student who is helping. A society organized so as to satisfy Nozick's justice as free transactions will be highly competitive while one organized to satisfy Rawls's justice as fairness will be highly cooperative. The relations among members of the society will thus differ significantly, and the distribution of the society's resources—grades in the case of a classroom—will differ significantly as well.

Because social work is an altruistic profession, concerned as a profession to empower and help others, social work must consider what is the most just society, what social structure will best achieve the end of helping those most in need. Justice as fairness and justice as transfer both presuppose that the economic organization of society ought to be capitalism, but, as Marx made clear, capitalism is only one form of economic structure and his argument is that it is inherently unfair.

Marx's attack on "bourgeois capitalism" sends a mixed message about what social work is obligated to do to fulfil its mission. On the one hand, Marx attacks the rhetoric of justice as "an ideological device for presenting bourgeois interests under the guise of allegedly universal values."[120] We may sometimes think an individual is trying to dress up an action done out of self-interest by giving us "ethical" reasons for it. "I only did it because I want to help you." Marx's critique is that capitalism has developed an entire "ethical" system simply to dress up unbridled self-interest so that it may appear just and responsible. Were we to take Nozick's justice as free transactions to its logical end and prohibit, as unjust, any interference by the government in how we engage in commerce, and so prohibit taxation that is used now to aid those in need, we would have a system without a safety net—or, more accurately, a safety net secured only by the kindness of those who have succeeded in the "dog-eat-dog rat race" of unbridled capitalism.[121] So for us to ask whether socialism is just is for us, from Marx's point of view, to use concepts that presuppose capitalism to query a system that rejects it. The answer ought to be "Not applicable."

And yet, on the other hand, Marx argues for a system of distribution that, in a pure form, would seem to distribute society's benefits "according to need."[122] A medical system that distributed health care on the basis of need would be far different than ours, which generally distributes health care on the basis of ability to pay, but it would still distribute health care. So it seems not unreasonable to ask, "Is that distribution just?" Indeed, part of the power of Marx's conception seems to derive from his critique of capitalism as being unjust, the exploitation of one by another, and from his description of a socialist system in which the benefits of society are distributed according to need as being inherently just, treating each member of society as a person entitled to have his or her needs satisfied merely by being a fellow human being in that society. That is why "the Marxian approach to justice [seems] essentially a Rawlsian one in that it concentrates on the alleviation of basic needs."[123]

When we lay out the competing visions of justice as free transactions and justice as fairness, we do not mean to exclude a vision of justice and thus a vision of society that may differ radically from those that would express the two visions we have examined, however briefly. It is one more reminder that we cannot assume that others share our vision of what is ethical. The first step in understanding the sources of conflict in an ethical situation is coming to see the issue from the point of view of those with whom we disagree. What may seem terribly unethical from our perspective may, within the boundaries of another ethical vision, be the only ethical thing to do. Only then can we properly begin to assess the competing judgments and determine what we ought to do, all things considered.

QUESTIONS

1. Distinguish between an instance of particular justice and one of social justice.

2. Some have argued that civil disobedience is impossible without the distinction between particular and social justice because being civilly disobedient can only take place within a political system that is basically just. Using Martin Luther King's protests as an example, explain how civil disobedience presupposes a just

system. In Case 1.2, *Dancing a Legal Dance,* could Mary have engaged in civil disobedience to protest the judge's decision?

3. What is the formal principle of justice? Give an example from social work practice or from the cases in the book of treating like cases unalike, and an example of treating unlike cases alike. Explain why they are prima facie wrong.

4. What is the difference between the formal principle of justice and substantive principles?

5. The formal principle of justice has substantive ethical weight. Explain how by using an example from your own experience or from the cases in the book.

6. Standing in line may seem an ethically unchallenging procedure for determining the order in which one is to be seen. But consider each of the following scenarios, first determining what is being distributed and the order in which individuals are being served, and then laying out the harms and benefits to all involved:

   a. In the emergency room of a hospital, those most severely injured are seen first regardless of the time of their arrival. So others may sit in the waiting room for hours for what are judged minor injuries by the staff on hand. Those waiting may include elderly individuals who are unable to sit for such long periods without extreme discomfort. Is this just? Is there anything that could be done to mitigate any harms?

   b. Two social work practitioners in an agency are seeing first-time clients on a first-come, first-served basis. The clients line up in two lines, one in front of each practitioner, the clients presumably judging which line will move the fastest, or deciding which practitioner they want to see.

   c. This time the clients line up in one line, the first in line going to whichever social work practitioner is free.

   d. The honor system is used. An elderly woman comes in, asks for a number, and when told that the honor system is used, says, "Good. I'm next."[124]

7. Now imagine yourself a social work practitioner who is being queried by a client about why the client is being treated in a way he or she perceives to be unjust and so harmful. For instance, a client waiting in the office when the elderly woman in question 6d enters and announces "I'm next" will not be seen by you as soon as she sees the elderly woman if you take her word for it. The honor system requires honor, that is, and disputes can readily break out that will need mediating. If you are the social worker, you will need to have at hand a procedure for mediation and an explanation of how it applies in the situation at hand. The mediation procedure will obviously itself need to be just. So lay out a mediation procedure for such disputes, one that is just, and apply it to the case at hand in which the elderly woman is taken ahead of others who have been waiting.[125]

8. Distinguish between perfect and imperfect procedural justice.

9. Explain how the welfare system is an instance of procedural justice. What is being distributed? How is it being distributed? Is the procedure imperfect or perfect? In either case, if either is applicable, why is it one or the other?

10. Suppose that the welfare system is a system of imperfect procedural justice. Could it be made perfect? What would that require?

11. The criminal justice system is imperfect, and it can be designed either to protect the innocent, which means that some who committed a crime will not be found guilty, or to ensure that those who committed a crime are found guilty, which means some who are innocent will be found guilty. Disagreements about what to do about "welfare cheats" center on where to put the burden of proof. Should we try to ensure that all who need help obtain it? Or should we try to ensure that those who do not need help do not obtain it? The former remedy will let some who do not need help get it, and the latter will not let some who do need it get it. Using the method of tracking harms, assess the relative merits of these two remedies and determine which is ethically preferable, if either is.

12. What are the conditions of justice? Give an example of something of concern to social workers that is so prevalent that we need not concern ourselves (at least overly much) with its just distribution. Why not? Give an example of something of concern to social workers that is so scarce that there is little sense concerning ourselves with its just distribution. Why not?

13. One of the powerful appeals of justice as free transactions is that we often obtain goods and services in our society through free transactions and no one thinks them unjust. We buy a blouse or shirt, when others cannot afford one, and we do not think that in itself is ethically wrong. Provide an instance from social work practice or from a case in the book in which those involved engaged in free transactions and everyone thought the result was just. What made it just—according to the theory in question?

14. What two particular problems come to the fore for social workers if the society is committed to justice as free transactions? Why are those problems the ones that come to the fore?

15. Is it ethically right to blame the client for a failure to achieve success within a social system organized to express justice as free transactions? Lay out the benefits and harms of such a practice and then assess the practice as a feature of justice as free transactions. That is, if it is harmful, is it so harmful that we ought not to organize our society to express justice as free transactions? If so, why? If not, why not?

16. What is the substantive principle of justice that animates justice as free transactions? What is the formal principle?

17. What is the substantive principle of justice that animates justice as fairness? What is the formal principle?

18. How might one argue on ethical grounds that natural features and social circumstances are morally irrelevant in the distribution of social benefits and burdens?

19. Explain how each different vision of a just society accentuates some human traits as being ethically more valuable than others. Compare the traits and assess, on those grounds alone, which theory is ethically preferable.

20. Justice as free transactions and justice as fairness mark out differing forms of social organization. Lay out how a classroom or any social structure would be organized under each view. Explain in particular how the differing forms of social organization would make different personal features and acts ethical. For instance, in a society that expresses justice as free transactions would individuals who help those who are least advantaged be acting justly? If not, what moral virtue would they be expressing? What about the same sort of act in a society that expresses justice as fairness?

21. If the same act expresses different moral virtues in different forms of social organization—as the answer to the previous questions suggests—what kind of moral character is each theory of justice holding up as the ideal? For instance, if someone who helps the least advantaged is just in the one society, but kind in another, does that make for a difference in the kinds of moral character each theory implies is ideal? What are those differences?

22. Marxist theory says that everyone ought receive according to their needs. Does justice as fairness go further than that? If so, in what way(s)? If not, how does it differ from Marxism? In what way(s) does justice as free transactions deny that claim?

23. The social system in which we live cannot be ethically right just because it seems "natural." It may seem natural just because we have been reared in it. Its arrangement of benefits and burdens is contingent and so can be changed. The questions are whether the arrangement ought to be changed, and if so, how and why. Assess the system and determine which of its features, if any, social workers have an obligation to examine and change if that is necessary. How are they to go about doing that?

APPENDIX I

Cases

CASE **1.1** **The Death of a Baby**

Sue had just bathed her five-week-old son, Jack, and put him in the middle of the double bed when one of her other three children called. She left Jack with her husband, Hal, who was playing with him when she left.

When she returned, she found Jack lying beneath Hal, who was sound asleep, and all she can remember is that Jack was blue and she had to pry him out from under her husband, who did not awaken.

She called 911, and what followed were three days of intensive care at the local hospital and then at the intensive care unit of the nearest major hospital. It took the medics ten minutes to get a heartbeat back when they first arrived after Sue called, and Jack had sporadic brain waves for awhile, but he was declared brain dead on the third day.

The physician ordered a drug test on the baby and a body scan to see if there were bruises or broken bones. Nothing unusual showed. So the physician wanted to call the death a "SIDS," a sudden-infant death syndrome of the sort that can occur to a child while sleeping in a crib.

The social worker involved, Deborah, thought that wrong. "There *is* an explanation. We just don't know what it is. There are some missing pieces here." Sue said that Hal had had two beers, and Hal admitted he had been drinking. But Jack was a big baby—eleven pounds at birth and thirteen pounds at five weeks. It seemed odd that Hal would not have sensed Jack's struggles as he tried to get air. But Deborah did not think that Hal had intentionally suffocated his son. He showed great remorse and guilt, he had stayed at the hospital the three days it took Jack to die, and the family seems to be a good family. They cared for their other children, and there were none of the usual causes of family disruption. He had a job, they had insurance, and so on.

Deborah felt she had a dilemma. If the death was reported as suspicious, Hal would be investigated, the parents might lose their other children, and they had clearly suffered a great deal already. But if the death was reported as a SIDS, a death that had an explanation would not be explained. "The doctor would be stretching the definition of SIDS." More importantly, Deborah felt she might be countenancing a situation in which the other children might be harmed. Unfortunately, a death certificate must be filed within forty-eight hours after death, and so Deborah had little time to make a decision about what to do.

CASE **1.2**   **Dancing a Legal Dance**

Martha and Kathy are twelve and fourteen years old and had been placed away from their home by the Juvenile Court because they claimed that their father sexually and physically abused them. Their father, Henry, then moved away from their original home. Hating where they were, the girls were placed back in their original home.

All of the members of the family were individually seeing Mary Todd, a social worker in private counseling under contract with Children's Protective Services. After asking Mary not to tell anyone, Martha told her that her father was sexually abusing her again. Mary had to put the information in her report, and the issue was taken to court where both Kathy and Martha were called to testify. The judge refused to see them in chambers, and faced with having to tell her story in front of her parents, and especially her father, whom she fears, Martha retracted it.

Kathy continued to insist that her sister was being abused, but the judge, given Martha's denial that her father was abusing her, declared that Martha was not sexually abused. When Mary Todd was called upon to testify about what Martha had told her and what she knew, the judge cut her off when she began reporting on the sexual abuse, saying that he had already declared that the child was not sexually abused and that only evidence of new sexual abuse would be admitted.

Henry is so obsessed with seeing the children that he has been coming over whenever he pleases. He has been there at least four times and was caught three times, and although the judge finally put him into jail for a month, he is still coming over whenever he wishes.

Martha has told Mary that she thinks Mary has betrayed her, and she has become extremely defiant. Whenever they meet for their counseling sessions, Martha stands with her hands on her hips, cusses Mary out, and flips out whenever sexual abuse is mentioned. She cannot trust her father; her mother cannot protect her; and now she cannot trust her social worker. Mary thinks that Martha has almost totally disintegrated. Martha cusses out everyone, hits and batters her mother, lies, and goes to the houses of friends and stays for days at a time. Her sister seems to be doing acceptably. Kathy is sticking to her story and is not being abused. "He won't mess with me 'cause he knows I'll tell."

No one is willing to consider criminal prosecution against the father because everyone except Kathy lies. The mother is a person with mental illness and will lie, for example, about the bruises on her arms caused by Martha. She will also lie about her husband. She was abused by her father and was picked up and cared for by Henry when she was 18. So she feels obligated to him.

Mary's coworkers keep asking her about the father, "Can you get him to confess?" But a caseworker at Children's Protective Services has suggested the case be dropped. "You're spending a great deal of time and getting nowhere. We've got other people to serve."

Mary does not know what to do. The judge is "dancing a legal dance," and she is forced to wait until the child is sexually abused again, but then has no guarantee the child will testify. "It is so unfair."

CASE **1.3**   Adoptive Children

The state has a registry for natural parents and adoptive children. A natural mother, for instance, may consent to have information about her given to the child she gave up for adoption if the child seeks it, or she may file a denial at the registry, refusing the child any information. But most people do not know about the registry since it is poorly advertised and underutilized by social work agencies.

LaShonda supervises adoptions for the county, and she often has adoptees come to her asking for information about their natural parents. She has a great deal of that information, but adoptees are only entitled to nonidentifying information. The law of the state she is in requires that, and when the natural parents gave the child up for adoption, the state agency promised them secrecy.

One woman came to see LaShonda. She had been to the registry without success and had tracked down the name of her natural mother, but it was a common name and she could not find her. So LaShonda gave her the father's name—a piece of identifying information. LaShonda is concerned about the interests of the natural parents, and so she does not give information to everyone who seeks it. She gives it only to those she judges as sensitive to the needs of their natural parents. She gives it to those who do not act only for selfish reasons, but work to change the law, and to those who work actively in support groups that exist for adoptive children, showing in that way that they care about others.

A young brother and sister showed up one day, without making an appointment, and asked her for help. She was concerned that they had not called her ahead of time. "That shows a lack of concern for me. I can't just see anyone who walks in the door!" And they said they would do whatever they had to do to find out who their natural parents were. LaShonda did not give them the information even though she knew.

LaShonda is concerned about what she does. She is breaking the law, and she knows it. "Do I really have the right," she asks, "to go above the law and say this person deserves it and this one does not?" Doing that puts her job at risk. At one time, the Court would contact the natural parents when they were sought by an adopted child and ask the parents if they wanted to use the registry. But a judge ruled that the State "has no right to interrupt their lives in that way." So LaShonda sometimes gives extra information.

She does it because she thinks the law as it now stands is unfair. Some are able to find out about their natural parents and others are not, based purely on accidents like whether the natural parents have heard of the registry.

CASE **1.4**   Doing What the Judge Orders

Jane got AIDS through a transfusion and is suspected of incestuous involvement with her fifteen-year-old son, Al, who is in foster care. Jane informed a social worker that she has AIDS, and when the social worker said, "There are people who ought to know about that," Jane told her, "If you tell anyone, I'll sue. I would rather my children find me dead than find out that I have AIDS." But the social worker told the caseworker for Al because Al may be a carrier. He has a girlfriend and claims to be sexually active, and his foster family may be at risk.

The caseworker, John, went to his supervisor and presented her with a hypothetical case. "If I knew that the natural mother of a young boy in my care has AIDS and might be involved incestuously with the boy, but I am not supposed to know that she has AIDS, what should I do?" They both went to the judge who had put the child in foster care and posed the same hypothetical. Al was up for review at the time, and he had been acting out. So the judge ordered a complete physical, asking that every test possible be done to see why he is acting out, including a test for HIV. Such a test is not a normal part of a physical, and the child is not to know.

John argued that "that will cover us for having a complete physical because it's a court order," and he remarked, "I've gone through all my channels so that if it came back on me, I could say, 'Hey, the judge told me to do it!'."

CASE 3.1   Refusing Help

Wilma was in her eighties, had lived in her home for forty-five years, and had lived alone for the eleven years since her husband died. Over the past few years, strangers had moved in with her, who, in several cases, wrote checks from Wilma's checkbook. She had been robbed three or four times. She is forgetful and often seems confused.

Her nephew was called by a multi-service agency for the elderly, and he closed her accounts, removed the unwanted guests, put new locks on the doors and windows, and asked neighbors to keep an eye on things. He felt that Wilma would be better off living in her home than going to a nursing home. He visits her twice a week.

One evening, a neighbor called the police because she had not seen Wilma and was worried. When Wilma answered the door, the police officer found that Wilma's house was unheated. It was winter and very cold, and the officer called an ambulance because Wilma seemed ill. But when it arrived, she refused to go. The officer left and called an agency that provides emergency service. The social worker there called the agency for the elderly, but since no one there could help until the next morning, the social worker went with the officer to Wilma's house with a blanket and small electric heater. Wilma did not answer the door, and, upon forcing entry, they found her dead. Four hours or so had passed since the neighbor had first called.

CASE 3.2   Depressed and Ready to Die

Juanita was diagnosed as having rectal cancer while she was also going through a nasty divorce. She had radiation treatment, but became very depressed and suicidal. She was diagnosed as schizophrenic, but was functional. She had her own apartment and car and cared for her two-year-old daughter. She came back into the medical hospital with inoperable cancer of the liver, but tried to sign herself out and stopped taking medication. She was sent to a psychiatric hospital.

The psychiatrist wanted her to have chemotherapy, but Juanita refused. "I don't want to do it. If I go through that again, I may prolong my life six months at most." She wanted to go back to her apartment. She had lived there with her cancer before, but the psychiatrist refused to release her from the hospital unless she had chemotherapy, and even then would only release her to foster care.

The other members of the multidisciplinary treatment team agreed with Juanita that she should be allowed to go home. They had explained the options to her and talked with her at some length. They agreed that "she could talk quite clearly about all of this and about what she wanted." When she had chemotherapy before, she became very ill physically, and she saw no point in such pain to prolong her life for so short a time.

But the psychiatrist told Juanita, "If you do not agree to accept chemotherapy, I will have to consider you suicidal, and I can't release a suicidal patient." The other members of the team attributed this response to the psychiatrist's having been trained as a pediatrician and to her having come to this country as an adult. "She has different cultural values and wants to save people in spite of themselves. So she treats them like children, which she finds easy to do."

The other members of the team thought about going to the director because the psychiatrist was essentially holding the patient for a medical condition, and that was inappropriate under the mental health code. But whenever they pressed the psychiatrist about this, she fell back on the claim that the patient was suicidal, and when staff members had gone to the director before, the director always backed the doctors, and they just got a reputation for causing trouble.

So they wrote up in their reports what they thought should have been done so that, whatever happened, they would be covered.

CASE 3.3   Low-Functioning Parents

"The parents met in the state hospital," Bianca said. "They're not psychotic." Their main problem is that they are low-functioning. Rob is ten, and he's smarter than they are. He's hyperactive. He's on medications. He's got sexual identity problems. He's a behavior problem. He tells his parents what to do.

"The school and a private agency want us to place him in foster care because the parents seem unable to handle him. The parents are like pack rats, collecting everything. So the house is filled with stuff, but it is not filthy. They were dressing him like a little girl and letting his hair grow into bangs, but once I explained to them what they needed to do, and provided them with funds to get a haircut and new clothes, they did what was needed. They clearly love their son. When he refuses to do his homework the mother calls me, worried that he will fail. They're not abusing their son, and they're not neglecting him. So I have no good reason to justify taking him out of the home.

"Besides, he would be a difficult placement, with all his problems, and I've seen the difficulties children have experienced in foster care—adjustment problems, attachment separation issues, and also abuse.

"The real issue is that this family is always going to need someone from the community to assist them in parenting the child. They are doing the best job they can."

CASE 3.4   Lying to Save a Marriage

"A married woman came to me. She is running around. I am also counseling her husband, and she asks me, 'Do you think my husband is running around?' I told her no. And he isn't. He's a good man. I wouldn't tell the husband that the wife is running around if he asks me, but I know damn well she is running around. I have to lie to the husband because if I say, 'I don't know' or 'I can't tell you,' or if I refuse to answer on the ground that I have a professional and confidential relationship with the wife, he will believe his wife is running around.

"Since I am a professional person, I will be believed if I say the wife is not cheating. I am patching up a relationship then. In our culture if you tell a lie with a straight face, it will be believed. Arab culture is a face-saving culture; American culture is a guilt-ridden culture. I will not feel guilt at lying. I would feel shame if someone found out that I was lying, but I will act to protect myself from being found out. I sometimes feel I shouldn't send an Arab client to an American social worker if there is an issue in which guilt and shame are involved."

CASE 3.5   Friends and Professional Relations

Raul was a recovering substance abuser who regularly attended meetings of Alcoholics Anonymous. He was also a social work therapist who worked with substance abusers. He encouraged Mark, one of his clients, to attend AA meetings. He had himself been attending meetings, but AA encourages those who come to the meetings to rely on each other, to call if they need help, for instance. Mark needed help and called Raul regularly.

Raul felt that he was doing therapy at Mark's beck and call rather than during their scheduled sessions. He confronted Mark, and Mark, feeling very rejected, stopped seeing Raul, dropped out of AA and out of treatment, and had a relapse.

CASE 3.6   Can You Help Me Now?

Angela had an alcoholic client who responded well to therapy. Although eventually the therapy ended, the client stayed in AA, still feeling the need for support.

Angela had liked the client as a person in the therapeutic relationship. The client was a massage therapist, and so, after a period of time had passed, Angela went to her to get massages.

The woman later relapsed, but did not come back to Angela. Angela later discovered that the woman had wanted to come back, especially in those shaky stages before the relapse, but felt that because they now had a different relationship, she could not.

CASE 3.7   Having Sex

Theresa came to see a therapist, Aubrey, in a family counseling agency. It came out over a number of sessions that Theresa had been in therapy before and had an affair with her previous counselor that began several months after the therapy ceased. She was married and was struggling with the affair's having ended and with her guilt at having had an affair.

Aubrey suggested that the counselor had crossed the proper boundaries between therapist and client in having a sexual relationship, even though the therapy had ended several months before the affair began. Theresa had not thought about that, but, as she did, she began to think that perhaps the initial stages of the affair started before the sessions with her therapist had ended, and she wondered if, as she said, "I somehow perhaps may have led him on."

Despite Aubrey's urging, Theresa decided not to press charges—partly because she did not want the publicity, which she thought would harm her relationship with her husband, and partly because she was not convinced that the affair was wholly the therapist's fault.

So Aubrey investigated on her own. She discovered that the therapist, who lived in a nearby community, was referred to as a licensed psychologist although the law required a Ph.D. for that title and the therapist did not have a Ph.D. Aubrey called a university where the therapist was to lecture, informing the university that the therapist was not a psychologist (it had advertised that he was), and she let it be known in the community that he was operating under false credentials.

CASE 3.8   Gift for Services

Jacinda is in therapy with Marie and has been diagnosed as having Post Traumatic Stress Syndrome. She is thirty-five and has a history of sexual and emotional abuse by her father and her stepfather. After her grandmother died, she became extremely agitated because she was emotionally close to her. She told Marie that she would like to give Marie a gift from among her grandmother's belongings.

Marie told Jacinda that she does not accept gifts. Jacinda was upset, and after some cajoling by Jacinda, Marie told her that she would accept a gift only in exchange for the time spent in calls with Jacinda between therapy sessions.

Jacinda came in the next week with seven of her grandmother's belongings and put them on the desk. Marie told her that she could not take all seven and asked Jacinda to pick one. Jacinda insisted that Marie pick out what she wanted, but Marie told Jacinda that Jacinda had to select one gift.

Jacinda picked out a vase, and Marie displayed it in her office. Marie looked at the vase when she came in for her next session and expressed pride at seeing it there. Jacinda does not know the vase's value and is afraid it may be very expensive. She is thinking of having it appraised and if it is expensive, crediting Jacinda for a number of therapy sessions.

CASE 3.9 A Social Visit

Tanika was a thirteen-year-old in therapy with Diane. She had been sexually abused by her father and was diagnosed as having Post Traumatic Stress Disorder. Diane had heard that Tanika had gone out socially both with her Protective Services worker and with the prosecutor of the case against her father.

Therapy terminated when Tanika had a baby and moved out of town. She came back in a year with a second baby and called Diane, asking to see her at Tanika's mother's house. She said she especially wanted Diane to see the babies. Diane tried to arrange to see Tanika at the office, but that did not work out and Diane went to visit her at her mother's.

Diane happened to mention that she would be driving to Florida for a vacation in a few days, and Tanika begged her to drive her to Georgia on her way so she could visit the father of one of the babies. Diane refused, and the situation became extremely uncomfortable.

Diane has not heard from Tanika again.

CASE 3.10 Hurting Oneself

Annette had been seduced by her former therapist. She is mentally ill and prone to extreme shifts in mood, but is consistently angry about her former therapist. She wants to pursue the case, take him to court, and see that he does not harm anyone else.

Her new therapist is concerned that Annette will hurt herself by pursuing the matter, that she is fragile emotionally, and will regress psychologically. Such cases are notoriously difficult to prosecute, and pursuing it will put a great stress on Annette when she is already very unstable. Besides, the therapist is not convinced that Annette will be believed, but thinks she will lose the case and lose what progress she has already made. So the therapist encourages her to drop the case.

CASE 3.11 Co-dependents

In an alcoholic's family, the spouse and children often need therapy as well. The need is severe enough that, without treatment for the other members of the family, the alcoholic is unlikely to cease using alcohol because the family members are unable to give support for the new forms of behavior necessary to remain off alcohol and, by their habitual practices, reinforce the alcoholic behavior.

But Rosemary cannot bill the company paying for treatment for treating anyone but the person who is abusing. "So sometimes," Rosemary says, "we put down 'family session' for the substance abuser when the focus was really on treating another family member. Other times we do not charge and see other family members for free."

CASE 3.12 Automatic Assignments

In one agency, social workers are assigned cases in the order in which they arrive. "If it is Monday, and I'm at the top of the list, I get the first case," Tamara said, and so she was assigned a case in which she was to do individual therapy for five children plus family therapy for the father and for the mother. The case was complicated by the various relations among the different members of the family, with some of the children having different fathers and some different mothers.

One day somewhat later Tamara was assigned another case—two young girls who had allegedly been sexually abused by their father, Marvin, who was no longer living with them, but was visiting them and seeking custody. She became close to the children, and especially to one child, and continued to see them for over six months.

Tamara then discovered that the boyfriend of the mother in the first family was Marvin, the father of the two girls in the second. She was concerned about sexual abuse in the new family setting and so told the woman there to be careful with her children around Marvin. She didn't tell the woman why, but the woman must have told Marvin that she was to be careful with him around the children and he was upset.

Tamara was asked to write a report for Friend of the Court, which was considering custody, and she wrote about the reports of sexual abuse that the two girls gave her. Friend of the Court put her name and position on the report, and since Marvin was acting as his own lawyer, he read it, put two and two together, and came into her office, angry and upset.

Tamara felt she had to choose between the two families, and she stopped seeing the little girls from the second family. She tried to have the one girl see another therapist, but the girl refused and stopped coming to the clinic. She apparently felt rejected, and although Tamara tried to explain to her that she was not being rejected, Tamara could not give the complete explanation.

CASE 3.13   Caring for the Family

A mother of low intelligence loves her three children, does well for them with what she has ("dresses the girls beautifully, irons their clothes"), and keeps in constant touch with the school and social workers. There has been a history of sexual abuse—the father first abusing the two girls when they were in the first and third grades and then a boyfriend abusing them. So Carrie, the social worker assigned to the family, allows the mother to stay with the children provided that certain rules are followed, which, it is hoped, will protect them from child abuse.

As it stands now, the family is entrenched in the social services system. "If we were not here for her, the family would not stay intact," Carrie says. The system cannot afford the time and resources to make that family a continual object of concern. So the family is likely to disintegrate, and, by law, the children must then be placed in foster care. When that happens, the mother will fall apart, Carrie thinks, and the children will be separated since no foster home is likely to take three children. The children will certainly be worse off in terms of losing a mother who truly loves them and in no longer being members of a family.

The family is so fragile that it is dependent upon the social services system. "What is needed," Carrie says, "is a foster home *for the entire family*." But that is not presently an option. The only option is to continue to treat the family until it is decided that too much has been spent on it and each of the children is then put into foster homes.

CASE 3.14   Self-Identity

Joanna had a client, Vicky, who was having difficulties with the consequences of her divorce. Joanna was black, Vicky was white, and Vicky's ex-spouse is black. In the course of Joanna's work with Vicky, Vicky brought in her oldest son, Tommy, who was six and having trouble in school primarily, the school thought, because his parents were going through a divorce. But when Joanna talked with him, she found out that he was upset because school officials had called him black.

Tommy was staying with his mother, who identified Tommy and the other two children as being white. When Joanna spoke with her, Vicky said she thought "her children would have a very hard time if they were identified as being black." She said she had told them that if you mix vanilla and chocolate, you get a combination, but "not black," something "closer to white."

But the children cannot pass for white. "They do not even have the features to pass for white," Joanna told Vicky. "Society is always going to see them as black, and the children need to feel good about that. You can't say he's brown. You can't say he's mulatto. You can't use those terms. You have to say he is a beautiful black child and you accept him. You have to validate that for the child."

Vicky said she couldn't tell Tommy that, that it would mean giving up her son. So Joanna was concerned that Vicky would stop coming in for therapy and particularly concerned that she would not talk to Tommy and tell him what Joanna thought he needed to hear. The situation was complicated by Tommy's fear that his mother would be upset with him—for not being white, Joanna surmised.

But Joanna persuaded the mother to go in and talk with Tommy and tell him that he is black, that she loves him, and that it is good to be black. The mother didn't believe any of that, but she did it. Afterwards, Tommy said, "I knew I was black all along."

C A S E 4.1 Peers?

A male social worker seduced and molested one of his clients, an adolescent male, who then molested his younger sister. The boy is now with his father and step-mother, but his present social worker, Malik, is pushing to reunite the boy with his mother and sister.

The girl's social worker, Margaret, is uncomfortable with this. She thinks the child needs more therapy, and that will end if the family is reunited. But most importantly, she is not sure the girl will be protected if the boy returns to the family.

Yet she says she is unwilling to "confront" the boy's therapist, as she puts it. "He has a Ph.D., and I don't; he's established, and I'm new to this community."

C A S E 4.2 Family Therapy

Jessica was a member of a family service agency that had brought in a person from outside to teach the agency personnel about structural family-centered therapy. Peer review was instituted, and the seven social workers would meet regularly, view videotapes, and talk about their cases.

Jessica was having a very hard time learning to use the new form of therapy. It requires that the social workers align themselves with a particular family member, but only for strategic purposes. One is never to form permanent alignments. But Jessica would form relationships with particular family members, the woman or a female adolescent, and not be able to break them. But that is harmful to the clients. Rather than achieving independence, they end up with a different form of dependence, unable to achieve a new balance of relationships within their family because of their attachment to the social worker.

When this was pointed out to Jessica, she became extremely frustrated, threw up her hands and said, "Well!" She cried another time, upset because, as she put it, "I was doing everything right, and yet you tell me it's all wrong."

The other social workers all agreed that she was not competent using this particular approach. "She was operating off a psycho-dynamic individual model, which is very different from a structural or strategic model." They all felt that Jessica was harming her clients, but although they had the evidence of their own eyes and could talk about how she failed to respond to suggestions, they said they could not prove her incompetence to the supervisor. Besides, she had been with the agency for almost 20 years and so had seniority over the other six.

CASE 4.3   Relapsing

Cynthia had been having problems with her work, but before her supervisor, Corliss, was able to talk with her about them, a client of hers who knew she was a recovering alcoholic reported that she had seen Cynthia drinking in a bar. A colleague also told Corliss that he thought Cynthia had begun drinking again. He had gone in to talk with her and saw that she was leaving little, empty whisky bottles in her wastebasket. Corliss then discovered that Cynthia had had periodic problems for some time before she had transferred to Corliss's department. "There is a history here," Corliss thought.

Corliss talked to Cynthia and explained that if her colleagues could see the empty bottles, her clients could too. Corliss and Cynthia agreed that she would have a month of residential treatment.

Cynthia did that, but although she was O.K. for awhile, after she came back, she relapsed. Corliss discovered that Cynthia had not followed through on her appointments, and, in addition, she was not doing her job well. So Corliss fired her.

Cynthia committed suicide, leaving a note blaming the colleague who had told Corliss that he thought she had begun drinking again. Corliss had told Cynthia that although she was fired, she could return if she "went into treatment and was sober for six months." So "she knew," Corliss added. "She had that option."

CASE 4.4   Bending over Backwards

Betsey had known of Jonathan for a long time and had met him as a colleague. He had been very successful working with clients and was well regarded in the community. She needed someone for a supervisory position and hired him after going through "the regular routine of references." Although Jonathan's director at his former agency complained and said he hated to see Jonathan go, he said he would prefer that he remain in the community.

The staff really liked Jonathan, but after a half-year or so, things began to go wrong. Jonathan did not handle his routine business well, failing to answer phone calls or respond to letters. He was writing letters for the agency even though those had to be approved by Betsey. And he was confused a great deal of the time, testifying in court, for instance, about a case but mixing up the details with some other case.

After documenting the difficulties, Betsey told him that "things are not going right" and would have to be corrected. The following Monday Jonathan's wife called and said he had been readmitted to an alcohol unit. Betsey had not known that Jonathan had problems with alcohol. He was off for six weeks, came back, did well for awhile, but then began to have problems again. It turned out that he needed a heart bypass operation.

Betsey was getting a lot of pressure to fire Jonathan from some of the staff and from the Board (see the Code of Ethics 2.09[a] & [b]). The agency was short-staffed anyway, and Jonathan's comings and goings over such a period of time, combined with the state of his papers and memos because of his confused state of mind, were creating extra work for everyone. In fact, the agency was audited seven times because of the problems Jonathan created and was beginning to get a bad reputation. But some of the staff were adamant that he be kept, and, as Betsey said, "I didn't feel I could fire someone who was going in for heart surgery."

But when Jonathan came back, he was no better. Betsey made him "a line worker" even though he was being paid as a supervisor, but he could not handle that either. Betsey suggested that Jonathan resign with disability, coming in to work on a contract basis whenever he felt able, but he refused, and after trying to get him to quit, she finally had to fire him. Jonathan was black, and he claimed racism on Betsey's part.

When she later talked to the director of the agency that Jonathan had worked at before, the director said that he had tried to warn her, but also that he didn't want Jonathan in his agency. Betsey thought that she had gotten anything but a warning from the director and that he had given her good recommendations in order to get rid of Jonathan.

CASE 4.5 Value Judgments

Jane works in private practice in a clinic that specializes in feminist therapy, with a strong emphasis on holistic health and "a general understanding of the mind-body connection." She works with several other social workers, one of whom, Daniela, she found naive about the risks involved in working with battered wives.

Daniela was encouraging one of her battered clients to confront her husband. Daniela thought that confrontation would help to resolve the problems between the couple. But it did not seem to help, and Jane thought Daniela was unable to cope with the husband of the woman she was counseling. The man kept coming to the clinic, threatening Daniela and other social workers, and putting all of them "in grave danger."

The group met without Daniela to talk about the problem and then spoke to Daniela about the harm they thought she was causing her client and the danger she was putting them all in, but Daniela refused to change her focus on this client. She thought it had to do with the client's right of self-determination. The client really wanted to stay in the relationship.

Jane disagreed with Daniela's understanding of the situation. As she put it, "If a woman's getting hit, and it could escalate to something worse, and she's telling you about it, but is not willing to leave, how long do you remain a part of that situation?" Battered women often have trouble leaving those who batter them, and Jane thought that Daniela's client was not really exercising self-determination and that Daniela was failing to intervene appropriately.

Daniela ended up leaving the group "under pressure." She did not want to leave, but the group was not willing to risk the danger to themselves or to the battered woman.

CASE 4.6   Harassment

Amy works in an agency associated with a hospital. She had been hired by her supervisor's boss, not by the supervisor, Don. Both Amy and the boss are African Americans; the supervisor is white. Both the supervisor and his boss are males. Amy was at the agency before Don came, and he told her that he resented her being there and did not want her there. He then proceeded to harass her, she says, for over two years in a variety of ways.

Don had the secretaries keep records of when Amy was on the phone and of how long she was gone from her office. Such records were not kept for other employees. He would pin memos to her door about what he thought she was doing wrong. He created a new schedule for her one day when she was gone to work on a case at the hospital and then, when she came to work at her normal time the next day, he said, "I've gotcha. Where were you?" He would not let her look in her personnel file (although she wanted to see the memos there). When she took leave to attend a funeral, he suggested she really was using that as an excuse to have lunch with a friend because she did have lunch with the friend before the funeral.

Don enforced a policy against Amy about not taking more than three sick or personal times in ninety days. She had to leave to take her sick child home from school, then to have minor surgery the next week, again to have the stitches taken out a week later, and then for something else for one other short period of time. He said, "I'm writing you up for dismissal because you've violated policy." But the policy had never been enforced before, and he did not enforce it against anyone else at the agency.

Don continually harassed Amy verbally, she said. He would call her into his office and find fault with her work, always taking her to task for not doing something right and saying how good he was compared with her and always complaining that she was getting selected for this or for that when he was the manager. He had, Amy said, "taunted" two African American secretaries until they finally left, and she was convinced that he was out to make the agency as white as could be.

Amy eventually filed a grievance, and when she went before the grievance board, she fully documented what she could of what Don had done. The board found no grounds for harassment, and Amy was told afterwards that the hospital's lawyer told the board that if they did find grounds, Amy would have had good grounds for a lawsuit. The board did find that there was "a gross misunderstanding" between Amy and Don, and, Amy learned, the whole agency was later to be reorganized, with Don's managerial responsibilities taken from him. She felt vindicated, but meanwhile the harassment continued.

CASE 4.7   Lying about Salaries

In an agency of about twelve employees, several who have been there for some years are earning significantly less than others more recently hired. The agency has such a good reputation that many were willing to work for it even though their starting salary was lower than what was then the normal going rate, but, as inflation has outstripped raises, their salaries have become significantly less competitive. As the agency's director puts it, "There are staff members who really have low salaries."

The director has pushed for increases, and was able to get an increase for one employee who pushed hard, but the agency has always been able to obtain very good employees at lower salaries. So the director has not been able to obtain a general increase for all employees.

One consequence is that some are not getting what they deserve. Another is that some who are equally situated are getting different salaries. As the director says, "The present situation supports dishonesty." If the news gets out that one employee has gotten an increase, then others, equally deserving, will demand increases as well. The agency does not have the money for that, and so the director has to be less than forthcoming with his staff about their salaries. Indeed, he told those employees who received raises not to tell the other employees.

CASE 4.8   Attention Deficit Disorder

Mark is an eighth grader with an attention deficit disorder. He has a high I.Q., and when he is on medication, he is extremely well-behaved and productive. But he does not now take his medication regularly. He is doing this as a form of rebellion, it seems, and that is what those his age are likely to do. So he is sometimes inattentive and disruptive in class.

His teacher hits Mark on the head with a folded-up paper when he is acting up, and it is not just harmful to him, but embarrassing and ineffective.

Mark told his school social worker, Janet, who is new to the job. She is unsure what to do. She can tell Children's Protective Services, or the principal, or talk to the teacher. Anything she does must be done carefully. She cannot be in the classroom all the time, and "when the door is closed to the classroom, the teacher has the power." But it is clear that the method the teacher has adopted to "control" Mark's behavior is counter-productive.

CASE 4.9   First Grader

Jerry was referred to the school social workers on the second day of school by a teacher who "knew his older brother and had had run-ins with the child's mother and didn't like the way they came out." Mike was the social worker assigned to assess the boy, and although he decided that the boy was a kinesthetic learner, having to touch everything to learn anything, he also decided that with some effort, the boy could be taught to behave as the teacher wanted.

Mike put together a program for the teacher with a check sheet where Jerry would receive points for behaving in certain ways and not behaving in other ways. The teacher filled it in, and he took it home every day. His mother signed off on it, and Jerry's behavior began to come under control.

But the teacher still was not happy because, although Jerry was improving, he was not one-hundred percent better. She wanted him to be certified as emotionally impaired. That would mean that he would then be removed from her classroom.

Mike interviewed the parents, the teacher, and Jerry again, and he found that Jerry was able to develop and maintain relationships, and he did not act out outside the classroom. So he was not emotionally impaired. "Actually," Mike said, "he's a pretty happy little kid."

The teacher was upset. She dropped the program that Mike had developed, and she put Jerry "in a box"—behind a set of room dividers so that he was screened off from the rest of the children. She had the support of the principal, and so finally Mike certified Jerry as emotionally impaired to get him out of the bad situation.

CASE 5.1   Skimming

Nina had been working at an agency for four years when she wrote a grant proposal that was approved and funded. It was one of four given out in the country.

After the grant money began to come in, the director of the agency, her boss, changed his salary in the grant, taking more. He also took part of the money from the grant to pay his secretary, who was not doing work on the grant, put Nina to work on other projects even though, by the grant, she was to work full-time on the grant, and skimmed off, or was about to skim off, part of the money to run the main office.

When Nina complained, she was put on probation and told, "If you do not do what I want here, you will be fired." When she complained to the federal representative for the project, her boss told her not to talk to that person, even though she had to in order to administer the grant and report on it.

The grant had an eight percent leeway built in so that some of what her boss had done could be hidden and perhaps even justified. Nina was not sure. At any rate, apparently as a consequence of her complaint, some governmental officials came and met with her director and local "heavies," as she called them. When they came out, they told her not to worry, that this happens all the time.

Nina and the grant were moved to another agency.

CASE 5.2   Buying Friendship

June is the director of a local agency and was called by a man, Don, who volunteered to give the agency money to help the needy. She arranged to meet him at a local cafeteria, where they met and had a long conversation about what the agency did, what more money could do, and what he was willing to provide.

June was struck by the man's appearance when he came up to her and, later, by his conversation. He did not look like someone who could afford to give money. "He looked like one of the people we try to help." In conversation, Don seemed somewhat confused, and June thought that he might be somehow mentally impaired, though in a minor way.

After the conversation, June received a check for several hundred dollars in the mail from a local bank, with a note that the contribution was from Don and that a like amount would be provided every month, "in perpetuity."

June was concerned that Don could not afford such a gift and called the bank to check. She was told that the information she requested about his financial status was private and that she would have to ask Don.

Don called June several days later and asked to meet her for lunch. She went to explain to him her concerns. She did, and he brushed them off, saying that he had enough money and that he wanted her to have it.

That lunch was followed by more invitations to lunch and by phone calls, in which Don called June his girlfriend. June went to several lunches with him, explaining that she felt that she owed that to him, but got more and more uncomfortable with going to lunch and with what he apparently expected from the relationship. At the same time, June felt that Don, like one of her clients, seemed to need help and that she might be able to help him.

CASE 5.3   A Pacifist

Helen works for an agency that has a contract with a company with significant defense contracts. She is a pacifist, but she was asked to coordinate the agency's work with the company. When Helen told her supervisor she did not want to have anything to do with this company, her supervisor told her that if she were serious in this, there was a real possibility she would be out of work. Besides, the supervisor added, it is not the company she is helping, but its employees.

The agency's general mission is to help workers who are too poor to afford purchasing help on their own, but the workers of this company are very well paid. So the contract departs from the agency's mission. On the other hand, the contract is lucrative, and, Helen tells herself, the profits allow the agency to further its mission. It is "taking from the rich to give to the poor." Besides, she thinks, if anyone needs help, those working in the military-industrial complex do.

Yet, Helen realizes, if she is successful in counseling them, she may make them more productive and thus herself be supporting the military-industrial complex. On the other hand, she thinks she may be counseling those who are having difficulty with the system at the company to leave the company. In addition, although the agency is taking from this particular corporation to help the poor, she thinks that, in general, the support we give the military-industrial complex takes away from what we could do for the poor.

Helen and her supervisor worked out a compromise in which she works with the employees, but is not the coordinator for the agency and the company.

CASE 5.4   Money or Care?

The state permits up to six children per foster home. The agency that places the children gets administrative money for each child placed—over $50,000 per foster home if the home takes in as many children as the state permits.

José is head of an agency charged, among other things, with placing children in foster homes. The money the agency makes from the placement that is not used for the placement itself or for training the foster parents is used to support other agency activities. Because the agency places a great many children, it makes a great deal of money that way and is able to support a wide variety of other programs for the poor.

The problems that the foster parents face with the children can be remedied if they are the result of lack of proper training, and in the worst of cases, children are taken from the home. But there are always going to be marginal cases, "gray areas," Ralph says, and the agency has a new problem because the kinds of kids it is now getting have more serious problems and are more difficult to care for.

The agency has solved the problem of what to do with cases that fall into the "gray areas" through "benign neglect," preferring to assume that the problems are not serious enough for the child to be taken out of the home. But this has caused problems for the social work practitioners who must work with the families. These problems cannot be resolved through training, and the practitioner can only tell the families that they must deal with them somehow.

The difficulty that some kids have more problems now is more serious, and the agency has responded by cutting the number of children it places in a foster home from six to four. That is better for the children, and better for the foster family too—except that the family is getting less funding and so is the agency. Indeed, the agency's program is now losing money because of the way it feels it must handle this new difficulty.

CASE 5.5   Limited Number of Visits

Pat is a social work practitioner in a hospital who helps clients with alcohol and drug problems. Most of her clients are covered by health insurance, but the insurance companies are demanding full records—partly in order to be sure that its clients are being served by properly accredited professionals and partly because, Pat thinks, "if they can find any little thing that doesn't look right to them, they can disallow the claim. So they are going to try to get as much information as possible."

But it is not in Pat's clients' best interests to have information that they are being treated for drug dependency or alcoholism getting back to their employers or even to the insurance companies. She had a client who gave permission for his insurance company to look at his files, but was later denied life insurance by the company because, it said, alcoholics die younger. The insurance company found out from the records the client released that he was in treatment for alcoholism. In addition, an employer can make life difficult for those of its employees it knows have been in treatment for drug dependency or alcoholism.

So one of Pat's problems is that she is caught in the middle, especially if the client refuses to give permission for her to reveal the complete record. She also thinks it is a mistake for clients to give her permission to reveal their records. She thinks that information ought to remain confidential. But if clients do ask her to send their records on to their health insurance companies and a company then refuses payment, the hospital will have to pick up the cost for those clients who cannot pay for the therapy themselves.

One consequence of this problem is that the hospital has dropped its outpatient program. Too many of the clients in that program were being supported by the hospital. It also limited the number of sessions for those in therapy in the hospital to ten unless the hospital can determine ahead-of-time that they will be covered by insurance or are able to pay their own way.

CASE 5.6   Taking On More Than It Can Chew

When crack cocaine hit the streets, its quick spread wrought social havoc, and, except for the police, human service agencies were the only institutions with any kind of experience in dealing with drug use and the harm it causes families and other social institutions. The crack epidemic spread so quickly, and so overwhelmed the agencies that traditionally dealt with drug dependency, that Aurelio's agency was asked to take on a new role to help with the problem.

The agency had no serious financial difficulties, and it was successful in its other programs. That was one reason it had been asked to take on this new problem. But it also had no experience in drug dependency programs, and taking on a new program would stretch its resources. There was no promise yet of any new money, and so the main problem, as Aurelio put it, was that he and the board "had to balance the long-term financial stability of the agency with the mission of responding to emerging social problems."

Aurelio was extremely reluctant to have the agency take on the new cause, but some members of the board argued that the problem was so overwhelming that they had no ethical choice but to help, despite the problems that might cause. They felt they could not just sit back and hope that the crack epidemic would run its course without significant harm to the community it was their mission to serve. They were also concerned that the problem might harm some of the activities the agency was currently engaged in and that they would end up having to take on the new mission in any event. "We might as well do it at the beginning," they said.

Aurelio agreed that taking on the new cause would further the agency's mission, but, he worried, unlike practitioners in other agencies whose mission had included working with drug dependency, the agency's employees had no special training or particular experience in working with drug dependency. They would need to be trained, and the new program and the need for training would take them away from the agency's regular programs and leave those programs underfunded as well as understaffed. Aurelio was thus concerned that the agency's practitioners were not the best ones for the job and that the agency's other programs would be jeopardized by the transfer of money and personnel to the new program.

CASE 5.7   Agency Misrepresentation

An agency advertises itself as taking care of the homeless. Its big promotion under its new popular director, Delores, who is a minister, is that it provides "A Home for the Homeless." Because of this campaign, and the way it has advertised itself, the agency under Delores has been able to raise significant funds in the community from foundations and from private citizens, and it now receives support from the county government.

But the agency provides only drop-in support for the homeless, and only in the day time. Delores went to the local motels and hotels asking for donations of small pieces of soap because, she said, "the homeless need to travel light on the street." There is no intent on the part of the agency to provide homes for the homeless.

In addition, the agency prides itself on providing help "no questions asked," and so is unable to direct those who need housing to other agencies that could help. It refuses to question those who drop in because, it argues, that would be an invasion of privacy, but that policy is also part of a campaign to attract those who need help. The agency tells them, "We don't ask; we just give."

Janet is the director of an agency that does provide homes for the homeless. She coordinated the original agreement among the various agencies in the area about how best to help the homeless, but Delores's aggressive advertising and fundraising have caused funds that would have gone to provide housing for the homeless to go instead to Delores's agency. In fact, county money that is earmarked for the county shelter to provide housing for the homeless is being sent to this agency on the mistaken assumption that it provides housing. The checks are made out to the agency, and Delores is using the money for the agency's programs. The agency's advertising has clearly caused confusion about what the agency does. The agency's accountant, who also works part-time for Janet, has told her of the misdirected funds, and is unsure what to do.

Janet's agency has not only lost funding, but it has had to spend additional money for "outreach therapy" at the agency. "We have to go in there," Janet says, to assess the needs of the clients so it can try to provide homes for those who need them. The agency was unwilling initially to provide office space for that, and, although it now does that, it charges them eight cents for each phone call and makes it difficult in other ways for Janet's agency to do its job.

CASE 5.8   An Adoption Agency

Adoption agencies are licensed by the state, and the state restrictions are all designed to ensure that the best homes are found for adoptive children. One agency, which we shall call "Homes for Babies," is advertising that "it will get you a baby," according to Joan, the director of another adoption agency. The advertisement also says that Homes for Babies does not always get "the cream of the crop," or, as Joan puts it, "a baby of Caucasian parents, with excellent medical backgrounds, no mental illness, prenatal care, a healthy attitude towards adoption, a willing father." So they are "tagging babies," Joan thinks, making distinctions among them that are inappropriate.

Joan has had several cases in which she or one of her social work practitioners has been working with a client for several months, only to go to the hospital to discover a representative of the other agency there. In most cases, the birth mother has said that she wants to work with the other agency.

Joan is concerned that such agencies are being licensed. They charge a great deal of money for an adoption, and the adoptive families pay the medical and other expenses. Her agency and the other nonprofit adoptive agencies charge their expenses and do not let the adoptive families pay any of the medical or other expenses. One former client told Joan that the Homes for Babies would allow her to meet with the adoptive parents when Joan's agency would not allow that, and Joan is concerned that the agency may be paying the birth mother, which is illegal.

Joan is even more concerned that the agency is not doing right by the children. One concern is that the home studies are not as thorough as they should be. The agency has an incentive to keep its costs as low as it can and so may not pay enough to provide a sufficient check on the adopting families. But the main problem for Joan is that while her agency starts with the children and tries to find the right home for them, Homes for Babies starts with those who want to adopt and makes a profit only if it finds a baby for them. It thus has a financial incentive to place children in homes that may not be best for them.

CASE 6.1   Still Waiting after All This Time

An agency had the opportunity to provide an Employee Assistance Program (EAP) for a number of local businesses. In such programs, businesses contract with agencies to provide such services as substance abuse or mental health counseling for their employees.

When asked whether the agency struggled with the issue of its serving fewer clients if it took on EAP clients, the director, Abe, responded by saying that without

EAP clients, the agency would be serving fewer clients. With EAP clients, the agency has the potential to see more clients at "full-cost reimbursement." "In fact," he said, "we're treating all of the clients exactly the same. The clients we had are still on the waiting list, *and* we are seeing the EAP clients. Those who pay up-front get quick service, and those who cannot continue to wait, just like before. It's just like the health-care system."

CASE 6.2 The Waiting List

There is a waiting list for service in a mental health agency. The list never gets shorter, only longer, and people stay on it "just in case." People are taken by priority of need, not by the time they spend on the waiting list, and priority of need is determined by, for example, whether a person needs hospitalization.

Some of those on the list injure themselves to get services, act out, "or do whatever" to be sure they are hospitalized, and Michael Jones, the person at the agency in charge of taking cases, must sort out those who are in real need from those who are not.

By the time a decision must be made because of an overdose, for instance, Michael has met with the prospective clients three or four times and so has some basis for judging whether they are a danger to themselves or others. In addition, he asks questions to determine the seriousness of the situation.

The most difficult cases are those in which the patient is borderline— enough of a problem to risk harm to those around and to themselves, but not enough to get hospitalized. Michael says he "puts those through their paces." If they want treatment, for example, they must come to therapy, three days a week for six months. If someone will follow through, then Michael will let him or her in.

He says he is right sixty percent of the time, and the rest of the time "we won't know what they will do." The decisions are complicated because the patients are very sophisticated in manipulation. One patient, Martha, wrote letters every three months asking for treatment, and Michael's assessment is that she wants to form more dependency-type roles.

CASE 6.3 Differing Social Circumstances

The social worker, Amena, is visiting a client in the city. The client has a son, Thomas, who is four years old. The woman lives generally by herself in a small, ramshackle house. She has a scar down her arm, put there by her occasional boyfriend who blowtorched it one night when he was angry. Her son has a hearing defect, and although he is intensely curious and talkative, Amena has a difficult time understanding him. He repeats what he hears, and what he hears is not clear.

Amena has finally found public housing for the woman and her son and explains the conditions. It costs, but her welfare payments will be increased to pay for it. Her boyfriend cannot live with her however.

They talk, and after pointing out that living in public housing will finally put Thomas in a position where his hearing impairment can be helped, Amena says, "It will also give you a reason for not seeing that man again. So he won't be able to hurt you."

The woman says, after a slight delay, and in tears, "You don't understand. He's my man, and any man is better than none." She refuses to move.

APPENDIX II

Additional Case Studies

CASE 1 **Dangerous to Self and Others**

Anna, a social worker in a family counseling unit, received a referral from the intensive in-home program for a severely depressed mother, Suzanne, and her children. Anna had worked with the family in the past when the daughter was depressed and actively suicidal. She had the daughter hospitalized, and Suzanne became furious with Anna and fired her for two weeks. Suzanne was having suicidal ideation and mentioned to another worker in the agency that she had a gun. Suzanne informed Anna that she had written good-bye letters to her children. She also put a dead-bolt lock on her door and would not answer when her children beat on the door. Anna was encouraging her to see a psychiatrist so she could get medication. Suzanne refused to go.

Anna waited two weeks while she tried to decide whether Suzanne was really suicidal. She then filed a petition to get Suzanne hospitalized since she would not get treatment. She decided not to tell Suzanne at their family therapy session of her intent to do this that very day. She was afraid that if she told Suzanne, she would kill herself rather than go to the hospital and may have killed her children since she is so enmeshed with them. The police came and handcuffed Suzanne because she would not go willingly. Suzanne's family threatened to call the ACLU and sue Anna. Anna lost sleep after she petitioned Suzanne. "It just violated everything I believed—being straightforward and letting her make her own decisions about treatment. She may have been just trying to get my attention."

CASE 2 **Foster Care**

Paula worked in a family counseling agency in a program that had a contract with community mental health to do specialized foster care with children and youth who needed intensive treatment. Allen, a fourteen-year-old-boy, had an alcoholic father and a mother who was paranoid schizophrenic. Allen was in treatment with Paula and in foster care for almost a year and was doing very well. His parents were emotionally abusive and extremely ineffective. In addition, their house was filthy. They were on the borderline of being neglectful and abusive. Paula did not report them to Protective Services, as these behaviors have to be grossly apparent.

Paula had to parent Allen's mother, Alicia. Alicia and her husband received resources from the Department of Social Services for years to support them in rearing their children, and it made little difference. Alicia would do better when she was on her medication, but she would go on and off it constantly. When Allen was doing well emotionally with his foster family, he would ask to go home and visit his family, and when he did, he would become angry, threaten to kill his mom, and sexually act out. He was hospitalized a number of times. Paula tried to get Alicia to release Allen so he could be adopted by his foster family, but she would not agree. Allen did not want to be adopted because he believed he would lose his identity with his family.

Community mental health did not want to pay for Allen's treatment any longer and expected that he would be returned permanently to his natural parents. It measures the success of the family counseling agency by whether children are returned to their parents. Paula's supervisor and the director of the agency believe strongly that children belong in their family no matter what; so they would not support Paula in going to court to have Allen removed from his family. Paula feels that the system let Allen down and there is nothing more she can do.

CASE 3 Coercive Contracts

A sixty-two-year-old Medicaid, managed-care patient enrolled in a physician-sponsored plan was admitted to the hospital for treatment of pneumonia associated with chronic obstructive pulmonary disease (COPD). She was treated with IV antibiotics and recovered well although she remains weak. She lives with her daughter who provides twenty-four hour care, but in order to go home she will require oxygen, a wheelchair, a hospital bed, a commode, and home nursing care. The social worker, Jean, tries to coordinate the discharge. Because this is a physician-sponsored plan, she contacts the primary care physician to obtain authorization for these home services.

The physician refuses to authorize any home care services and equipment for two reasons. The first is that he feels the care would be too costly. It is to be noted that payment for these services would come out of the capitation rate/payment he receives from Medicaid. The second reason is that the physician knows this patient is an alcoholic, smokes despite the COPD, and is generally noncompliant in her health care. He instructs Jean to put the patient in a nursing home. That care will be financed by a different Medicaid program.

The patient adamantly refuses to go to a nursing home. Jean believes home discharge is best for the patient, and so she tries to convince the physician. Authorization is again refused. Jean went back and forth between the patient and physician for a week beyond the discharge order written by the hospital doctor.

Jean informed the hospital's medical director that she was contacting someone at the managed care company to file an appeal. The medical director contacted the chief financial officer of the hospital who negotiates all managed care contracts. He provided Jean with his counterpart at the managed care company, whom Jean called. A supervisor of case management services acted as a go-between with the primary care physician and patient/social worker and negotiated a plan. The physician would agree to authorize all of the home care services if the patient agreed to quit smoking, to have the visiting nurse do weekly urine/alcohol tests, and to keep all of her scheduled follow-up appointments with him. Failure to comply would result in the physician revoking authorization. The patient agreed and was discharged home. Jean felt the contract with the patient was coercive and ethically problematic.[125]

CASE 4   The Hummel Figure

Betty had an eighty-eight-year-old client, Ethel, who became quite attached to her after working with her for two months. Betty mentioned she had a collection of Hummel figures after noticing Ethel had a Hummel calendar. On Betty's next visit to Ethel's house, Ethel was beaming and proudly handed her a wrapped gift. She said "I am giving this to you, because I like you." Betty opened the gift, which turned out to be an antique Hummel. She estimated to herself that it was worth $2000. Betty knew that her client had a need to give, but could not accept the gift because it might appear she extorted it from her client. Ethel was crushed and said, "But you are my friend." Betty said, "I like you too, but it is too valuable to accept. I heard you are an excellent cook, and I would like you to bake cookies for me."

On Betty's next visit, Ethel gave her cookies, which she shared with her colleagues in the office. The next time Betty visited Ethel, Ethel handed her a brown bread she had baked. Betty was surprised and said, "I am watching my weight. Please do not make any more food for me. I will get fat." Betty does not want Ethel to feel that she must pay her for each visit, but she also does not want to offend Ethel. She also knows Ethel is poor and cannot spare the resources to feed her.

CASE 5   Should He Know?

Evelyn was a social worker in community mental health who had a chronically mentally ill, nineteen-year-old client, Michael, who could not make good decisions or care for himself well. Michael did not accept that he had a mental illness and would often not take his medication. He was in adult foster care and so was being supervised. He also had a payee handling his money. Thus, he was relatively safe. Evelyn decided not to go to court to seek guardianship for him.

One of Michael's family members became concerned about him because he wandered off for a few days. Evelyn was opposed to having a guardian appointed for him because Michael came back in good shape, indicating to her his judgment was not so impaired. She felt that having a guardian would make him feel like a child, lower his self-esteem, and take hope and motivation away from him. Evelyn explained that a temporary guardianship could be arranged if Michael leaves again and there is a concern about him. She felt that this family member should not be the guardian because some of Michael's delusions included this family member. Evelyn thinks it could lead to a further deterioration in Michael's mental health.

Evelyn found out six months later that the family member had become Michael's guardian. She should have been called to court to advocate on Michael's behalf. Michael was not even at the hearing, and he has not been told that he has a guardian. His legal rights were violated. Evelyn is trying to decide whether to go to court to ask for the guardianship to be revoked. She knows the family member has Michael's best interests at heart. Putting Michael through the legal process could possibly trigger his psychosis and land him back in the hospital.

CASE 6   Right Diagnosis, Wrong Treatment

Judy, a senior social worker at a substance abuse agency, had a client, Amy, whom she assessed as having a dual diagnosis—an avoidant personality disorder and chemical dependency. Amy's HMO utilized Judy's agency as a preferred provider of substance abuse services, but had no preferred provider for dual diagnosis. Amy was accepted into the inpatient treatment program although it was not equipped to provide mental health services for her. Amy would not engage with other clients in group treatment. She refused to share her life story with her peers, and this is a requirement for everyone in the group. Judy made the decision to ask Amy to leave the program because she was not receiving appropriate one-to-one treatment for her diagnosis.

The Employee Assistance Program worker put pressure on Judy to get Amy back in the program. Judy knows it is an influential EAP from a large employer in the community that has lots of dollars to spend and is a key source of revenue for her employer. Amy cried and begged Judy to let her back in the program, saying she will try harder and be more successful this time. She knew that she could lose her job without getting treatment, and this program was the only option she was offered. Amy's insurance company did an assessment over the telephone and concluded that she needed to try harder and did not need dual diagnosis treatment.

Judy decided she would not permit Amy to reenter the program because it would set Amy up for failure and would be too stressful for Judy's staff and other clients. Judy was hoping that her decision would encourage the EAP case manager to put pressure on the insurance company to pay for appropriate services for clients in the future. She stated, "I know that Amy is going to hurt a little more because I made this decision, but overall, I am giving the message, 'We have to provide proper services, that we're just not going to try to be everything to everybody and pick up the pieces'." Judy does not know whether Amy lost her job or received further treatment after her dismissal from the program.

CASE 7   The Ghost

Jane is a medical social worker in a renal program in a hospital. One of her clients, Marie, has renal disease as well as terminal cancer. Marie is bedridden, incontinent, and semicomatose. Jane is concerned because Marie is suffering, but her husband and son cannot seem to let her die. Marie had told family members before she lost consciousness that she wishes "the Lord would take her." Her husband is torn about what to do because Marie cannot tell him what she wants now, and her son does not want to let his mother go. Jane believes the husband is holding on because Marie made all the decisions, and he is afraid that he cannot make it without her. She believes that although the son states that the sanctity of life should take precedence over all other values, his primary motivation for keeping his mother alive is his guilt about living far away and not having closure in his relationship with his mother. Jane feels an obligation to advocate for Marie who seemingly wants to die. On the other hand, Jane does not feel she can encourage the family to let Marie die because she must support the family, especially the husband. She is helping him process his issues and hopes it will enable him to make the decision to let Marie die. Jane believes that Marie is like a ghost, and so her client in effect becomes Marie's husband because he is the conscious, verbal person. Jane states, "Can I work through thirty-three years of marriage in time enough to advocate for the ghost (Mary)?"

CASE **8**   **Kidneys Are Scarce**

Paulene is a hospital social worker in the renal unit who serves in the role of transplant coordinator. She works to facilitate a client's access to transplant programs at other hospitals. Maryann, a new, nineteen-year-old dialysis patient in the unit, is mildly mentally retarded and works in a sheltered workshop. She does not have a guardian. Maryann received an evaluation for a kidney transplant. She was told about the option of a transplant and was very excited about the prospect of not having dialysis and being more independent. She will not die because of a lack of a kidney transplant, but it very likely would improve the quality of her life. There are no contraindications medically to Maryann getting the transplant.

Paulene has concerns about Maryann socially, psychologically, and cognitively. She discovered that Maryann rules her family with temper tantrums and verbal abuse. She has a history of noncompliance with her medical care and does not understand the connection between taking medicine and not losing her kidneys. Those who have a kidney transplant must take anti-rejection medication every day or risk losing the kidney.

Paulene referred Maryann and her family for therapy especially to help Maryann learn new ways of coping and being medically compliant with her dialysis. Maryann has been told the goal of behavioral therapy is to ready her for a transplant. Maryann has made minimal strides in treatment, but will need years of therapy before Paulene and the physicians think she may be ready for a transplant. Maryann has not been informed of this, nor does she know she has a right to go to another hospital for an evaluation. It is very possible that she would have a transplant by now if she went to another hospital because most hospitals do not do psychosocial screening of potential transplant patients.

Paulene feels uncomfortable because her hospital does not have a policy to support denying a transplant based on nonmedical criteria. She is also concerned that it is "almost like playing God" to deny Maryann this kidney. However, if

Maryann loses the transplanted kidney because she doesn't take care of it, another girl her age does not get a kidney and waits several more years.

CASE 9   I Have Got a Secret

Jon, a school social worker, has two clients, a brother and sister, who are classified as educably mentally impaired and pre-primarily impaired. Their mother, Ethel, has a major, untreated mental illness and seems to be functioning reasonably well. When Jon took the initial family history from her, Ethel denied the illness, but there were so many parts of the history that did not fit together that he was suspicious. Jon wrote up the history without knowing this information.

In a second discussion with Ethel, she revealed her history of manic depression and the problems she is still experiencing. She does not want anyone else to know because she is afraid of treatment and does not want to be labeled "crazy." She also believes it will have negative repercussions for her children. Jon decided to not reveal this information to anyone at school because Ethel has a right to privacy, and she is not abusive to her children. She is just minimally neglectful of them. Jon believes if teachers at the school know about Ethel, they will be prejudiced against her and her children. Jon believes that if school officials view Ethel as being mentally ill, they will ignore her, and then she will be less able to be the best kind of mother she can be for her children. Jon has encouraged Ethel to agree to go into treatment for her illness.

CASE 10   Only Time Will Tell

Elena, a school social worker, has a sixteen-year-old client, Janice, who talked to her about feeling suicidal and experiencing hallucinations. Janice has asked Elena to keep this information confidential, including not talking to her parents. Elena wants her to have a psychiatric exam to assess whether she is psychotic. Janice is afraid of having an assessment, as she believes she will be labeled "crazy" and will be institutionalized. Janice asserts that her parents will not pay for the exam anyway. Elena knows her parents and believes they will not pay unless Janice gives her permission to reveal to them what she has confided to Elena. Since Elena is a minor, Janice must get her parents' permission to do the assessment, as she already had to do to see Elena in the first place.

Elena is trying to convince Janice to agree to let her talk to her parents. She wants to convince them to pay without breaking her client's trust. Elena is not willing to take the risk of breaking confidentiality because she believes Janice would feel betrayed and may never trust anyone again. She is worried about the possibility of Janice killing herself, but she thinks it will not happen unless there is a "major loss." For example, a man that Janice is in love with will be home from the service at Christmas. He has said he just wants to be friends. Janice is counting on the relationship to evolve into something more, so this could trigger a crisis. "I am really worried about those kind of things happening."

CASE **11**   **Poor Medical Risk**

An elderly woman, Marge, who has a history of strokes and hypertension, was visiting her daughter in another state when she had a stroke. Her daughter took her to a rehabilitation hospital where she stayed for two weeks receiving medical care and physical therapy. After two weeks, the hospital social worker called Marge's insurance company about payment. The social worker found out that Marge had Medicare managed care. The policy of the company would have been to put this patient in a nursing home rather than a rehabilitation hospital, even though it is the most expensive alternative.

The case manager from the insurance company was angry about Marge's stay at the hospital and threatened not to pay the hospital for her stay. The case manager from the insurance company demanded that the social worker provide her with all of the information from Marge's records before the company would decide whether to pay.

Upon entering the hospital, Marge, like all patients, was asked to sign a consent form to release all information from her record to any person or organization responsible for the payment of her hospital bills. The social worker knew that Marge needed to stay at least two weeks longer and then be released to her daughter's house, with twenty-four hour skilled nursing care provided. The case manager was not a social worker and was primarily interested in saving money. Marge was seen as a high stroke risk.

The social worker released Marge's records and decided to try to convince the case manager that there would be cost savings in keeping Marge in the hospital longer and discharging her to her daughter's house with only a nurse's aid provided and without twenty-four hour care. She knew it was a compromise because Marge would still have major cognitive and emotional impairment, but thought it was the only way the insurance company would agree to pay for Marge.

CASE **12**   **Homeless and Without Insurance**

Damon, a homeless man in his fifties, was admitted into an acute care hospital with multiple injuries that he had sustained as a result of a pedestrian-train accident. He was drunk and walked on the train tracks. Damon had limited family contact and, thus, was without support. He did not have Medicaid because he was regarded as able-bodied although he had not worked in years. Damon needed to be qualified for Medicaid after the accident because it was medically necessary for him to receive long-term respiratory care and neuro-rehabilitation to stay alive. His social worker in the hospital made a number of attempts to reach the welfare department to get the Medicaid process initiated, but Medicaid did not follow up promptly. The social worker was eventually told that Damon could not get a Medicaid number until he was discharged from the hospital.

Nursing homes did not want to accept Damon because they were concerned about losing money due to his extensive medical needs. Even the nursing home connected to the hospital, of which the social worker was an employee, did not agree to accept Damon. The social worker was feeling pressured by the hospital to discharge Damon since he was there for a month and was costing the hospital a lot of money. She convinced a nursing home to reconsider taking him. The nursing home did not even have a respiration therapist, let alone neuro-rehabilitation. Damon died two weeks after being placed in the nursing home.

CASE 13   Abandonment

A sixty-year-old woman, Claire, had a long history of multiple sclerosis. She lived with her eighty-year-old mother who was caring for her. Claire went into a rehabilitation hospital because of increased weakness and confusion. She was in a hospital for acute care and needed intense therapy in a rehabilitation hospital so she could live more independently with her mother. Claire needed to be precertified by her HMO managed care company so it could decide whether it would pay for rehabilitation in the hospital. The nurse case manager in another state asked the social worker at the rehabilitation hospital to set up a discharge plan with all supports in place for when Claire would leave the hospital. The social worker set up a plan for physical and occupational therapy in Claire's home and asked for two and one-half weeks to work with Claire in the hospital.

The case manager denied the request for therapy in the hospital and approved only a nurse's aid with no wheelchair for Claire. The rationale given was that the social worker had already done too much for Claire and she did not need rehabilitation. The social worker appealed the decision to a physician reviewer in yet another state, and he denied the social worker's requests as well.

The hospital received no reimbursement for the week Claire was in the hospital while the discharge plans were made. The social worker believes the insurance company did not want to pay for services to a person with a chronic illness, as it is costly. The social worker knows that Claire is not receiving adequate care, but feels powerless because the hospital can absorb only so much uncompensated care. The hospital is much more likely to provide uncompensated care if it is for children.

CASE 14   Set Her Off

Mary Ellen, a Protective Services worker, has a client, Alice, who has had three of her five children taken away from her. They were legally taken away by the courts after different Protective Service workers petitioned the court for their removal. Alice has been diagnosed with schizophrenia, and at times, she refuses to recognize her illness and stops taking her medication. The first three of her children were taken away because there was evidence of abuse.

At present, Alice is doing well and taking her medication. Mary Ellen is mandated to work with the family to assist them in functioning. Mary Ellen is torn about what to do because she is afraid that Alice will go off her medication and her children will be harmed. Ellen is thinking of trying to set Alice off by pressuring her, so she can go to court and tell the judge that Alice "is talking crazy and hallucinating." She would convince the judge that Alice's mental illness is a risk to her children. She may then be hospitalized. This way, Alice's remaining children will be removed so she cannot harm them.

CASE 15   You Are My Girlfriend

A male client of seventy is lonely and needy. He has no family other than a sister he has not seen in twenty years. He is covertly sexual with his social worker and indicates that he believes they are special to one another. He initiates hugging and hand-holding, and he calls her endearing names. His social worker tells him that she is not his girlfriend, and he accepts that for awhile. He invariably goes back to flirting with her and trying to touch her.

CASE 16   Spending His Money as He Pleases

Many clients in the assertive community treatment program have representative payees in the guardian's office. An assertive community treatment team is given power by the guardian's office to decide how its clients' personal money will be spent.

The client of one team has a substance abuse problem, and the team must decide whether to give the client his money to spend as he pleases even though team members know there is a good chance he will spend it on drugs. They decide, based on the treatment implications of the decision and their belief in self-determination, to give the client his money. They base their decision on the fact that the client does not have a previous history of getting into trouble with the law or of hurting others. If the client decides to spend the money on drugs rather than provide for such basic needs as food, they will take away his freedom to spend his money. The team leader states that "our clients are citizens of the community and deserve the same rights and responsibilities as other citizens."

CASE 17   Rigidity

Carol had hired Joyce because, she said, the two complemented each other. Joyce's "structured method of operating and my sort of nonstructured method met well in the middle." But after hiring her, Carol discovered that Joyce was extremely rigid in her application of the rules.

Joyce went by the book, and though, as a consequence, many things were done well, a lot of things that needed doing were not getting done. For instance, she did a superb job of licensing foster homes, but when "it got to be the implementation of the programs and not the logistics, we started having trouble." When it came to working out with agencies and individuals the difficulties that arose because of the rules, Joyce simply asserted that the rules were the rules. She had no room for compromise. She allowed no exceptions for anything, and so Carol began to "get a lot of flack from referral sources."

Carol eventually gave Joyce three months to find another job, with the threat of being fired after that period of time.

CASE 18   Bail or Jail

An assertive community treatment team has two clients who live together. The male client beat up his female roommate and was arrested. The team must decide whether to pay bail for the client or leave him in jail. Team members would only bail him out if they could find a supervised alternative living arrangement for him.

The team has the power to make this decision about bail. It also has influence with the prosecutor's office. The team must decide whether to advocate for the client to remain in the criminal justice system or receive treatment for his offence in the mental health system. The decision is based upon whether team members think the client's offense stemmed primarily from his mental illness. They also base their decision on the seriousness of the offense. If the offense is less serious (e.g., malicious destruction of property, shoplifting, simple assault), they are inclined to advocate for keeping the client in the community and recommending that he receive probation and do community service.

The team decides that as long as the client lives away from his roommate in a supervised setting, he will not hurt her. The team decides to leave him in jail for the weekend and recommend probation and community service, but use the client's money for the bail payment to show him that his actions have consequences. The team is concerned that his having to stay in jail and not having his money may set him off and result in his being unwilling to stay away from his roommate, and will thus result in further harm to her.

CASE 19   Abuse and Care

Thirteen-year-old Jean disclosed to her therapist Doris that she had been sexually abused by her father, stepfather, and grandfather from the ages of eight to thirteen. Jean was diagnosed as having posttraumatic stress disorder and was also developmentally disabled with an IQ of 80. She was having a lot of flashbacks, and medication was not helping her. She lacked physical and emotional boundaries. Jean drew an ecogram with herself in the middle and her family and Doris on top of her and overlapping with one another. Emotionally and physically she needed to be enmeshed, and her mother reinforced it.

Jean was a large child who needed and wanted to be held. She would aggressively come up to Doris and hug her and wanted to hold hands during sessions.

She invited Doris to her birthday party. While Jean was waiting for her session, she would wander through other therapists' offices, use their phones, and take pens and paper.

Doris wondered what would be a way to respond to Jean's needs for hugs and handholding that would not reinforce the abuse she had suffered. How can she provide Jean with the safety and nurturing she needs?

Doris recommended that Jean be placed in foster care because of her mother's poor judgment and inability to establish boundaries. Jean went into foster care, became suicidal, and was hospitalized. She remains in the hospital and is doing much worse than when she was with her mother.

CASE 20   "I Thought You Cared about Me!"

A thirty-year-old woman named Ann has been emotionally, sexually, and physically traumatized by all of her family members. She originally had a diagnosis of borderline personality disorder. She was self-mutilating, prostituting, abusing alcohol and drugs, and engaging in abusive relationships with men. After her first child, Ann corrected herself somewhat, and her diagnosis became posttraumatic stress disorder. She has a great deal of anxiety and depression. The current issue for which Ann came into treatment was that her son raped her after she blacked out from drinking.

For the first six months of therapy, Ann was very tangential and controlling about what could be discussed. She would not discuss parenting issues with Sue, her therapist, as she refused to take any responsibility for her son's problems. She has very poor boundaries and is likely to call Sue two or three times a week after her weekly session. If Sue does not call her back quickly, she may call back a number of times that day. Ann often pours out personal information to whomever answers the phone, whether it is a secretary or another therapist.

During the first six months of therapy, Sue would make sure to call Ann back quickly or sometime the same day because Ann engaged in suicidal ideation and Sue was very concerned about her. Ann constantly tests boundaries and then engages in black-and-white thinking. "I thought you cared about me, but I guess you don't." Sue does not want to alienate Ann by not calling her back because she wants to win her trust. Ann has had other therapists whom she did not trust. After eleven months of therapy, Ann has ceased her suicidal ideation, and Sue is considering waiting a few days before calling Ann back. Sue's ultimate goal is not to process issues at all with Ann between sessions.

Ann becomes distraught when Sue does not call her back for a few days. She starts calling Sue's office many times a day and her suicidal ideation increases. Ann makes a suicide attempt and ends up in the emergency room. She blames Sue for not calling her back. At their next session, Sue tells Ann that she will be terminating therapy with her and is referring her to another therapist. She tells Ann that it is for her own good, as she has become too dependent on her.

ENDNOTES

1. *NASW Code of Ethics* (Washington, DC: National Association of Social Workers, 1996).
2. When we say that many ethical cases are easy, we do not mean to deny that they can be hard for those participating to decide what to do, or that once they decide what they ought to do, hard to do it. People may be ignorant of the proper ethical considerations, for instance, or weak-willed—unable to bring themselves to do what they ought to do or unwilling because it runs so counter to their own self-interest. What we do mean to say is, first, that once the ethical considerations are clear, it is clear in many cases what ought to be done, ethically, no matter how difficult it may be for participants to do it. Indeed, as we shall see when we examine cases, some cases that appear quite impossible turn out to be easy once we apply the method we propose and get clear on what needs to be considered ethically. And, second, we mean to say that we are concerned with those cases that are difficult because there are competing ethical demands—not because there are, for instance, competing demands of self-interest.
3. The difficulties with codes of ethics as the final arbiter of ethical issues are notorious. We will consider some of the major problems in Chapter 2. For further reading about the matter, see note 35.
4. We have tried to reproduce the original language used by those providing us these cases. The social worker here said that the children "had been placed away from their home," and the implications of that choice of words should be noted. To say of a person that he or she is *placed* somewhere is to treat what is placed as some sort of object, a thing to be maneuvered. Talking in that way is perhaps necessary to gain distance and thus objectivity, but we should be aware of how the usual language of our profession—and we think this talk of *placing* people is common—can encourage an unfortunate attitude toward them, as though they were objects, not persons. We do not mean to suggest that Mary had this attitude. We only mean to warn against what may be the implications of certain word choices.
5. Child Prevention and Treatment Act of 1974, Pub. L. No. 93-247, 88 Stat. 4. See Robert Adler (1995), To tell or not to tell: The psychiatrist and child abuse, *Australian and New Zealand Journal of Psychiatry* 29 (2), 190–198; Butz Randell (1985), Reporting child abuse and confidentiality in counseling, *Social Casework* 66 (2), 83–90.
6. Bok, S. (1983). The limits of confidentiality. *The Hastings Center Report*, 13 (1), 24–31; Dickson, D. T. (1998). *Confidentiality and Privacy in Social Work: A Guide to the Law for Practitioners and Students.* New York: Free Press.
7. Barker, R. A. (1988a). "Client dumping": Some ethical considerations. *Journal of Independent Social Work,* 2 (1), 1–5.
8. See Joel Feinberg, *Harm to Others* (New York: Oxford University Press), Vol. I of *The Moral Limits of the Criminal Law.* His analysis of harms as setbacks to interests as well as his analysis of what it is to wrong someone are implicit in our analysis of how ethical issues are raised and resolved. Anyone interested in pursuing the theoretical aspects of harms should begin with Feinberg's work, not just the volume mentioned, but also the others in the series, especially *Offense to Others,* in which he makes clear how different harming someone is from offending them.
9. Not always successfully, obviously. If there were one acceptable criterion that weighed ethical harms one against another and did that efficiently and in a way that left no doubt about which were the greater and which the lesser harms, we would have at our disposal an acceptable theory of ethics and no ethical dilemmas. It is because we have disagreement about how to weigh harms one against another—disagreement, that is, about what

constitutes the right ethical theory—that we have disagreements about how to weigh harms against each other and even disagreement, as we shall see, about what constitutes a harm since what is a harm by one ethical theory may not be a harm by another.

10. We give more guidance about giving arguments in Chapter 2. For those who wish to pursue further discussion of the criteria for constructing arguments, an introductory text in elementary logic will suffice. We suggest some edition of Irving Copi, *Introduction to Logic*, 6th edition (New York: MacMillan, 1982), Alec Fisher, *The Logic of Real Arguments* (Cambridge: Cambridge University Press, 1988), or Bruce N. Waller, *Critical Thinking: Consider the Verdict* (Englewood Cliffs, NJ: Prentice Hall, 1988).

We should add that what we are doing is hypothesizing what the person would have given as a justification for his or her actions or omissions. But a person might do a particular thing for a variety of different kinds of reasons, and so we cannot know for sure, just because we figure out what persons might have been thinking that would justify what they did, that that is what they had in mind or would have had in mind had they attempted to justify what they did. We need independent evidence for the premises we attribute to the person. We can get that, in part, by seeing whether our hypothesis fits in with other features of the person and the situation.

11. Kutchins, H. (1991). The fiduciary relationship: The legal basis for social work responsibility to clients. *Social Work, 36* (2), 106–113.

12. And looks like a factual issue, but it is not ethically neutral for at least two different reasons. First, it will sometimes require an ethical judgment to determine who is a participant and who is not or, more generally, who is affected or who is not. One way of saying that the father did not intentionally fall asleep on the baby is to decide that he is not a participant—or at least not a willing participant.

Second, it is an essential principle in every ethical theory except forms of egoism that those making ethical decisions step back from the situation they are concerned about and take a general point of view. John Stuart Mill says that no one is to count for more than one in calculating how to produce the greatest happiness for the greatest number, and Kant demands that the maxims on the basis of which we are to act be what he calls universalizable. What they both mean is that the person involved—Mary in *Dancing a Legal Dance,* Deborah in *The Death of a Baby*—not take their own interests as being any more important than the interests of anyone else.

To universalize one's maxim, according to Kant, is to ask whether everyone can act in the way you are proposing to act, and that is just to ask whether you are treating yourself as someone special to be distinguished from others, or whether everyone ought to do what you are about to do, in which case you are counting for no more than anyone else would in your situation.

When Mill says that no one is to count for more than one in calculating out to determine the greatest happiness for the greatest number, he is saying that you are just as important as, but no more important than—worth as much as, but no more than—anyone else. It would thus not be ethical to make a decision that elevated your interests over those of anyone else.

Step 1 forces those considering a case to get out of their own point of view and consider the views of others involved in the case. That is an essential first step in making an ethical decision—in assuming the general point of view. But we shall discuss this at greater length and provide references when we come to examine ethical theories.

13. Slonim-Nevo, V. (1996). Clinical practice: treating the nonvoluntary client. *International Social Work. 39,* 117–129.

14. Abramson, M. (1990). Keeping secrets: Social workers and AIDS. *Social Work, 35,* 169–173; Kagle, J. D., & Kopels, S. (1994), Confidentiality after Tarasoff. *Health and Social Work, 19,* 217–222; Gray, L., & Harding, A. K. (1988). Confidentiality limits with clients who have the AIDS virus. *Journal of Counseling and Development, 66* (5), 219–223; Kain, C. D. (1988). To breach or not to breach. Is that the question? *Journal of Counseling and Development, 66* (5), 224–225.

15. On why it is wrong to tell a lie, see Immanuel Kant, "On the supposed right to tell lies from benevolent motives," in Thomas Kingsmill Abbott, trans., *Kant's Critique of Practical Reason and Other Works on the Theory of Ethics* (London: Longman, 1909), pp. 361–365. See also Sissela Bok, *Lying: Moral Choice in Public and Private Life* (New York: Pantheon, 1978).

16. See the first section of Chapter 4 where we talk about the values of treating one's colleagues as peers. See also Olson, E., Chichin, E., & Meyers, H. (1994). Early experience of an ethics consult team. (Jewish Home and Hospital for the Aged, New York City). *Journal of the American Geriatrics Society, 42,* 437–441; Reamer, F. G. (1995). Ethics consultation in social work. *Social Thought,* 18 (1), 3–16.

17. Much has been written about how to brainstorm. A brief but insightful introduction is Chapter 17 of Murray Gell-Mann, *The Quark and the Jaguar* (New York: W. H. Freeman & Co., 1994), pp. 261–273. A very helpful introduction to brainstorming in regard to ethical issues is Chapter 3, "Finding the Best Problem," of Anthony Weston, *A Practical Companion to Ethics* (New York: Oxford University Press, 1997), 29–48.

18. When we have a serious question about whether to inform, the issue about the potential harm is always a question of judgment about which people may disagree. If it were not and if everyone agreed that certain, severe harm was going to occur or that no harm of any sort would occur, no one would dispute a decision to inform the authorities, in the first instance, or not to inform, in the second. So when we have a serious question about whether to inform, it is because it will not be obvious what risk, if any, there is. No one suggests informing the authorities when there is only the slightest possibility of the smallest of harms.

    We might also have a serious question if, for some special reason, maintaining the trust of the relationship were deemed crucial—and this would again be a matter of judgment—and worth breaking the law when the law requires informing. We should never break the law lightly, particularly when by doing so we may end up having harm caused to others as well as to our clients. So this is not a likely possibility. But a social worker might properly think that holding off informing the authorities had some value—so that, for instance, the names of the persons being put at risk by one's violence-prone client could be determined.

19. See Stuart A. Anfang & Paul S. Appelbaum (1996), "Twenty Years After Tarasoff: Reviewing the Duty to Protect," *Harvard Review of Psychiatry,* Vol. 14 (2), 67–76; Rebecca Stanard & Richard Nazler (1995), Legal and Ethical Implications of HIV and duty to warn for counselors: When does Tarasoff apply?, *Journal of Counseling and Development,* Vol. 73 (4), 397–400; Swartz, M. S. (1990). Is there a duty to warn? Does safety ever warrant releasing confidential information about HIV-infected people? *Human Rights,* 17, 40–45; Lewis, M. B. (1986). Duty to warn versus duty to maintain confidentiality: Conflicting demands on mental health professionals. *Law Review,* 20 (3), 579–615; Polowy, C. & Gorenberg, C. (1996). Office of General Counsel Law Notes: *Confidentiality and Privileged Communications.* Document of the NASW Press, Washington, DC; Kopels, S., & Kagle, J. D. (1993). Do social workers have a duty to warn? *Social Service Review,* (March), 101–126.

20. It may appear that our method is utilitarian. After all, we are concerned with tracking what harms will come from an act or omission and so with the consequences of acts and omissions. But we mean for the method to be neutral between competing ethical theories. The harms we have in mind may include wrongs, and we may wrong someone—by lying, for instance—without causing any bad consequences. Indeed, lying may happen to produce only good effects. One consequence of our method of tracking harms is that if we lie to someone, and so wrong that person, we must weigh that wrong against whatever good effects the wrong, i.e., that harm, may produce.

    We do not mean to be choosing between ethical theories by including wrongs among the harms that we consider or by considering the consequences of acts and omissions. We are rather trying to sort out all the possible harms—as identified by any of the relevant theories of ethics—to be sure we understand a case thoroughly before proceeding on to determine what we ought to do.

21. See Faya Rozovsky, *Consent to Treatment: A Practical Guide* (Boston: Little, Brown, 1984); Jane Cawles, *Informed Consent* (New York: Coword, McCann, and Geoghegan, 1976); Michael Parker (1995), Commentary on "True Wishes," *Philosophy, Psychiatry and Psychology* 2 (4), 313–314; & Cheryl Regehr & Beverly Antle (1997), Coercive Influences: Informed consent in court-mandated social work practice, *Social Work* 42 (2), 300–306; Freedberg, S. (1989). Self-determination: Historical perspectives & effects on current practice. *Social Work*, 34, 33–38. Rothman, J. (1989). Client self-determination: Untangling the knot. *Social Science Review*, 63, 598–612; Regehr, C., & Antle, B. (1997). Coercive influences: Informed consent in court-mandated social work practice. *Social Work*, 42, 300–306; Swartz, M. S. (1988). AIDS testing and informed consent. *Journal of Health Politics, Policy and Law*, 3 (4), 607–621; Schoeman, F. (1980). Rights of children, rights of parents, and the moral basis of the family. *Ethics*, 91, 6–19.

22. We shall be examining the issue of self-determination with more thoroughness in Chapter 3, but, in any event, the following are worth examining: Felix P. Biestek, Client Self-Determination, in F. E. McDermott, ed. *Self-Determination in Social Work* (London: Routledge and Kegan Paul, 1975); Saul Bernstein, Self-Determination: King or Citizen in the Realm of Values, *Social Work* (1960), 5:3–8; Alan Keith-Lucas, A Critique of the Principle of Client Self-Determination, *Social Work* (1963), 8:66–71; Helen Harris Perlman, Self Determination: Reality or Illusion?, *Social Services Review* (1965), 39: 410–421; R. F. Stalley, Determination and the Principle of Client Self-Determination, in F. E. McDermott, ed., *op. cit.*, pp. 93–117.

23. Abramson, M. (1996). Reflections on knowing oneself ethically: Toward a working framework for social work practice. *Families in Society, 77*, (April), 195–202. See also Manning, S. (1997). The social worker as moral citizen: Ethics in action. *Social Work*, 42, 223–230.

24. Goldstein, H. (1998). Education for ethical dilemmas in social work practice. *Families in Society*, 79 (3), 241–253.

25. This has the look of a principle, and we mean this to be the basis for deciding. Yet, as we have pointed out, what counts as a harm on one theory may not be a harm on another, and this appeal always to act so as to minimize harm will sometimes be unclear and sometimes unhelpful. It will be unclear when we examine a case and discover that different theories give us different conceptions of what has gone wrong and so give us different understandings of what counts as a harm in that case. It will be unhelpful when the harms seem of such relatively equal weight, within or without the theories in question, that we have no way to choose between them. This difficulty of sometimes not knowing what we ought to do is, we think, part of what it is to be a human being, trying to be ethical in a complex world. Sometimes we do not know what is ethical.

26. For a rich variety of examples, see Terrence Real, *I Don't Want to Talk About It: Overcoming the Secret Legacy of Male Depression* (New York: Scribner, 1997). It turns out, according to Real, that sometimes the crucial factor in creating the momentum for change is for a person to come to the insight that the behavior in question is abusive to others. What a man may think of as a temper tantrum, quickly dissipated (and so, he may think, doing no lasting harm), is a way of controlling others, and once the man can see his own behavior in that way, he has made the first step necessary to changing it. But that first step can be extremely difficult—if for no other reason than that no one likes to see his or her own behavior as abusive.

27. Asserting this truth does not make it true. A detailed examination of the relationships between self-interest and ethics would require us to come to grips with the view of ethical egoists that we ought always to act in our self-interest and of psychological egoists that we cannot help but act in our self-interest. We shall not pursue these questions here because their analysis would take us far astray, but interested readers may look to the references provided in the section on ethical theories. In addition, material on egoism of both kinds is in most anthologies.

28. Of course, being honest and clear does not mean that she will have succeeded in communicating her position to Martha. That case is conceptually problematic because we can disagree on what would be sufficient for Mary to have informed Martha—telling her at the initial

meeting? Telling her each time they meet? Telling her just before it looks as though Martha is about to speak about the issue? That is, although we may agree that Mary ought to be honest and clear to further her long-term interests, and Martha's, we can disagree about what would count as being clear and so would count as being prudent.

29. Again, it is no argument to assert that acting in our long-term self-interest is not necessarily to do what is ethical. For an examination of the difficult questions the assertion bypasses, see the material listed in the endnotes in the section on ethical theories.

    The core idea is simple, however. It is that each person's acting in his or her own long-term self-interest is a form of egoism. When conflicts occur between the long-term interests of one person and those of another—conflicts that are inevitable when the resources are fewer than the needs they must meet—each person's acting on prudence does not resolve the problem, but exacerbates it. No problem of distributive justice can be resolved, that is, if we each take our own long-term interest as the basis for action. It may be that we cannot resolve such issues and that appealing to prudence simply makes clear what is true, but it is some evidence against such a theory of how we ought to act that it cannot handle questions of distributive justice. For we do handle at least some of these questions and handle them relatively well.

30. Jayaratne, T. C., & Mattison, D. (1997). Social work professional standards: An exploratory study. *Social Work, 42*, 187–199; Duncan, B. J. (1998). A response to "Social work professional standards." *Social Work, 43* (1), 70–72.

31. See Charles S. Levy, *Social Work Ethics* (New York: Human Services Press, 1976), pp. 50–51, 141–142; Susanna J. Wilson, *Confidentiality in Social Work* (New York: Free Press, 1978) Shemmings, Daniel. Client Access to Records: *Participation in Social Work.* Avebury, 1991; Alves, Joseph T., *Confidentiality in Social Work.* Greenwood Publishing Group: 1984.

32. Think here of the problem psychiatrists have when patients tell them they are going to go out and do something harmful to themselves ("I'm going to commit suicide") or to others ("I'm going to get even!"). Such statements by patients are not proof that the patients will do what they say they will do. They are signs for a psychiatrist to interpret—quite typical, in fact, of psychiatric encounters—and the burden the psychiatrist has is determining, in each particular case, just how serious the threat is—what the risk is. If the code for psychiatrists said only to breach confidentiality when harm will occur—is "foreseeable"—then no psychiatrist—would ever breach confidentiality.

33. This right is a prima facie right. That is, it is a right that we can breach when we have more weighty rights that compete. Someone who comes to a physician with an infectious disease that can only be transmitted in what the patient finds to be an embarrassing manner may find that the physician has an obligation to inform authorities about the disease, and even to name the patient, in order to protect others from potential infection.

34. We touch here on the difficult issue of how we are to make reasonable and ethical decisions in situations of uncertainty, in which we do not know exactly what will happen from some act. For an examination of the nature of the problem, with a large bibliography of source material, see Wade L. Robison, *Decisions in Doubt: The Environment and Public Policy* (Hanover, NH: The University Press of New England, 1994).

35. For a thorough examination of the problems and benefits of codes of ethics, see John Kultgen, Evaluating Codes of Ethics, in Wade L. Robison, Michael S. Pritchard, & Joseph Ellin, *Profits and Professions: Essays in Business and Professional Ethics* (Clifton, NJ: Humana Press, 1983), 225–264.

36. On the need to think for oneself, see Anthony Weston, *op. cit.*, 13–27.

37. One way in which we can harm another person is not to act when action is called for. When we see a person drowning, are in a position to save the person, have the capacity to save the person, and yet fail to try to do so, we have caused that person harm. So, although we shall generally concern ourselves with acts, we mean to include omissions to act as well.

38. We also need to make it clear that this analysis, though drawn from different descriptions of ethical theories both by their main exponents and by commentators, is not to be found in any of those. In particular, thinking of these theories as promoting different ethical visions based on different features of us is unique.

   There are many introductory texts that one may find useful in fleshing out the rather brief descriptions we provide of ethical theories. Among the better ones is Tom L. Beauchamp's *Philosophical Ethics: An Introduction to Moral Philosophy* (New York: McGraw-Hill, Inc., 1991), 2nd edition, Chapters 4–6 (pp. 127–252). This text contains a superb set of references and a list of supplementary readings for those who wish to pursue any particular details of these theories.

   In addition to Beauchamp's book, you may wish to examine in some detail any or all of the following general texts in ethics: Joseph Ellin, *Morality and the Meaning of Life* (Fort Worth, TX: Harcourt Brace, 1995); William K. Frankena, *Ethics* (Englewood Cliffs, NJ: Prentice-Hall, 1963); Robert L. Holmes, *Basic Moral Philosophy* (Belmont, GA: Wadsworth, 1993); William N. Nelson, *What's In It For Me?* (Boulder, CO: Westview Press, 1991). Bernard Williams, *Ethics and the Limits of Philosophy* (London: Fontana Press, 1985).

39. This shift from pleasure to happiness is not innocent. We shall discuss its implications when we compare the scope of the different ethical theories.

40. One might object that all living things feel, but some may argue that worms, for instance, cannot feel a thing even though they are obviously alive. For instance, Descartes thought that only human beings could feel and that dogs and other animals were automatons, reacting to stimuli mechanically as a watch responds to being wound. See Rene Descartes, *The Discourse on Method*, Part Five (in J. Cottingham, R. Stoothhoff, & D. Murdoch; *The Philosophical Writings of Descartes*, Vol. I (New York: Cambridge University Press, 1985), pp. 139–141).

41. For further reading on utilitarianism, see William Frankena, *op. cit.*, 29–46; Anthony Quinton, *Utilitarian Ethics* (New York: St. Martin's Press: 1973); and, for a very brief but thorough introduction to the theory and to some of the theories to which it has given rise, see Philip Peffit, Consequentalism, and Robert E. Goodin, Utility and the good, in Peter Singer, ed., *A Companion to Ethics* (Oxford: Blackwell, 1993), 230–248.

   Also, rather obviously, there is John Stuart Mill's *Utilitarianism*, which is widely available. Some of its more pertinent sections, along with critical essays by others and other original material, are in Jonathan Glover, ed., *Utilitarianism and Its Critics* (New York: Macmillan, 1990). For a selection of critical essays, see Harlan B. Miller & William H. Williams, *The Limits of Utilitarianism* (Minneapolis, MN: University of Minnesota Press, 1982).

42. For a sustained set of examples and a theoretical explanation for why events are not always foreseeable, see Wade L. Robison, *op. cit.*, pp. 15ff.

43. This is a variant of an example that Kant gives in the *Foundations of the Metaphysics of Morals*, trans. Lewis White Beck (Indianapolis, IN: Bobbs-Merrill, 1976), 13. Anyone who wants to explore deontology in all its details needs to read Kant, but that is best done with an additional set of readings. A good collection of essays combined with a translation by Beck of the *Foundations* is found in *Foundations of the Metaphysics of Morals with Critical Essays*, ed. Robert Paul Wolff (Indianapolis, IN: Bobbs-Merrill, 1969).

44. Immanuel Kant, *Foundations of the Metaphysics of Morals, op. cit.*, p. 10.

45. For additional reading on Kant's theory, see the brief essay by Onora O'Neill, Kantian Ethics, in Peter Singer, *op. cit.*, 175–185; Chapter 2 of William K. Frankena, *op. cit.*, 11–28; J. B. Schneewind, Autonomy, obligation, and virtue: An overview of Kant's moral philosophy, in *The Cambridge Companion to Kant*, ed. Paul Guyer (Cambridge: Cambridge University Press, 1993), 309–341; the eight essays by various authors in Part II of the anthology, ed. Robert Paul Wolff, *Kant: A Collection of Critical Essays* (Garden City, NY: Doubleday Anchor, 1967), 211–336; and Marcia W. Baron, *Kantian Ethics Almost Without Apology* (Ithaca, NY: Cornell University Press, 1995).

46. Gilligan, C., et al. (eds.). (1988). *Mapping the moral domain: A contribution of women's thinking to psychological theory and education.* Cambridge, MA: Center for the Study of Gender, Education &

Human Development, Harvard University Graduate School of Education: Distributed by Harvard University Press; Kohlberg, L. (1976). Moral stages and moralization: The cognitive-developmental approach. In T. Likona (ed.), *Moral development and behavior: Theory, research and social issues* (pp. 31–53). New York: Holt, Rinehart and Winston; Rhodes, M.L. (1985). Gilligan's theory of moral development as applied to social work. *Social Work*, 30 (2), 101–105.

47. For a particularly insightful analysis of the kinds of problems professionals can have integrating their professional lives into their ordinary lives, and vice versa, see Gerald J. Postema, Moral Responsibility in Professional Ethics, in Robison, Pritchard and Ellin, *op. cit.*, 37–63.

48. For further reading on virtue theory, see Aristotle, trans. Martin Ostwald, *Nicomachean Ethics* (Indianapolis, IN: Bobbs-Merrill, 1962); Greg Pence, Virtue theory, in Peter Singer, *op. cit.*, 249–258; R. Kruschwitz & R. Roberts, *The Virtues: Contemporary Essays on Moral Character* (Belmont, CA: Wadsworth, 1987), and especially the bibliography, 237–263; and Alasdair MacIntyre, *After Virtue* (Notre Dame, IN: University of Notre Dame Press, 1981).

49. See the section on ethical principles and the particular principle that "social workers respect the inherent dignity and worth of the person."

50. Murdach, A. D. (1996). Beneficence reexamined: Protective intervention in mental health. *Social Work*, 41, 26–32; Abramson, M. (1985). The autonomy-paternalism dilemma in social work practice. *Social Casework*, 66, 387–393; Abramson, M. (1989). Autonomy vs. paternalistic beneficence: Practice strategies. *Social Casework*, 70, 101–105; Reamer, F. G. (1983). The concept of paternalism in social work. *Social Service Review*, 57, 254–271; Galambos, C.M. (1997). Resolving ethical conflicts in providing case management services to the elderly. *Journal of Gerontological Social Work*, 27 (4), 57–67; Harold Lewis, Self determination: The aged clients' autonomy in service encounters, *Journal of Gerontological Social Work* 7 (3), 51–63; Paul Spicker, Social Work and Self-Determination, *British Journal of Social Work* 20 (3), 221–236.

51. Timothy B. Kelly, Paternalism and the marginally competent: An ethical dilemma, no easy answers, *Journal of Gerontological Social Work*, 23 (1–2), 67–84.

52. The example is a variant of one John Stuart Mill gives in *On Liberty*, ed. Currin V. Shields (Indianapolis, IN: Bobbs-Merrill, 1956), 117.

53. Salmon, M. (1997). Ethical considerations in anthropology and archaeology or relativism and justice for all. *Journal of Anthropological Research*, 53, 47–63; Crandall, L. A. (1990). Advocacy of just health policies as professional duty: Cultural biases and ethical responsibilities (part of a symposium on: Justice and the health care industry), *Business & Professional Ethics Journal*, 9, 41–53.

54. Holstein, M. (1995). Multidisciplinary ethical decision-making: Uniting differing professional perspectives. *Journal of Elder Abuse & Neglect*, 7(2–3), 169–182; Csikai, E.L., & Sales, E. (1998). The emerging social work role on hospital ethics committees: A comparison of social worker and chair perspectives. *Social Work*, 43 (3), 233–242.

55. Wesley, C. A. (1996). Social work and end-of-life decisions: Self-determination and the common good. *Health and Social Work*, 21, 115–121.

56. Fleck-Henderson, A. (1998). The family as a moral community: A social work perspective. *Families in Society.* 79 (3), 233–240.

57. Pope, K. S., & Bajt, T. R. (1988). When laws and values conflict: A dilemma for psychologists. *American Psychologist*, 43 (10), 829–833.

58. One of the most serious problems concerns informed consent. It happens all too frequently that someone who does not understand because of cultural or linguistic differences nods yes. In regard to the general problems that arise concerning informed consent, see Tom Beauchamp and Ruth R. Faden, *A History and Theory of Informed Consent* (Oxford University Press: New York, 1986).

59. Those who wish to pursue the issue of ethical relativism more fully should look to the bibliographies of the general texts in ethics cited in Chapter 2.

60. Linda M. Jorgenson, Audrey Hirsch, & Kathaleen M. Wahl (1997), Fiduciary duty and boundaries: Acting in the client's best interest, *Behavioral Sciences and the Law* 15 (1), 49–62; Marilyn Peterson, *At Personal Risk: Boundary Violations in Professional-Client Relationships* (New York:

W. W. Norton, 1992), 184–186; Smith, D., & Fitzpatrick, M. (1995). Patient-therapist boundary issues: An integrative review of theory and research. *Professional Psychology, Research and Practice, 26*, 499–506.

61. Jill D. Kagle (1994), Dual Relationships and Professional Boundaries, *Social Work* 39 (2), 213–220; Jeffrey N. Younggren & Darlene Skorka (1992), The nontherapeutic psychotherapy relationship, *Law and Psychology Review* 16, 13–28; Debra S. Borys & Kenneth S. Pope (1989), Dual relationships between the therapist and client: A national study of psychologists, psychiatrists, and social workers, *Professional Psychology: Research and Practice* 20 (5), 283–293; Mary Valentic & James Gripton (1992), Dual Relationships: Dilemmas and Doubts, *Canadian Journal of Human Sexuality* 3, 155–166; Keith Brownlee (1996), The ethics of nonsexual dual relationships: A dilemma for the rural mental health practitioner, *Community Mental Health Journal* 32 (5), 497–503; Herlihy, B., & Corey, G. (1992). *Dual Relationships in Counseling,* Alexandria, VA: American Association for Counseling and Development; Anderson, S. K., & Kitchner, K. S. (1996). Nonromantic, nonsexual posttherapy relationships between psychologist and former clients: An exploratory study of critical incidents. *Professional Psychology: Research and Practice, 27* (1), 59–66.

62. Sloan, L., Edmond, T., & Rubin, A. (1998). Social workers' knowledge of and experience with sexual exploitation by psychotherapists. *Social Work, 43* (1), 43–53; Gechtman, L. (1989). Sexual contact between social workers and their clients. In G. Gabbard (Ed.), *Sexual exploitation in professional relationships* (pp. 27–38). Washington, DC: American Psychiatric Press; Pope, K. S. (1987). Preventing therapist-patient sexual intimacy: Therapy for a therapist at risk. *Professional Psychology, 18* (6), 624–628.

63. Frank M. Loewenberg (1987), Another look at the unethical professional's professional conduct, *Journal of Applied Social Sciences* 11 (2), 220–229; Alan Davis & Daniel Yazak (1996), Supporting a Colleague in Ethical Conflict: Resolving Problems of Commonsense, *Journal of Applied Rehabilitation Counseling* 27 (3), 11–16; Layman, M. J., & McNamara, J. R. (1997). Remediation for ethics violations: Focus on psychotherapists' sexual contact with clients. *Professional Psychology, Research and Practice, 28*, 281–292; Gannon, L. (1982). The role of power in psychotherapy. *Women and Therapy,* 1 (2), 3–11; Gartrell, N., Herman, J., Oarte, S., Feldstein, M., & Localio, R. (1987). Reporting practices of psychiatrists who knew of sexual misconduct by colleagues. *American Journal of Orthopsychiatry,* 57, 287–95.

64. Philosophers disagree about exactly what the minimal ethical conditions are for each profession. The Code of Ethics for social work contains a set, but rather than take philosophers head-on and argue that it is complete, we will rest content providing what we take to be relatively clear instances of conditions that any social worker must satisfy to be engaged in ethical social work practice.

    For further reading about professional ethics and virtues in the professions, see Robison, Pritchard, and Ellin *op. cit.,* esp. Part I, 3–73; also see Michael D. Bayles, *Professional Ethics,* 2nd ed. (Belmont, CA: Wadsworth, 1989); and Peter Y. Windt, Peter C. Appleby, Margaret P. Battin, Leslie P. Francis, & Bruce M. Landesman, *Ethical Issues in the Professions* (Englewood Cliffs, NJ: Prentice-Hall, 1989).

65. Woody, R. H. (1998). Bartering for psychological services. *Professional Psychology, Research and Practice, 29* (2), 174–178. See also the Code of Ethics at 1.13(b).

66. J. David Kinzie & James K. Boehnlein (1993), Psychotherapy of the victims of massive violence: transference and ethical issues, *American Journal of Psychotherapy* 47 (1), 90–102; Thomas Gutheil (1989), Borderline Personality Disorder, Boundary Violations, and Patient and Therapist Sex, *American Journal of Psychiatry* 146 (5), 597–602; George E. Vaillant (1992), The beginning of wisdom is never calling a patient a borderline, *Journal of Psychotherapy: Practice and Research* 1 (2), 40–57.

67. There are disagreements about what the virtues for a professional are, disagreements about how to classify them in any perspicuous way, and disagreements about whether social workers, as a kind of professional, are to have special virtues that are peculiar to social work, or must display certain professional virtues that are common to all the professions, in special ways.

68. This is a variant of Aristotle's list on the ways in which we can go wrong ethically. See the *Nicomachean Ethics*, op. cit., 43. As Aristotle puts it there, "[T]here are many ways of going wrong, but only one way which is right." A child might send a note to a grandparent with thanks for a present for a birthday, but wait ten or eleven months; the note may disparage the gift and so not really thank the grandparent, and so on.

69. Glasser, P. H. (1984). Being honest with ourselves: What happens when our values conflict with those of our clients? *Practice Digest, 6* (4), 3–29.

70. The Code says in this regard, "Social workers should establish and maintain billing practices that accurately reflect the nature and extent of services provided and that identify who provided the service in the practice setting" (3.05). Appealing to the Code might thus seem to end any question that Rosemary might have, but it does not remove the ethical dilemma she faces. Following the Code in regard to billing will mean serving only the alcoholic, but, as we go on to point out, that will be harmful to the alcoholic, and so Rosemary will be unable to meet her "primary responsibility. . .to promote the well-being of clients" (1.01).

71. Strom, K. (1992). Reimbursement demands and treatment decisions: A growing dilemma for social workers in private practice. *Social Work, 37* (5), 398–403.

72. The Code tells her to "avoid conflicts of interest" (1.06[a]) and "to seek agreement among the parties involved concerning each individual's right to confidentiality" and so on (1.06[f]), but, of course, Tamara's problem is that the conflict of interest was thrust upon her: She was unable to avoid it. Now, if she follows the Code and seeks agreement among all the parties involved, she has effectively made a decision about how to proceed. Perhaps that decision is the one she ought to make, but she ought not to make it just because the Code tells her to. She needs to think through the implications for all of the parties involved and try to choose the alternative that causes the least harm. That may mean that she is to do what the Code tells her, but there is no guarantee of that.

73. John P. Ronnau & Christine R. Marlow (1993), Family Preservation, Poverty and the Value of Diversity, *Families in Society* 174 (9), 538–544.

74. The Code requires social workers to "obtain education about and seek to understand the nature of social diversity and oppression with respect to race, ethnicity," and so on (1.05[c]). But it is no easy task trying to understand how it is that someone who is oppressed feels about the oppression, how it is that such a person is likely to take the social worker as part of the oppressive system, or how a social worker can respond ethically while yet being part of the system.

75. Kanvanagh, K., & Kennedy, P. (1992). *Promoting cultural diversity: Strategies for health care professionals.* Newberry Park, CA: Sage Press; Longres, J. (1991). Toward a status model of ethnic sensitive practice. *Journal of Multicultural Social Work, 1* (1), 41–56; Lum, D. (1992). *Social work practice and people of color.* (2nd ed). Belmont, CA: Brooks/Cole; Gallegos, J. (1984). The ethnic competence model for social work education. In White, B. (ed.), *Color in white society.* Silver Springs, MD: National Association of Social Workers; Baruth, L., & Manning, M. (1991). *Multicultural counseling and psychotherapy.* New York: Macmillan Publishing.

76. Pelligrino, E.D. (1991). Informal judgments of competence and incompetence. In M.A.G. Cutter & E.E. Shelp (eds). *Competency* (pp. 29–39). The Netherlands: Kluwer Academic.

77. Borders, L. D. (1991). A systematic approach to peer group supervision. *Journal of Counseling and Development, 69* (3), 248–52; Greenberg, S. L., Lewis, G. J., and Johnson, J. (1985). Peer consultation groups for private practitioners. *Professional Psychology: Research & Practice, 16* (3), 437–447.

78. Myers, L. L., & Thyer, B. A. (1997). Should social work clients have the right to effective treatment? *Social Work, 42,* 288–298; Raw, S. D. (1998). Who is to define effective treatment for social work clients? (comment on L.L. Myers and B. A. Thyer). *Social Work, 43* (1), 81–86.

79. Harrar, W. R., VandeCreek, L., & Knapp, S. (1990). Ethical and legal aspects of clinical supervision. *Professional Psychology: Research and Practice, 21* (1), 37–41; Hopkins, K.M. (1997). Supervisor intervention with troubled workers: A social identity perspective. *Human Relations,* v.50 (Oct. 97), 1215–1238; Brashears, F. (1995). Supervision as social work practice: A reconceptualization. *Social Work, 40,* 692–699.

80. *Guidelines for Clinical Social Work Supervision* (1994). NASW Press (Washington, D.C.); Sims, E. (1995). Judicial decisions concerning dismissals: Some recent cases. (ILO's Convention concerning Termination of Employment at the Initiative of the Employer). *International Labor Review*, 134 (6), 675–703; Springer, B. (1996). Terminating problem employees. *Public Management*, 78, 16–17.

81. Coombs, R. H. (1997). *Drug-impaired professionals.* Cambridge, MA: Harvard University Press; Reamer, F. G. (1992). The impaired social worker. *Social Work*, 37, 165–170.

82. Sovereign, K. L. (1999). *Personnel Law* (4th ed.). Saddle River, NJ: Prentice-Hall; Edelman, L. B., Abraham, S., & Erlanger, H. S. (1992). Professional construction of the law: The inflated threat of wrongful discharge. *Law Society Review*, 26, 47; Preventing wrongful discharge litigation. In Sovereign, K. L. (4th ed.), *Personnel Law*, (pp. 171–185), *op. cit.*, Martucci, W. C., & Boatright, D. B. (1995). Immunity for employment references; *Employment Relations Today*, 22 (2), 119–123; Kleiman, L. S., & White, C. S. (1994). Opinions of human resource professionals on candor of reference-givers. *Psychological Reports*, 74, 345–346; Balancing employee privacy rights and employer's right to know. In K. L. Sovereign (4th ed.), *Personnel Law*, (pp. 186–209), *op. cit.*

83. Springer, B. (1996). Protection from termination lawsuits. *Public Management*, 78 (March), 10–11; Employee dismissal: justice at work; ed. by S. Henry (symposium). *The Annals of the American Academy of Political and Social Science*, 536 (Nov. 1994), 8–170.

84. Accommodation for religion and physical handicaps. In K.L. Sovereign (4th ed.), *Personnel Law*, (pp. 67–88). Saddle River, NJ: Prentice-Hall.

85. Lerman, H. & Porter, N. (1990). *Feminist Ethics in Psychotherapy.* New York: Springer Publishing; Glassman, C. (1992). Feminist dilemmas in practice. *Affilia*, 7(2), 160–66.

86. Baker, L. D. (1995). Racism in professional settings: Forms of address as clues to power relations (part of a special issue on managing diversity: anthropology's contribution to theory and practice). *The Journal of Applied Behavioral Science*, 31, 186–201; Pinderhughes, E. (1989). *Understanding race, ethnicity, and power.* New York: Free Press (1997); Racial masques: Black women and subtle gendered racism (Chapter 4). In Y. St. Jean & J. R. Feagin, *Subtle Sexism*, (pp. 179–200). Thousand Oaks, CA: Sage Publications.

87. Collier, J. (1998). *Theorizing the ethical organization. Business Ethics Quarterly*, vol. 8, No. 4 (Oct. 1998), 621–654.

88. Bocage, M. D., Homonoff, E.E., & Riley, P.M. (1995). Measuring the impact of the fiscal crisis on human service agencies and social work training. *Social Work*, 40 (5), 701–105.

89. Lewis, H. L. (1988). Ethics and the Managing of Service Effectiveness in Social Welfare. *Administration in Social Work*, vol. xi, #3–4 (Fall-Winter), 1987, 271–284.

90. Robin, D., Reidenbach, R. E., & Babin, B.J. (1997). The nature, measurement, and stability of ethical judgements in the workplace. *Psychological Reports*, 80 (Apr.), 563–580; Victor, B., & Bullen, J. (1988). The organizational bases of ethical work climates. *Administration Science Quarterly*, 33 (Mar.), 101–125.

91. Lewis, H. (1985). The whistle blower and the whistle-blowing profession. *Child and Adolescent Social Work Journal*, 2 (1), 3–12.

92. Bissell, G. (1996). Personal ethics in social work with older people. *International Social Work*, 39, 257–263.

93. Verschelden, C. (1993). Social work values and pacifism: Opposition to war as a professional responsibility. *Social Work*, 38, 765–769.

94. See the Code of Ethics 4.06(a). Also, Carpenter, M. C., & Platt, S. (1997). Professional identity for clinical social workers: Impact of changes in health care delivery systems. *Clinical Social Work Journal*, 25, 337–350; Loewenberg, F. (1992). Notes on ethical dilemmas in wartime: Experiences of Israeli social workers during Operation Desert Shield. *International Social Work*, 35 (4), 429–439.

95. We owe this example to Gerald Postema, in Moral Responsibility in Ethics, *op. cit.*

96. Doherty, W. (1995). *Soul searching: Why psychotherapy must promote moral responsibility.* New York: Basic Books; Jeffries, V. (1998). Virtue and the altruistic personality. *Sociological Perspectives*, 41 (1), 151–166.

97. Beauchamp, T., & Childress, J. (1989). *Principles of biomedical ethics* (3rd ed.). New York: Oxford University Press.

98. Rationing health care (an informed debate about explicit choices is better than pretending that rationing does not exist). *The Economist,* 331 (1994), 17–18; Kelly, M. (1994). Theories of justice and street-level discretion (part of the Berkeley symposium on public management research). *Journal of Public Administration Research and Theory,* 4 (April), 119–140.

99. Corcoran, K., & Winslade, W.J. (1994). Eavesdropping on the 50-minute hour: Managed health care and confidentiality. *Behavioral Science and the Law,* 12 (4), 351–365; Edwards, H. B. (1995). Managed care and confidentiality. *Behavioral Health Management,* 15, 25–27.

100. Moskowitz, E. H. (1998). Clinical responsibility and legal liability in managed care. *Journal of the American Geriatrics Society,* 46 (3), 373–377; Strom-Gottfried, K. J. (1998). Is "ethical managed care" an oxymoron? *Families in Society,* 79 (3), 297–307; Newman, R., & Bricklin, P. M. (1991). Parameters of managed health care: Legal, ethical and professional guidelines. *Professional Psychology: Research and Practice,* 22 (1), 26–35; Christensen, K. T. (1995). Ethically important distinctions among managed care organizations. *Journal of Law, Medicine, and Ethics,* 23 (3), 223 229; Gibelman, M., & Whiting, L. (1997, December). *Negotiating and contracting in a managed care environment: Considerations for practitioners.* Unpublished paper, New York: Yeshiva University; Feldman, S. (1992). Managed mental health services: Ideas and issues. In Feldman, S. (Ed.), *Managed mental health services* (pp. 3–26), Springfield, IL: Charles C. Thomas; Davidson, J. R., Davidson, T., & Weinstein, D. (1997, May). Managed care and social work practice: A call for action. *Currents,* 39 (7), 4, 8; Davidson, J. R., & Davidson, T. (1996). Confidentiality and managed care. *Social Work,* 21 (3), 208–215; Corcoran, K. (1997). Managed care: Implications for social work practice. In R.L. Edwards (Ed. in Chief), *Encyclopedia of social work* (19th ed.), 1997 Suppl. (pp. 191–200). Washington, DC: NASW Press; Corcoran, K., & Vandivir, V. (1996). *Maneuvering the maze of managed care.* New York: Free Press; Wineburgh, M.L. (1997). Ethics, managed care and outpatient psychotherapy. *Clinical Social Work Journal,* forthcoming Romirowsky, R. L. (1997). Managed care and caring: Ethical issues in service delivery. *Association of Psychiatric Outpatient Centers of the Americas* (POCA Press), 24 (3), 5–7; Jackson, V. H. (1996). Behavioral managed care: A social work perspective. *Behavioral Health Management,* 16, 22–23; Poole, D. L. (1996). Keeping managed care in balance (editorial). *Health & Social Work,* 21, 163–166; Stoil, M. J. (1995). Ethical dilemmas rife in behavioral managed care. *Behavioral Health Management,* 15, 5–7.

101. Strom-Gottfried, K.J. (1998). Informed consent meets managed care. *Health and Social Work,* 23 (1), 25–33; Manning, S. S., & Gaul, C. E. (1997). The ethics of informed consent: A critical variable in the self-determination of health and mental health clients. *Social Work in Health Care,* 25 (3), 103–117; Manning, S. S. & Gaul, C. E. (1995). The ethics of informed consent: A critical variable in the self-determination of health and mental health clients. A paper presented in Israel, January, 1995. Reprints available from Susan Manning, School of Social Work, University of Denver, Denver, CO 80208; Chambers, T. (1998). Letting the patient backstage: Informed consent for HMO enrollees. *Journal of the American Geriatrics Society,* 46 (3), 355–358.

102. Orentlicher, D. (1998). Practice guidelines: A limited role in resolving rationing decisions. *Journal of the American Geriatrics Society,* 46 (3), 369–72.

103. Bok, Sissela (1982). Secrets: On the Ethics of Concealment and Revelation. New York: Vintage, 1989.

104. Wittmer, D., & Coursey, D. (1996). Ethical work climates: Comparing top managers in public and private organizations. *Journal of Public Administration,* 6 (Oct.), 559–572; Lewis, H. L. (1989). Ethics and the private, nonprofit human service organizations. *Administration in Social Work,* 13 (2), 1–14.

105. Lynch, R. S. & Mitchell, J. (1995). Justice system advocacy: A must for NASW and the social work community. *Social Work,* 40 (Jan.), 9–12.

106. For a thorough but brief discussion of the formal principle of justice and its difference from substantive, or material, principles of justice, see Joel Feinberg, *Social Philosophy* (Englewood

Cliffs, NJ: Prentice-Hall, 1973, pp. 99–103). The text contains some references on justice that provide a good beginning for anyone interested in pursuing the topic.

107. For a more detailed examination of the differences between these two principles of procedural justice and another variant, see John Rawls, *A Theory of Justice* (Cambridge, MA: The Belknap Press of Harvard University Press, 1971), pp. 83ff.

108. For a useful discussion of this concept, though drawn within the law, see Ronald Dworkin, *Taking Rights Seriously* (Cambridge, MA: Harvard University Press, 1977), pp. 31–39, 68–71.

109. Lubove, R. (1965). *The professional altruist.* Cambridge, MA: Harvard University Press; Hutchinson, E.D. (1993). Mandatory reporting laws: Child protection case finding gone awry? *Social Work,* 38 (Jan), 56–63.

110. Roby, P. A. (1998). Creating a just world: Leadership for the twenty-first century. *Social Problems,* 45 (1), 1–20; Gill,D. (1994). *Confronting social injustice and oppression: Concepts and strategies for social workers.* New York: Columbia University Press.

111. Withorn, A. (1998). No win . . . facing the ethical perils of welfare reform. *Families in Society,* 79 (3), 277–287.

112. The classic examination of the conditions of justice is found in David Hume, *A Treatise of Human Nature,* Book II, Part II, Section II, ed. L. A. Selby-Bigge (Oxford: The Clarendon Press, 1960), pp. 484ff.

113. Robert Nozick, *Anarchy, State, and Utopia* (New York: Basic Books, 1974), esp. Section 7 of Part II, pp. 149–231.

114. This analogy has been developed at greater length in Wade L. Robison, *Monopoly* with Sick Moral Strangers, in *Reading Engelhardt: Essays on the Thought of H. Tristram Engelhardt, Jr.,* eds. Brendon Minogue, Gabriel Palmer-Fernandez, and James E. Reagan (The Netherlands: Kluwer Academic Publishers 1997), pp. 95–112.

115. The phrase is Rawls's, *op. cit.,* p. 3.

116. Rawls points out the obvious in saying that "each person finds himself placed at birth in some particular position in some particular society, and the nature of this position materially affects his life prospects" (*op. cit.,* p. 13). Similarly, each person is born with a set of physical and mental characteristics that can materially differ and be valued in differing ways within different societies and different positions within a society. Yet these "accidents of natural endowment and. . .contingencies of social circumstance" are not features they "can be said to deserve" (*op. cit.,* p. 15). As we shall see, Rawls devises a theory of justice which mitigates the harms produced by some being "better endowed, or more fortunate in their social position," than others (*op. cit.* p. 15), and Nozick does not. So in introducing the concepts of natural features and social circumstance in order to critique Nozick's view, we are appealing to the two features of our lives Rawls cites as having the most effect on the just distribution of life's resources.

117. For an extensive overview of Nozick's theory and its virtues and failures, see Jeffrey Paul, ed., *Reading Nozick: Essays on Anarchy, State, and Utopia* (Oxford: Basil Blackwell, 1981). The essays in this collection cover the field and themselves contain a great number of references for those who wish to pursue particular aspects of Nozick's theory to investigate.

118. An additional reason no one complains is that they can choose to play or not to play *Monopoly.* One does not choose to be born and particularly to be born into any particular social position.

119. Rawls, *op. cit.* The literature on Rawls's theory is extensive. For those interested in pursuing its details, see the following: Norman Daniels, ed., *Reading Rawls: Critical Studies of A Theory of Justice* (New York: Basic Books, 1989); *Ethics,* Vol. 99, No. 4 (July 1989), A Symposium on Rawlsian Theory of Justice: Recent Developments; Kai Nielsen and Roger A. Shiner, eds., *New Essays on Contract Theory* (Guelph, Ontario: Canadian Association for Publishing in Philosophy, 1977); and Michael J. Sandel, *Liberalism and the Limits of Justice* (Cambridge: Cambridge University Press, 1982). This listing is not meant to be exhaustive of the various kinds of comments on Rawlsian theory, but is an introduction to those comments that themselves can lead to further references and further study.

120. Tom Campbell, *Justice* (Atlantic Highlands, NJ: Humanities Press International, 1988), p. 180. Campbell's description of Marxism is brief, but clear.
121. The phrase "'dog-eat-dog rat race" is one of those wonderful mistakes that yet nicely captures, in this case, the feel of a highly competitive situation.
122. Campbell, *op. cit.,* p. 180. See also Diquattro, A. (1998). Liberal theory and the idea of communist justice. *The American Political Science Review,* 92 (1), 83–96.
123. Campbell, *op. cit.,* p. 196.
124. This example is drawn from Enid Nemy, Metropolitan Diary, *The New York Times* (January 24, 1999), p. 40.
125. Dr. Karen Neuman, an Assistant Professor in the School of Social Work at Western Michigan University, provided this case.

INDEX

The first occurrence of the cases discussed are in **bold**. Cases are *italicized*. Endnotes are indicated with an *n* followed by the note number.

An index ought to list all and only those items needed by those who use a book. Unfortunately, the process of picking items is an instance of an imperfect procedure, and we would appreciate information about any failing or problematic reference you find. Please e-mail the authors at the addresses listed in the Preface.